PROBLEMS IN THE U.S. AVIATION RELATIONSHIP WITH THE UNITED KINGDOM AND JAPAN

(104–59)

HEARINGS

BEFORE THE

SUBCOMMITTEE ON
AVIATION

OF THE

COMMITTEE ON
TRANSPORTATION AND
INFRASTRUCTURE
HOUSE OF REPRESENTATIVES

ONE HUNDRED FOURTH CONGRESS

SECOND SESSION

MARCH 27 AND APRIL 30, 1996

Printed for the use of the
Committee on Transportation and Infrastructure

U.S. GOVERNMENT PRINTING OFFICE
24–087CC WASHINGTON : 1996

For sale by the U.S. Government Printing Office
Superintendent of Documents, Congressional Sales Office, Washington, DC 20402
ISBN 0-16-054141-7

COMMITTEE ON TRANSPORTATION AND INFRASTUCTURE

BUD SHUSTER, Pennsylvania, *Chairman*

DON YOUNG, Alaska
WILLIAM F. CLINGER, JR., Pennsylvania
THOMAS E. PETRI, Wisconsin
SHERWOOD L. BOEHLERT, New York
HERBERT H. BATEMAN, Virginia
HOWARD COBLE, North Carolina
JOHN J. DUNCAN, JR., Tennessee
SUSAN MOLINARI, New York
WILLIAM H. ZELIFF, JR., New Hampshire
THOMAS W. EWING, Illinois
WAYNE T. GILCHREST, Maryland
Y. TIM HUTCHINSON, Arkansas
BILL BAKER, California
JAY KIM, California
STEPHEN HORN, California
BOB FRANKS, New Jersey
PETER I. BLUTE, Massachusetts
JOHN L. MICA, Florida
JACK QUINN, New York
TILLIE K. FOWLER, Florida
VERNON J. EHLERS, Michigan
SPENCER T. BACHUS, Alabama
JERRY WELLER, Illinois
ZACH WAMP, Tennessee
TOM LATHAM, Iowa
STEVEN C. LATOURETTE, Ohio
ANDREA SEASTRAND, California
RANDY TATE, Washington
SUE KELLY, New York
RAY LAHOOD, Illinois
BILL MARTINI, New Jersey
DAN FRISA, New York
TODD TIAHRT, Kansas
RICHARD H. BAKER, Louisiana

JAMES L. OBERSTAR, Minnesota
NICK J. RAHALL II, West Virginia
ROBERT A. BORSKI, Pennsylvania
WILLIAM O. LIPINSKI, Illinois
ROBERT E. WISE, JR., West Virginia
JAMES A. TRAFICANT, JR., Ohio
PETER A. DEFAZIO, Oregon
BOB CLEMENT, Tennessee
JERRY F. COSTELLO, Illinois
PETE GEREN, Texas
GLENN POSHARD, Illinois
BUD CRAMER, Alabama
BARBARA-ROSE COLLINS, Michigan
ELEANOR HOLMES NORTON, District of Columbia
JERROLD NADLER, New York
PAT DANNER, Missouri
ROBERT MENENDEZ, New Jersey
JAMES E. CLYBURN, South Carolina
CORRINE BROWN, Florida
JAMES A. BARCIA, Michigan
BOB FILNER, California
EDDIE BERNICE JOHNSON, Texas
BILL K. BREWSTER, Oklahoma
KAREN MCCARTHY, Missouri
FRANK MASCARA, Pennsylvania
THOMAS C. SAWYER, Ohio
GENE TAYLOR, Mississippi
JUANITA MILLENDER-MCDONALD, California
ELIJAH E. CUMMINGS, Maryland

SUBCOMMITTEE ON AVIATION

JOHN J. DUNCAN, JR., Tennessee, *Chairman*

JERRY WELLER, Illinois, *Vice-Chairman*
WILLIAM F. CLINGER, JR., Pennsylvania
HOWARD COBLE, North Carolina
WILLIAM H. ZELIFF, JR., New Hampshire
THOMAS W. EWING, Illinois
Y. TIM HUTCHINSON, Arkansas
JAY KIM, California
VERNON J. EHLERS, Michigan
SPENCER T. BACHUS, Alabama
ANDREA SEASTRAND, California
RANDY TATE, Washington
SUE KELLY, New York
RAY LAHOOD, Illinois
BILL MARTINI, New Jersey
BUD SHUSTER, Pennsylvania *(Ex Officio)*

WILLIAM O. LIPINSKI, Illinois
JERRY F. COSTELLO, Illinois
JAMES A. TRAFICANT, JR., Ohio
PETER A. DEFAZIO, Oregon
BUD CRAMER, Alabama
BARBARA-ROSE COLLINS, Michigan
JERROLD NADLER, New York
PAT DANNER, Missouri
ROBERT MENENDEZ, New Jersey
JAMES E. CLYBURN, South Carolina
CORRINE BROWN, Florida
PETE GEREN, Texas
JAMES L. OBERSTAR, Minnesota *(Ex Officio)*

CONTENTS

TESTIMONY

MARCH 27, 1996

PREPARED STATEMENTS SUBMITTED BY MEMBERS OF CONGRESS

PREPARED STATEMENTS SUBMITTED BY WITNESSES

ADDITION TO THE RECORD

APRIL 30, 1996

PREPARED STATEMENT SUBMITTED BY A MEMBER OF CONGRESS

Page

PREPARED STATEMENTS SUBMITTED BY WITNESSES

SUBMISSION FOR THE RECORD

ADDITIONS TO THE RECORD

PROBLEMS IN THE U.S. AVIATION RELATIONSHIP WITH THE UNITED KINGDOM AND JAPAN

WEDNESDAY, MARCH 27, 1995

U.S. HOUSE OF REPRESENTATIVES,
SUBCOMMITTEE ON AVIATION,
COMMITTEE ON TRANSPORTATION AND INFRASTRUCTURE,
Washington, DC.

The committee met, pursuant to notice, at 2 p.m. in room 2167, Rayburn House Office Building, Hon. John J. Duncan, Jr. (chairman of the committee) presiding.

Mr. DUNCAN. I call this meeting of the Aviation Subcommittee to order.

Before we get started, I want to thank all of the distinguished witnesses today for adjusting their very busy schedules in order to accommodate the subcommittee. Many of our members are returning from their districts right at this time, since the House will not begin voting until 5:00 o'clock.

I must say that it is always a pleasure for me, and I think I can speak for all of my colleagues, to have two very talented and knowledgeable business executives from outstanding and very successful companies testifying before the subcommittee today. On the first panel, Mr. Smith, of course, has testified before the subcommittee in the past. And I thank him for being here with us again today.

I had the pleasure of meeting with Mr. Weidemeyer a few days ago, and I also would like to thank him for being here. Federal Express is a very important company to the State of Tennessee, and I have a very large UPS operation in my own district. And these are two very fine companies.

The purpose of this hearing is to review the current stalemate in aviation negotiations with the United Kingdom and with Japan. Although we have made some progress since last July with Japan and I hope that it was at least in part a result of this subcommittee's hearing on that issue, we still have not seen adequate movement entirely from the Japanese government. However, I do understand that an agreement was reached late last night in Tokyo for our cargo carriers. And I hope that this will eventually lead to successful passenger traffic negotiations in the very near future.

This is the second time this has happened, and I hope that it's, as I said, in part a result not only of our earlier hearing, but the Senate Aviation Committee held a hearing on this, and of course, everyone knew we had this hearing scheduled today. Unfortunately, for the most part, our aviation negotiations with the United Kingdom have not been as productive. Despite the success of the U.S. Air-British Airways code sharing relationship, our progress, or lack thereof, has been very discouraging to our aviation industry as a whole. Of course, the major issue here is more access for U.S. carriers to Heathrow and the need for U.S. cargo carriers to fly to points beyond London.

It's kind of disappointing that the market share for U.S. airlines between the United States and the United Kingdom continues to decline. Currently, British airplanes fly 59 and a half percent of the passengers between the U.S. and the U.K., while U.S. carriers carry only 40.5 percent. The U.S. share is down from the 1994 level of 46 percent, which I think is something that we all need to work on.

In my opinion, the Administration should be doing everything within its power to move these negotiations with Japan and the United Kingdom forward. I think that we need to place a much higher priority on these negotiations, and that we must be decisive and tough. We cannot afford to be timid in our positions.

Moreover, I do not think that our negotiators should buy into the Japanese strategy which pits one U.S. carrier against another. The fact is that we currently have a huge trade imbalance with Japan. And as I said last July, our Government should be embarking on a cohesive policy which protects our carriers in one of the only markets that the United States currently experiences a surplus with Japan.

In my opinion, we must negotiate these agreements from a position of strength. And by standing together, I think we can accomplish these goals, not only for U.S. carriers and passengers, but for our Japanese and British counterparts as well.

I look forward to hearing from the witnesses today on these very important issues, and I now yield to the ranking member of the subcommittee, Mr. Lipinski.

Mr. LIPINSKI. Thank you, Mr. Chairman.

Mr. Chairman, first of all, I want to say I have a formal statement which I would like to have permission to insert into the record at the appropriate time. And I'm sure you'll have no objection to that, right?

Mr. DUNCAN. Fine.

[Mr. Lipinski's prepared statement follows:]

CONGRESSMAN WILLIAM O. LIPINSKI
Ranking Democratic Member
Subcommittee on Aviation

Opening Statement
U.S. Aviation Relationship with the United Kingdom and Japan
March 27, 1996

Mr. Chairman, this afternoon's hearing focuses on an issue of tremendous importance to me and to the entire aviation community, international aviation. I'm thrilled that we are holding this hearing this morning and have scheduled a second hearing on the subject when we return from the April recess.

In the over 13 years I have been a Member of this Subcommittee and in particular since I became the Ranking Member last year, I have come to realize the importance of international air routes to American carriers and to the nation. International business is the key to long term profitability, and so the carriers will do all they can to assure their access around the globe.

I gave a speech in January in which I was critical of the Department of Transportation and Department of State's ability to negotiate bilateral agreements which provide U.S. carriers the rights they deserve. There are quite a few cases, I will concede, in which DOT and State have been successful in opening markets to U.S. carriers and negotiating open skies agreements. I commend the negotiators for their hard work and success with these nations. The problem, unfortunately, is that we have not had the same success with the two most critical nations, the United Kingdom and Japan.

Mr. Chairman, these hearings will focus on the U.K. and Japan because they are the real problem. I encourage our negotiators to continue pushing for open skies in every country in the world, including Japan and the U.K. Open skies is good for American carriers and good for America. But in the cases where open skies cannot happen, where the traditional approaches to negotiating bilaterals go nowhere, we need to be willing to consider alternative approaches. Thinking or acting the same way because "that's they way we have always done it" is simply not acceptable.

Today we will hear from representatives of the U.S. airlines with a vested interest in this subject. We are all too aware that U.S. carriers rarely agree when it comes to this subject. In Japan, there is a schism between the 1952 carriers and the MOU carriers. In the U.K., two U.S. carriers have Heathrow while the rest do not. Because of the inherent conflicts, it is impossible to find a solution which provides every American carrier what it wants. What we must strive toward is creating increased opportunities for U.S. carriers in every market around the world. **Our priority should be expanding markets for all U.S. carriers to use their competitiveness against foreign competitors rather than pitting them one against the other to trade the rights we already have.**

Unfortunately, as a result of scheduling conflicts, not every American carrier with an interest in this subject could be here this afternoon. We will be hearing from other carriers at our second hearing on April 24th, as well as the Department of Transportation and others interested in this important issue.

Mr. Chairman, I want to thank you for working with me to schedule this hearing. I know there are other Members who wish to make statements so at this point I will yield back the balance of my time.

Mr. LIPINSKI. Thank you.

I welcome the two gentlemen here today. The Chairman got in a plug for Federal Express in Tennessee, so I have to get in a plug for United Parcel. United Parcel has two of the largest facilities in their gigantic empire located in the Third Congressional District in the State of Illinois, which I just happen to be fortunate enough to represent.

So now that the commercials and the plugs are even, I want to say I welcome the two gentlemen here. I think this is a very important hearing that we are going to have today. I am looking forward to the opinion both from Federal Express and from United Parcel on the agreement that apparently was agreed to in Japan within the last 24 hours.

Now, I understand that nothing has been committed to writing as of yet. But I understand that a handshake deal has been agreed to. I have some preliminary information about that. I will be looking forward to ascertaining from both of you gentlemen what information you have about it and what your views are on it.

As the Chairman mentioned, aviation and international aviation in particular is extremely important to the United States of America. It's one of the places where we certainly have a very significant lead over the rest of the world. And I think it's the duty and the responsibility of the United States Government to see to it that all our carriers, whether they be passenger carriers or cargo carriers, have the opportunity to expand their service all over the world.

And I think that we should do everything possible to see that that comes into play, whether it be the Executive Branch or the Legislative Branch. And I want to at the present time conditionally compliment our negotiators in Japan for apparently putting together an agreement where we are really getting what we are entitled to, plus expanding our other carriers, such as United Parcel, service that will benefit American consumers and Japanese consumers.

And Mr. Chairman, as I say, I'll put my formal statement in the record. I'll be anxious to hear the two gentlemen testifying, so I yield back the balance of my time.

Mr. DUNCAN. Thank you very much, Mr. Lipinski.

Mr. Cramer.

Mr. CRAMER. Thank you, Mr. Chairman.

Just very briefly, I would like to submit a statement for the record. I am very interested in this hearing. I represent north Alabama, the Fifth District of Alabama, certainly our region of the country feels like to some extent we've been left out of service to Japan. We have a space camp down there at the Marshall Space Flight Center. We have a lot of participants, young people, that come in there from Japan. We have now worked out a partnership to open a space camp in Japan as well. So needless to say, we have those issues on our minds when we think about this.

But this is a very important subject matter today, and I will be listening as well for any agreement or understandings that perhaps have already been reached.

Thank you, Mr. Chairman.

[Mr. Cramer's prepared statement follows:]

STATEMENT OF REPRESENTATIVE ROBERT E. 'BUD' CRAMER FOR THE COMMITTEE ON TRANSPORTATION AND INFRASTRUCTURE SUBCOMMITTEE ON AVIATION

- Throughout history trade and travel have been consistent engines of prosperity. They have also lowered barriers between nations, enabling peoples of various cultures and traditions to live harmoniously.

- Trade and travel, including tourism, is still the foundation of much of the world's prosperity. The pace and distances involved, however, have changed enormously as technology advances.

- Businesses seeking new markets or tourists seeking new vistas need to be able to get there from here. Cities, regions and nations have the best chance to maximize growth if they have the air transit options they need.

- That is why the US pushes to liberalize the bilateral agreements that govern air service between our country and our trading partners. Namely, with Japan and the United Kingdom.

- Currently, whole regions, including the South are virtually shut out of the market all together.

- Allow me to cite one example from my own district. We have in Huntsville, Alabama a tremendous educational facility - Space Camp.

- It provides an opportunity for kids from ages 10-17 to learn about space travel. They learn the engineering and physics involved in putting people into space. They learn astronomy and other space-related sciences. Importantly, they also learn how to work and cooperate with other campers from around the world.

- Space camp wants to attract participants from Japan -- and more significantly, it wants to open a space camp program in Japan. That requires dependable and affordable air travel, so program directors and participants can travel with efficiency. With the current state of air service, that's going to be difficult to do.

- Let me emphasize, I understand the limitations of the marketplace. Even with expanded service, I don't expect nonstop service direct from Tokyo to Huntsville. I do, however, expect better service to the South.

- The business and the people needed to support it are there.

- Mr Chairman, in my district, there's space camp and hundreds of other enterprises that need air service. In your district, there are other local ventures that would benefit from better service. When we put together all the big and small opportunities, we're talking a significant national need.

- I think this is a very important issue for the U.S. We need to make it easier and cheaper to travel between the United States and Japan. We need to improve service and price by introducing competition.

- I am pleased to hear an agreement was reached with Japan yesterday, and I look to a more open relationship with them in this arena.

- There's just too much at stake to continue on with the restrictions now encumbering US-Japan travel and economic growth.

Mr. DUNCAN. Thank you.

Ms. Danner.

Ms. DANNER. Thank you, Mr. Chairman.

Although as you know I usually submit my statement for the record, this morning, or this afternoon, I should say, I would like to voice it.

I'm pleased that the Aviation Subcommittee is holding this hearing on the U.S.-U.K. aviation relationship. At a time when the United States, along with many other countries, is attempting to liberalize bilateral aviation agreements, the United Kingdom appears to be resisting these efforts. Under the current aviation agreement, known as Bermuda II, only two U.S. airlines are granted access to Heathrow Airport. Because of such restrictions, British airlines currently carry 60 percent of the air travelers between the United States and the United Kingdom.

For some time the United States has attempted to negotiate a more equitable air agreement. After more than 1 year, these negotiations have led only to a mini-deal that does not address the major concerns of the United States. In the past, the United States has taken many steps to prove that it is negotiating in good faith. These steps include the approval of code sharing agreements and the granting of several additional U.S. routes to British carriers. These gestures, however, have not convinced British negotiators to address U.S. concerns fully.

While much of the negotiating process is highly technical, the effects of closing off Heathrow to additional U.S. service has real cost to our Nation's airline and to our economy.

And now I come to the crux of my statement. Missouri-based TWA has been attempting to gain approval for a New York to Heathrow frequency. The benefits such a service would provide are enormous. TWA forecasts annual revenues of more than $100 million annually resulting from this route. Such gains would go a long way toward ensuring the continued recovery of our airline, TWA. With tens of thousands of employees and more than $1 billion in revenue, the continued success of TWA is vital to both our national economy and the economy of our State of Missouri. The United States must continue to do all that it can to negotiate a fair bilateral aviation treaty with the United Kingdom. I believe such a treaty should include provisions granting TWA access from New York hub to Heathrow.

I would also like to take a moment to welcome Scott Gibson of TWA, who will be testifying later in this hearing. And I know that if I have failed to convince you of the importance of this matter, I feel assured that Scott will.

Thank you, Mr. Chairman.

Mr. DUNCAN. Well, thank you very much, Ms. Danner.

Mr. Ewing, do you have a statement you wish to make at this time?

Mr. EWING. Mr. Chairman, were you talking to me? I had too many people whispering.

Mr. DUNCAN. Do you have an opening statement?

Mr. EWING. I do not, but I am pleased to be here. I think the subject matter of this hearing is one of extreme importance, and I'm pleased to be here to participate in it.

Mr. DUNCAN. Thank you very much.

Mr. Hutchinson.

Mr. HUTCHINSON. None, thank you.

Mr. DUNCAN. All right, then. Mr. Ehlers

Mr. EHLERS. Thank you, Mr. Chairman.

Just a comment. I agree with the gentleman from Illinois that this is an extremely important issue. As you know, international agreements and negotiations are very difficult and touchy, one might say. But one thing I would want to point out. I think it's something extremely important to recognize and remember in all these discussions on this issue, is to maintain the fifth freedom rights, or the beyond rights that we currently have in Japan.

Those are so difficult to obtain. We do have them. We're using them judiciously. They are beneficial to our airlines and our Nation. I think whatever position this committee might take or might get involved in or the position adopted by the Administration in their negotiations should do whatever is possible to ensure that we maintain those rights. And I would like to have that entered in the record with my opening statement.

Thank you.

Mr. DUNCAN. Thank you very much, Mr. Ehlers.

Mr. Costello.

Mr. COSTELLO. Mr. Chairman, I'll put my statement in the record.

[Prepared statements of Mr. Costello and Mr. Traficant follow:]

JERRY F. COSTELLO
12TH DISTRICT, ILLINOIS

PLEASE RESPOND TO THE OFFICE CHECKED BELOW:

COMMITTEES:
BUDGET
TRANSPORTATION & INFRASTRUCTURE
SCIENCE
(ON LEAVE)

Congress of the United States
House of Representatives
Washington, DC 20515–1312

OPENING STATEMENT OF CONGRESSMAN JERRY F. COSTELLO

SUBCOMMITTEE ON AVIATION

HEARING ON PROBLEMS IN THE U.S. AVIATION RELATIONSHIP WITH THE UNITED KINGDOM AND JAPAN

March 27, 1996

Mr. Chairman, I want to thank you for calling today's hearing so that our Subcommittee will have the opportunity to receive testimony from witnesses who are concerned about the future of U.S. airlines. This is an extremely important issue that deserves our close attention.

Restrictions on travel to both the United Kingdom and Japan should be significantly reduced so that the market can freely operate. The "Open Skies" approach taken by the United States benefits all consumers and will lead to a more competitive airline industry.

International service must be available as intended under the existing bilateral negotiations. To counteract unfair activities from other countries, the U.S. Department of Transportation should take a hard look at applications made by foreign carriers to ensure their country's compliance with existing agreements. We must not continue to approve requests of foreign countries when they refuse to cooperate with U.S. carriers.

Mr. Chairman, I look forward to our Subcommittee's in-depth

☐ 2454 RAYBURN BUILDING, WASHINGTON, DC 20515, TEL: (202) 225-5661, FAX: (202) 225-0285
☐ 327 W. MAIN ST., BELLEVILLE, IL 62220, TEL: (618) 233-8026, FAX: (618) 233-8765
☐ 1363 NIEDRINGHAUS AVE., GRANITE CITY, IL 62040, TEL: (618) 451-7065, FAX: (618) 451-2126
☐ 250 W. CHERRY ST., CARBONDALE, IL 62901, TEL: (618) 529-3791, FAX: (618) 549-3768
☐ 8787 STATE ST., EAST ST. LOUIS, IL 62203, TEL: (618) 397-8833
☐ 1330 SWANWICK ST., CHESTER, IL 62233, TEL: (618) 826-3043

look at these problems and hope that we will be able to formulate some solutions.

STATEMENT OF THE HONORABLE

JAMES A. TRAFICANT, JR.

TRANSPORTATION AND INFRASTRUCTURE

SUBCOMMITTEE ON AVIATION

HEARING ON U.S. AVIATION RELATIONSHIP

WITH UNITED KINGDOM AND JAPAN

MARCH 27, 1996

Thank you Chairman Duncan for holding this hearing – I think it is vitally important for Congress to work closely with the Clinton Administration to aggressively expand passenger and cargo air service between the United States and Japan, as well as the United Kingdom.

I am especially concerned over our aviation relationship with Japan. The Pacific Rim is one of the fastest growing markets in the world. Expanding U.S. airline service -- passenger and cargo -- to the Pacific Rim will depend, on the large part, on the ability of U.S. airlines to expand their hubs and presence in Japan.

Of particular importance is the ability for U.S. airlines to use Japan as an important stopover point to other destinations along the Pacific Rim.

I would like to make a few comments about the U.S.-Japan aviation relationship. The history of the trade relationship between Japan and the United States over the past forty years should teach Congress one thing: unless the United States stands firm in protecting its own interests, Japan will run roughshod over U.S. business.

Page Two

I strongly support expanding access of U.S. airline companies into Japan and other markets in the Pacific Rim. I believe we can -- and should -- achieve such expansion without compromising one inch on the inroads we have already made through the U.S.-Japan Aviation Agreement.

I would caution my colleagues on this panel not to support any proposal that benefits one sector of the U.S. passenger industry at the expense of other sectors.

Congress and the Administration should work together with the airline industry on a plan of action to force Japan to further open up its aviation markets to U.S. competition -- without making any concessions to Japan that would, in the end, result in less access and less competition.

The goal should be a truly open and free market. This overarching goal should be applied to both the U.S.-Japan relationship and the U.S.-UK relationship. The U.S. airline industry has made remarkable strides in recent years. Given the opportunity to compete with interference and roadblocks, I know they will continue to do quite well.

Once again, Mr. Chairman, thank you for holding this hearing. I look forward to working with you and the distinguished ranking member from Illinois, Mr. Lipinski, on this issue in the weeks and months ahead.

###

Mr. DUNCAN. All right. Thank you very much.

We have two very distinguished panels, and we will hear later from representatives from Northwest Airlines, TWA, United Airlines and the Economic Strategy Institute. But at this time, we're very pleased to have with us Mr. Frederick W. Smith, Chairman and Chief Executive Officer of the Federal Express Corporation, and Mr. Thomas H. Weidemeyer, who is President of United Parcel Service Airline Company. So thank you, gentlemen, for being here. And Mr. Smith, I suppose we'll start with you.

TESTIMONY OF FREDERICK W. SMITH, CHAIRMAN AND CEO, FEDERAL EXPRESS CORPORATION; AND THOMAS H. WEIDEMEYER, PRESIDENT, UNITED PARCEL SERVICE CO

Mr. SMITH. Well, thank you very much, Mr. Chairman. I would like to personally thank you and the committee for the leadership you've shown on this issue. I believe that if the United States makes any significant progress in these aviation disputes in large measure the credit will go to the Congress. And the significant support for U.S. interests has been demonstrated by key members on both the Senate and the House sides and on both sides of the aisle.

I'd also like to say to Mr. Cramer, just to ingratiate myself to him, it's not only Japanese youngsters that go to space camp. I'll have a daughter in space camp in June down there. So we'll be adding to the north Alabama economy.

[Laughter.]

Mr. SMITH. I have a prepared statement, Mr. Chairman, that I'd like to submit, and just try to make some brief comments to bring this issue into focus. I'd like to say at the onset that cargo issues are vastly different than passenger issues. The passengers issues have a different set of circumstances. Just for starters, they are bilateral in nature, because we all like to come home when we go some place. Cargo only goes one way.

So flexible operating agreements, for that reason, and increased variability of seasonality and the demand for goods in various parts of the world require very flexible operating agreements for all cargo carriers, whether it's traditional or the integrated express carriers like ourselves and UPS to be successful.

In the hearings in the Senate last week or the week before, the GAO testified, and I thought there were a couple of telling points that were made in that testimony. The first was the observation that historically, and almost incredibly, the United States has done little if any econometrics analysis of its air service agreements to determine whether the agreements reached were in the best interests of the United States as a whole, and what the respective values of the aviation rights that were being afforded to the various parties represented in terms of economic advantage.

And second, and perhaps even more telling, was that the United States had no strategy whatsoever to resolve the dispute with Japan and the United Kingdom. Now, to understand the profundity of those observations made by the GAO, and observations which by the way we strongly agree with, you have to recognize the historical context in which all aviation treaties are constructed. And they are based on a bilateral aviation trading regime established in 1944 over the objections of the United States, which required individual treaties between each country that wanted to engage in air commerce one with the other.

This so-called 1944 Chicago Convention was built around an agreement which was importantly called the Five Freedoms of the Air. The first and second freedoms were the ability to fly over a country and the ability to fly through a country with a technical stop without enplaning traffic. Third and fourth freedom traffic was the ability to move traffic from one's homeland to another country and vice versa. And fifth freedom, or beyond traffic rights, were the ability of a U.S. carrier to go to another country and enplane traffic from that country to yet a third country and vice versa, back to the treaty signatory.

The opposite economic opportunity in the agreement in 1944 was called anterior fifth freedom rights. So U.S. carriers were to receive fifth freedom rights, foreign carriers were to receive anterior fifth freedom rights.

About 20 years or so, for reasons best known to U.S. officials at the time, the United States let foreign interests begin to advance a new concept. And the term anterior fifth freedom traffic or beyond rights was supplanted by the term sixth freedom traffic rights. And sixth freedom traffic rights are the ability of a foreign carrier to pick up traffic destined to the United States, making a stop over that carrier's homeland. So in the case of Great Britain, a sixth freedom traffic flow would be a Polish shipper or citizen moving over the United Kingdom and the United States, and in Japan, an example of it might be a shipment or a passenger from Thailand moving over Japan into the United States.

Note importantly that what I am describing is U.S. trade. In the case of cargo, it is something that has been bought or sold by a U.S. interest.

In 1952, when the United States established an air service agreement with Japan, which was based on the principles of the 1944 Chicago convention, this air service agreement predictably called for reciprocal or relatively equal beyond rights for the two parties, as was conceived in the 1944 bilateral trade agreement. And so the Japanese carrier, which at that time was Japan Air Lines, just arising from World War II, and three U.S. carriers, Northwest, Pan American, whose rights were bought by United Airlines, and an all cargo carrier, Flying Tigers, which was purchased by Federal Express.

And with the purchase of those rights by FedEx and United, we received, under the treaty between the United States and Japan, the ability to move traffic to and from the United States and Japan and from Japan to any point and from any point to Japan, which was the opposite economic opportunity the Japanese carriers were receiving.

And in fact, the charts which we have over there represent these opportunities. The first chart shows that Japanese carriers exercising their anterior fifth, or now so-called sixth freedom rights, have access to the entire population of Asia, some two billion people, that they can flow goods and of course passengers, which again is a different issue, but goods over Japan into the United States. On the other side of the coin, we have the rights, as does United or

Northwest, to take traffic to and from points in Japan to other points and vice versa.

If one measures the relative economic value of those two beyond rights, you can see that the Japanese have a 9.3 to 1 advantage over the United States, because there is much more trade going to the United States traveling many more miles. Despite this, the Japanese, over the past 2½ years, have attempted to restrict FedEx's ability to operate, utilizing our beyond rights. And in fact, this intransigence and unwillingness to honor the terms of the treaty, which has been confirmed by our U.S. Department of Transportation, costs FedEx in excess of $100 million.

Now, the agreement which we understand has been reached with the U.S. and Japan today, we applaud. It is a major step in the right direction, in our opinion. But we wanted from these negotiations only one thing. And that was for the United States and Japan to assure that we would be able to enjoy the rights which we hold. And if those rights were not honored, the United States would move swiftly and decisively to restrict Japan's huge sixth freedom traffic opportunities in order to permit us to engage in our fifth freedom traffic opportunities.

I also understand that the agreement gives some new rights to UPS, which we applaud. Because we support the concept of open skies. And perhaps during the question period, we can return to this.

In the case of the U.K., I'll just make one comment. I see my time is up. If one measures those relative economic opportunities between Japan and U.S. interests in terms of third, fourth, fifth and sixth freedom markets combined, which is the only way that one can really look at the totality of the market, and which is in total accordance with the 1944 regime which the United States acceded to, in the case of the United Kingdom, that ratio would be 43 to 1 in favor of the United Kingdom.

And the United Kingdom's intransigence in this regard is directly related to the fact that the U.S. gave them, in the Bermuda II agreement, a trading advantage of unprecedented proportions. And we believe strongly that the United States should press the United Kingdom to liberalize that agreement. And in fact, we were assured that that was in fact the case in the so-called mini-deal that was done last year, and then which was conveniently abandoned several months later.

So I will yield now to my friend, Tom Weidemeyer, and answer questions as you want, or come back to any of these subjects during the question period as you want, Mr. Chairman.

Mr. DUNCAN. All right, thank you very much, Mr. Smith.

Mr. Weidemeyer.

Mr. WEIDEMEYER. Thank you, Mr. Chairman, and members of the committee. And sometimes you have opportunities for coincidence or good fortune. And I likewise have a son and daughter that are going to space camp in August this summer.

[Laughter.]

Mr. DUNCAN. Let's keep this going now.

Mr. WEIDEMEYER. I'm out of children.

I have a number of prepared statements here. I have one that I've submitted for the record, a formal statement with some exhibits. And I'm going to try to paraphrase some of what's in there. Much of what's in there has changed overnight, as Mr. Lipinski alluded to.

I think as time goes by and the information age begins to become a reality, and we look around and we see information moving at the speed of light or faster, we see the monetary system almost mirroring the same thing, there's one great difficulty that still exists. And that's the limitations that are put on the movement of people and goods.

There has to be a recognition which driving the economy of the U.S. and other economies of the world is very different today than it was a generation ago, and move from a regulatory climate to one that enhances and helps develop world trade. We have the opportunity as the U.S. has great potential to be effective in these markets, we have the opportunity to lead the way by asking for, demanding in the appropriate manner, the opportunity for open skies. Mr. Smith has alluded to it. UPS likewise agrees with the comments of Federal Express that open skies is in the best interests of U.S. carriers and consumers in the U.S. We have no fear of being able to compete, being put on an even playing field with our foreign competitors.

As Mr. Smith mentioned, last year there was a mini-deal that was struck between the U.S. and the U.K. We were given assures that when that mini-deal was being negotiated that shortly thereafter, perhaps in as few as several days, that cargo liberalization and open skies would take place. Nine months has passed. To my knowledge, there hasn't even been a meeting to discuss the issue.

I think it once again is time to help our cause by taking a firm stand with the U.K. to get additional access. UPS is in an interesting position, because we are one of three carriers designated with beyond rights out of the U.K.

However, we operate out of East Midlands, which is 150 miles from London. And fortunately, one of the beyond points we have goes to Germany, which is where our international hub is located in Europe. If we wanted to go to places other than where designated, such as France or Spain or Italy, at this point in time we are precluded from doing so. We think that we should have the unfettered rights to do whatever is safe and what the customers, the consumers around the world, desire services to be rendered.

On the issue of Japan, the testimony that has been submitted has a series of exhibits which were intended to show that the negotiating position of the U.S with regard to Japan was very vital to UPS. We certainly hope that open skies is the ultimate outcome of ongoing negotiations with Japan. But we certainly recognize as well that with the difficulty we've had in negotiating those agreements that we had to take a step phased-in approach. And we also recognize that there are carriers that have become known as the incumbents that had rights that were already existing that our Government should protect and should not jeopardize.

We had suggested to the U.S. Government that there were ways to do that, that the 1952 agreement should be held without further negotiation. Both parties think they know what it means, and that should not encumber the negotiations to create greater opportunities for aviation liberalization.

We also said we did not fear additional Japanese cargo carriers having additional rights in the U.S., and that was fine with us. And at the end of the day, the worst possible position for us was the status quo. That is, that no agreement could be reached whatsoever. In that situation, the incumbents, although how much they've been able to exercise certainly has been subject to debate with the Japanese, the incumbents nevertheless have substantial rights.

We as an MOU, memorandum of understanding, carrier, one of the new fellows on the block, have very restricted operations. Basically, six frequencies a week into Narita, no beyond rights. If no agreement is reached, or if no agreement had been reached, in the future, that was the limit of the rights that we could have. Because they were specifically spelled out in the agreement. Unlike the 1952 incumbent carriers, who theoretically and in practice have been able to put up as many routes as necessary to meet the demands of the business.

As a consequence, the handshake, which we only have sketch reports of at this point, which has recognized the rights of the incumbents, as well as granted additional opportunities for UPS to have frequencies to Japan as well as beyond rights to at least one point beyond Japan to link up with our intra-Asia hub, have given UPS the opportunity to be able to provide even more access for our consumers.

We applaud those actions of both our U.S. negotiators, as well as the Japanese negotiators, in finally taking a step forward. And we at UPS hope that this is just the first step in many towards the liberalization of aviation agreements around the world.

And I would also recommend if perhaps we can use this in negotiation with a very tough trading partner as a basis to use a similar negotiating strategy with the U.K. to perhaps, let's get off the dime and get something negotiated and truly get to an open skies arena.

Thank you very much, and I'm available for questions.

Mr. DUNCAN. Thank you very much, Mr. Weidemeyer.

We've now been joined by several other members of the subcommittee, and I would like to ask any of them if they have an opening statement at this time, before we get into the questions. And we'll go first to our vice chairman of the subcommittee, Mr. Weller.

Mr. WELLER. Well, thank you, Mr. Chairman. I have no questions. Thank you for the courtesy.

Mr. DUNCAN. Thank you very much.

Mr. DeFazio.

Mr. DEFAZIO. No, thank you, Mr. Chairman.

Mr. DUNCAN. Mr. Menendez.

Mr. MENENDEZ. No, thank you, Mr. Chairman.

Mr. DUNCAN. All right. And Mr. LaHood.

Mr. LAHOOD. No, thank you, Mr. Chairnnan.

Mr. DUNCAN. All right, thank you very much.

Mr. Smith, I'll be very brief so we can move to other members. But what, how much of your cargo, roughly what percentage of your cargo that you carry from Japan to points in Asia originate in the United States? You know, there's been some concern expressed by the Japanese in regard to the local traffic.

Mr. SMITH. I can't give you the specific numbers, but let me address that question this way, Mr. Chairman. In the air service agreement between the United States and Japan, Article 12 states very clearly that the primary purpose of the air transportation services between the two countries must be to accommodate third and fourth freedom traffic flows. In the passenger side of the house, the Japanese have taken the position that that means 50 percent of the people on board the airplane must originate or terminate in the United States. U.S. carriers have predictably objected to that.

In the cargo side of the house, all of our flights throughout the Pacific, on the other side of Japan, are scheduled with Article 12 in mind, meaning that the primary purpose of those flights is to serve the third and fourth freedom markets. That's not too hard to do when one understands that Japan today represents 70 percent of the gross national product of all Asia.

Japanese carriers, on the other hand, carrying this sixth freedom traffic, in the 5 years prior to today, increased their all cargo capacity by 57 percent while growth of Japan to other points in Asia traffic increased by 10 percent. So where did that capacity, what was it being used for? It was being used to carry U.S. trade on a sixth freedom traffic basis in the United States.

So we have no problems in terms of that mix of utilizing our beyond rights and have expressed to the Japanese the opinion that if you want to have any kind of a reasonable control on fifth freedom traffic flows, we're happy to accommodate that, so long as you're willing to accede to the same type of controls on your sixth freedom traffic.

It's important to recognize the Japanese have never advanced such a theory in cargo. Because if they're concerned about the percentage of our traffic on the other side of Japan being fifth freedom traffic, you ought to look at some of their planes, and you'll find that they are chock-a-block full of American trade being moved in sixth freedom traffic.

Let me make one other, I think it's very significant, about the agreement that was just reached, as we understand it. The important point from our part is that the United States representatives expressed in the strongest possible terms to the Japanese that they expected our rights to be honored, and if not, that we would respond in kind to embargo of sixth freedom traffic flows on Japanese carriers in the United States.

The new services which were provided for by Japanese carriers in this agreement, again, as we understand it, are from any point in Asia that they serve into their United States points. The new services which are provided for United States carriers, specifically UPS, which we applaud, and is a step in the right direction, specifically limit that from one point in Asia to one other point in Asia, not to all of the points in Asia.

So it needs to be just a first step towards further liberalization. And it is very important that the United States protect these incumbent rights that we hold. And we have been assured at the highest levels of the United States Government that the U.S. will, in fact, protect our rights in the Pacific, and respond in kind.

And this is hugely important to us. Let me say again what I said in the testimony. For 2½ years, we were kept from flying routes in the Pacific to which we were legally entitled. And over $100 million of our business was confiscated.

So this is the only issue we wanted out of these negotiations. We support the further liberalization and believe that open skies is where we ought to get to. There were also some points, the way we understand it, where incumbent carriers could go to several additional points in Japan. But there are no "beyonds," which means that those additional authorities are not meaningful.

Mr. DUNCAN. I turned to Mr. Schaffer when you mentioned the $100 million figure a while ago in your testimony and asked him were you talking about each year. But you meant the $100 million over that 2½ years?

Mr. SMITH. Yes, that's right.

Mr. DUNCAN. Let me ask you this. When you were here a few months ago, when we got into this issue, you mentioned your hub in Subic Bay. And I believe you mentioned some threats that the Japanese had made to shut it down or take other actions. How has your Subic Bay hub worked out?

Mr. SMITH. Well, other than the fact that the Japanese delayed us from opening it about 6 months, and was the largest portion of those costs that I just mentioned, and other than the fact that obviously, I'm sure a lot of our shippers can't be too thrilled that the Japanese, as late as a month ago, put down on the negotiating table, not a verbal threat, but a written threat, that if the United States did not accede to what they wanted done that they would shut FedEx down.

Now, we're very grateful to the Government for calling the Japanese to task on that. And in fact, they did remove it. I would simply point out that the basic framework of the agreement that was being discussed at that time is essentially what's now been agreed to.

Mr. DUNCAN. Mr. Weidemeyer, Mr. Smith mentioned a 9 to 1 disparity with Japan, and said the comparable figure would be 43 to 1 with the United Kingdom. You have in your prepared statement a paragraph that I think is interesting, in regard to the bilateral relationship with the United Kingdom. It says, we approached our own U.S. DOT to help us solve this misinterpretation of the agreement.

To our amazement, our DOT told us that the U.K. was right, and that they had always interpreted the agreement this way. They further told us that they would be happy to redesignate us as directed by the U.K. DOT, but that they would not pursue the matter with the U.K. DOT.

Is it fair to say that you have been surprised or disappointed by the position of the Department of Transportation in that regard? Do you think that—I assume that you're pleased with this latest agreement or this progress that's been made in regard to Japan. But you see that much more needs, I assume you would say that much more needs to be done in regard to the United Kingdom.

Mr. WEIDEMEYER. Mr. Chairman, I think the situation that I alluded to in the testimony is an example of what we're also talking about with Japan, and that's the framework of the bilateral agreements themselves. The difficulty with bilateral agreements is that they are negotiated by regulators, they are put in place and then they are subject to interpretation somewhere down the road where perhaps the people that negotiated them are no longer available.

In the case of our difficulties with the U.K., we had a designation that we could fly at one point, at that point in that time, that was Stanstead. We decided for operational purposes that we wanted to shift our flight to East Midlands, which is 150 miles or so away. The understanding that the two governments had was that the agreement, once you changed designated points, took away your fifth freedom rights.

We obviously heartily opposed that, and went to our DOT and say, you know, they can't do this just because we're going to a different airport for our operating convenience. Certainly there is not a flood of business at either Stanstead or East Midlands, as is the case at Heathrow. It's a very different situation. And because of the lack of understanding of these bilateral arrangements, there was an inability of DOT to come to the same conclusion we had. So we went out on our own and were able to establish with folks in the U.K. that indeed there was nothing wrong with us changing our point.

Mr. DUNCAN. Let me ask you this, and then I need to move on. You mentioned just now that these bilateral agreements are negotiated by regulators.

Do you feel that the Department of Transportation should have a closer relationship with your company, or with both of your companies, in regard to negotiations at this time? Do you think you could provide information that would be helpful to them? Do you find that you have to get your side or your position or your story out in hearings like this? Or do they, does our Department of Transportation ask you for your input in regard to these negotiations or these agreements before the negotiations get down to the nitty-gritty?

Mr. WEIDEMEYER. Over the last few years, there has been a great increase in the ability of carriers like FedEx and UPS to provide input to our negotiators. What I was really referring to was regulators such as the folks that put together bilateral agreements, rather than trade negotiators whose business it is to make sure that the world economy, or the U.S. economy in our case, has an opportunity to expand and grow and foster trade through the agreements we reach with other nations. When trade becomes involved with the regulatory climate, people get a much more realistic idea of what needs to be accomplished, rather than providing regulations to be enforced to prevent commerce, you can come up with trade agreements which enhance commerce.

Mr. DUNCAN. Just to sum up the positions, from the positions of both of you, is that you want to see, you don't want any special protections or considerations, you just want to see the skies as open as possible, so you can compete on a fair basis with companies all over the world. Is that correct?

Mr. WEIDEMEYER. That would be correct.

Mr. DUNCAN. All right, Mr. Lipinski.

Mr. LIPINSKI. Thank you very much, Mr. Chairman.

Mr. Smith, based upon what you said, it seemed to me that the Japanese delayed giving you your rights because they were attempting to capture some cargo for their cargo airlines over the course of 2½ years that they delayed you, and it cost you $100 million. Is that what you were conveying to me, or to us?

Mr. SMITH. Well, yes, sir, except I would just like to correct you on one thing. They didn't deny us our, what they did is they would not approve our flight schedules. We got the rights in 1952, or our predecessor company did. They just wouldn't approve our flight schedule. We then in essence took a complaint about that to the U.S. Department of Transportation. And the U.S. Department of Transportation issued an order finding in our favor. And they put on a sanction which they withdrew for various reasons. And so we sat there for 2 years.

Then we filed our flight schedule for the Subic Bay operation, which we had fully briefed the Japanese operation about, and the U.S. Government about. The Japanese said, we're not going to approve that schedule.

Mr. LIPINSKI. What was their rationale, though, for not approving that particular schedule?

Mr. SMITH. What was our reaction?

Mr. LIPINSKI. No, what was their rationale for not doing it? Why did they say they weren't doing it?

Mr. SMITH. Because they wanted new authorities and rights for their carriers. And they decided to use us as the point of leverage, as the whipping boy.

Mr. LIPINSKI. No, that I understand. I was saying, what rationale, though, did they express any rationale publicly?

Mr. SMITH. Yes. The rationale that was expressed publicly was why I went through that history lesson, is that somehow the beyond rights that the U.S. 52 incumbent carriers had, that these were somehow illegitimate, that these were imposed upon them when they were a war-ravaged economy, and had they been stronger, they never would have agreed to it. The reality is that fifths and anterior fifth freedom opportunities were known in 1944 and 1952 to be equivalent economic opportunities.

What led the Japanese to take this position, and bear in mind, for 40 years, they had honored the agreement. It was only in 1993 that they came to this new interpretation. And what made the Japanese very aggressive in this are the economic problems of their own carriers. I think they did have some legitimate issues about wanting more freedoms for their carriers, which we fully supported, as we do today, the agreement that was just reached.

And then third, and I don't think the importance of this can be underestimated by this committee, they saw the tremendous success of the British, under their moving from Bermuda I, which was very similar to the 1952 air services agreement with Japan, to Bermuda II, which took away almost all of the United States' beyond rights, but was moot about the British anterior fifth or sixth freedom traffic flows.

Well, this gave them an incredible inherent advantage over the United States. And in fact, the ratio, if you take the revenue ton mile opportunities for all of the British carriers' sixth freedom markets into the United States, and compare them to the U.S. fifth freedom or beyond opportunities, the ratio is 43 to 1.

The one final point, Mr. Lipinski, that's very important, and I agree with Tom, I mean, what we would support is a liberal open skies regime worldwide. But what has created a lot of these problems has been that many of these agreements that the United States has entered into have not been based on any economic analysis whatsoever. And that is one of the two criticisms that the GAO made of them.

And I would just request, what I would suggest to the committee, if you really want to get into this and see what the issue is, ask for the supporting analysis on any agreement that they make, and I think you'll be amazed.

Mr. LIPINSKI. Well, we have an excellent turnout here for the committee today, and it's obvious that people have a tremendous amount of interest in this subject. You were talking about the sixth freedom rights. Now, correct me if I'm wrong. That means a Japanese carrier can pick up cargo in Peking, fly and stop in Tokyo, and fly into Los Angeles, correct?

Mr. SMITH. Correct.

Mr. LIPINSKI. Now, are there any of those routes that exist for Japanese cargo carriers that do not exist for American cargo carriers?

Mr. SMITH. Well, under the terms of the 1952 agreement—

Mr. LIPINSKI. No, I'm talking in reality, today.

Mr. SMITH. Well, I'm trying to answer the question. Under the terms of the 1952 agreement, in the plain, unalterable language, there is no such difference. Under the interpretation that the Japanese adopted since 1993, there are huge differences. And hopefully this new agreement will resolve those.

Again, as I mentioned to you, we had only one objective in these negotiations. We wanted the United States to unequivocally inform the Japanese that FedEx's or the incumbent carriers' rights would be protected, and if not, the United States' response would be to take down Japanese carriers' ability to move sixth freedom traffic flow. It's quid pro quo.

Now, if in fact that has been clearly communicated, and it has been clearly communicated to us by the highest levels of the U.S. Government that that will be the case, then we are very, very happy and think this is a great progress. And we applaud any additional rights that we can get for other U.S. carriers moving towards open skies. I would point out, however, Mr. Lipinski, that the Japanese did not in writing confirm that. And in fact, the agreement, we understand, will specifically say that both sides retain their interpretation.

So I hope I am wrong on this. But it would not surprise me if I'm not up here a year from now or 2 years from now.

Mr. LIPINSKI. I assure you, if it is not put into writing and the American carriers are not satisfied with it, you'll be back here much sooner than that. Because I'm sure the Chairman will see to it that you have the opportunity to be back here.

Let me go to another question for you, Mr. Smith, and then we'll get over to Mr. Weidemeyer. In regards to negotiating these bilaterals, do you think it would be wise to have the U.S. trade representative be involved in this?

Mr. SMITH. I think that the involvement of the U.S. trade representative might well be a good solution. Today it is the statutory responsibility of two departments, Department of State and Department of Transportation. One of the problems has been historically, in the years I have been in the business, has been, as the GAO said, the lack of econometrics analyses as to what the respective economic opportunities are. It's been simply a political battle.

And many times, the political battle has been fought utilizing the multiplicity of U.S. interests against the singular or near singular interests of foreign carriers. So we tend to get a horse trade, which makes a lot of sense for an individual carrier, getting some new right. But in the scheme of U.S. interests overall, it's been a very poor agreement. That really is the case in Bermuda II.

So one of the things that the U.S. trade rep might perform is the role of scorekeeper with an institutional memory based on trade. And furthermore, I think that an idea which may be worth evaluation by the Congress would be U.S. trade reps involvement on the cargo side of the house. Because you see, the ability to move goods back and forth by air represents today almost 37, about 37 percent of the total value of U.S. trade. Our estimate is, FedEx, it will be 60 percent of the value.

So if U.S. carriers can't be involved in U.S. trade and a foreign entity can use one of these air service agreements to sit like Gibraltar over an airborne trade route, it will be a serious impediment to our ability to trade internationally. So I think there might be a real rationale to get USTR in as a scorekeeper and perhaps give them some sort of portfolio on the cargo side of the house.

Mr. LIPINSKI. Thank you very much, Mr. Smith.

Mr. Weidemeyer, what are your feelings in regard to the U.S. trade representative being involved in these negotiations?

Mr. WEIDEMEYER. As I said earlier, I think what we're facing in today's economy and the future global economy is, we have to recognize that trade has to take precedence over regulation. As a consequence, I think they should be involved.

Air cargo, and you just heard Mr. Smith's figures of where we think it's going, and I'll accept his figures, 60 percent is a pretty attractive number looking out in the future, air cargo becomes the facilitator of that trade, and as such is really an arm of trade rather than a regulated transportation mode. It becomes the facilitator of trade.

Mr. LIPINSKI. Thank you very much, Mr. Weidemeyer. Mr. Weidemeyer, one last question before I give the microphone back to the Chairman. But I'll be back for other questions later on.

According to the report that I have, United Parcel is going to obtain 12 new flights to Osaka, including six fifth freedom flights to Taipei. Is that your understanding of the agreement?

Mr. WEIDEMEYER. That is what we would hope it is. We have not been given a specific designation of a point. But the point that we requested was Taipei.

Mr. LIPINSKI. Mr. Smith, do you have—is that the information you have also? Because we're trying to put together what was agreed upon in Japan.

Mr. SMITH. Yes, our understanding is that United Parcel Service will get 12 additional flights to the new Kansai Airport in Osaka, 6 of which may be continued to another point in Asia, restricted to the fifth freedom traffic flows between the Kansai point and that point, and six blind sector, which means that they could fly to that point and beyond. And again, I think that's excellent progress. I really do think our negotiators have done an outstanding job of moving the ball down the field. But I would hope that it would be—

Mr. LIPINSKI. Only the first step, by any account.

Mr. SMITH. The first step.

Mr. LIPINSKI. Mr. Weidemeyer, do you want to add anything to what I said, what you said, or what Mr. Smith said here?

Mr. WEIDEMEYER. No. I think just for clarification, I think all that's been agreed is that there will be one beyond point. It's our hope that, we will request that it be Taipei.

Mr. LIPINSKI. Well, my information tells me it's Taipei. That doesn't necessarily mean it's true, but that's what my information tells me at the present time.

Thank you, Mr. Chairman. I have questions I'd like to talk to these panelists later on, but I know there's a lot of people here. Thank you.

Mr. DUNCAN. Thank you very much.

Mr. Weller.

Mr. WELLER. Thank you, Mr. Chairman, and like my friend Mr. Lipinski, I come from the Land of Lincoln, the State of Illinois, which is very, very trade dependent. The economy and many, many jobs in our State are very dependent on international trade and opportunity and access to overseas markets. And frankly, my questions are a little bit similar to Mr. Lipinski's.

As I understand it from testimony, both FedEx and UPS are supporting the agreement that was reached as of yesterday. And I was wondering, particularly, going a little further than what we've already discussed, you were talking about the need for economic analysis as part of the discussions and seeing what the results of an agreement would be. I was wondering, can you give us, from the standpoint of working families back home, your best estimate of what the economic impact is for the United States as a result, what benefits we will get economically as a result of this agreement, Mr. Smith?

Mr. SMITH. Well, we've done our own independent analysis of this. And I'm not ducking the question here, Mr. Weller. But you have on the next panel one of the leading experts on this particular subject in the form of Clyde Prestowitz, who recently published, last weekend, published a comprehensive paper on this. And he might be better to answer that more objectively than us.

In his report, it made the point, if you looked at open beyond environments in future years, the difference to U.S. economic interests was measured in the multiple billions of dollars and in the tens of thousands of additional employees. And we concur with that wholeheartedly and think that the analyses in his report may well be understated. And I'm sure in terms of the relative relationships of the U.S. and Japan interest in this particular case, he could probably give you a more objective picture of it than I could.

Mr. WELLER. From your own company's standpoint, can you project, will you be hiring additional employees, will you be purchasing additional equipment?

Mr. SMITH. Well, we have been a major purchaser of McDonnell Douglas MD-11 intercontinental aircraft. And assuming that our beyond rights in the Pacific are protected by the U.S. Government, I'm sure we will continue to buy the MD-11 or perhaps other airplanes, like 747-400s. But the MD-11 is really our primary airplane. We just bought five more of them, or are having five more delivered.

And in fact, another airplane order was hanging on the balance, depending on what this negotiation turned out to be. So if it is as we understand it and we have those assurances that our rights are going to be honored, we'll go on and take that airplane, which I'm sure will be very good news to McDonnell Douglas, since it's already in our colors, I understand.

Mr. WELLER. From your perspective, Mr. Smith, for Federal Express, what do you see is the economic benefit to the United States as a result of the agreement that was reached yesterday?

Mr. SMITH. You mean Mr. Weidemeyer?

Mr. WELLER. Excuse me, Mr. Weidemeyer. Excuse me.

Mr. WEIDEMEYER. From UPS' perspective or from a U.S. perspective?

Mr. WELLER. Well, from UPS.

Mr. WEIDEMEYER. Up to now, because of the limited rights we had in Asia, we really had a competitive disadvantage with being able to serve customers in southeast Asia. This will give us the opportunity to open up those markets, not only between points in Asia, but also to make that service available to and from the U.S.

Historically, for UPS, every 70 packages we add to our network creates another job. I think there is a recognition in our work force, particularly with Rod Carey, who is the President of Teamsters, he understands that as well. And although we're not always on the best of terms, he has written a letter to President Clinton fully endorsing our position in this, that additional rights are necessary to help protect and create additional jobs.

Mr. WELLER. You say your formula is for every additional 70 packages, that's one more job? Is that 70 packages a day, or—

Mr. WEIDEMEYER. Yes.

Mr. WELLER. Okay, is one more job. How many more packages do you feel that this will generate in trade between the United States and Japan and the markets around Japan?

Mr. WEIDEMEYER. Based on the size of the aircraft we have to fly between Asia and the U.S., Fred talked about MD-11s, we operate 747s. The size of the packages we handle are in the neighborhood of 10,000 or more. And in order for us to be successful, we have to develop markets that will fill up those aircraft. Obviously, day one, they're not going to be full with packages. But that's ultimately what we need to do. So that gives you an idea of what the scope may be.

Mr. WELLER. That's a lot of boxes.

Mr. WEIDEMEYER. A lot of boxes.

Mr. WELLER. Following up on some of the questions that my colleagues have also brought up, about the role of the special trade

24-087 97 - 2

representative as part of these negotiations, from your perspective, you've indicated that you feel the STR should be more actively involved in this process, because of the trade issues.

Mr. WEIDEMEYER. Yes, sir.

Mr. WELLER. Involved here. Do you feel that there would have been a better agreement had the STR been involved?

Mr. WEIDEMEYER. This particular instance, I'm not sure. And I'd like not to speculate on it because I don't know what underlying data would have been available. Mr. Smith has given some pretty graphic illustrations of the imbalances. And taking for granted his information is right, it's pretty obvious on its face that the imbalance needed to somewhat corrected. And every step we could take towards ultimately open skies, but along the way liberalizing it, is going to create additional opportunities for U.S. carriers.

Mr. WELLER. With just a quick follow-up, I realize I'm running out of time, Mr. Chairman, and if you'll just grant me just a couple more seconds or another minute here, it appears we do have the agreement with Japan. Of course the U.K. issue still remains to be resolved. Just from the experience that we've had, do you feel that the Department of Transportation or do you feel that the special trade representative should take the lead in resolving the U.K. issue?

Mr. WEIDEMEYER. At this point in time, I'd recommend that it be a joint effort. The Department of Transportation certainly is trying with every capability they have to obtain additional international rights for U.S. carriers, and Canada and Germany and now Japan are all indications that they are making progress. The U.K. may be a special situation. They have proven to be and continue to be rather intransigent in this area. And perhaps bringing some pressure to bear with trade issues as well could indeed enhance the opportunity to get an agreement.

Mr. WELLER. Okay. Mr. Smith, do you agree with Mr. Weidemeyer, or do you feel that one agency should have lead over the other, between STR and DOT in the U.K. negotiations that are still underway?

Mr. SMITH. Well, our belief about the negotiations with the United Kingdom goes directly back to the point I made about equating sixth and fifth freedom traffic flows. And that the GAO noted the United States didn't have a strategy. It doesn't make any difference whether you get the USTR or anybody else involved, unless you have a strategy for dealing with the intransigents, why would they change? They have a marvelous situation.

So I don't think the issue is the agency involved. I think it's the adoption of a strategy to get the British to liberalize. And I think that the appropriate response to the British is again, the relationship of fifth freedom and sixth freedom traffic flows.

There's a lot of difference, by the way, I might point out, to the air services agreement between the United States and Great Britain today and the air services agreement between the United States and Japan. And those subtle differences are hugely, hugely important, which we certainly don't have the time or the inclination to go into those legal nuances. But they are very significant differences between the two treaties.

Mr. WELLER. Well, thank you, and thank you, Mr. Chairman.

Mr. DUNCAN. Thank you, Mr. Weller.

Mr. DeFazio.

Mr. DEFAZIO. Thank you, Mr. Chairman.

I just want to follow up on the negotiating strategy a little bit with Mr. Smith. Tell me about comparative values here. What is, the way I always look at these issues is, what clout do we bring to the table? And what percentage of the revenues are derived by British traffic into the U.S. for some of your competitors versus what percentage you derive with traffic to the U.K. and beyond?

What I'm getting at here is normally when you're dealing with a country of that size, we are the much more lucrative market. And their companies are much more at risk if we decide to get tough in the negotiations. Is that a correct assumption?

Mr. SMITH. Precisely.

Mr. DEFAZIO. So you'd be willing to take a risk here, that is in terms of, if when they, back 20 years ago, unilaterally renounced our original agreement, I mean, if we got really tough and said, look, we're just not going to tolerate this any more, I mean, if we got tough, don't you expect that those firms over there are so much more at risk that they would be putting extraordinary pressure on their government to say, look, they're finally getting serious over there in the United States. They're not going to be kicked around any more. FedEx can go for 20 years without access to our market, but we can't go for 6 weeks without access to theirs. "I mean, I don't know that that's a good comparison." But I assume there's some sort of comparison like that.

Mr. SMITH. Mr. DeFazio, I like to think of myself as a student of history, and particularly commercial history. And the United States' willingness to accede to this position over the last 20 some odd years, led by the British, that somehow our beyond rights were unfair, illegitimate and what have you, but yet their beyond rights were sacrosanct, has been one of the damndest product positioning scams I've ever seen pulled off.

And to this day, there is a reluctance on the part of many in this Government to equate those two economic opportunities. And the theory is, well, we hadn't said much about it until you folks started screaming about it. So ergo, we don't want to do it. And as I tried to explain in my background on the 1944 Chicago convention, framework that was put together, fifth freedoms for both sides were called fifth freedoms. One was fifths, and one was anterior fifths.

So the proper strategy of dealing with a carrier that has an air service system which is viable only because of its sixth freedom traffic flows, which is certainly the case in the example that you said, to say that there's not a potential strategy for changing the agreement seems to be not well thought out.

Mr. DEFAZIO. Well, I wish we could divine the root cause of the reluctance. I mean, I know in the past, of course, when we were locked in the cold war struggle with the Soviet Union, you know, basically State told Commerce or DOT, "look, we've got to accede to our allies, or our bulwarks overseas against the evil empire here, and so what if it's to the disadvantage of our commerce, we're going to do those things."

But I guess in today's competitive world, where I see the competition shifting to economics, I'm puzzled as to why the United States would continue this position. Is there any insight you can give me to any discussions you've had that aren't confidential with principals in our Government as to why they won't take that more consistent reciprocally tough line?

Mr. SMITH. Mr. DeFazio, if I could tell you the number of hours that my business partners, some of whom are sitting behind me, have sat and speculated about that, I mean, I've spent days. I cannot understand why. I don't know why.

Mr. DEFAZIO. Okay. Well, perhaps we'll have some Administration witnesses at a soon future hearing, and maybe they can—

Mr. SMITH. Well, as I mentioned a moment ago, I would recommend to the Congress that they simply ask two questions. One, to be shown some of the economic analyses on these air service agreements that are made. And I think you will be thunderstruck. If the numbers that we and United Parcel and some of the other people, that we have, all of which, ours are produced not by us, these are produced by external consultants.

Just ask to see those. And then ask why the United States Government does not equate beyond rights for foreign interests, which is U.S. trade—again, this is not foreign trade, this is U.S. trade—why the United States has been unwilling to equate the two. I cannot answer why the Government has been unwilling to do either of those two things.

Mr. DEFAZIO. Okay, I thank you. I thank the Chairman for the time.

Mr. DUNCAN. Thank you, Mr. DeFazio.

Mr. Ehlers.

Mr. EHLERS. Thank you, Mr. Chairman.

Just a brief question for both of you. I gather that you are reasonably happy with the agreement that was reached yesterday, reasonably satisfied with it. Mr. Smith, is that—

Mr. SMITH. Well, we are extremely pleased and very grateful to the U.S. Department of State and the Department of Transportation for asserting in the last meeting this equivalency of economic rights and stating unequivocally that these rights would be protected by countermeasures against Japanese sixth freedom movements in the event that our rights were not honored. And we have been very gratified that that has been confirmed to us by the highest levels of the United States Government.

And we think this agreement marks great progress, assuming that is correct. I simply point out to you that the written agreement that will be signed will simply state that both sides adhere to their interpretation of the agreement. And that means that the Japanese, should they desire to do so, can take the position 6 months, a year from now, 18 months, that the interpretation which they adopted in 1993 is again on the table and our flight to wherever is not going to be approved.

And that is exactly what we've been going through for the last 2, 2½ years. And it has been extremely, an extreme impediment to running our business and taken a huge amount of time. And as I mentioned to Mr. DeFazio, it has done nothing short of amaze me that we've been permitted to be treated this way.

Mr. EHLERS. Just a follow-up. Later on in today's hearing we'll be discussing passenger service to Japan and beyond. And there's a move by some American airlines, I understand, to say that we should give up some of our fifth freedom rights in exchange for more routes between Japan and the U.S. I take it from your comments you would advise against that?

Mr. SMITH. Well, it's our understanding, by the way, Mr. Ehlers, in having heard this from my counterpart at American Airlines and Governor Baliles, who is the chairperson of the ACCESS U.S.-Japan Coalition, that that is not their position, that they do not want to trade away U.S. beyond rights for additional access. And certainly that is the case in the cargo side of the house.

I can't speak authoritatively on the passenger side. I can tell you in the cargo side that were the United States agree to limit or to eliminate beyond authorities for U.S. interests and trade for those interests strictly third and fourth freedom rights, it would be a poor trade at the most incredible levels. And again, to the Government's credit, they've made it very clear to the Japanese government, according to our information, that they will not countenance any such trade.

Mr. EHLERS. Thank you.

Mr. Weidemeyer, do you have anything to add to that, in response to my questions?

Mr. WEIDEMEYER. Yes, Mr. Ehlers. I would just support what Fred has just said. It's our understanding as well that the U.S. Government has taken the firm position that the existing rights are not touched in any way by this and that these are additional rights, therefore enlarging the pie rather than splitting up a standard size pie in smaller pieces. We've made the pie bigger so that there are more entrants and more competition.

Mr. EHLERS. All right. We'll learn more about it in the second panel.

Mr. Chairman, I'll reserve the remainder of my time for questions during the next panel.

Mr. DUNCAN. All right. Thank you very much.

Mr. Cramer.

Mr. CRAMER. Thank you, Mr. Chairman.

And I'll be able to be brief, because many of the questions I had on my mind have already been asked of you. Both of you, you indicate your companies have had to be aggressively involved in negotiations in spite of what our Government was trying to do. And you've indicated that both the United Kingdom and Japan have presented challenges, certainly, to the old way of thinking and the old way of negotiating. And I hope we've learned from this.

On the U.K. side, would either of you care to comment about the progress we seem to be making and where we are, and where you think we are with regards to getting an agreement there?

Mr. WEIDEMEYER. I may be in the dark, but I'm not aware of any progress that has been made. I have seen things in recent weeks that we're considering getting back together and hopefully we can make some progress. But I have no independent knowledge that that has taken place or meetings have even been scheduled.

Mr. SMITH. Well, it's important to recount just a very small bit of history. Last year when the so-called mini-deal was put on the table, we objected very strongly to the fact that cargo was not included in the mini-deal. And I think UPS did as well.

At that time, we were informed very directly by U.S. Government representatives that we should not oppose the mini-deal, because liberalization of cargo was "a done deal," and that it would be very shortly thereafter addressed.

In actual fact what happened is the Secretary of Transport of the United Kingdom left his post and took over a political position with Prime Minister Major, and a new group, a new Secretary of Transport came into the Secretary of Transport situation that did not feel bound by that agreement, I suppose, that had led to those comments to us.

And in fact, the British position, when talks were held in September, were significantly regressive from even the most modest proposal the United Kingdom had put forward before. So far from being any progress since the mini-deal, there has been a significant retrograde movement, as far as we can tell.

Mr. CRAMER. All right. Mr. Weidemeyer, you recounted a history in your efforts to move from the Stanstead Airport to the East Midlands Airport, negotiating that. How long did that take you to finalize that?

Mr. WEIDEMEYER. It seems like ancient history now. But it took a period of months. And I just want to reemphasize, the difficulty with the situation was not with the U.S. representatives. The difficulty with the situation is the bilateral agreements which are subject to interpretation and misinterpretation. And that's exactly what occurred in that situation.

Mr. CRAMER. So that's what you mean when you distinguish between the bilateral relationship versus the bilateral agreement?

Mr. WEIDEMEYER. Yes, sir.

Mr. CRAMER. All right. Thank you. I yield back my time.

Mr. DUNCAN. Thank you very much, Mr. Cramer.

Ms. Danner.

Ms. DANNER. No questions.

Mr. DUNCAN. All right, thank you very much. Mr. Geren.

Mr. GEREN. No questions.

Mr. DUNCAN. All right. Mr. Kim.

Mr. KIM. Mr. Chairman, thank you for recognizing me. And I'm sorry I was so late. I had to go to another hearing.

I don't have any questions at this time, Mr. Chairman.

Mr. DUNCAN. Mr. Lipinski, do you have any other comments?

Mr. LIPINSKI. I have a couple of questions, if you don't mind, Mr. Chairman.

Mr. DUNCAN. Go ahead.

Mr. LIPINSKI. I have a fax over here which is a document from the White House Office of the Press Secretary, then it goes on, it says United States Department of Transportation. And it's pertaining to the handshake agreement that we have achieved in Japan. And there's a paragraph in here I just want to ask both of you gentlemen, well, I don't have to ask you, Mr. Weidemeyer, because it doesn't pertain to you, only you, Mr. Smith. It pertains to you.

And it reads the following: The agreement also provides additional operating flexibility for Northwest Airlines, Federal Express, and United Airlines. It permits these carriers to operate from any

U.S. city and serve three additional Japanese points which may be combined with these carriers' existing Japanese rights.

Now, is your interpretation of that that Northwest, FedEx and United are going to get three each, or is it one per each one? Do you want me to read it to you again?

Mr. SMITH. No. My interpretation of that, as I understand it today, is that each of the incumbent carriers could serve three each. The point that you should recognize, again, I point out to the information that I mentioned to you, the ability to serve those three points on the third and fourth freedom basis are of marginal, if any, economic utility to any of the carriers.

Mr. LIPINSKI. Run that one by me again?

Mr. SMITH. Well, let's take a real life example, Mr. Lipinski. I mean, the profundity of these traffic flows is very, very huge. If I'm a U.S. carrier flying from Memphis or Louisville or California or what have you, and I can serve one additional point in Japan, or three additional points, but I cannot serve any beyond, then I am limited only to the traffic which I can pick up in that catchment are in the United States, and to the catchment area in Japan.

The Japanese carriers, on the other side, can fly from any point in Asia to any one of those three points, and do. And pick up traffic all over Asia and commingle it with traffic originating in that catchment area in Japan and move it to the United States, and conversely, in their movement from any point in the United States, they can pick up traffic not just to Nagoya or Fukiyoko or Sapporo, they can pick up traffic from any point in the United States to any point in Asia that's connected by that airport. There's no economic benefit of having those three points.

Mr. LIPINSKI. But under your interpretation of our agreement with Japan, in my interpretation of it, if you are going to be stamped approved by Japan to fly into three new sites in Japan, should you not then be able to fly beyond that?

Mr. SMITH. Yes, sir. That would be real liberalization there, from our standpoint.

Mr. LIPINSKI. But underneath your interpretation and my interpretation, it would seem to me that this here is nothing particularly new. You should have had this ability in the first place.

Mr. SMITH. Well, no, sir. The existing air service agreement limits FedEx, at least, to service three points in Japan. Tokyo's Narita Airport, Osaka, which is now the new Kansai Airport, and Okinawa.

Mr. LIPINSKI. And now with those three you have beyond rights, correct?

Mr. SMITH. That's correct. The three additional points, there are no beyond rights whatsoever.

Mr. LIPINSKI. But in your interpretation and mine, there should be beyond rights with those?

Mr. SMITH. Well, the air service agreement would have to be modified to include those points on an unrestricted basis. You see, the air service agreements have rights and points. And we are restricted to three points in Japan: Tokyo, Osaka and Okinawa. And from those three points, according to the air service agreement that we have, our interpretation, DOT's interpretation, we can fly from those three points to any point.

Mr. LIPINSKI. But if you—

Mr. SMITH. As long as we meet the test of Article 12.

Mr. LIPINSKI. Out of this latest agreement, Article 12, that's where—what is Article 12?

Mr. SMITH. Article 12 states that, there are a lot of technical issues, but that the primary purpose of the air carrier service conducted between the two points shall be the movement of third and fourth freedom traffic. Let me give you a real life example, and it's something that doesn't apply to us, but which you can ask Mr. Hirst about from Northwest.

Several years ago, Northwest wanted to fly over Japan to Australia, which sounds a little convoluted, but actually it's a fairly efficient routing. The percentage of seats on that flight sold between the United States and Australia were relatively small percentage. The Japanese objected to that under Article 12, and said it doesn't meet the primacy test. Well, where is that primacy test? Is it 5 percent? Is it 50 percent?

Mr. LIPINSKI. They were maintaining it was 50 percent in that case, weren't they?

Mr. SMITH. In the passenger side of the house. But I noted to you before they've been silent on the cargo side of the house, for obvious reasons. The three additional points for the incumbent carriers as far as cargo is concerned will be of marginal benefit. Now, they may be of great benefit to Northwest and United. I don't know.

But as I tried to describe before, Japanese carriers at these three points, any service that they have to any other point can be carried into the United States. Whereas our service to those points can only be carried between very small catchment areas between the two. So that is a very limited economic opportunity.

Mr. LIPINSKI. But if you were to get beyond rights with these three new locations, then it would be very advantageous economically to you, correct?

Mr. SMITH. And that is why we support open skies with Japan. Because we would like to have the ability to serve any point in Japan to any other point, not just the three points that we're currently authorized to do. And we are more than willing to see our "advantage" under our 1952 agreement go away, and let the market decide who's winners if we had that. But this agreement, again, it's not open skies. But we applaud the negotiators. It's a tough thing, and it is progress. And we appreciate it.

Mr. LIPINSKI. Well, I applaud the negotiators also. And I hope we can get it totally and completely firmed up. Because it is a step in the right direction, but a great deal more has to be done, I believe, in regards to Japan and the United Kingdom.

I thank both you gentlemen for being here. I have many other questions, but I know we have to move on to a second panel, and I've had two opportunities to speak already. So Mr. Chairman, I turn back the microphone.

Mr. DUNCAN. Thank you very much, Mr. Lipinski. And we do need to, we have some other witnesses that we need to move to.

Gentlemen, let me say this. I just want to thank you once again, and we are going to continue to look very closely at this relationship with the United Kingdom. And as I understand it, and from the information, I received a call from Secretary Pena shortly before this hearing, and if the information that we've gotten from the White House and from the Department of Transportation about this agreement, apparently there's been a handshake agreement so far that will be formalized by mid-April.

If the Japanese do not fully comply with that, if you have "scheduling difficulties," Mr. Smith, after that, then you let us know. Because I can assure you, and I think you know this from the earlier hearing a few months ago, there is a very strong majority on this subcommittee that would be very willing to fashion some sort of legislative remedy if it was necessary to do that. We really want to avoid that. But the Japanese need to fully comply with this agreement that was reached yesterday, and we need to work toward other agreements of this nature as we move down the road.

But thank you very much for coming to be with us today. Your testimony has been very helpful.

Mr. SMITH. We appreciate the support. Thank you.

Mr. WEIDEMEYER. Thank you very much.

Mr. DUNCAN. We will call our second panel at this time. And panel number two consists of Mr. Richard B. Hirst, who is Senior Vice President for Northwest Airlines; Mr. Scott C. Gibson, who is Vice President for Planning and Corporate Strategy of Trans World Airlines, Inc.; Mr. Cyril D. Murphy, who is Vice President for International Affairs of United Air Lines; and Mr. Clyde V. Prestowitz, Jr., who is President of the Economic Strategy Institute.

Gentlemen, thank you very much for being with us. And we'll begin your testimony at this time. And I suppose that we'll just go in the order as we move down the table. And Mr. Gibson, we'll start with you, and then Mr. Hirst, we'll go to you, and Mr. Murphy will go third. And thank you very much. Mr. Hirst, you may begin your testimony. Mr. Gibson, I'm sorry.

TESTIMONY OF RICHARD B. HIRST, SENIOR VICE PRESIDENT, NORTHWEST AIRLINES, INC.; SCOTT C. GIBSON, VICE PRESIDENT, PLANNING AND CORPORATE STRATEGY, TRANS WORLD AIRLINES, INC.; CYRIL D. MURPHY, VICE PRESIDENT, INTERNATIONAL AFFAIRS, UNITED AIR LINES, INC.; AND CLYDE V. PRESTOWITZ, JR., PRESIDENT, ECONOMIC STRATEGY INSTITUTE

Mr. GIBSON. Thank you, Mr. Chairman and members of the committee. TWA appreciates the opportunity to appear before you today to present testimony on the important issues raised by the U.S.-U.K. bilateral negotiations.

Our aviation relationship with the United Kingdom has been difficult for many years. And it's resulted in high fares and limited service on the most important trans-Atlantic route of our Nation. The restrictive bilateral also produced a market in which the two British flag carriers have a 60 percent market share compared to 40 percent for six U.S. flag carriers. One issue for the United States is how to change this situation, how to expand service for the benefit of the traveling public, and enhance the competitive opportunities of U.S. airlines.

I would also suggest that another major public policy issue related to these negotiations is how to give TWA the opportunity to succeed as a viable trans-Atlantic competitor. TWA provides important

U.S. flag service to 12 major destinations in Europe and the Middle East. Although TWA has suffered a decade of financial adversity, it has turned the corner and begun the return to profitability. The strengthening of TWA's route system on the Atlantic will benefit the U.S. balance of payments, enhance U.S. flag competitiveness and preserve the jobs of TWA's 23,000 employees.

As you know, in the last round of negotiations in October 1995, the United Kingdom made a proposal that would have allowed a limited transfer of service from Gatwick to Heathrow, and in a precedent-setting move, would have removed the ability of the U.S. Government to pick which carriers and which routes would receive this new service. It would have totally precluded TWA's proposal for new service between New York-JFK and Heathrow. TWA believes that the U.S. Government acted properly in rejecting this inadequate British proposal, and while we urge that negotiations be resumed and we hope that the end result will allow the United States to designate TWA in the JFK to Heathrow route.

In this testimony I will briefly review the history of TWA's financial difficulties, our attempts, with the dedicated support of TWA's employees, to return to sustained financial strength, and the public benefits that would be achieved by TWA's New York to Heathrow route. Finally, I will review the course of the bilateral discussions and make recommendations for future steps. I also ask permission to submit a more detailed statement for the record.

TWA has suffered massive financial problems over the past 2 years. It has endured two bankruptcies and has begun the arduous climb back to financial strength. We recognize that we still have substantial work to do. We succeeded in 1995, but it was a very good year for the industry, and we have to be prepared for the inevitable downturn. We have to take several more steps, including the following. We have to modernize our fleet, and last month we ordered 20 Boeing 757s with an option for another 20, which is TWA's first new equipment order in 10 years. We are negotiating with manufacturers for additional aircraft and are planning to hushkit our existing DC-9 fleet.

We have to reduce our costs. We are reviewing all phases of our operation to increase efficiency, reduce costs and become more competitive. Our employee task forces have already identified over $100 million in cost savings.

Finally, we have to fill the void at the heart of our trans-Atlantic route structure. To do this, we need a New York-Heathrow route.

The New York-Heathrow route is not only of immense importance to TWA, but it's also the single most valuable route that the U.S. could achieve in these negotiations. While other airlines are proposing to switch existing service from Gatwick to Heathrow, only TWA is proposing entirely new service in a competitive market. TWA has worked hard to develop its major international hub at JFK and connects 26 domestic U.S. cities with 11 major European destinations. However, it is weakened because it lacks access to London, which accounts for almost one-third, and actually in 1994, it was 32 percent of all U.S.-Europe passengers.

TWA's inability to carry traffic between its major gateway and London, has an adverse impact on our trans-Atlantic system. Without access to London, we lack market identity at New York and cannot compete effectively for corporate traffic, because companies desire to contract with one airline for all major trans-Atlantic markets. Without the support of connecting London passengers, our domestic spokes are weaker, which limits our ability to expand on these domestic segments. A JFK-Heathrow route would give TWA badly needed market identity in the trans-Atlantic market, the support of connecting traffic and the ability to turn our international system into overall profitability.

TWA forecasts that it will achieve $100 million annually in operating revenues on this route. In addition, we will earn between $20 million and $40 million in revenue on other trans-Atlantic routes that we do not today have access to, because of our inability to offer a comprehensive route system across the Atlantic.

TWA recognizes that other U.S. carriers have legitimate desires for access to Heathrow, and would like to transfer current flights that now serve Gatwick. However, the public benefit for such transfers cannot match the gain that would be achieved by a new route for TWA. Only TWA would add entirely new service on this route, its daily Boeing 747 would provide additional U.S. flag competition for British carriers at New York, where TWA has traditionally been a major trans-Atlantic carrier, as well as new on-line service for the numerous points served by TWA's New York hub.

The British remain intransigent. Their last offer was sharply circumscribed to allow switching of existing service from Gatwick to Heathrow while precluding any possibility of TWA providing its new service from New York. We are pleased that the Government stood firm. It was correct to be extremely dissatisfied with the nature of the British proposal, particularly after the United Kingdom had promised in the first round of 1995 negotiations to be more forthcoming with Heathrow authorities.

We are well aware that other carriers have also suggested that TWA would be happy to take the Gatwick route offered by the British and give up our attempts to return to Heathrow. TWA rejects this advice, because we want to be an effective competitor in the New York-London market, and we know this requires access to Heathrow. In this market, Gatwick is a distant second choice.

We accept the testimony of Sir Colin Marshall, the Chairman of British Airways, who recently told the U.K. inquiry on the construction of Terminal 5 at Heathrow that expansion at Gatwick was not an alternative. He noted that Gatwick had the disadvantages of greater distance, time and cost for most passengers from the main markets in the southeast of the U.K. and was limited by a single runway.

In the current negotiations, the British have also claimed that a route for TWA would be simply too much, that it would result in an imbalanced agreement that is far beyond the scope of the limited and balanced exchange of Heathrow routes that was intended. This argument comes with poor grace from a government whose airlines carry 60 percent of total U.S.-U.K. traffic. Only a government that believes in mercantilism rather than competition can be concerned about the impact of one flight by one carrier in a market the size of New York-London.

TWA believes that negotiations should be resumed and that both the U.S. and U.K. should attempt to reach an agreement that will expand service opportunities between our countries. We do believe it will be possible to reach an agreement. Mr. Malcolm Rifkind, the British Foreign Minister, has recently indicated a willingness to resume negotiations on the basis of the last British offer. While that was inadequate, there are possible counteroffers that may lead to the British being more generous.

In this regard, I believe that Senator Pressler's recent speech to the International Aviation Club was very helpful in moving this discussion forward. To encourage a bigger, bolder and braver approach to negotiations by the British, he suggested movement by the U.S. on two issues, foreign ownership of U.S. airlines and foreign carriage of Fly America traffic. TWA endorses both these proposals in a regime of true reciprocity, but believes that the current British proposal would not justify granting its carriers benefits in either category.

If we are not successful in reaching an agreement in this round of negotiations, what do we do next? Because there is nothing left for U.K. carriers to gain from the U.S., there is no incentive for the United Kingdom to undertake negotiation to allow U.S. carriers to achieve their goals of entry into Heathrow and expanded access to the U.K. market. TWA believes since the British have nothing to gain, the only solution is to create a threat of loss. In my written testimony, I have discussed in detail our ideas for attacking British airways' excessive reliance on sixth freedom traffic, which we propose purely as a market opening tactic.

Thank you for this opportunity. I'll be pleased to answer questions you may have.

Mr. DUNCAN. Thank you very much, Mr. Gibson.

Mr. Hirst.

Mr. HIRST. Thank you, Mr. Chairman. On behalf of Northwest Airlines, by the way, I'd like to mention that we are a carrier that also has an interest in serving Heathrow. We also have strong views about Bermuda II, which we think was a disaster for the U.S. And we have views as to what the proper way is to deal with that. And I'll be happy to discuss those at some point.

But I'm here mainly to talk about Japan, and I have limited time. I would like to say that we congratulate the negotiators on the U.S. side on the cargo agreement today. Northwest is also, as you may not know, the largest operator of heavy cargo, or the largest operator of heavy cargo across the Pacific. We have eight 747s that are devoted entirely to cargo.

And we are a strong supporter of open skies in the Japan air cargo market, as well as in the Japan passenger services market. We think this agreement is a step in that direction, an important step. And specifically, I would like to congratulate Mr. Turillo and Mr. Spiro, of the State Department, as well as Mr. Hunnicutt and Mr. Oppler of DOT on this agreement. Mr. Spiro was also the lead negotiator in the China agreement last December that led to Northwest's ability to serve Beijing non-stop from Detroit.

And so we think they're doing a good job in defending U.S. interests. And I think that is the proper perspective from which to examine the relationship with Japan, that is, not from the perspective of the parochial interests of Northwest Airlines or any other airlines, but from the standpoint of what is in the U.S. interest.

And from that perspective, we believe that what is most important is I think was implicit in Mr. Smith's testimony, that is, not so much the relationship in service between the U.S. and Japan directly, but rather, service between the U.S. and Asia. And the reason that I would say that is shown by the top map over here. See those lines, what they demonstrate is service into Japan and then from Japan into points like Bangkok, Singapore, Beijing, Taipei, many points in Asia, which can only be reached via Japan.

Most of the markets there are too thin or too distant to be served directly. And so the U.S. must have access to Asia via Japan. And that, we believe, should be the focus of U.S. policy in dealing with Japan at this time, although it's very important to open the Japan market to the extent possible directly.

But the reason we say that is really twofold. First, the U.S. is actually winning the competition between the U.S. carriers and Japan carriers, and winning it very decisively. As shown by this next chart, a bit over 500 flights each way per week between the U.S. and Japan, the U.S. has two-thirds of those. The U.S. has 343, Japan has 158. So we have essentially two-thirds of the market, Japan has one-third. And this market advantage has generated a $4.8 billion trade surplus for the United States in its trade with Japan, one of the two major surplus areas in a trade that overall has a $60 billion deficit.

Consumers are well served by the current market structure between the U.S. and Japan, contrary to what has been alleged by some other airlines. The market between the U.S. and Tokyo is less concentrated than the market between the U.S. and Heathrow, as measured by the HHI concentration index that the Justice Department uses, substantially less concentrated. Fares are comparable on a seat per mile, or cents per mile basis, between the U.S. and Japan versus the U.S. and the U.K. Load factors are actually lower across the Pacific than they are across the Atlantic.

And as I think we've shown in a variety of places, there are actually more flights between the U.S. and Japan than there are between the U.S. and the U.K. when you include all of the U.S., such as Hawaii, in your calculations. We've produced a study, because there's been a lot of misinformation on these points, called Getting It Right, which addresses the nature of the U.S.-Japan market.

And we're releasing it today, it's a thorough study. It builds in part on work done by Mr. Prestowitz at the Economic Strategy Institute. And his excellent report was released last week. And Mr. Chairman, I would ask that it be placed in the record with your permission.

Thank you, sir.

As a summary point here, notice the trend in market share from 1975 forward. The bottom chart shows the trend in the U.S.-Japan market share. Often the Japanese, by the way, argue that the present agreement is unbalanced in the U.S. favor.

But 10 years ago, even 15 years ago, Japan had more than half the market. Over the last 10 years, with United entering the market, and with United and Northwest both become more efficient as a result of deregulation, we have captured share from the Japanese carriers, under the agreement. The agreement hasn't changed substantially except to some degree against the U.S. during that period.

During the same period, under Bermuda II, where beyond rights were capped, and eliminated eventually, the U.S. share has dropped from approximately 60 percent to approximately 40 percent.

The U.S. is doing fine as a country in this market, although we recognize that there are carriers that would like to participate in it and there are localities that would like more direct service.

But again, turning to Asia, Asia is likely to be the most important market in the world to the U.S. by the year 2010. It's the fastest growing market in the world. Asian economies beyond Japan are growing three times as fast as those in Japan and Europe. It will be the largest market, the largest market, for U.S. exports by the year 2010. And over half of the U.S. international passenger traffic by the year 2010 will travel to Asia and points beyond Japan.

So the U.S. must have access to Japan, and it should have access by its own carriers, whose costs are about half those of the carriers in Japan. But in order to provide that service, the U.S. must have hubs in Japan. You can only operate this kind of traffic via hubs. You need to aggregate traffic in one point, combine it with local traffic flows and flow it on. Japan is the only place that has the kind of flows and the kind of geography that allows that to happen.

If the U.S. doesn't have hubs in Japan, it cannot compete with Japanese carriers for those flows, and Japan will dominate that traffic. So that's why this is so important.

Japan understands this, and has used every negotiation since 1982, beginning with United's attempts to gain the right to serve Japan from Seattle. Japan has used every negotiation as an opportunity to restrict U.S. beyond rights. And we are concerned that as we move into passenger negotiations, as we should, in order to move in the direction of open skies in the passenger area, that Japan not be given that opportunity again.

We're concerned partly because of Japan's history in this regard and partly because some carriers have called for a trade in which the U.S. would be asked to exchange a cap on beyond rights which are essential to U.S. access to Asia, in exchange for additional third and fourth freedom rights for them. They have opened that door, and if we don't close it before talks begin, Japan will take advantage of it.

So we believe there should be the following sequence pursued toward passenger talks. First, Japan should be required by the U.S. to grant pending fifth freedom applications by U.S. carriers. There are two that Northwest has and two that United has. We have the right, under the 1959 minute to the aviation agreement, to have those applications granted without any process by Japan. And if Japan believes they're not operated in compliance with the agreement, then Japan has the right to challenge that, ex post facto, after 6 months, in consultation. So they should grant those rights first, so they can't be used as leverage in a passenger negotiation.

Second, we should move on to negotiating an agenda with the Japanese addressing what the passenger talks will consist of after all other pending fifth freedom issues are resolved. By that, I mean talks should be held under Article 12 which JAPAN has requested to settle the ground on fifth freedom issues after our applications have been granted and after we've resolved those pending Article 12 issues, pending fifth freedom issues, we're then in a position to move into passenger talks without having them contaminate the attempt of the U.S. and Japan to exchange additional opportunities for both sides.

We believe if we follow that sequence, first pending applications are granted, second, other fifth freedom issues are addressed in talks as the Japanese have requested and as they have the right to request, and then third, we proceed to an agreed agenda that would exclude any fifth freedom issues from passenger talks, that the U.S. has a good opportunity to expand the pie, to gain new access to Japan, to do it without being leveraged by pending applications or other fifth freedom issues, and potentially to move in the direction of open skies in passenger as we've done in cargo.

Thank you.

Mr. DUNCAN. All right, thank you very much, Mr. Hirst.

And next we'll go to Mr. Murphy from United Airlines. Mr. Murphy.

Mr. MURPHY. Thank you, Chairman Duncan, Congressman Lipinski and members of the subcommittee. I want to thank you for inviting me to appear today. I've prepared a written statement and I'd like to submit that for the record, with your permission.

I would like now to summarize the points made in that document. There are three questions I would like to answer today. First, where are we in our aviation relationships with Japan. Second, what brought us to this present impasse. And third, what do we do to move forward in a way that advances U.S. interests.

In 1952, the U.S. started out with a liberal open-entry agreement with Japan. I cannot improve on the words of Chairman Shuster when he described that agreement as, "extremely liberal; so liberal that Japan has spent decades engrafting restrictions upon its basic terms. It is these restrictions that need to be removed. However, it seems that Japan wants to bring all of the rights granted in the 1952 agreement under its tight regulatory control. This should not be permitted."

If its provisions had not been whittled down over the years, there would be no Japan access issue today. The 1952 agreement guaranteed the U.S. the right to designate as many carriers as it wanted to serve Japan, with as many frequencies as those carriers felt the market required, and to continue those flights beyond Japan to Asia.

How, then, did we get from there to here? Well, according to a recent article by Mr. Hanyu, the Chairman of Japan's Aviation Delegation, the impetus for change was the British success in negotiating the highly protective Bermuda II agreement with the U.S. in 1977. To the Japanese bureaucrat, that agreement was a regulator's dream come true. With the Pacific version of Bermuda II, not only could Japan control every aspect of competition by U.S. carriers, but it constructed the environment to favor Japanese carriers, even when, as is the case today, U.S. carriers are more competitive.

According to Mr. Hanyu, in 1977, Japan had decided that it, too, wanted a Bermuda II style agreement with the U.S. It called for renegotiations. To its credit, the U.S. had learned its lesson with the British. We did not jump at this opportunity to shoot ourselves in the other foot. Then in a tactic that has served it well over the subsequent years, Japan simply ignored its commitments under the agreement. When the U.S. Government, in the late 1970s, designated a new carrier, United, to operate to Japan from the Pacific Northwest, Japan refused to honor the designation. What followed was a series of agreements and actions that step by step effectively gutted the liberal provisions of the 1952 agreement. These steps are outlined on this chart.

In 1982, to resolve the dispute over United's new authorization, the U.S. agreed that all new designations would be negotiated with Japan and they would not have the ability to operate hubs in Japan. This ensured that all subsequent awards would be in the form of point to point authority, with no rights to operate beyond Japan. The MOU carrier concept was born.

In 1985, the restrictions were expanded to include the 1952 carriers. The U.S. carrier operations were capped to those U.S. points that the CAB had previously named in the 1952 carrier certificates at that time. Because of that, the U.S. cannot today integrate its highly efficient domestic hub structure with its international routes to the Pacific, even for the original 1952 carriers.

For instance, United, the biggest U.S. carrier to Asia, can fully integrate its Pacific routes with only one of its principal domestic hubs, San Francisco. In 1986, Japan designated a second Japanese carrier to perform international services, and it began developing Asian hubs and seeking access from them to the United States. In 1989, Japan expanded the number of U.S. routes and capacity under its regulatory control by limiting the expansion of new points to those only under MOU conditions. In 1994, Japan announced a freeze on both U.S. carrier, passenger and cargo airport operating slots when the new Osaka Airport opened, foreclosing long-awaited growth in Japan's second largest city, and with Narita's locked and strained since 1989, the only potential for growth into and beyond Japan for the foreseeable future.

Under domestic pressure, Japan agreed with the U.S. carriers on a multi-year schedule of constrained growth at Osaka, then reneged on that agreement only months later, by disapproving our sole service and FedEx Subic Bay service in early 1995. In 1995, Japan and the U.S. reached an understanding that Japan would honor most of the beyond rights of U.S. cargo carriers. In March of 1996, Japan has again threatened to withdraw those promised U.S. cargo rights. Evidently yesterday we have now reached some limited agreement on cargo. But U.S. passenger rights beyond Japan remain both frozen and unaddressed.

What we are left with now is a Bermuda II agreement without a formal document. The only remaining item outside Japan's formal control is the 1952 carriers rights to operate hubs in Japan in order to serve the rest of Asia. And even there, as FedEx has experienced, and our own demonstrates, Japan now has its eyes on that last regulatory prize. Because of the rights previously surrendered, Japan can dangle the carrot of allowing some new service in front of our communities and carriers, if in return they will support Japan's negotiating efforts before the U.S. Government. That is where we find ourselves today with ACCESS U.S.-Japan.

And that is why the Japan Times can confidently predict as these excerpts from its February 15th edition show, that ACCESS U.S.-Japan "is likely to be a stronger supporter of Japan," and leading an MOU official to say that "Tokyo welcomes the efforts of the MOU carriers." Sad to say, Japan has succeeded in pitting U.S. carriers against each other and should Japan succeed in its strategy, the economic loss for the U.S. economy will far outweigh the incremental gains by one or two U.S. carriers.

The Asian market is enormous and growing faster than any other. As this chart shows, by the year 2010, there will be 10 Asian air transport markets that will match or exceed in size today's two largest markets in Asia. Why then is Japan so set on tightly regulating U.S. participation? The answer is that Japan's Ministry of Transport seeks to salvage a disastrous regulatory policy that has left JAL and ANA unable to compete effectively with U.S. and other lower cost carriers.

This chart is illustrative. It plots a comparison of JAL and United's costs based on ICAO statistics. That's in the first chart. As you can see, as late as 1985, JAL's costs were below ours. By 1993, however, they were dramatically above ours and were continuing to trend in the wrong direction. Not surprisingly, it was after 1985 that the U.S. carriers' share of the trans-Pacific market began to exceed that of Japanese carriers. Clearly, the answer is relative costs. But to admit that, Japan's MOT must confess that its regulatory policies are an abject failure. It is far easier, they believe, to repeat their myth that the underlying 1952 agreement is somehow unfair.

Let me show you something interesting: the performance of Japan Air Lines against those of its Asian neighbors with more liberal aviation policies. As you can see from this chart, the airlines of Korea, Singapore and Taiwan, all of which have liberal aviation agreements with the U.S., have a rate of growth that has far outstripped that of the Japanese carriers in expanding their global coverage of the world's most important trade centers. Similarly, as you can see from this next chart, those same carriers have more than doubled their share of the U.S.-Asia market, while Japanese carriers' share has almost been halved.

Also on a global basis, their participation in the global market has nearly tripled, while Japan's carriers show no growth over the past 18 years. Japan wants to salvage the reputation of its bureaucrats and carve out a protected market for its uncompetitive carriers by denying U.S. and foreign carriers the means to compete effectively. Japan's current objective, therefore, is to eliminate the rights of U.S. carriers to operate hubs in Japan to serve the growing Asian market.

Equally important, we must recognize that no U.S. carrier today operates any non-stop service to any Asian point except Japan unless that carrier also operates a hub in Japan. These non-stop and hub services are complementary, giving U.S. carriers a presence in an Asian city that is competitive with both Japanese and other Asian carriers. If we lose hub access beyond Japan, then all U.S.

carriers will be in the same position that a number of U.S. carriers, most recently Delta, have been in when they tried and failed to maintain a system of service to other Asian points without a hub in Japan. It would leave Japan with the only efficient carrier networks in the Pacific.

Simply put, Japan intends to gain through regulation an advantage that carriers cannot win in the marketplace. What should we do about it? Just last month, Charles Hunnicutt, DOT's Assistant Secretary for Aviation and International Affairs, stressed the need for U.S. policy makers to concentrate on the long term. "It is important to underscore that in our dealings with Japan we ought not settle for short-term gains at the cost of sacrificing long-term needs into the next century." His comments echoed those of Secretary Pena in conjunction with his recent extended trip throughout Asia.

We agree completely. It has been our concern about the future consequences of any negotiations with Japan that it led us to commission Booz, Allen and Hamilton to look at what the Japanese policies would mean to the U.S. in the coming decades. We believe that no policy can be relied upon if it is not based on economic reality. That is why we took the lead in gathering these facts. The study conducted by Booz, Allen and Hamilton concluded that over the next two decades, the cumulative reduction in U.S.-Asian trade balance from restrictions on the U.S. expansion of passenger travel in Asia through Japan could exceed $100 billion. Japan, the Booz, Allen study suggests, would be the primary beneficiary.

A subsequent independent study conducted under the supervision of Clyde, here, at the Economic Strategy Institute, reached much the same conclusion. In that analysis, as we will probably hear more from in a few minutes, U.S. job losses could reach as high as 213,000. There are real dollars and real jobs that will be lost to the U.S. economy if Japan has its way.

And just as now it is easy to criticize the mistake we made in Bermuda II, it will be easy to recognize in 2010 to recognize in retrospect the damage done by concessions to Japan in 1996. The challenge is to recognize those downsides in advance and negotiate accordingly. In this regard, the economic analysis of Booz, Allen, as well as the Economic Strategy Institute, have armed the U.S. Government with the knowledge it requires. What is needed now is the political will to act and avoid the dominance of another successful U.S. industry by Japan.

In our view, and we hope in yours, the responsible course requires the U.S. first reconcile its well crafted international aviation policy with its negotiating objectives. That policy states, "Carriers wishing to establish global networks require a higher quality and quantity of supporting route authority than they have sought in the past. Airlines will become increasingly concerned with every market that enables them to flow passengers over any part of their system network. These airlines will be looking for broad, flexible authority to operate beyond and behind hub points in addition to the hub to hub markets between two countries. At present, governments operating in a bilateral context naturally focus on opportunities for their respective carriers to serve the local market between two countries. In a bilateral context, services destined for or coming from third countries receive less consideration. In the future, governments will have to adjust their focus to bargain for the bundles of rights that will permit airlines to develop global networks."

We cannot continue to proceed by committing the same mistakes in the 1990s as we did in the 1980s. As the international policy recognizes, adjusting our focus should mean that integrating domestic and international hubs has to have the highest priority. Specifically, it means that undoing the damage of the 1980s must be undertaken so that those carriers that can still hub in Japan can once again have the ability to integrate those hubs with their domestic systems. Japan recognizes this need for its carriers. We can do no less for ours.

In addition, as this chart illustrates, we should approach negotiations with the following framework in mind. First, insist that Japan honor its current agreements. Second, steadfastly refuse to fall into Japan's trap of accepting restrictions on existing rights as a way to secure other opportunities. And third, set as our negotiating goals objectives which are first determined by economic analysis to be in the best interests of the U.S. as a whole. United has committed itself to supporting the results of negotiations conducted in accordance with these principles, and we firmly believe they are an absolute prerequisite to the success of our industry and the fastest-growing and soon to be the largest international market in the world.

Thank you.

Mr. DUNCAN. Thank you very much, Mr. Murphy, and we'll go now to Mr. Prestowitz.

Mr. PRESTOWITZ. Thank you, Mr. Chairman, and thank you for inviting me this afternoon.

As the last speaker on the last panel, it's always hard to find something new to say. I'd like to introduce my statement for the record, and just take a very few minutes here to emphasize two or three key points.

The first point is that in an age of globalization, the aviation industry is like basic infrastructure. You can't have globalization, you can't be competitive in a global economy without a strong aviation services industry. Second point is that the U.S. has such an industry. The U.S. air service industry is far and away the world's most competitive. We are the low cost operators. And as many of these charts have shown, even in restrictive markets, our carriers gain market share which says that consumers vote with their feet and their dollars when given even half a choice.

I like to think of the U.S. aviation industry a little bit like the Japanese electronics industry. You remember back in the 1960s and 1970s, when the Japanese became the most competitive players in making video tape recorders and television sets and a range of consumer electronics products, they came to dominate world markets, because the U.S. market was open, the European markets were relatively open. They were allowed to make acquisitions, to invest, to achieve distributors, and basically they wiped out everybody else in the business worldwide.

We saw a similar development in the case of the Japanese auto industry. They became the low cost producers in the 1980s. They were able to leverage that capability to gain large market shares in global markets.

One of the problems is that despite the tremendous competitiveness of the U.S. industry, it is hampered in its ability to do what Japan did in consumer electronics by the regulatory regime of a couple of key countries, i.e., Great Britain and particularly Japan. The Japanese regulatory regime is particularly important, because as, again, these charts showed, aviation is not only a basic industry, it's a rapidly growing one. And the growth is in Asia. So we're looking at a strategic question here, as to not only what is going to be the ability of the U.S. to exploit its competitiveness in a key industry, but beyond that, what is going to be the impact on the U.S. economy of not being able to do that.

And what we've done in our recent study, Turbulence Over The Pacific, is to model a few scenarios, looking at what would happen to employment in the United States, what would happen to U.S. carrier revenue, what would happen to economic GDP activity in the U.S., and finally to U.S. trade receipts. And the answer is, overwhelmingly, an open sky scenario is the preferred scenario. Under an open sky scenario, by the year 2010, the U.S. would add 700,000 jobs to the present trend line, $30 billion in GDP and roughly $18 billion in trade receipts. Any other scenario is inferior to that.

But most importantly, any scenario which restricts the rights of U.S. carriers beyond where they are now, any scenario which would further restrict fifth freedoms, any scenario that would add any restrictions to what we have now, comes out a poor third and fourth best.

Now, the significance of this to me is that we have with Japan about a $55 billion trade deficit. We had just in the past week two carrier task forces sitting off the coast of Taiwan to provide stability and peace in the Pacific. And of course, that's important to us. But if it's important to us, the last time I looked at the map, Japan is closer to instability in Asia than we are. Japan is a member of APEC, and the APEC countries have committed themselves to free trade by the year 2010 for developed countries, and 2020 for developing countries.

So to me, it just seems inconceivable that the U.S. could accept a negotiating agenda that was anything less than an agenda committed to achieving open skies. Of course, there can be transitional periods. But it seems to me that the U.S. has the justification, the economic, the moral justification and the cards in this case to insist on that kind of a negotiating agenda, in particular because one of the really striking results we found in our study was that an open skies scenario would actually increase Japanese GNP by a half a percentage point.

We're talking about an economy that has had no growth in 5 years, a half a percentage point in GDP just by liberalizing their aviation, almost one full percentage point in increased GDP for most of the other countries in Asia because of the benefits they would achieve from gaining greater aviation service in the Pacific. Japanese travelers would pay lower fares. They would have more flight frequencies. The only people who win out of restrictions in Japan are Japan airlines and the bureaucrats at MOT.

So there is every reason for Japanese consumers, Japanese political leaders, Japanese academic and business leaders, to support a

U.S. position dedicated to open skies. It seems to me that's where we should go.

Thank you.

Mr. DUNCAN. Thank you very much, Mr. Prestowitz.

On this round of questioning, I'm going to go last. I'm going to go first to Mr. Oberstar and then to Mr. Ehlers. And we're always pleased to have the ranking member of the full committee, Mr. Oberstar, here with us. And Mr. Oberstar, you may make any comments or ask any questions.

Mr. OBERSTAR. Thank you very much, Mr. Chairman. I apologize for not being here at the outset of the hearing. We had rail safety hearings at the same time and I was trying to cover both bases. I therefore ask unanimous consent to include my statement in the record, especially since it is a commendation of you for initiating these hearings and Mr. Lipinski for participation in shaping them. And I think this is a very important time, and we couldn't have timed it any better, coming right on the heels of the agreement reached with Japan on cargo service.

And in the context of this hearing, without exploring any of the details of that cargo agreement, what I would like to ask our panel, what are its implications for passenger service? Frankly, it's an agreement I never thought would be reached so readily with Japan, given their protection of domestic carriers, protection of their market, protection of their beyond rights, their policy of resisting change. But they seem to have had a very significant change of heart and embarked on a policy that certainly I concur in. But what are its implications, if any, for the passenger side? Mr. Hirst?

Mr. HIRST. Thank you, Mr. Oberstar. I think one should be cautious in drawing implications for the passenger side on the basis of this agreement. In our experience, Japan views the cargo environment as distinct from the passenger environment. And in fact, these talks began on the premise that both sides agreed that there needed to be liberalization in cargo and both sides, particularly the Japanese side, was very clear that it did not treat and did not want these talks to be regarded as a precedent of any kind on the passenger side.

Having said that, it seems significant to us that for the first time within my memory, since 1952, Japan has agreed that a new U.S. carrier should have fifth freedom rights, which UPS has accomplished. And that's important.

But I guess in summary, in looking toward passenger talks, we think it is very important, as I said, that they should be sequenced, if there are passenger talks, to be held, they should not be held with any pending fifth freedom issues on the table. We believe they would be used under those circumstances as leverage in a way that would not be in the U.S. interests.

Mr. OBERSTAR. Well, I won't ask the other members of the panel to respond, because we really have limited time here. But it has long been U.S. policy, enunciated first by this committee through hearings in the Investigations and Oversight Subcommittee, through hearings at a time when Mr. Gingrich and I were working together on this issue, that we separate cargo issues from passenger issues. We do not trade cargo rights for passenger rights or vice versa.

So this agreement ought to be as it is, a separate agreement, and should not be a precondition to anything in the passenger arena. And certainly, the implication is that Japan is willing to look at fifth and sixth freedom rights given by a reading of this agreement. But as you rightly say, we've got to wait and see. They are a separate set of issues.

Everybody that I have talked with, both recently and in my memory, about aviation issues with Japan, says that existing rights, especially beyond rights, should not be negotiated away to get more access for U.S. carriers, whose access now is limited. That is, the MOU carriers. Everybody else says more access for more U.S. carriers to Japan is in U.S. overall interest. How do we get to both of those goals, keeping what we have and the rights to serve Japan and serving beyond Japan, of gaining better access for those MOU carriers?

Mr. Murphy, I'll let you respond to that one.

Mr. MURPHY. Thank you, Mr. Oberstar.

I guess if I could maybe kind of combine your two questions, I would say first of all, we're throwing cautions to the wind. We're very disappointed with the cargo agreement. Because we'd like to kind of measure ourselves against our goals and not simply against our results. And frankly, if our goal is and was, as it was announced, to achieve liberalization in cargo, then this agreement fails by all accounts.

What we've gotten in this cargo agreement is a few spokes. And it's an illusion to believe that those few spokes are going to have any significant impact on the nature of competition or the marketplace on the cargo side.

And I think that is, in effect, the same problem with our goals and ambitions on the passenger side. If we go into the passenger negotiations with nothing more than the ambition, as we seem to have had in the cargo negotiations, to pick up a few spokes, and let the Japanese continue to enhance their hub access to the United States, then I suspect we're going to be disappointed once again.

In fact, I would say that when it comes to the U.S. international aviation policy, the Japanese are doing a much better job of being faithful to that policy than we are. We seem to be mired in the approach of the 1970s, where getting a few more carriers into a marketplace was considered an accomplishment.

But I would point out to you that if in 1978, when we deregulated the domestic marketplace, and the tremendous effort that went into that, if the net result had been we got a few more spokes for a few more carriers, I don't think we would have considered it to have been much of an achievement.

Thank you.

Mr. OBERSTAR. So you don't have an observation on how we can leverage more access for MOU carriers while retaining the rights of the 1952 treaty rights carriers?

Mr. HIRST. I do, Mr. Oberstar, if I could take a crack at it.

Mr. OBERSTAR. Yes.

Mr. HIRST. I think that it's, as discussed earlier, the U.S. has to first and foremost protect its access to Asia. And that means the fifth freedom rights that the U.S. has. The U.S. has a responsibility to do that, and it's very fundamental. If we don't do that, we're going to be very sorry we didn't in 10 and 15 years, as that market grows dramatically.

And so I think that in order to do that, the fifth freedom issues must be separated from the third and fourth freedom issues. And the fifth freedom issues that are pending should be addressed first. And that includes the applications that United has on file, and the two applications that Northwest has on file, which by the way, we don't believe present serious problems for Japan.

Japan has certain issues regarding traffic composition under Article 12, and it has requested consultations under Article 12 to address those issues. And we believe the U.S. has a responsibility. Once pending applications have been granted to agree to those consultations and let them be held, then I believe those issues can be resolved.

Once they're resolved, then there are no pending fifth freedom issues that should prevent negotiations from going forward on an agreed agenda in which both sides would say, we're going to discuss the expansion of opportunities for our carriers to serve the Japan-U.S. market. If it is possible in the context of those negotiations for rights to be further expanded to include additional fifth freedom rights for U.S. carriers, then we would applaud the U.S. negotiators in that regard. We think they have the freedom to seek that.

But that's the sequence that should be followed in our view. Otherwise, the risk is that pending fifth freedom issues will become chips in the third and fourth freedom negotiations. And that shouldn't be. The U.S. shouldn't be put in that position. It's not in the U.S. interest to let itself be put in that position.

Mr. OBERSTAR. Frankly, I must say, I'm somewhat ambivalent about hearings about negotiating policy, Mr. Chairman. On one hand, we do all this in open forum, we've done it for years. And even with the Japanese television and press in attendance recording our comments while their discussions all take place in camera, in chambers, and they don't let it all out. However, that's the nature of our society, and I think it's important to send a message to our trading partners that we are united on a viewpoint and that is that we do not sacrifice one set of rights for another. We don't advance the total cause of aviation in that regard.

May I ask one further question, Mr. Chairman?

Mr. Prestowitz, you are the preeminent Japan trade observer in this country. Your book, Trading Partners, your current document, Turbulence Over The Pacific, give you a particular insight into these issues. Do just a thumbnail sketch of your analysis of how capping beyond rights will actually result in less third and fourth freedom service.

Mr. PRESTOWITZ. Sure. U.S. carriers, United, Northwest, are now carrying on, the traffic that goes between say, Bangkok and Tokyo, or Hong Kong and Tokyo, whatever point it is in Asia, roughly half of that traffic is originating at some point in Asia, transiting Tokyo and coming to the U.S., or originating in the U.S., transiting Tokyo and going on to Asia.

So that means that for every two of those beyond flights, they're supporting one trans-Pacific flight. So if you cap those beyond flights and the carriers are not able to grow with that market, that means that they will then not be able to grow in the trans-Pacific market either.

Now, by trading those beyond rights for further access to Japan, you could argue that you would pick up that trans-Pacific traffic with other carriers. And you will pick up some of it with other carriers. The problem is that you can't pick up enough of it. You would do it by code sharing, but the ratio on code sharing is about 10 to 1. That is, it takes 10 beyond code share flights to make trans-Pacific flight.

So you just can't be efficient enough in picking up that lost beyond traffic with new code sharing arrangements. And the result is that you actually wind up, even though you try to get more access to Japan, you actually wind up with fewer frequencies U.S. to Japan than you had under the old arrangement.

Mr. OBERSTAR. Thank you, Mr. Prestowitz.

Thank you, Mr. Chairman.

Mr. DUNCAN. Thank you, Mr. Oberstar.

Mr. Ehlers.

Mr. EHLERS. Thank you, Mr. Chairman. I appreciate the questions and comments of the ranking member. I find myself certainly in agreement with them.

It strikes me in hearing the testimony in the first half of this hearing, before the first panel, it seems very clear that we made a very serious mistake with Bermuda II in giving up the beyond rights or the fifth freedom and getting very little in return. And yet it appears that there is a proposal to do much the same thing now. I am curious about one item, perhaps this panel can clarify.

I asked Mr. Smith about the ACCESS U.S.-Japan position of being willing to give up fifth freedom in exchange for additional routes to Japan. He stated that he had been informed unequivocally that they definitely did not want to do that. If they were here, I would ask them that. But since you're the panel, I wonder if you could verify whether that's true, or whether that's not your impression at all. Because it seems to me that's the crux of whether or not we go down the wrong path and create, not an other Bermuda II, but perhaps Hawaii II or wherever the conference might be.

Mr. GIBSON. Mr. Ehlers, I was happy to hear Mr. Smith's comment. But we have seen nothing to indicate that there has been a change in position. In the ACCESS materials that were presented publicly on February 21, ACCESS indicated that from its perspective, it believed that Japan would welcome a trade in which there would be a cap on U.S. fifth freedom rights in exchange for additional third and fourth freedom operations. And it certainly implied by saying that that it supported such a cap, or such an exchange. And a principal supporter of ACCESS, a founding member of ACCESS, is American Airlines.

And last October, the Chairman of American Airlines, in a speech in Washington, said the following: "In our view, a U.S.-Japan agreement premised on limiting the expansion of beyond operations would be good for consumers, good for competition within the U.S. and across the north Pacific, good for the U.S. trade balance with Asia overall, and fully consistent with the DOT's international aviation policy statement."

So that's the position, stated position of American Airlines, which is a member of ACCESS. And we have heard nothing to indicate that ACCESS is——

Mr. LIPINSKI. Would the gentleman yield to me for a moment?

Mr. EHLERS. Yes, as long as I don't lose too much time.

Mr. LIPINSKI. You won't lose too much time. I simply want to say, I've heard this statement made a number of times by this panel. And I want to go on record, I want to inform you that I have talked to former Governor Baliles, who heads this ACCESS U.S.-Japan. And he maintains that it's not his position nor the position of ACCESS U.S.-Japan committee that any beyond rights be given up.

And in regards to the President or Chairman of the Board of American Airlines, I've spoken to him as recently as Monday. And he has said that he has no interest in the United States negotiating away any of the beyond rights of United Airlines, Northwest Airlines, or Federal Express. He does want access to Japan and he wants beyond rights for Japan.

But that is his position, that's the commission's position. So I'd like to put that in the record, because I believe that is truly the position.

Thank you.

Mr. EHLERS. Thank you, Mr. Lipinski. I certainly appreciate that clarification and I hope that it's accurately recorded. I think this committee should go on record as being opposed to giving up any of the current fifth freedom rights, and perhaps expanding them. There can be a matter of semantics here, I presume, and one says that we don't want to give away any fifth freedom rights, and one might mean we won't give any of the fifth freedom flights we have right now, but we're going to give away any expansion of them. So I think that's something that has to be clarified and put on the record as well at some point.

Question for this panel is then, if the hope is to get additional routes and we're not exchanging any fifth freedom rights, what negotiating leverage do we have, what position can we take as a Nation to increase the number of routes available? I certainly believe in that. In fact, I get a little confused about third freedom, fourth freedom, sixth freedom. As an American, I guess I'd like full freedom. And that's what I believe you call open skies.

But if the other nations don't agree to that, what can we do? Mr. Prestowitz, looks like you're ready to—

Mr. PRESTOWITZ. Well, I think there are several things. First of all, Japan has carriers who want more access as well. So that should give us some allies in Japan for further opening or liberalizing the agreement. Second, I think the point I made earlier, that maybe we shouldn't look at this strictly in terms of the airline situation, but we after all have had a long running trade deficit with Japan at the same time that we perform a number of important politico, diplomatic, military services for Japan.

It's kind of bizarre when you think about it, that a country that provides still the market for about a third of Japan's output and that provides Japan's security and that somehow, and we're dealing with a country which has in the WTO and in the APEC agreements, has reaffirmed time and again its commitment to free trade. And in the case of APEC, to free trade in aviation services.

It seems to me it's kind of bizarre that we would even consider talking to them about anything other than the mechanisms, the steps and the timetable by which we get to open skies. I think that, you know, if you step back and look at this, you know, if you were the negotiator and looked at this broadly, I think you feel that you had pretty significant leverage.

Mr. EHLERS. I would certainly hope so. But I happen to be a resident of Michigan. And I'm familiar with several decades of negotiations about automobile imports and so forth. And I just remain somewhat skeptical about any success in negotiations we might enter into without being very, very tough in our negotiating position. And I certainly hope that the DOT and the entire Administration would show considerable backbone in these and make it abundantly clear we're not going to give up any fifth freedom rights. And that we are wiling to negotiate exchanges of routes or an increase in the number of routes on their part in conjunction with the increase in number of routes on our part, and that's all we will talk about. I take it that's the position of this panel as well.

Mr. PRESTOWITZ. Absolutely.

Mr. EHLERS. Mr. Gibson.

Mr. GIBSON. Mr. Ehlers, let me say that having had some experience myself with Japan, I would agree with Mr. Prestowitz that you can effectively shame them into such a mode with the U.S. We are in full agreement with Governor Baliles that you do not need to trade beyond rights and in fact can improve upon beyond rights if the U.S. industry stays firm and united on that issues, in return, and at the same time get expanded third and fourth freedom rights in Japan. In this one industrial sector the Japanese are so entirely inconsistent with their policy across the board that in a sense, linkage on this issue is probably the best way to shame the Japanese. And shaming them works quite well into expanding U.S. rights.

Mr. EHLERS. You're more optimistic than I am.

That's all I have, Mr. Chairman. Thank you.

Mr. DUNCAN. Thank you very much, Mr. Ehlers.

Mr. Geren.

Mr. GEREN. Thank you, Mr. Chairman.

Mr. Chairman, I represent an area where the Texas Rangers baseball team resides. And for the 22 years they've been there, we've always said, gosh, if we just had pitching. And when I got to know people from around the country, almost no matter who you talk to, wherever they're from, whatever baseball team may be in their area, they say, well, you know, if we just had pitching.

And it seems to be the same with the international routes. That's looking at it from the perspective of a north Texan. We keep thinking, gosh, if we could just have access to some of these international markets, if American and Delta just had more access to international markets. And you sit down with folks from Michigan, folks from almost anywhere and it's the same story over and over and over.

It seems that every part of our country, there aren't enough pitchers to go around, there are not enough international routes to go around. And I just wonder if we're going about it the right way. And perhaps Mr. Prestowitz would be the best to comment on it, I'd like to hear the observations of the rest of the panel, in looking at how the, this is more of a big picture question, how the other countries do it, compare it to how we do it. And Mr. Oberstar talked about how the Japanese do it in camera, we do it in front of the world's television audiences.

It's always seemed to me that we don't play as hard ball as some of our competitors do in pushing our interests, particularly in this area. I think it's going to become increasingly important with the globalization of trade, whether it's NAFTA and expanding aviation routes into Canada, or as Asian countries open up more and more, if it's easier for a company in Great Britain to get to an expanding market than it is for a company in Fort Worth or Chicago, those companies are just going to have that little bit of an advantage in penetrating that market.

So we have the USTR open up some markets. But if it's easier for some company in Great Britain to get to that market, not only are we losing out on the international route and the trade, but we're not going to penetrate that market as we should. And I'd like to just hear the panel's thoughts on what we could do as a country to restructure the way we go about this to do a better job of ensuring that American interests are advanced in this area. Because it's so tied to every other aspect of globalization of the economy.

Mr. PRESTOWITZ. Well, that's a really good question, and it's applicable beyond just the airline situation. And I think that the first thing is really a change of psychology, which means putting, a change of priorities, and putting a greater emphasis on the questions like access through Japan and aviation services and other industries equivalent to the priority that we put on other issues.

Let me give you an example. I had a call this morning from a friend of mine in Tokyo, a former U.S. trade negotiator, who recounted to me an incident that occurred this week at the ACCJ, the American Chamber of Commerce in Japan. One of our present State Department negotiators was addressing a breakfast meeting of the chamber. And he was asked, well, how are things going for the President's trip. And he said, oh, things are going terrific, fine. And then he apparently realized that he was talking to a bunch of businessmen and caught himself, and said, oh, of course, there's not much progress on trade.

Well, I think you have it right there. Too often in these and other negotiations, our negotiators' top priority is a vote in the U.N., a donation of aid money to Rwanda, an assurance of bases.

I mean, right now, the President's preparing to go to Japan for a summit meeting. And the top priority for the U.S. in the summit meeting is to assure base rights at Okinawa and to conclude a satisfactory security arrangement with Japan. And because the Japanese know that that is our top priority, they feel perfectly at ease in telling our trade negotiators to take a hike.

Because in the end, they know that we want the bases worse than we want the airline rights, or worse than we want access on semiconductors, whatever it is. And we then, our trade negotiators wind up in a very difficult negotiating position.

So I could go through a lot of detail about who should do the negotiation, should it be DOT, should it be USTR and things like that. But I think that the heart of the matter is that until we adopt the view that our ability to realize the benefits of our competitiveness is as or more important to our national security as base rights and exercise rights and so forth, we will always be at a disadvantage.

Mr. GEREN. Another point, I think we need to expand our notion of the significance of it, just be specific. You're seeing tremendous opportunities for natural resource companies to develop mineral resources in the Far East. And if somebody from, if it's hard to get there from Houston, it's likely that that Houston company is not going to be a competitor.

So it isn't just the hundreds of millions or billions we lose in the transportation sector. It really limits our domestic industries' ability to cross over there. I don't think the big picture is—yes, sir?

Mr. MURPHY. If I could add, I agree with Mr. Prestowitz completely on the question of attitude. And you can see this in many instances. Our chairman, Mr. Greenwall, likes to tell a story about his experience in automobiles as well, where he was formerly the Vice Chairman of Chrysler. And he talks about his experience in the international arena. And to him, it comes down to one thing. Most of the foreign countries that he had to deal with were interested in only one thing in the economic arena, and that was leverage. It was a constant search for leverage to try and achieve their economic goals.

When we go into a situation, leverage is not our number one priority. It's a fair outcome, a balanced outcome, it's fair trade, free trade, whatever. But it is not leverage. And as an example, yesterday, we haven't discussed this, but yesterday there was an agreement with France. Now, from our standpoint, why did we have an agreement with France yesterday? Yesterday, what we offered the French was 500 new frequencies that are going to be subsidized to enter the United States. In return, we got something that we already had a right to, and that is to replace a carrier that had pulled out of Boston.

So we gave them 500 new frequencies in spite of their subsidies to Air France and then in return, we got them to talk to us. And it seems as if the main rationalization, the main thing we looked for, was a conversation. That is no leverage.

Mr. GEREN. Mr. Hirst.

Mr. HIRST. Just a brief observation. It may be that some of our trading partners believe that the best thing that they can do to advance their interests with the U.S. is to get the U.S. to make a really bad agreement like we did with the U.K. in 1977. But I think Mr. Prestowitz' work shows that certainly the next best thing they can do is agree to open skies. And in the case of Japan, the economy in Japan would benefit significantly, and the economy's link to Japan would also benefit.

And I've been impressed with the progress that the Administration has made in developing that theme and developing open skies agreements in Europe. And in time, I believe that those agreements will put pressure on the British to liberalize their relationship with us, and that that's the best way of doing that, as traffic basically moves from the U.K. as a gateway to other markets such as Amsterdam and Frankfurt.

So I believe that the U.S. is on the right track, but we have to be very careful not to put ourselves in a position where leverage can be used against us and force us into making a bad deal, rather, keep moving toward the open skies goal. Which by the way, I'm not saying this altruistically, from our standpoint, Northwest Airlines would benefit from open skies in Japan, as again, Mr. Prestowitz' study showed, as compared with an extension of the current agreement. In 2010, we would have more flights under an open skies environment, so would United.

Thank you.

Mr. GEREN. Thank you, Mr. Chairman.

Mr. DUNCAN. Thank you very much, Mr. Geren. Mr. Lipinski and I have agreed to go last on this round, so that means that Mr. DeFazio is next.

Mr. DEFAZIO. Thank you, Mr. Chairman. I thank the senior members of the committee for deferring.

I have a concern that I direct to Northwest and United, and particularly some statements made by United, and that is, there's another strategy which the Japanese, and other competitors can pursue. One is to distract us into our highest priority as begging the Japanese to allow us to continue to spend $70 billion a year defending their interests in the Pacific Rim, which has worked for a long time. And we're having trouble getting beyond that.

But the other is to divide the industry. Because they know in part our regulators and our policy makers are responsive to our own domestic industries and their concerns. And I'm concerned that they're having some success there. Rather than going forward and saying, okay, let's all come together, those who are 52 carriers, those who are MOU carriers, and agree that our highest priority is that the United States Government should go into these talks saying, look, open skies is where this is headed.

We're into this, well, we want to get our 52 rights first, and then we want to get this, and then, you know, we can go on to open skies. And the derogatory comments about the MOUs, the concern, particularly, to United I have expressed is, United does not serve parochially Orient to the Orient. It serves Seattle to the Orient. Now, from Chicago, maybe it all looks the same. It isn't, we're competitive. And Delta serves Japan.

And to say that the MOU carriers are a failure, which is an assertion made by United, I don't believe is supportable. I mean, they're not doing that out of the goodness of their heart. We're making money so far as I know, we're so much more competitive than Japanese airlines. We'll beat the heck out of them if we have open skies.

So I guess I'd just like to ask if that's a viable strategy. Why not take the optimal strategy, have all of the competitors agree to push our Government to do that, and go in using Mr. Prestowitz' work to show, look, you may think that we're doing this just to advantage our industry. We're not, your country's going to benefit, too. Obviously maybe their individual carriers are going to feel threatened, but they would benefit as a people as a whole.

Is that a possibility?

Mr. MURPHY. If I could respond.

Mr. DEFAZIO. Certainly.

Mr. MURPHY. About a month before United Airlines made the filing that you refer to, in referring to the MOU carriers as failures,

Delta Airlines went to Japan and held meetings with Japanese government officials, with Japanese press officials, and asked a Japanese government to intervene on their behalf against the interests of other U.S. firms. Now, when we see a company do that, deal directly against our commercial interests, we are going to respond.

Mr. DEFAZIO. Sure—

Mr. MURPHY. We will respond with an argument that we think is a valid argument, and that is, we do not believe that the idea of simply adding more carriers from more points is necessarily a successful strategy in terms of enhancing consumer choices in the marketplace. This is the old point to point strategy that we abandoned with the new international aviation policy and yet, in spite of the fact that at least in theory we've abandoned that approach, we continue to pursue it.

And specifically with respect to Portland, Portland could have had rights, in the original 1952 agreement, the United States had the ability to operate from any point in the United States to points in Japan and beyond. It was carriers such as the MOU carriers, American and Delta, that were supportive of giving up those rights in 1985 because they found it in their parochial interests to do so.

So if you were to ask what you asked earlier to Mr. Smith, what do we keep doing wrong, well, part of what we keep doing wrong is we never really sit down and examine in depth what we're doing. We look at our immediate parochial interests and we pursue that without a further examination of what does this mean to the country and what is this going to mean over the long term.

I think Senator Pressler has been very articulate on the principle that this division between U.S. carriers is a major impediment to us making progress. But the answer to that is not trying to prove one right or wrong. The answer to that is, do an economic analysis, determine what is the best course for the United States, and then pursue that.

Mr. DeFazio. Okay. And is the best course the open skies policy?

Mr. MURPHY. Absolutely. And United will take second fiddle to no one in open skies. We were the only major carrier that supported domestic deregulation when Delta was saying it was going to be a disaster.

Mr. DEFAZIO. Okay, but today, if we had all of the major competitors at the table, couldn't we get consensus that, in this case, in the negotiations with Japan, would disadvantage no one, and would be in the best interests of us as a Nation?

Mr. MURPHY. If I could just maybe, Mr. Hirst wants to respond as well. But if I could just respond.

First of all, I think one of the things that you might sit down and come to a determination of if you were to do an economic calculus, is that in some instances it might be the wisest thing to do to defer certain interests. That you cannot pursue all things simultaneously. And you have to work towards these goals in a step by step way. I think we are doing that in Europe. We have just signed an open skies agreement with Germany which I think is going to be a critical change in that marketplace and is going to commercially derive that marketplace in the open skies.

But at least in Europe, we had a strategy, we pursued it, we were successful, now we're the second largest country, I think we've changed the nature of the marketplace. Unfortunately in Japan, we haven't got a willing partner yet.

Mr. DEFAZIO. But if I could just, if you were here for my earlier question, and it was certainly restated by Mr. Prestowitz, you know, we've got the clout here, I mean, if we decided to play hard ball with Japan, we're going to be less disadvantaged than the Japanese. Our carriers are less at risk than theirs in terms of, you know, any difficult negotiations we might get into, or threats of curtailment.

Mr. MURPHY. I can tell you, up until yesterday, we had tremendous leverage with the French. I mean, every good argument you want, we had available to us with the French.

Mr. DEFAZIO. But we gave it away.

Mr. MURPHY. And we gave it away. That's why I say, the problem—

Mr. DEFAZIO. And that's inexplicable.

Mr. MURPHY. The problem is not simply the question of who's negotiating or something. I think Mr. Prestowitz had that exactly right. It's the attitude with which you approach these things. Even in a situation where we had leverage by any standard, we gave it away.

Mr. DEFAZIO. Well, maybe it's this problem that he's also pointed to where we get all these 29 year old kids negotiating these things who have never negotiated anything before, and they're looking at their next job, which is going to be as foreign agents, where most of them go. But that's another issue to deal with.

[Laughter.]

Mr. HIRST. Mr. DeFazio, if I could, a couple of observations. One is, my experience with the U.S. negotiators in this area is that they, the people who are doing this now are mature individuals. And I think they're doing a good job.

I think we don't have the leverage in this sector that we might in other sectors, because we have a huge surplus with Japan. And that's at risk in any negotiation. Other sectors where we are at a deficit and don't have a surplus, we have less to lose. So we have to be somewhat careful about how we approach the negotiation with Japan.

So I think that if it is true that the ACCESS group does not advocate capping fifth freedom rights in exchange for additional thirds and fourths, if that is true and if that is Delta's position, as well as American's position now, then it seems to me that the ACCESS group, as well as those carriers, should welcome the kind of sequence that United and Northwest are advising. Because I believe it's the best way to get to an open skies agreement, or to an agreement that truly expands the market between the U.S. and Japan.

And the reason is that if Japan believes when it goes into passenger negotiations that it can in fact negotiate some limits on fifth freedom operations, they will seek those. They will seek those instead of seeking to liberalize the market. We have to take away from Japan the objective of capping beyonds, or limiting beyonds by addressing those issues first.

I don't believe that is a huge problem. I believe that can be done successfully. And then we can move into a negotiation that addresses directly the concerns you're raising and the concerns that Delta and others have. And it's conceivable in that context that they could get rights beyond Japan, it seems to me, on the basis of this cargo negotiation.

So that's what I would suggest. And I think perhaps in light of what's happened in cargo, other carriers will take a second look at their position and perhaps we will have a united group.

Mr. DEFAZIO. I thank the Chairman for the time.

Mr. DUNCAN. Thank you very much, Mr. DeFazio.

Ms. Brown.

Ms. BROWN. Thank you, Mr. Chairman.

I guess I'll ask Mr. Gibson a question. Mr. Gibson, how would you compare air service between the United States and Japan and say, the United States and the United Kingdom?

Mr. GIBSON. Well, the United States and Japan, believe it or not, the U.S. carriers today are winning, which is not the case with the United Kingdom. And I think earlier, I can't remember whether it was Northwest or United, put some charts up to say that we actually do have more flights than the Japanese carriers and do have a better market share. It is at risk if the U.S. does not follow through and continue to be strong with the Japanese.

But the U.K. has been the clear beneficiary of the 1977 agreement and has taken great advantage of it. And we see it in declining U.S. market shares and increases in British carrier frequencies and their market shares.

Ms. BROWN. Mr. Prestowitz, given the air fares between the United States and Japan, on a revenue per passenger mile basis, averaged 29 percent more than theirs between the same cities and principal cities of Europe, and that this substantial difference in fares can be attributed significantly to the inadequate access of U.S. airlines to Japan, isn't it time for the United States to address the issue of additional access for the passenger airlines not included in the 1952 bilateral agreement with Japan?

Mr. PRESTOWITZ. Well, certainly, the U.S. should be exerting every effort to achieve greater access for all of our carriers to Japan. I think that the so-called MOU carriers have a legitimate right and complaint. They should have more access to Japan. And our negotiators should be attempting to get that.

I think the first part of your statement, where you talked about differences in air fares across the Pacific and the Atlantic, I'm not sure that I would agree with that. We've just looked into that very carefully in this study that we did. We've looked at comparison of air fares at all levels across the Pacific and the Atlantic, and we've found that they're pretty much the same.

Where there is a big difference, there's a huge difference in fares in the beyond markets, between Tokyo and points in Asia, fares are two, even three times higher than they are trans-Pacific or trans-Atlantic. But trans-Atlantic, trans-Pacific, we found the fares are very comparable.

Ms. BROWN. Do I have time for one more question? Thank you, Mr. Chairman, I yield back the balance of my time.

Mr. DUNCAN. All right, thank you very much, Ms. Brown.

Mr. Lipinski.

Mr. LIPINSKI. Thank you, Mr. Chairman. I promise the Chairman that the Democratic side would be finished by 5:00 o'clock, so I have very little opportunity here to ask anybody any questions.

[Laughter.]

Mr. LIPINSKI. And I had a ton of them to ask you.

But I want to say while I have an opportunity that, Mr. Murphy, I have a solution to our negotiations with Japan. And I'm going to recommend this to the ACCESS U.S.-Japan Coalition, that they persuade, because I like your attitude very much. You're not even happy with the cargo agreement that was negotiated within the last 24 hours. And I like your aggressive attitude.

But I'm going to recommend to them that they persuade you to leave United Airlines—

[Laughter.]

Mr. LIPINSKI.—and you become the principal negotiator for ACCESS U.S.-Japan for American, Delta, and UPS and anybody else that's in that coalition. But that's just an observation on my part. But I am going to make that recommendation very strongly.

I asked a member to yield a little bit earlier to express myself in regards to a situation pertaining to the Chairman of the Board of American, and also to the head of the ACCESS U.S.-Japan Coalition, former Governor Baliles. I also what to say for my part that I certainly do not advocate in any way curtailing your beyond rights, or any of your future beyond rights. I think that would be a terrible mistake.

But by the same token, as I've told Mr. Murphy individually, I am a very strong proponent of getting additional rights into Japan for other carriers. I am also a strong proponent of beyond rights for them, because I think that the Asian market, as has been stated here on a number of occasions, is going to be a fantastic market in the future. And I'm very happy that Northwest is in a position to cash in on it. I'm very happy that United is, and that Federal Express is. But I'd like to see the other American carriers have the same opportunity.

Now, Mr. Hirst, you mentioned that you have two applications pending at the present time? What are they?

Mr. HIRST. Yes, sir, there are two. Indonesia, we've just had very successful talks with the Indonesians who have maintained closure on that market. And in conjunction with the U.S. Government down there, they have now indicated a willingness to accept our flights via Japan. And so we filed an application with the Japanese for authority to do that.

And we have also filed an application to transfer a flight that we're operating from Tokyo to Shanghai to Tokyo to Guangzhou in southern China, which doesn't have any service from Tokyo right now. And as I said, I'm reasonably optimistic that Japan will not object to those.

Mr. LIPINSKI. What about United?

Mr. HIRST. I'm always open to offers, by the way.

Mr. LIPINSKI. Yes, he said you had a couple of routes that were pending.

Mr. MURPHY. Yes, we have, actually in our business plan we have filed actually three different things. We are commencing freighter operations this fall, so I'm not totally opposed to what was

24-087 97 - 3

done yesterday. I mean, it will at least, it allows us to exercise the rights that we had to fly freighters. And we're going to do that this fall.

We also had pending applications to fly beyond Osaka to Seoul, that's the application that has been denied for over a year now. And we also have a pending business plan application with the Japanese for Osaka-Bangkok.

Mr. LIPINSKI. Thank you. I have 30 seconds left, according to my watch. And I simply want to recommend to the gentleman from TWA over there, Mr. Gibson, that instead of maybe flying from New York to Heathrow, why don't you try to fly from your big hub in St. Louis to Heathrow. You might have a better opportunity to get into that. Go ahead if you want to respond. But you only get about 10 seconds, because the Chairman's going to cut you and me off.

Mr. GIBSON. Mr. Lipinski, we'd be delighted to do both.

[Laughter.]

Mr. LIPINSKI. Thank you, Mr. Chairman.

Mr. DUNCAN. Thank you, Mr. Lipinski.

We have other legislation we're supposed to mark up here in just a few minutes. But Mr. Gibson, let me ask you, since you haven't been asked any questions here today, a few years ago TWA sold its access to Heathrow to American Airlines. What would you say to somebody who might say that you're now asking the Government to negotiate back something that you sold a few years ago?

Mr. GIBSON. Mr. Chairman, many people may remember at the time TWA was owned by someone named Carl Icahn, which I think would be familiar to most people in this room. And Mr. Icahn was effectively pursuing a strategy of liquidating the company. If Carl Icahn had sold every route to London except those two from our hub, we might be a little more stable than we were over the subsequent years. But he did sell those routes. He did it over the objections of Congress, over the objections of TWA employees, and over the objections of a lot of the management that was in place at that time.

The management that has come into TWA, of which I am a part, in 1994, decided that to rebuild the company it's absolutely essential that you have to fly from your major east coast hubs, which happen to be your trans-Atlantic gateway to London. Mr. Icahn, I suspect, had a little understanding of the airline business, didn't feel this was important, and besides which, he thought he wasn't going to have an airline, he was going to have lots of pieces that he was going to dismember. So he was not thinking in a way of running a business.

We have to worry about running a business. And I think most people, when they look at that era of the 1980s can possibly forgive a company who was owned by a financial raider.

Mr. DUNCAN. Let me ask you this. If the British refuse to give this country additional, and its airlines additional access to Heathrow, what do you think would be the effect of this Nation restricting British access to our slot controlled airports, such as Kennedy and O'Hare?

Mr. GIBSON. That's certainly one possibility. We've suggested, in my written testimony, that possibly a more effective mechanism may be limiting the sixth freedom rights. British Airways now is a major participant in sixth freedom traffic. And we see it from cities we serve, such as Barcelona, Milan and Athens.

British Airways today carries more traffic from Barcelona to the U.S. than either TWA or Iberia combined. And if we find ways to restrict that as a tactic, not as a permanent measure, but as a tactic to bring them to the table, I think BA would find it very, very painful economically. And I think it would cause the British government to move quite quickly to try and deal with the United States. And we have those rights under the current bilateral.

Mr. DUNCAN. Mr. Hirst, or Mr. Murphy, you know that in the past, the Japanese have sometimes said that their airport capacity is limited. And they now have a new airport in Osaka, the Kansai Airport. And they are already saying that it's full. Do you believe that there is airport capacity in Japan, both to expand your beyond rights and to expand the number of fights coming from the United States for other airlines such as American and Delta?

Mr. HIRST. Mr. Chairman, I think there's additional capacity in a couple of respects. My understanding is there is some additional capacity at Kansai that is not totally capped out at this point.

But more significantly, the second runway that's been constructed in Narita, or largely constructed, there are half a dozen landowners who own plots of ground on the runway. Japanese authorities, for the first time this year, have become quite optimistic about being able to complete their land acquisition program and complete construction of that second runway. And they're projecting that that will be done in 1997. It will double the capacity of Narita. So I think that's a very significant development.

Mr. DUNCAN. Mr. Murphy, anything you wish to add?

Mr. MURPHY. Yes. We believe that any airport, especially one that's used as a hub, quickly develops peaking problems. And that is essentially what's happened at Kansai Airport. Kansai is actually under-utilized as an airport, probably by about 30 percent. But in certain time frames, certain peaks, essentially about a 3 hour time frame in the afternoon, it is quickly approaching saturation.

On point to point services, that's of little concern. It's of much more concern to carriers that are operating hubs or at least attempting to operate hubs, such as United and Northwest. You might say we're fortunate at this point that we haven't been allowed to do so. Because we haven't run into this problem.

But our total collection of beyond operations from Osaka today, by virtue of Japanese regulation, is one, which was operated by Northwest to Manila. So we think there is plenty of capacity there, and before too much longer, I would agree with Mr. Hirst, we expect to see additional capacity coming on and on-line.

But again I would stress that this is a Japanese decision. They are responsible for building an infrastructure. And the Japanese have chosen to limit that infrastructure in a way that maximizes their control over air transportation. So we think that is just part and parcel of the Japanese approach to controlling the marketplace.

Mr. DUNCAN. All right, thank you very much.

Mr. Prestowitz, I understand that there is a Coopers and Lybrand study financed by American or Delta or by ACCESS, the

ACCESS group or somebody, that claims that much of the value that Northwest and United receive from their current beyond rights derives from their monopoly status or a semi-monopoly status, earned on capacity restricted routes. What do you think about that? I understand that Mr. Murphy and Mr. Hirst might question that. What do you say about that?

Mr. PRESTOWITZ. Well, I think that's pretty much the same question as the pricing question. And we looked at that in our study. What we found was first of all that load factors across the Atlantic are actually higher than they are across the Pacific. And nobody claims that there's a monopoly across the Atlantic. So if the load factors are higher there than they are across the Pacific, that would suggest that there's not a great deal of restriction trans-Pacific in terms of traveler choice.

And then we looked at air fares. We looked at the lowest advertised fares in the first calendar quarter. And what we found was, for example, we're using city fares with Tokyo as an index. So Chicago-Tokyo is $100, Chicago-Paris is $140, Chicago-Frankfurt $137, Chicago-London $135. That would suggest that fares trans-Pacific Chicago are better than fares trans-Atlantic Chicago. And that kind of suggests that if there's a monopoly, it's not very good.

Mr. HIRST. Mr. Duncan, if I could make one or two observations?

Mr. DUNCAN. Sure.

Mr. HIRST. That is essentially one of the claims that we respond to in this pamphlet that we're releasing today. There are 13 major factual assertions made by the ACCESS group which we believe are either serious distortions or flatly wrong. In this case—

Mr. DUNCAN. We would like for you to give that to the Aviation staff, and I'm sure you would be glad to do that.

Mr. HIRST. We plan to do that. In this case, one of the principal problems with the Coopers and Lybrand study appears to be that they focused on published fares versus the fares that actually sell in the market. And there's a huge differential in the Japan market. It's much larger than in other markets, including the U.S.-U.K. market, although in every market the published fare is often generally higher than the discount fare, the fares that actually sell.

What Mr. Prestowitz did was to take a look at the actual fares, the ones that are actually sold to consumers, and found that there was essentially no difference on a cost per mile basis between the U.S.-U.K. market and the U.S.-Japan market. There are not monophonic profits in that market.

Mr. MURPHY. If I could add something to that.

Mr. DUNCAN. Yes, sir.

Mr. MURPHY. We have had a study done, too, which we would be glad to provide for the committee, which looked at the question of the beyond routes and the impact of U.S. carriers in terms of prices beyond Japan. And basically it showed that the impact of U.S. carriers in the beyond Japan market, the intra-Asia markets, was anywhere from about 16 percent to 43 percent a decrease in fares in those markets, compared to the intra-Asia markets where U.S. carriers did not participate.

And since this is largely United and Northwest, I think it's an illustration that in effect, we use price quite effectively to compete with Japanese and other Asian carriers.

Mr. DUNCAN. Well, thank you very much. We've got to mark up some NTSB legislation. I might say that we have very important aviation relationships with many countries throughout the world, most countries. Canada, of course, is one of the most important. But certainly our relationships with Japan and the United Kingdom are among the most important of those aviation relationships.

And so we set up 2 days of hearings. But I understand, or I'm told that we have so many people who want to testify that we may have to go to a third day. Mr. Lipinski mentioned the CEO of American Airlines and the Chairman, Mr. Crandall, will be testifying at our next hearing on this issue, along with some other witnesses. And we'll get into that shortly after we come back in April.

But your testimony has been very helpful and very informative. And we thank you very, very much for being here with us today.

Mr. DUNCAN. And that concludes this hearing.

[Whereupon, at 5:13 p.m., the subcommittee proceeded to other business.]

PREPARED STATEMENTS SUBMITTED BY WITNESSES

TESTIMONY OF

SCOTT C. GIBSON

VICE PRESIDENT PLANNING & CORPORATE STRATEGY

TRANS WORLD AIRLINES, INC.

BEFORE THE

SUBCOMMITTE ON AVIATION
COMMITTEE ON TRANSPORTATION & INFRASTRUCTURE

HOUSE OF REPRESENTATIVES

MARCH 27, 1996

TESTIMONY OF

MR. SCOTT C. GIBSON
VICE-PRESIDENT PLANNING AND CORPORATE STRATEGY
TRANS WORLD AIRLINES

March 27, 1996

Mr. Chairman and members of the Committee, TWA appreciates the opportunity to appear before you to present testimony on the important issues raised by the U.S.-U.K. bilateral negotiations. Our aviation relationship with the United Kingdom has been difficult for many years, and has resulted in high fares and limited service on the most important transatlantic route. The restrictive bilateral has also produced a market in which the two British flag carriers have a 60% market share, compared to 40 % for the six U.S. flag carriers. One issue for the United States is how to change this situation -- how to expand service for the benefit of the traveling public and how to enhance the competitive opportunities of U.S. airlines.

I would also suggest that another major public policy issue related to these negotiations is how to give TWA the opportunity to succeed as a transatlantic competitor. This is important not only for the 23,000 employee-owners of TWA, but also for the strength of the U.S. flag industry on the Atlantic. TWA provides important U.S. flag service to 12 destinations in Europe and the Middle East. Although it has suffered a decade of financial adversity, it has turned the corner and begun the return to profitability. The strengthening of TWA's route system on the Atlantic will benefit the balance of payments, enhance U.S. flag competitiveness, and preserve the jobs of TWA's 23,000 employees.

As you know, in the last round of negotiations in October, 1995, the United Kingdom made a proposal that would have allowed a limited transfer of service from Gatwick to Heathrow, but would have totally precluded the U.S. from even considering TWA's proposal for new service between New York and Heathrow. TWA believes that the U.S. Government acted properly in rejecting this inadequate British proposal. We urge that negotiations be resumed, and that the end result will be an agreement that will allow the United States to designate TWA for the New York-Heathrow route.

In this testimony, I will briefly review the history of TWA's financial difficulties, our efforts, with the dedicated support of TWA's employees, to return to sustained financial strength, and the public benefits that would be achieved by TWA's New York-Heathrow route. Finally, I will review the course of the bilateral discussions and make recommendations for future steps.

I. TWA IS WINNING THE STRUGGLE TO RETURN TO PROFITABILITY.

While everyone is aware that TWA has suffered massive financial problems over the past few years, has endured two bankruptcies, and has begun the arduous climb back to financial strength, it may be useful to place those bare facts in some historical perspective.

TWA is one of the great companies in aviation history. It has operated continuously since the 1920's. This year, we are celebrated the 50th anniversary of TWA's first transatlantic flight -- a distinction no other U.S. carrier can claim. At the time of deregulation, TWA had both a large domestic route system, and an international operation that connected the United States with Europe, the Middle East, India, and points beyond. By 1985, TWA was the largest transatlantic carrier -- bigger than any U.S. or foreign flag carrier[1] -- and the sixth largest airline in the U.S. However, in that year, TWA was caught up in the competitive financial manipulation that destroyed so many companies during the 1980's. In 1991, the company was forced into bankruptcy.

TWA's first bankruptcy did not work. Despite sacrifice by employees, TWA emerged from bankruptcy in November, 1993 with a financial structure that was still heavily burdened with debt and a unrealistic financial plan. When I joined the company in April, 1994 as part of a new management team, it was clear that further steps were necessary for TWA to survive.

Our new team quickly worked with our unions to identify further employee concessions that would reduce our costs to more competitive levels. Employees reduced their ownership share from 45% to 30%. With the cooperation of our creditors and lessors, we were also able to create a new financial structure that gives TWA the opportunity to become viable over the long term. In June, 1995, we filed a pre-packaged bankruptcy plan, and emerged from bankruptcy six weeks later, having eliminated $500 million in debt and $60 million per year in interest payments.

---

[1] Aviation Week & Space Technology, March 9, 1987, p. 208.

TWA is still an employee-owned company, with a new sense of purpose and a realistic expectation that we can survive.

The financial results that we announced last month demonstrate the extent of our turnaround. We reported our first annual operating profit since 1989, along with significant improvements in both quarterly and annual operating and net results. Our operating income of $25.1 million was an improvement of $ 304.6 million over the operating loss of 1994. We did have a significant net loss on an annual basis, in large part due to restructuring charges. However, our fourth quarter net loss of $27.8 million was an improvement of $217.4 million over the same quarter of 1994. The chart attached as Chart 1 shows our improvement in several important economic indices over the last year.

We recognize that we still have substantial work to do. We succeeded in 1995, but that was a very good year for the industry, and we have to be prepared for the inevitable downturn. There are several more steps that we have to take:

- We have to modernize our fleet. Last month, we ordered 20 B-757's, with an option for a further 20 -- our first order of new equipment in ten years. We are negotiating with manufacturers for additional aircraft, and are planning to hushkit our existing DC-9 fleet.

- We have to reduce costs. We are reviewing all phases of our operation to increase efficiency, reduce costs, and become more competitive. Our employee task forces have already identified over $100 million in cost savings.

- Finally, we have to fill the void at the heart of our transatlantic route structure -- to do this, we need a New York-Heathrow route.

II. NEW YORK-HEATHROW AUTHORITY FOR TWA IS THE SINGLE MOST IMPORTANT ROUTE THAT THE U.S. COULD ACHIEVE IN THE CURRENT ROUND OF NEGOTIATIONS.

The New York-Heathrow route is not only of immense importance to TWA, but also is the single most valuable route that the U.S. could achieve in these negotiations. While other airlines are proposing to switch existing service from Gatwick to Heathrow, only TWA is proposing entirely new service in a competitive market.

TWA has worked hard to develop its major international hub at JFK. As shown by Chart 2, its New York hub connects 26 domestic cities with 11 major European destinations. However, it is weakened because it lacks access to London, which accounts for almost one/third of all U.S. - Europe traffic. In 1994, 32 percent of all U.S.-Europe passengers use the London gateway.

	Total Passengers Year 1994 (INS data)
U.S. - Europe Total	31,761,166
U.S. - London	10,110,721
% London	32%

TWA's inability to carry traffic between its major gateway and London has an adverse impact on our entire transatlantic system. Without access to London, we lack market identity at New York, and cannot compete effectively for corporate traffic, because companies desire to contract with one airline for all major transatlantic markets. Only one U.S. airline can offer this one-stop shopping today, but it does so by code sharing on the flights of a British carrier. At TWA, we want to fly American aircraft with American crews. Without the support of connecting London passengers, our domestic spokes are weaker, which limits our ability to expand on those domestic segments. A JFK-Heathrow route would give TWA badly-needed market identity in the transatlantic market, the support of connecting traffic, and the ability to become a strong U.S. international competitor.

TWA forecasts that it will achieve $100 million annually in operating revenues on the JFK-Heathrow route. In addition, we will earn between $20 and $40 million in revenue on other transatlantic routes because of our ability to offer a more comprehensive transatlantic route system (Chart 3). We will be competitive for corporate travel, and for multi-destination passengers who enter or leave Europe at London. We would also be able, with the support of Heathrow, to institute nonstop service from New York to U.K. regional points. Such service is not economically feasible if we are not also serving Heathrow. It is clear, therefore, that achieving a JFK-Heathrow route is the stepping stone to development of a much stronger international system for TWA.

TWA recognizes that other U.S. carriers have legitimate desires for access to Heathrow, and would like to transfer current flights that now serve Gatwick. However, the public benefit from such transfers cannot match the gain that would be achieved by a new route for TWA. Because of the frequency limits of the bilateral, these carriers will not be allowed to increase service. Thus, they will not increase U.S. flag capacity to London.

Only TWA would add entirely new service on a new route. Its daily B-747 would provide additional U.S. flag competition for British carriers at New York, where TWA has traditionally been a major transatlantic carrier, as well as new online service for the numerous points served by TWA's New York hub.

The British remain intransigent. Their last offer was sharply circumscribed to allow switching of existing service from Gatwick to Heathrow, while precluding any possibility of TWA providing its new service from New York. In a precedent-setting move, it would have removed the ability of the U.S. government to pick which carriers and which routes could be authorized for new service. We are pleased that the government stood firm. It was correct to be extremely dissatisfied with the nature of the British proposal, particularly after the United Kingdom had promised in the first round of 1995 negotiations to be more forthcoming with Heathrow authority.

III. THE BRITISH ARGUMENTS AGAINST ADDITIONAL SERVICE TO HEATHROW ARE INVALID.

We are well aware that other carriers have suggested that TWA should be happy to take the Gatwick route offered by the British and give up on our attempts to return to Heathrow. TWA rejects this advice because we want to be an effective competitor in the New York-London market, and we know that this requires access to Heathrow. In the New York-London market, Gatwick is a distant second choice airport.

The limited attraction of service to Gatwick is demonstrated by examining the schedules of the incumbent JFK-London carriers, all of whom have authority to serve both Heathrow and Gatwick. Of the 17 daily flights offered by these carriers, only one goes to Gatwick, and it is operated by a carrier that has a hub at that airport. The remainder go to Heathrow for a perfectly valid reason -- that is where the traffic wants to go. I should note that Virgin has moved, by choice, its JFK and Newark-London operations from Gatwick to Heathrow, and that Continental clamors to do the same.

Business passengers, who are particularly significant in this market, overwhelmingly prefer Heathrow. U.S. business travelers are accustomed to Heathrow's ease of access to the central city. U.K.-originating passengers are far more likely to depart from homes or offices that are nearer to Heathrow than to Gatwick. In this regard, we accept the testimony of Sir Colin Marshall, the chairman of British Airways, who recently told the U.K. inquiry on the construction of Terminal 5 at Heathrow that expansion at Gatwick was not an alternative. He noted that Gatwick had the disadvantages of greater distance, time and cost for most passengers from the main markets in the Southeast, and was limited by a single runway[2]. Like British Airways, TWA would prefer to serve Heathrow rather than Gatwick.

The United Kingdom has traditionally rejected claims by the U.S. for new Heathrow authority on the grounds that Heathrow is overcrowded, and cannot accept additional carriers. During the 1980's, the United Kingdom even adopted Traffic Distribution Rules that precluded additional airlines from moving existing service or starting new service at Heathrow. These rules were rescinded in 1991 for the airlines of every nation but the United States. Since then, the expansion of service at Heathrow has demonstrated that there is ample room for a new carrier from New York. Thus, a comparison of Heathrow service in July, 1990 and 1995 shows the following:

- 34 new carriers have started service at Heathrow.
- These carriers have added 1799 flights per month.
- Total departures from Heathrow have increased by 26 percent.

---

[2] The Guardian City Page, p. 19, November 9, 1995

Moreover, we know that Virgin had no problem getting slots for its new Heathrow-Dulles service, or for its Heathrow-Johannesburg flights.

The current public hearings in England over the construction of Terminal 5 at Heathrow demonstrate the potential for future growth at Heathrow. British Airways has testified there that the new terminal will allow it to increase its traffic there from 23.5 to 36 million passengers per year. There can be no doubt that any claim that there is no room for additional service at Heathrow is a mere smoke screen designed to obscure protectionism.

In the current negotiations, the British have also claimed that a route for TWA would simply be too much -- that it would result in an imbalanced agreement that is far beyond the scope of the " limited and balanced" exchange of Heathrow routes that was intended. This argument comes with poor grace from a government whose airlines carry 60 percent of total U.S.-U.K. traffic. TWA's proposed route cannot be an economic threat to British carriers. It is proposing initially to add one flight per day in a market that currently receives 17 daily flights from both British and U.S. flag carriers. This single flight, which terminates in London, can hardly threaten British Airways, when its hub is at Heathrow, the largest international airport in the world. British Airways has publicly stated that 39 percent of all its Heathrow traffic is sixth freedom -- traffic connecting at Heathrow, but destined to countries beyond the United Kingdom which will not be affected by a single TWA flight terminating in Heathrow. Moreover, the other British carrier, Virgin Atlantic, has a code share Alliance with Delta that protects its position on the route and gives it a hub at JFK. Only a government that believes in mercantilism rather than competition could be concerned about the impact of one flight by one carrier in a market the size of New York - London.

IV. THE BRITISH SHOULD BE INVITED TO RESUME NEGOTIATIONS FOR A REASONABLE AGREEMENT

TWA believes that negotiation should be resumed, and that both the U.S. and U.K. should attempt to reach an agreement that will expand service opportunities between our countries. Ultimately, we would like to see an open skies agreement similar to the just initialed U.S.-Germany agreement, but the United Kingdom has set so many additional requirements, including cabotage, that the idea is not worth discussing at this time.

We do believe that it will be possible to reach an agreement. Mr. Malcolm Rifkind, the British Foreign Minister, has recently indicated a willingness to resume negotiations on the basis of the last British offer. While that was inadequate, there are possible counteroffers that may lead the British to be more generous. In this regard, I believe that Senator Pressler's recent speech to the International Aviation Club was very helpful in moving the discussion forward.

To encourage a "bigger, bolder and braver," approach to the negotiations by the British, he suggested movement by the U.S. on two issues -- foreign ownership of U.S. airlines and foreign carriage of Fly America traffic. TWA endorses both these proposals in a regime of true reciprocity.

TWA has long believed that the current limitations on foreign ownership of U.S. carriers are obsolete, and that capital should be allowed to move across international boundaries in the airline industry just as in the rest of the economy. We appreciate the concern of labor about the impact of foreign ownership of U.S. jobs, but we believe that the infusion of foreign capital into U.S. companies is more likely to preserve jobs than to destroy them. We also appreciate the arguments of those who are concerned about the support provided by U.S. airlines in times of war. However, U.S. companies remain U.S. citizens and will be subject to the needs of the nation. We do not believe that there should be any concern about the commitments of U.S. airlines to the CRAF program simply because they may be partially owned by foreign nationals. The 49% limitation proposed by Chairman Pressler is a reasonable compromise between those who see no need for any limitation on foreign ownership and those who are concerned about its impact on U.S. jobs and security.

Fly America traffic is certainly an appropriate subject for negotiation. We strongly object to the current system under which foreign carriers transport Fly America traffic under the guise of code shares with U.S. carriers because it is a violation of both the letter and spirit of the Fly America legislation. However, if there were an adequate quid pro quo, it may well be worthwhile to grant foreign carriers access to Fly America traffic.

While we support liberalization of foreign ownership and grant of access to Fly America traffic, we do not believe that the current British proposal would justify granting its carriers benefits in either category. When the British are ready to offer more access to Heathrow, including a route from JFK for TWA, we should consider granting them more access to Fly America traffic. When they are ready to offer open skies, they may then receive the right to own a U.S. carrier. Until then, however, we should withhold this privilege.

V. OVER THE LONG RUN, WE MUST FIND A WAY TO ENCOURAGE THE BRITISH TO RENEGOTIATE THE BILATERAL

If we are not successful in reaching an agreement in a new round of negotiations, what do we do next? Because there is nothing left for U.K. carriers to gain from the U.S., there is no incentive for the United Kingdom to change its protectionist ways and to undertake negotiations to allow U.S. carriers to achieve their goals of entry into Heathrow and expanded access to the U.K. market. TWA believes that, since the British have nothing to gain, the only solution is to create a threat of loss.

A. The nature of British Airways operation that are subject to bilateral challenge.

The transatlantic operations of British Airways are subject to challenge under the bilateral because they rely to an excessive extent on the carriage of sixth freedom traffic, i.e, traffic that originates or terminates at points behind the United Kingdom. As a result, British Airways offers far more capacity on the Atlantic than would be justified by natural traffic flows between the U.S. and U.K., and can compete with frequencies that the U.S. carriers cannot match. British Airways's hub at Heathrow allows it to capture traffic flows between numerous European, Asian and African countries, including Italy, Greece, Poland Spain, and India, and the United States.

British Airways compounds its competitive edge by offering low off-tariff fares for this sixth freedom traffic. Because the proportion of its traffic that comes from a particular European country is small, it can offer fares priced on a marginal cost basis without threatening the revenue it receives from passengers originating in its primary U.K. market. British Airways offers such off-tariff fares through two devices -- it sells through consolidators who resell to the public, or it offers override commissions that allow travel agents to rebate part of the fare to the passenger. As a result, it undercuts the fares of the primary carriers in its sixth freedom markets, or forces them to reduce yields to uneconomic levels.

Because it drains so much traffic from the sixth freedom markets, British Airways offers far more capacity between London and American destinations than it could justify on the basis of the third and fourth freedom U.S. - U.K. traffic that, under the terms of the bilateral, is supposed to be its primary justification for transatlantic operations. It also reduces the base traffic of direct U.S. - Europe services, making flights operated by U.S. carriers uneconomic. British Airways's schedule is heavily oriented to larger capacity B-747s, and includes double daily nonstop operations to several major U.S. destinations. These schedules are sustainable only because sixth freedom traffic accounts for at least 40% of British Airways's transatlantic traffic. However, if the principles of the U.S.- U.K. agreement were correctly applied, the U.S. would not allow such disproportionate reliance on this traffic.

B. The Current Bilateral Restricts British Airways's Reliance on Sixth Freedom Traffic, But is Not Enforced by the U.S.

The current bilateral agreement with the United Kingdom contains a traditional capacity provision, based on the one first negotiated in the Bermuda I agreement of 1946. Under Article 11(3) of the agreement,

> Services provided by a designated airline ... shall retain as their primary objective the provision of capacity adequate to the traffic demands between the country of which such airline is a national and the country of ultimate destination. The right to embark or disembark on such services international traffic destined for and coming from third countries ... shall be exercised in accordance with the general principles of orderly development of international air transport ... and shall be subject to the general principle that capacity should be related to:
>
> (a) the traffic requirements between the country of origin and the countries of ultimate destination of the traffic;
>
> (b) the requirements of through airline operations; and
>
> (c) the traffic requirements of the area through which the airline passes, after taking account of local and regional services.

In the context of the British Airways's operation, this means that the primary objective of British Airways's capacity should be to meet the requirements of traffic originating in the U.K. and traveling to the U.S. or points beyond, or vice versa. While it can carry traffic from third countries, its capacity must not be based on such traffic volumes, but must be related to the requirements of third and fourth freedom traffic. Its capacity should not be related to the traffic that it siphons from Continental Europe over its London hub. Unfortunately, in the last ten years the U.S. government has paid little attention to the capacity provisions of its bilaterals. It has taken the position that it does not care where the other country's traffic originates.

The pricing provisions of the bilateral should also restrict British Airways's ability to divert sixth freedom traffic by limiting its ability to undercut published fares of direct carriers by published fares of its own. Under Article 12, carriers are required to file tariffs, which can be disapproved by the authorities of the other. Because the U.K. has restricted the ability of U.S. carriers to offer through fares from points behind their gateways, the U.S. has required British Airways to publish only fares for beyond points in Europe that match the fares of carriers providing direct service in those markets. British Airways however, has been allowed to "game" the system by filing fares from other nations (such as France) on numerous occasions that undercut approved tariffs. While the U.S. disapproves them, British Airways has already loaded them in CRS's and sold them for a week before withdrawal. Moreover, the U.S. has done nothing to limit the ability of British Airways to compete through off- tariff pricing. The U.S. limitation on British Airways's pricing is, therefore, ineffective.

C. How to Bring the British to the Negotiating Table

We believe that the only way to exert pressure on the British is to start enforcing the bilateral and to focus the attention of both the U.K. and other countries on British Airways's sixth freedom operation. We suggest three specific steps, all permitted under the current bilateral agreement:

1. Ask for consultations about British Airways's excess capacity and restrict its reliance on sixth freedom traffic. There are specific provisions in Annex 2 to the British bilateral that govern challenges to seasonal frequency changes, and which the British may argue are the exclusive method of handling capacity disputes. However, there are also more general provisions for arbitration and consultation about the correct interpretation of the bilateral. The U.S. should go on the attack about this issue.

2. Require British Airways to file all off-tariff fares in all markets beyond the U.K. Once the fares are filed, the U.S. should review their economic justification and disapprove them if found to be unreasonable. British Airways should not be allowed to steal sixth freedom traffic by undercutting the fares of the third and fourth freedom carriers in those markets.

3. Require British Airways to file schedules of all override commissions paid to agents on sixth freedom countries. Where such overrides amount to rebates, action should be taken against British Airways to require it to adhere to its tariffs. The level of overrides should be publicized in such countries, so that the aviation authorities of those countries will be aware of the impact of British Airways on their national carriers.

Once attention is focused on British Airways's sixth freedom traffic, and its reliance on such traffic is threatened, we believe that the British may be more interested in coming to the negotiating table.

I should emphasize that we wish that there were no need for us to urge the government to enforce the capacity and pricing provisions of the bilateral. We believe that consumers benefit from price and service competition free from artificial constraints. We propose these tactics as measures to open the U.S.-U.K. market, not as an ongoing policy. Our ultimate goal is open skies between the U.S. and the U.K., but we will never get there unless there is a drastic change in the attitude of the British government.

Chart 1

TWA IS SUCCEEDING

	Year 1994	Year 1995	Change
Employee Productivity Is Improving			
Number of Employees	25,184	22,927	-13.0%
ASMs (Millions)	39,450	38,186	- 3.2%
Unit Costs Are Down			
Operating Expense per ASM	8.41c	8.16c	- 3.0%
Revenue Performance Is Improving			
Load Factor	63.6%	65.7%	+2.1pts
Yield	11.31c	11.39c	+2.5%
Revenue per ASM	7.19c	7.48c	+4.0%
Financial Results Have Improved Dramatically			
Operating Profit/(Loss) (Millions)	$ (279.5)	$ 25.1	
Net Profit/(Loss) (Millions)	(435.9)	(227.5)	
Excluding Restructuring - Related Expense		(71.7)	

* Excluding GETAWAY Vacation Trans World Express subsidiaries

Chart 2

TWA'S JFK HUB
TWA Online Service Between 26 U.S. Cities And 11 Cities in Europe and the Middle East

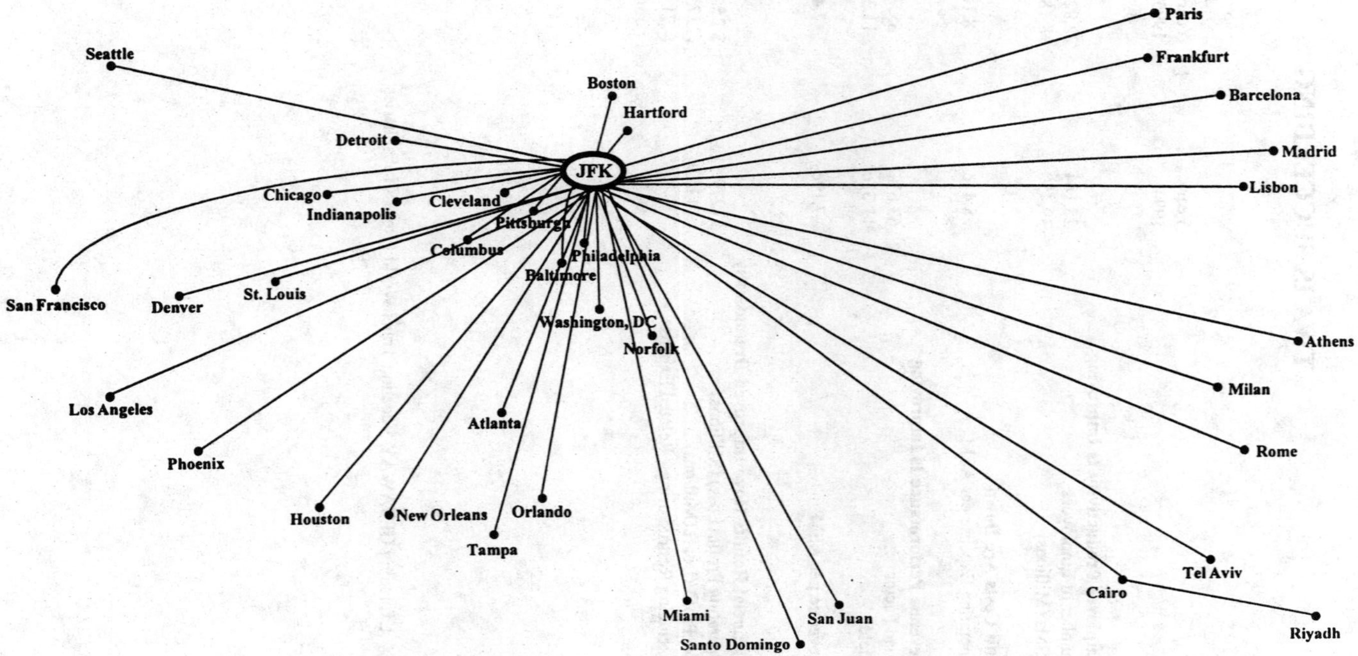

Chart 3

THE INITIAL VALUE OF TWA OF A JFK - HEATHROW ROUTE IS MORE THAN $100 MILLION ANNUALLY IN ADDITIONAL REVENUE

	$ in Millions
U.S. - Heathrow	
Passenger Revenue*	$84.4
Cargo Revenue	12.0
Total	$96.4
Effect on Other Transatlantic/ Transcontinental Revenue	$20 - $40

* 66% annual load factor, $400 average System fare, including segment beyond JFK

TESTIMONY OF RICHARD B. HIRST

BEFORE

THE SUBCOMMITTEE ON AVIATION,
HOUSE COMMITTEE ON TRANSPORTATION AND INFRASTRUCTURE

MARCH 27, 1996

Richard B. Hirst
Senior Vice President
Northwest Airlines, Inc.
5101 Northwest Drive
St. Paul, MN 55111
phone: 612-727-4774

Summation of Northwest Airlines Testimony, delivered by Richard B. Hirst

Current Aviation Rights Critical to U.S. Trade with Japan

- The U.S. Aviation Agreement with Japan has become a critical positive factor in U.S. trade with Japan and Asia.

$4.8 Billion Trade Surplus for U.S.

- Due to the competitiveness of the U.S. carriers the U.S. has captured two-thirds of U.S.-Japan market. Most significantly, the U.S. enjoys a $4.8 billion aviation trade surplus with Japan - one of only two trade sectors with Japan where a U.S. surplus exists.

Beyond Rights Key to Success

- Continued success in this market is highly dependent upon the current rights of U.S. carriers to fly "beyond" Japan to Asia. These "beyond rights" allow for full competition with Japanese carriers. Without these rights, the U.S.-Asia market would be ceded to high cost Japanese carriers.

Beyond Rights are the U.S. Ticket to Asia for Aviation and for Export Generally

- These "beyond rights" will become even more critical to the U.S. trade picture as Asian economies grow. Every global economic forecast considers the Asia region to be the fastest growing trade market in the world. The U.S. cannot relinquish these rights without relinquishing its foothold in this market.

Japan Seeks Curtailment

- Japan recognizes the significance of the "beyond rights" and has adopted a consistent pattern of negotiation to curtail them. The current cargo negotiations - where Japan has first sought and then threatened curtailment - are only the most recent example.

Jobs Lost if Surrender Rights; Parochial Interests Must be Measured in Trade Context

- Open skies with Japan would be the best aviation relationship, but it is not available because Japan wants less U.S. access, not more. Recognizing the Japanese position on open skies, the ACCESS U.S.-Japan airlines have encouraged the Administration to trade exactly beyond rights for more Japan access for them. This should be opposed by the U.S. There can be no surrendering of beyond rights. Whatever the benefits to individual carriers of increased access to Japan, none can compare to the value to the U.S. of current rights. According to ESI, the ACCESS proposal (capping beyond rights in exchange for new service to Japan) would produce 18% *less* service to Japan in the year 2010 than extending the current regime. It also risks imposing a net revenue loss to U.S. carriers of $3.9 billion; a net loss in U.S. economic activity of $6.4 billion; a net loss in U.S. trade receipts of $3.7 billion; and a net loss of U.S. employment of 168,000 jobs.

Negotiation Only if Current Rights Honored

- The facts show the consumer is well-served today. Nonetheless, we welcome competition and fully support expanded opportunities for U.S. carriers. However, the U.S. must insist on these conditions before opening negotiations with Japan:

    - Japan must show that it is honoring the Aviation Agreement with the United States by approving all current applications for fifth freedom operations.

    - The Administration should firmly announce to Japan that it will not negotiate new opportunities between the U.S. and Japan that it will not negotiate new opportunities between the U.S. and Japan on the basis of restricting existing rights of U.S. carriers.

    - When Japan demonstrates through its actions that it is complying with the Aviation Agreement, the U.S. should seek talks with Japan based on an agreed agenda that talks will address the expansion of opportunities for both sides, but that neither will propose curtailment of rights held by the other.

TESTIMONY OF RICHARD B. HIRST
SENIOR VICE PRESIDENT, NORTHWEST AIRLINES, INC.,
BEFORE THE SUBCOMMITTEE ON AVIATION,
HOUSE COMMITTEE ON TRANSPORTATION AND INFRASTRUCTURE

MARCH 27, 1996

I would like to thank the Subcommittee for affording me the opportunity to present Northwest Airlines' views concerning our nation's critical aviation relationship with Japan.

Northwest Airlines has a long-standing major investment in the U.S.-Japan-Asia market. Northwest serves Tokyo nonstop from New York, Chicago, Detroit, Minneapolis/St. Paul, San Francisco, Seattle/Tacoma, Los Angeles and Honolulu. In addition, Northwest has established convenient hub and spoke networks at Detroit, Minneapolis/St. Paul and Seattle/Tacoma which allow passengers throughout the United States to make convenient connections at these hubs on their way to Japan and the Far East.

Northwest also provides services to U.S.-Asia traffic through Japan under the terms of the Aviation Agreement with Japan. Via Northwest's Tokyo hub, we fly to Seoul, Singapore, Beijing, Shanghai, Bangkok, Hong Kong, Manila and Taipei. We have applications pending in Japan to add Jakarta, Indonesia (via Osaka) and Guangzhou, China (via Tokyo).

These hearings are timely in light of the current state of U.S.-Japan cargo discussions; recent initiatives by some carriers to seek passenger negotiations; and the President's upcoming trip to Japan.

We want to state at the outset:

- This is not a debate about whether other carriers should be allowed greater access to Japan. Northwest has a long history of supporting open skies between the U.S.-Japan. Northwest also supports greater access through the Memorandum of Understanding process that was used in 1985 and 1989.

- This is a debate about the current and future U.S. trade position in Japan and Asia.

- Japan has no interest in open skies or liberalization of the current passenger agreement. Since 1982, when Japan authorized United to serve Seattle-Tokyo on the condition that no beyond rights would be connected with the route, Japan has pursued a strategy of negotiation to curtail the existing rights of U.S. carriers to fly to Asia via Japan.

- The current cargo negotiations clearly demonstrate Japan's desire to curtail beyond rights. Japan has pursued a two-fold agenda throughout months of discussion: first, expansion of Japanese carriers' rights, and second, curtailment of the beyond rights of U.S. carriers. In the face of U.S. resistance to this agenda, Japan threatened to cancel certain existing beyond routes operated by Federal Express.

- Japan wants curtailment in U.S. passenger and cargo rights because it knows that U.S. carriers are in an extremely competitive position in U.S.-Japan-Asia market, the fastest growing aviation market and the fastest growing trade market in the world. Curtailment could allow Japan to dominate this market.

- Whatever the benefits to individual carriers of increased access to Japan, none can compare to the surrendering of existing U.S. rights to fly to Asia. At risk is the $4.8 billion aviation trade surplus with Japan, one of only two trade sectors where a U.S. surplus exists. Beyond jobs in aviation, also at risk are jobs in the export industries and the tremendous opportunity for future U.S. growth in aviation and export trade.

However, the U.S. must insist on these conditions before opening negotiations with Japan:

- Japan must show that it is honoring the Aviation Agreement with the United States by approving all current applications for fifth freedom operations.
- The Administration should firmly announce to Japan that it will not negotiate new opportunities between the U.S. and Japan that it will not negotiate new opportunities between the U.S. and Japan on the basis of restricting existing rights of U.S. carriers.
- When Japan demonstrates through its actions that it is complying with the Aviation Agreement, the U.S. should seek talks with Japan based on an agreed agenda that talks will address the expansion of opportunities for both sides, but that neither will propose curtailment of rights held by the other.

1. <u>The Best Aviation Policy, Open Skies, Is Not Available With Japan</u>

In its 1995 statement on United States international air transportation policy, the U.S. Department of Transportation made clear that it will push for procompetitive aviation regimes in which air service patterns are set by marketplace demand rather than by governmental fiat. According to DOT, "[o]ur approach is a practical one: . . . to advance the liberalization of air service regimes as far as our partners are willing to go, and to withhold benefits from those countries that are not willing to move forward."[1/]

1/ U.S. Department of Transportation, <u>U.S. International Air Transportation Policy Statement</u>, April 1995, at 10.

Consistent with this policy, the U.S. government would, and appropriately should, favor an open skies regime with Japan. Under such a regime, all Japanese and U.S. carriers -- including Northwest -- would have the unfettered right to compete with one another in U.S.-Japan markets and U.S.-Asia markets via Japan. According to a recent Economic Strategy Institute report, an open skies regime would optimize economic benefits for both the United States and Japan.[2/]

Unfortunately, however, Japan wants less competition in aviation, not more. Even the ACCESS Coalition recognizes this in its position paper:

> An "open skies" agreement with Japan may be the ultimate goal of U.S. government officials, the aviation industry, and communities, but achieving it will take time -- perhaps years.[3/]

ACCESS further has observed, quite correctly, that "the Government of Japan historically has resisted U.S. proposals for such an agreement. . . ."[4/]

Faced with this reality, the United States in recent years has focused on negotiating limited additional market access for U.S. carriers in exchange for additional Japanese carrier access,

---

2/ Economic Strategy Institute, Turbulence Over the Pacific, March 21, 1996, at 60.

3/ ACCESS U.S.-Japan, Expanding the U.S.-Japan Aviation Market: Economic Opportunity, Growth and Jobs, February 21, 1996, at 10.

4/ Coopers and Lybrand L.L.P., U.S.-Japan Aviation Options, Technical Analysis, February 21, 1996, at 1.

without giving up existing rights. After much effort, the United States has had several "access-for-access" successes. In the current climate, however, even that type of deal does not appear possible. Japan has made clear that it wants passenger negotiations in order to cut back the fifth freedom beyond-Japan rights of U.S. carriers. Japan also has focused on obtaining a comparable cutback in the cargo area, by proposing a freeze on fifth freedom operations and then threatening the cancellation of existing U.S. carrier operations if an agreement is not reached.

2. Under The Current Aviation Agreement, U.S. Airlines Have Captured Two-Thirds of the Market and Generated a $4.8 Billion Annual Trade Surplus With Japan

The existing U.S.-Japan aviation agreement provides substantial trade benefits to the United States. In the last fifteen years, U.S. carriers have been able to utilize industry-wide efficiency gains spurred by domestic deregulation, and, since the late 1980s, when these gains took firm hold, have achieved impressive commercial success in Japan. Northwest and United, the "1952" carriers, and American, Delta and Continental, the "MOU" carriers,[5] are together able to operate 61% of the

---

5/ Three U.S. airlines, Northwest, United and Federal Express, are authorized to provide service pursuant to the original bilateral aviation agreement signed in 1952. These three carriers have the right to carry (1) traffic between the United States and Japan; (2) traffic between the United States and Asia via Japan; and (3) traffic between Asian countries and Japan ("fifth freedom traffic"). These are known as the "1952" carriers.

(continued...)

capacity offered between the United States and Japan; JAL and ANA operate 33%.[6] The U.S. and Japanese carriers garner about the same shares of the traffic pool. Before these efficiencies emerged, i.e., as recently as the mid-1980s, the Japanese airline industry held a market share advantage. In 1982, under the same aviation agreement that exists today, the Japanese market share was 58%.[7]

As a result of this impressive trade achievement, U.S. carriers generated $5.4 billion in export revenue in 1994, and contributed a $4.8 billion offset to the U.S. deficit with Japan.[8] This surplus with Japan represents almost 75% of the U.S. worldwide trade balance in air transportation.

The U.S.-Japan cargo story is the same. Northwest has estimated that, in available ton miles, U.S. carriers out-perform their Japanese counterparts between the U.S. and Japan by 67% to 33%.

5/(...continued)
In 1985 and 1989, the U.S. and Japan signed Memoranda of Understanding ("MOUs") permitting American Airlines, Delta Air Lines, and Continental Airlines to enter the Japan-U.S. market on discrete city pair routes, with no more than seven flights per week on each route, and with no rights to fly beyond Japan into Asia. These are known as the "MOU" carriers.

6/ OAG Flight Guide, August 1995. The remaining 6% is operated by other foreign airlines, principally Asian airlines operating fifth freedom services between Japan and the United States.

7/ U.S. Department of Transportation, U.S. International Air Passenger and Freight Statistics.

8/ U.S. Department of Commerce, Survey of Current Business.

3. <u>The Key Element Of The Aviation Agreement Is That It Gives U.S. And Japanese Airlines The Right To Carry Traffic Between The United States And Asia Via Japan, Thus Allowing Northwest, United And FedEx To Establish Japan Connecting Hubs To Compete With JAL, ANA and NCA</u>

Northwest, United and FedEx have secured their positions in Japan by investing literally billions of dollars in aircraft and facilities and by establishing hub-and-spoke networks in Tokyo and Osaka. These networks enable the U.S. carriers to combine traffic flows from many U.S. cities to Japan and beyond to the Pacific Rim, and to augment their U.S.-Japan-Asia services by carrying Japan-Asia passengers on flights from Tokyo or Osaka to places like Singapore, Bangkok, Manila, Hong Kong, Beijing, Shanghai, Seoul and Taipei. With these networks, Northwest, United and FedEx can compete on roughly equal terms with their powerful Japanese and Asian competitors, which of course have their own Asia hubs.

A Japan hub is critical to U.S. carrier participation in U.S.-Asia markets. Most Pacific Rim countries are either too distant from the U.S. mainland, or too thin in traffic, to support nonstop service. These cities can be served only via a hub-and-spoke network in Asia, and Japan is the only suitable place in Asia to locate such a network. As the Economic Strategy Institute recently noted:

> The reason for the intensity and bitterness of the U.S.-Japan aviation negotiation is that Japan holds the key to the future of the Asian portion of any global network by dint both of location and the size of its market.

> Today's aircraft are unable to fly nonstop from North America to many important Asia-Pacific destinations beyond Japan, and even though ranges will be extended in the future, other Asian destinations do not generate sufficient demand to justify high-frequency service. Thus, Japan, and particularly Tokyo's Narita Airport, is the natural, and the only practical, hub for aviation service between North America and the Asia-Pacific region. . . . [N]o other Asian destination can match it. If you want to have a global network and be a serious player in Asia, you have to hub out of Tokyo.[9/]

Were it not for the fifth freedom rights of United, Northwest and FedEx to carry Japan-Asia traffic, Japan Air Lines, All Nippon Airways and Nippon Cargo Airlines would be the only carriers with hubs in Japan, and, thus, the only carriers economically positioned to carry U.S.-Asia traffic. The loss of fifth freedom rights would hand over to high-cost Japanese carriers a virtual monopoly on U.S.-Asia business.

4. Since Japan Is Losing The Battle Against U.S. Airlines, Which Have Become More Competitive Since Deregulation, It Is Seeking To Change The Rules That Allow Carriers From Both Countries To Carry U.S.-Asia Traffic Via Japan

As indicated, Japan is losing the competitive battle with U.S. carriers. Its carriers are highly protected and find it difficult to compete head to head against their more efficient

---

9/ Economic Strategy Institute, Turbulence Over the Pacific at 32.

American rivals. JAL's costs per available ton kilometer are twice that of Northwest and United.[10/]

Rather than encourage its carriers to address the root cause of their inefficiencies, Japan instead is attempting to handicap its American rivals by cutting back on their fifth freedom rights, and thus curtailing their ability to maintain hub-and-spoke networks in Japan. As reported by the Economic Strategy Institute, negative effects are felt even within Asia:

> With inefficient carriers, but a crucial hub location, Japan's Ministry of Transportation has used regulation to protect its airlines and attempted to give them the immense leverage that control of Asia's key hub entails. This has led to significant constriction of traffic through Tokyo. While transpacific service has been maintained at a level comparable to that over the Atlantic, intra-Asian load factors and fares are sky high. As shown below, this constriction and Japan's manipulation of the agreement has led to clashes with U.S. carriers and difficult U.S.-Japan negotiations.[11/]

Japan's efforts in this regard are not of recent origin. For a number of years, it has tried to place impediments on the U.S. carrier exercise of fifth freedom rights. Recently, these efforts have intensified -- for instance, in the round of cargo negotiations held in Washington last month.

The rights to carry traffic between the U.S. and Asia via Japan, however, have been available in the U.S.-Japan aviation

---

10/ Booz Allen & Hamilton Inc., Shaping Pacific Aviation in the 21st Century, September 25, 1995 at II-11F.

11/ Economic Strategy Institute, Turbulence Over the Pacific at xi (emphasis added).

agreement to Northwest, United, FedEx and their predecessors since 1952. To maintain the access of U.S. passengers, shippers and airlines to U.S.-Asia markets, the United States has consistently refused to entertain Japan's persistent requests to cancel, cap or restrict U.S. fifth freedom rights. Under a policy followed by every Administration since 1959, the United States laudably has defended the rights of U.S. carriers to fly fifth freedom routes beyond Japan into Asia.

5. Japanese Efforts To Restrict U.S. Carrier Competition Have Serious Adverse Implications In The Area of U.S.-Asia Trade

I have already described the positive impact that U.S. carrier Pacific services have on the U.S. trade position. The impact is manifest in the $4.8 billion trade surplus experienced in the air transport sector in 1994. The effects, however, go far beyond this trade surplus figure, reverberating throughout the U.S. economy. The Economic Strategy Institute estimates the 1995 impact on economic activity at $29.3 billion.[12/]

I would like, moreover, to underscore the particular importance of the Pacific market. No one of renown would dispute that this is where future global economic growth lies. As the FAA recently indicated, China had the world's highest GDP growth in 1995, with a 10.5% gain for the year, and:

> Asia leads the world in economic growth. Besides China, the Pacific Basin -- Hong

12/ Economic Strategy Institute, Turbulence Over the Pacific at 56.

> Kong, Indonesia, Malaysia, the Philippines, Singapore, South Korea, Taiwan, and Thailand -- experienced growth of 7.6%, higher than any other region of the world.[13]

The FAA predicts that the economies of the Pacific and developing Asian countries -- with a projected average annual rate of 5.0% over the next 12 years -- will continue to experience growth rates exceeding most of the world's economies.[14] Consistent with this economic growth, the FAA also has forecast that the Pacific region will be the fastest area of U.S. carrier passenger growth. During the 1995-2007 period, according to the FAA, Pacific entity enplanements will grow at an average annual rate of 6.0%, far higher than domestic or Atlantic enplanements and even above rapidly growing Latin America enplanements.[15]

The Economic Strategy Institute has reached the same conclusion. It points out, for instance, that the Asia-Pacific market already accounts for more than a third of scheduled international passenger traffic, and that the figure is expected to grow to over 50% by the year 2010.[16]

It is imperative that the U.S. maintain U.S. flag competitiveness in the rapidly growing Pacific region.

13/ Federal Aviation Administration, FAA Aviation Forecasts -- Fiscal Years 1996-2007, March 1996, at II-2.

14/ Id. at II-14.

15/ Id., Table I-2.

16/ Economic Strategy Institute, Turbulence Over the Pacific, at 13. See also id. at 45-47 (discussing various Pacific and intra-Asia air traffic growth projections).

Maintenance of the U.S. trade position and the ability of U.S. businesses to access Asian markets depend on it.

6. Consumers Are Well-Served By The Existing U.S.-Japan Market Structure

The ACCESS U.S.-Japan coalition would have the United States disregard all these considerations and instead focus on the economic benefits that supposedly would flow from improvements in the U.S.-Japan market structure. Northwest would be the first to agree that more competition certainly would be better. However, Northwest does not agree that the market today is suffering the adverse effects of inadequate competition. The U.S.-Japan passenger market already receives service from a total of two Japanese carriers, five U.S. carriers and five third-country carriers. The market is well-served, as demonstrated by a variety of measurements.

First, load factors across the Pacific are comfortable and, indeed, are lower than load factors across the Atlantic. According to the FAA, there was a 4.5 percentage point difference in 1995, and the difference should average three percentage points annually through the year 2007.[17/] This means that it is now easier, and will remain easier, for consumers to obtain passage on the flights of their preference to destinations in the Pacific than to destinations in the Atlantic.

17/ Federal Aviation Administration, FAA Aviation Forecasts -- Fiscal Years 1996-2007 at III-31, III-33.

Second, fares between the United States and Japan are comparable to fares between the United States and the United Kingdom, notwithstanding significantly higher costs of doing business in Japan. (Landing fees are five times higher at Tokyo than at London-Gatwick, for example.) The ACCESS U.S.-Japan Coalition claims that fares in the Japan market are as much as 60% higher than fares in comparable European markets. This is not true. Retail prices in the U.S.-Japan market (as opposed posted prices) are virtually identical to those across the Atlantic when measured on a price per mile basis. Data compiled by the Economic Strategy Institute show that beyond Japan fares are indeed very high compared to transatlantic prices, but transpacific fares are quite comparable to fares across the Atlantic.[18]

Third, there is no shortage of service in the U.S.-Japan market. There are 5% more flights, and 32% more seats offered between the U.S. and Japan than between the U.S. and Britain.[19] Claims by the ACCESS U.S.-Japan coalition that the U.K. market receives almost twice as many flights as Japan are based on "cooked" numbers, and are spurious. ACCESS concocted its conclusion by omitting from its calculation all flights between

18/ Economic Strategy Institute, Turbulence Over the Pacific at 36-37.

19/ In the week of January 15, 1996, the same period analyzed in the Access U.S.-Japan Coalition's study, there were 1042 roundtrip flights, and 363,050 roundtrip seats between the U.S. and Japan, but only 988 roundtrip flights, and 275,726 roundtrip seats between the U.S. and the U.K.

Japan, on the one hand, and Hawaii, Guam and Saipan, on the other. Japan-Hawaii is the single most heavily travelled route between the U.S. and Japan. Almost one-half the U.S.-Japan market consists of travel to and from Hawaii. Recognizing the unique importance of Hawaii to our aviation relationship with Japan, three of the nine routes obtained by the United States in the 1985 and 1989 MOUs were allocated to new Hawaii service (Honolulu-Tokyo, Honolulu-Nagoya, and Honolulu-Fukuoka). Moreover, one of the ACCESS Coalition carriers (Continental) is seeking talks with Japan to enable it to add more service to Hawaii (as well as Guam and Saipan).

The Economic Strategy Institute has attempted to quantify the economic effects of various possible outcomes of U.S.-Japan aviation. Under its analysis, the United States would be significantly better off with the status quo than under a scenario in which new U.S.-Japan rights are obtained at the expense of existing fifth freedom rights.[20/]

According to ESI, the likely impact in 2010 of a trade in which the U.S. receives additional frequencies for the MOU carriers in exchange for a cap on the beyond rights of Northwest and United is:

Revenue of U.S. carriers	$3.9 billion less
U.S. economic activity	$6.4 billion less
U.S. trade receipts	$3.7 billion less
U.S. employment	168,000 less

20/ Economic Strategy Institute, Turbulence Over the Pacific at 60-63.

7. <u>The Access Coalition Would Lead The United States Into A Disastrous Exchange Which Would Make U.S. Airlines Less Competitive And Reduce -- Or Even Eliminate -- The Aviation Trade Surplus</u>

The ACCESS Coalition recognizes that Japan is interested in curtailing U.S. access, not expanding it. The Coalition's answer to this is to urge that the United States give Japan exactly what it has been seeking for almost twenty years: a Bermuda II type arrangement that (1) curtails U.S. fifth freedom rights, and (2) adds U.S.-Japan city-pair routes for allocation to them:

> [T]here have been indications recently that Japan would be willing to permit expanded competition on routes between the United States and Japan (third and fourth freedom markets) in exchange for some negotiated limits on future increase in beyond operations by U.S. airlines (fifth freedom markets). . . . Thus, the current situation poses the fundamental question as to whether U.S. national interests would be better served by trading expanded U.S. carrier access to third and fourth freedom markets in exchange for some limitation on the future expansion of beyond rights by U.S. airlines.[21]

Protests by the Coalition that it is not calling for curtailment of fifth freedom rights are thus disingenuous and disproved by the Coalition's own written proposal.

Implementation of the Access Coalition's agenda would be disastrous for United States interests. It would lead to a

---

21/ Coopers and Lybrand, <u>U.S.-Japan Aviation Analysis, Technical Analysis</u> at 1.

negotiation in which Japan, aided by division within the United States, would seek to:

- Foreclose U.S. airline access to U.S. Pacific Rim markets, the fastest growing and most dynamic markets in the world;
- Dismantle the U.S. trade surplus with Japan in air transportation; and
- Reduce U.S. airline flights to Japan. ESI concluded that because about 50 percent of traffic on beyond legs [of United and Northwest] is flow-through traffic, the loss of two beyond frequencies entails the loss of one U.S.-Japan frequency. The ACCESS proposal to cap beyond rights in exchange for new service to Japan, therefore, produces a net decrease of 18% in service to Japan compared to the level of service that would be provided by extending the current regime.

8. A Similar Negotiation In 1977 Produced Bermuda II, The Worst Aviation Rights Exchange In U.S. Commercial Aviation History

In 1976, the United Kingdom renounced the Bermuda I agreement, which was substantially the same as the current U.S.-Japan Aviation Agreement. The new Bermuda II agreement that replaced Bermuda I effected a dramatic reduction of U.S. access to Britain, including the virtual elimination of U.S. carrier fifth freedom rights beyond London. This capitulation to U.K. demands to "balance" the aviation relationship resulted in a U.S. market surplus turning into a significant trade deficit that remains the single most troubling aspect of U.S. international aviation. Since 1977, U.S. market share has declined from 55% to 41%, and the U.K. market has remained highly restrictive.

Bermuda II has been widely criticized in the United States, and the U.S. has determined that it should take all available steps to avoid a repeat of the Bermuda II debacle with Japan. The central purpose of U.S. aviation policy toward Japan has been to maintain a political framework that would permit the preservation of United States fifth freedom access to Asia. To date, this strategy has succeeded.

9. By Publicly Aligning Itself With Japanese Interests, The ACCESS Coalition Already Has Undermined The U.S. Negotiating Position

In July 1995, the United States and Japan agreed to enter into all-cargo talks. There was no agreed agenda, other than an expectation on the part of the United States that the talks would produce liberalization.

During the first three rounds of talks, Japan sought expansion of opportunities for its carriers, but curtailment of fifth freedom expansion rights for U.S. carriers. This was unacceptable to the United States. On February 21, 1996, less than a week before commencement of the fourth round of talks, the ACCESS Coalition held a press conference to propose that the U.S. exchange fifth freedom[22] rights for additional access to Japan for its carrier sponsors. The effect was predictable. At the talks six days later, Japan made a new and unprecedented demand. Not only was it seeking to curtail fifth freedom expansion rights; it was threatening that if the United States did not

---

22/ See attached correspondence regarding statements by Coalition leadership on relinquishing fifth freedoms.

accept its air cargo proposal, Japan would cancel seven fifth freedom all-cargo routes currently operated by Federal Express.

10. Policy Recommendations

The ACCESS Coalition is proposing that the United States negotiate with itself in dealing with a party that desires only to curtail existing U.S. rights. The current air cargo negotiation demonstrates where this would lead.

From this experience, it is clear that the United States should not enter into passenger talks unless there is an agreed agenda that excludes the possibility of discussing a curtailment of existing rights. The United States must not allow Japan to use as negotiating leverage threats to cancel fifth freedom operations or refusals to grant applications to expand fifth freedom services that are authorized by the Aviation Agreement.

U.S. aviation policy toward Japan thus should consist of three elements:

- The Administration should firmly announce to Japan that it will not negotiate new opportunities between the U.S. and Japan on the basis of restricting existing rights of U.S. carriers.

- Japan must show that it is honoring the Aviation Agreement with the United States by approving all current applications for fifth freedom operations.

- When Japan demonstrates through its actions that it is complying with the Aviation Agreement, the U.S. should seek talks with Japan based on an agreed agenda that talks will address the expansion of opportunities

for both sides, but that neither will propose curtailment of rights held by the other.

UNITED AIRLINES

March 18, 1996

World Headquarters

The Honorable Gerald L. Baliles
Hunton & Williams
Riverfront Plaza, East Tower
951 East Byrd Street
Richmond, Virginia

Dear Governor Baliles:

It is our understanding that *Access U.S.-Japan*, the lobbying group represented by your law firm, now suggests that the U.S. not give up existing operations by U.S. airlines to Asia (individual flights actually being flown today). It is clear, however, that Access is fully prepared to have the United States give up the existing rights of U.S. airlines to fly to locations they are not currently serving (and perhaps also capping the frequency of service to locations that are currently being served), so that the airline members of the lobby group -- American, Delta and Continental -- can be given additional point to point routes by Japan in exchange.

In such an exchange, the United States would give up the right of its carriers to grow service to points in Asia beyond Japan -- the fastest growing market in the world. As the Chairman of American Airlines candidly acknowledged in his October 12, 1995 speech to the International Aviation Club, "U.S. carriers without the right to use Japan's airports as intermediate hubs are simply unable to participate in the U.S.-Asia market."

This, of course, is an exciting prospect for the Japanese, who are actively encouraging the kind of exchange advocated by Access so that their carriers can dominate the Asian market without competition from far more efficient U.S. carriers. Markets that U.S. carriers would give up in such an exchange include Vietnam (projected to be the fasted growing aviation market in the world), Malaysia, most of China, India (over the Pacific), Indonesia, and Singapore.

Let's look at the evidence:

- American Airlines and Delta Airlines founded Access U.S.-Japan and provide the bulk of its financial support. This was confirmed in the February 26, 1996 edition of *World Airline News* (copy attached) by American Airlines' director of government relations and by other members of the lobby group.

- American Airlines has openly and notoriously expressed its view that U.S. negotiators should trade the existing rights of U.S. carriers to fly in the future to points in Asia beyond Japan so American Airlines could begin new point-to-point service to Japan.

Box 66100, Chicago, Illinois 60666, • Location: 1200 East Algonquin Road, Elk Grove Township, Illinois 60007

March 18, 1996
Page Two

1.) In a speech given at the International Aviation Club on October 12, 1995, the Chairman of American Airlines stated:

"The Japanese government does want to constrain the further growth of [Northwest's and United's] beyond operations. A U.S.-Japan agreement premised on limiting the expansion of beyond operations by [United and Northwest], in exchange for a substantial increase in operating rights between various U.S. cities and Tokyo and Osaka, would be good.....Such an agreement would trade beyond-Japan rights that Northwest and United do not now use, and may never use, for authority that American and other 'have-not' U.S. carriers are prepared to operate today."

2.) The March 8, 1996, *Aviation Daily* quotes the President of American Airlines as stating that "there have been indications that Japan would be willing to permit expanded competition on routes between the United States and Japan in exchange for limitations on the future rate of growth of operations by incumbent U.S. airlines beyond Japan." That same statement appeared in a filing made on February 21, 1996 by American Airlines.

Presumably, you expect us to believe that after setting up and financing the *Access* lobby group with Delta, hiring a "coalition" public relations firm, hiring your law firm to represent the "coalition" and scouring the country to find "coalition" members -- all at substantial expense -- that Access is not pushing for a trade of existing U.S. carrier rights in exchange for new point-to-point service for American, Delta and Continental, while the *Access* lobby group's founder and principal financial supporter is publicly and vocally seeking such an exchange. Let's continue to examine the record.

- Your letter of February 14, 1996 to Jerry Greenwald states that *Access* seeks to achieve "greater third and fourth-freedom access to the U.S. -Japan aviation market . . . without reducing [our] current fifth freedom operations.

- The so-called "study" prepared for Access by American Airlines' long-time consultant Dan Kasper also states that "[Access] believes the best policy option for the United States (and for Japan as well) would be to expand air service on routes between the United States and Japan, while preserving beyond rights currently being exercised by U.S. carriers.

March 18, 1996
Page Three

- *World Airline News* attributes to American Airlines' director of governmental affairs the statement that Access does not necessarily wish to eliminate all future fifth-freedom opportunities by United and Northwest. "Even if the other side [Japan] puts only some restrictions on the future growth of fifth freedoms, but does not eliminate those opportunities, then it's easier to reach some agreement with the Japanese," the American Airlines representative said. Just what kind of agreement is he referring to? Trading those fifth freedom opportunities for additional point to point service for American and Delta?

It is clear to us that the Access lobby is trying to obfuscate the reality that its plain purpose is to fulfill the parochial interests of its founders and financial supporters, principally American and Delta Airlines, to obtain point-to-point service from the United States to Japan the only way they can -- the same way the Japanese have suggested -- by sacrificing existing United States carrier rights to serve points beyond Japan.

Finessing the question won't work. Claiming that Access only wants passenger talks to obtain more U.S.- Japan access, and refusing to answer questions about how that access should be obtained won't work. Stating that U.S. negotiators will "know what to do" about obtaining that access in exchange for U.S. rights to fly beyond Japan (while Access' airline members lobby hard for their clearly defined parochial position) won't work.

If *Access U.S.-Japan* has changed its position, or if its position is different than that of its founders and principal financial supporters, we would be pleased to hear about it. Does Access U.S.-Japan believe that the United States should exchange existing rights of U.S. carriers to fly beyond-Japan in the future in order to obtain additional point to point access for the U.S. 'MOU' carriers? If the answer is 'NO', we would welcome your publicly clarifying that view and so advising the Department of Transportation and the State Department so that they may take that view into account in any discussions with the Japanese.

Very truly yours,

Stuart I. Oran
Executive Vice President
Corporate Affairs and
General Counsel
United Airlines

Very truly yours,

Richard B. Hirst
Senior Vice President
Corporate Affairs
Northwest Airlines

Aviation Coalition for Competition and
Expanded Services Between the United States and Japan

March 21, 1996

Mr. Gerald Greenwald
Chairman, United Airlines
1200 Algonquin Road
Elk Grove Township, Illinois 60007

Dear Jerry:

I am very disappointed in the letter dated March 18 and sent to me, co-signed, by a member of your staff. I am particularly disappointed that I read about the letter in *Aviation Daily* before I had received my own copy a day or so later.

In view of the stridency of that letter, let me state again that, in my public statements and in my private conversations with U.S. government officials, and others, I have stated our agenda clearly: "ACCESS U.S. - Japan is in favor of increasing -- not decreasing -- service in the U.S. - Japan market, and beyond. Anyone who claims differently mis-represents our agenda and our analysis of the U.S. - Japan market."

I am leading a nationwide coalition of more than 400 members. They include governors, mayors and other civic leaders, corporate chief executives, labor and consumer leaders. Naturally, I cannot control every view and utterance of every member -- particularly when they were expressed two and-a-half months before I ever became involved as chairman of this coalition. The references in the March 18 United letter to speeches made by others last October are hardly relevant to the agenda of a coalition formed February 21, 1996. The coalition subscribes to the idea that the national interest is best served by the expansion of the U.S. - Japan aviation market, and also agrees on the goal of more flights to more cities by more airlines between the U.S. - Japan, and beyond.

Finally, the United letter of March 18 refers to my letter to you of February 14, specifically language about "current beyond operations." Let me be clear: our position on this issue as stated in my February 14 letter was in response to your specific concern that ACCESS U.S.- Japan was willing to trade current beyond operations for new U.S. - Japan

700 Thirteenth Street, NW Suite 1180 Washington, DC 20005 Phone: 202.434.8312 Fax: 202.393.

service. The coalition's position clear: we support increased service in the U.S. - Japan market, and beyond.

Although you and I have had two very pleasant conversations about the agenda of ACCESS U.S.- Japan, your staff continues to mis-represent that agenda. I assume they continue to do so without your knowledge or direction. If you have any continuing questions about our agenda, ask me directly. In the meantime, please advise your staff that their letters and press releases of personal invective and careless misrepresentation do not reflect favorably on their chief executive or on the corporate image of United.

Sincerely,

Jerry

Gerald L. Baliles

BEFORE THE

SUBCOMMITTEE ON AVIATION

OF

THE COMMITTEE ON

TRANSPORTATION AND INFRASTRUCTURE

OF THE

UNITED STATES HOUSE OF REPRESENTATIVES

STATEMENT OF

CYRIL D. MURPHY

VICE PRESIDENT - INTERNATIONAL AFFAIRS

UNITED AIR LINES, INC.

MARCH 27, 1996

STATEMENT OF

CYRIL D. MURPHY

VICE PRESIDENT - INTERNATIONAL AFFAIRS

UNITED AIR LINES, INC.

Chairman Duncan, Congressman Lipinski, Members of the Subcommittee. Thank you for allowing me to appear before you today.

Your hearings focus on aviation relations with two of our most important air transportation trade partners. The policies of both exemplify protectionism in the extreme. In the case of the U.K. we labor under an agreement -- Bermuda II -- that represents one of the worst bargains we have ever struck. Our Government and our carriers are of the uniform belief that we must negotiate a much more liberal regime with the British.

In Japan, on the other hand, we have a very liberal basic agreement. Indeed, in the words of Chairman Bud Shuster, that agreement is "extremely liberal; so liberal that Japan has spent decades engrafting restrictions upon its basic terms. It is these restrictions that need to be removed. However, it seems that Japan wants to bring all of the rights granted in 1952 under its tight regulatory control. This should not be permitted."[1] The problem arises from the fact that the 1952 Agreement has been whittled down over the years to the point that it provides for

---

[1] Letter dated February 27, 1996, from Bud Shuster to Federico Peña.

that it provides for only a fraction of the opportunities originally exchanged. This has produced a regime that is in fact quite similar to what we have with the U.K. By now offering to exchange a few point-to-point routes in return for the surrender of the rights that allow United, Northwest and Federal Express to compete in the Asian market, Japan hopes to duplicate the U.K.'s position under Bermuda II. The irony is that since 1985 it is frequently the loudest U.S. carrier critics of the U.S.-U.K. agreement that are the strongest advocates of its repetition in the Pacific.

The restrictive bent of the U.K. and Japan policies may be similar but there is one fundamental difference in our aviation relationships with them. The United Kingdom (and the United States) honor scrupulously the agreement that they signed; Japan does not. Japan's actions represent a direct political challenge to the U.S. I trust that this Subcommittee recognizes that this challenge must be met head on.

In December, 1994, Japan unilaterally decided to prevent United, Northwest and Fed Ex from any further exercise of the rights we hold to extend our transpacific flights beyond Japan to other points in Asia. For instance, for over a year now Japan has refused to allow United to operate one of its flights beyond Osaka to Seoul, Korea. This is, as the Department of Transportation acknowledges, a clear violation by Japan of the provisions of the Air Services Agreement. Japan earlier threatened and now has threatened again, to withdraw approval for key beyond rights being exercised by Federal Express and other U.S. cargo carriers unless the U.S. negotiates a new cargo agreement by the end of this month.

Japan has thus made it plain that it is willing to ignore any provision of its aviation trade agreement that it believes to be working in favor of U.S. air carriers. If we turn a blind eye to that behavior -- as some urge we must do -- we would be ratifying it. We would also be sending a message that U.S. businesses operating under a variety of trade agreements with Japan, do so only at that country's sufferance. The message to U.S. companies would be: "Being too successful will place your rights at risk."

This transcends aviation issues. It is a matter of international trade principle on which the U.S. must not waiver. The U.S. must expect its trade partners to honor their bilateral obligations and must demand that they do so.

How did we get ourselves in this position with Japan? As Mr. Jiro Hanyu, Deputy Director General of the Civil Aviation Bureau and Chairman of the Japanese aviation negotiating delegation recently pointed out it began "in the wake of the U.K. government's successful renegotiation of the U.S.-U.K. aviation agreement which introduced a limit on the number of flights that could be operated by the U.S. carriers."[2] It was Bermuda II that prompted Japan in 1977 to

---

[2] J. Hanyu, "Japan-U.S. Aviation Negotiations--In Pursuit of Elimination of Inequalities," Transport, Feb. 1996,pp.34-36.

seek a similar "comprehensive revision of the bilateral agreement." There can be little doubt about the outcome the Japanese seek from that revision.

Japan and the U.S. have now been "renegotiating" for almost 20 years. Those negotiations have moved step-by-step toward a U.S.-Japan aviation regime which mimics that which we have -- to our serious disadvantage -- with the U.K. At each step in the process, which is illustrated in Chart 1, the overall scope of U.S. rights was restricted.

In the early 1980's Japan refused to honor its obligation to accept the designation of United Airlines to operate on a route from the Pacific Northwest to Tokyo. In June, 1982, the U.S. Government acquiesced in that violation, accepting an arrangement whereby United became the first "MOU carrier" with its frequencies and beyond rights limited by Japan's insistence. The U.S. accepted the principle that henceforth any new U.S. carrier serving Japan would be precluded from developing a hub in that country. All service by new carriers would be point-to-point, without beyond authority and limited as to the frequency, without a provision for growth.

In 1985, at the urging of Delta and American, the U.S. agreed to cap the rights of the so-called "1952 carriers" to those gateway points already listed in their certificates. In conjunction with what it had surrendered in 1982, this step backwards precluded any U.S. carrier from providing non-stop service to Japan from a large number of cities, including Atlanta, St. Louis, Salt Lake City, Las Vegas, Pittsburgh and Philadelphia unless Japan was willing to agree to it. It also precluded the U.S. carriers from integrating their highly efficient domestic hub structures with international routes to the Pacific. For instance, United, the largest U.S. carrier to Asia, can fully integrate its Pacific routes only with San Francisco of its principal domestic hubs.

The unwillingness of the U.S. to stand up to Japan at these critical junctures placed us in the position where we are today.

In 1986, Japan authorized ANA as its second international flag carrier, and it began developing Asian hubs and seeking access to them from the U.S.

In 1989, Japan expanded the number of U.S. routes and capacity under the control of Japanese regulators by limiting the expansion of new points to those only subject to MOU conditions.

In 1994, the first opportunity in years for expanded U.S. flag services -- the opening of the new Kansai Airport at Osaka -- took place. Japan immediately moved to block its expanded use by American carriers by announcing a freeze on their airport slots at prior levels. When the U.S. carriers agreed to restraints on the pace of their growth as the price of expansion, Japan accepted it, yet only months later reneged on the understanding and blocked all new beyond services.

This left U.S. carriers with a single beyond flight from Osaka; the same number of beyond flights that U.S. carriers now operate at Heathrow.

In 1995, the U.S. believed it had reached an agreement with Japan to honor all of the fifth-freedom rights of Federal Express as well as other U.S. cargo operators, except for the potentially most important -- China. In March 1996, Japanese officials threatened to renege on that agreement as well. U.S. passenger rights beyond Japan remain both frozen and unaddressed.

It is clear that over the past two decades, Japan has gained enormous regulatory control over what once was a very liberal regime. It has created a class of U.S. carriers and a class of U.S. cities which must act as supplicants to the Japanese government if they are to gain even point-to-point access to Japan.

It is this control that now allows Japan to dangle the carrot of new service in front of those cities, and new designations for U.S. carriers to serve them. The price is that they support Japan's negotiating objectives before the U.S. government. That is why the *Japan Times* reported that Access U.S.-Japan "is likely to be a strong supporter of Japan" and led an official of Japan's Ministry of Transport to say that Tokyo "welcomes the efforts of the MOU carriers." See Chart 2.

Our negotiators often point to the difficulties that they encounter because of the conflicting objectives of our cities and our carriers. In this instance, I hope the

Subcommittee will recognize that those "conflicting objectives" could have been avoided entirely if in the 1980's the U.S. had resisted Japan's effort to restrict the 1952 Agreement and demanded that its provisions be honored.

Japan maneuvered the U.S. into accepting the concept of "second tier" rights for certain of our cities and our carriers despite the 1952 Agreement's open designation provision. Japan now hopes to use the frustrated aspirations of those same cities and carriers to eliminate the remaining liberal provisions of the basic agreement: our beyond rights. If that attack is successful all U.S. cities and carriers will become "second tier" when it comes to direct services to much of Asia.

In 1995, the Clinton Administration released its Statement of U.S. International Aviation Policy. Its specific acknowledgment of (i) the necessity of regional networks if U.S. air carriers are to compete on a global basis and (ii) the need for the U.S. to negotiate to secure the bundles of fifth-freedom rights needed to construct those networks, was a rejection of the approach followed with Japan in the 1980's and received widespread, bipartisan support in Congress as well as general support in our industry.

Japan has taken the policy statement conclusions to heart and is acting on them. It realizes that by unravelling the "bundle of fifth freedom rights" that United, Northwest and Federal Express now hold it can cripple their competitive abilities by emasculating their hubs in Asia, just as they limited U.S. carrier access from their domestic hubs in the 1980's. At the same time, it is supporting the networks of JAL and ANA by allowing them to develop Asian hubs at the new Osaka Airport as well as at Tokyo, and encouraging them to enter into marketing arrangements with U.S. carriers to assure broad coverage of the U.S. via U.S. domestic hubs, just as British Airways has done with U.S. Air and now, it seems, with America West. Japan's hope is that the U.S. will focus its attention on the fringes of the Agreement: gaining some additional point-to-point flying at the expense of the greater U.S. interest in the future growth of Asia.

The stakes, of course, are enormous. Asia is the fastest growing air transportation market in the world. The dimensions of the forecast passenger growth for key cities in that region over the next 14 years are truly amazing. By 2010, as you can see from attached Chart 3, ten Asian markets will have matched or exceeded in size today's two largest Asian markets, while the Japan market itself will have jumped from 35 to 91 million passengers per year.

Of the countries in Chart 3, six lie well beyond the non-stop range of even the B-747-400 aircraft from Los Angeles (Singapore, Thailand, Indonesia, Malaysia, India and Pakistan). To serve them effectively, a stop in Asia is essential. Agreements that the U.S. has today position us to participate in that growth -- if they are maintained and enforced. Japan is doing its best to see that our participation is minimal and that their carriers alone can make use of Japan's natural geographic and economic position as an Asian hub. To their minds it has worked for the U.K. in Europe; it can work for them in Asia.

Why, with the projected growth in the market, is Japan being so protectionist? Why is Japan so insistent that the "fault" in their carriers' market performance lies not with their carriers' business decisions but with the Agreement?

The answer is that Japan's Ministry of Transport has had the responsibility for regulating the economic health of Japan's aviation industry. The simple, inescapable fact is that it has failed miserably.

That failure is evident even in Asia. The Japanese carriers are rapidly being eclipsed in growth by the more competitive carriers of those Asian countries with which we have essentially an "open skies" agreement: Taiwan, Singapore and Korea.

As you can see from Charts 5 and 6, since 1978 the other Asian carriers have more than doubled their share of the U.S.-Asia market while Japanese carrier share has been almost halved. Also, on a global basis their participation in the global market has nearly tripled, while Japan's carriers show no growth over the past eighteen years.

The reasons the Japanese carriers have fallen behind both U.S. and other Asian carriers lies in relative efficiencies. Since deregulation, U.S. international carriers have become among the most efficient in the world. It is not surprising, therefore, that our carriers' share of the U.S.-Japan market has increased significantly. Rather than acknowledge that our traffic gain is in part of function of MOT policies that protected Japanese carrier inefficiencies, Japan's bureaucrats contended that the underlying agreement was "unbalanced." While this may have served to divert attention from the real problem, there is no question that, factually, the argument is nonsense. Under the same agreement JAL had no problem gaining approximately 50 percent of the total U.S.-Japan traffic, until its costs began to diverge sharply from those of its competitors. See Chart 4. That cost disparity, as measured by ICAO statistics is remarkable. It reflects the cost of regulation by MOT. In 1985, Japan Air Lines was more efficient than was United on a cost per available ton kilometer basis. By 1993 the equation had changed dramatically. United's efficiency edge was enormous and growing. See Chart 4.

Rather than acknowledge its own bureaucratic mistakes, Japan has taken a predictable tack. It blames its carriers' performances on foreigners; in this case foreigners abetted by an "unfair" air services agreement. By characterizing the agreement as unfair, of course, they can rationalize ignoring it. And by ignoring it, they hope to buy time to salvage their own position.

From the U.S. standpoint, however, we are being asked to sacrifice our nation's future in the Asian transportation market to protect the reputation of Japan's bureaucrats and their ill-conceived policies. This is a burden we cannot accept.

Equally important, we must recognize that no U.S. carrier today operates any nonstop service to any Asian point (except Japan) unless that carrier also operates a hub in Japan. These nonstop and hub services are complementary, giving U.S. carriers a presence in an Asian city that is competitive with both Japanese and other Asian carriers. If we lose hub access beyond Japan, all U.S. carriers will be in the same position as a number of U.S. carriers, most recently Delta, which have tried and failed to maintain a system of service to other Asian points without a hub in Japan. It leaves Japan with the only efficient carrier networks in the Pacific.

What should be done?

Just last month, DOT's Assistant Secretary for Aviation and International Affairs, Charles Hunnicutt, stressed the need for U.S. policy makers to concentrate on the long-term: "It is important to underscore that in our dealings with Japan, we ought not settle for short-term gains at the cost of sacrificing long-term needs

24-087 97 - 5

into the next century."[3] His comments echoed those of Secretary Peña in conjunction with his recent extended trip trough Asia.[4] We agree completely. We believe that no policy can be relied upon if it is not based on economic reality. That is why we took the lead in gathering those facts.

A study conducted for us by Booz Allen and Hamilton concluded that over the next two decades the cumulative reduction in U.S.-Asian trade balance from restrictions on the U.S. expansion of passenger transportation in Asia through Japan could exceed $100 billion. Japan, it believes, would be the primary beneficiary.

A study conducted under the supervision of Clyde Prestowitz of the Economic Strategy Institute reached much the same conclusion. In that independent analysis, a cap on U.S. carrier beyond rights would mean that in the year 2010, U.S. carriers as a group would earn almost $3.2 billion less in the best case and $5.4 billion less in the worst. In that same year, the cap would reduce U.S. employment by between 111,000 and 213,000 jobs and reduce U.S. trade receipts by up to $5.1 billion in that year alone. Unfortunately, we believe the worst case is more likely to prevail.

These are real dollars and real jobs that will be lost to the U.S. economy if Japan has its way. And, just as it is now easy to criticize the mistake we made in

---

3 Response of Assistant Secretary for Aviation and International Affairs, Charles Hunnicut, to Access U.S.-Japan Announcement, February 21, 1996.

4 "Pena Asserts Shift in Focus from Europe to Asia," Aviation Daily, November 1, 1995, p. 179.

Bermuda II, it will be easy in 2010 to recognize the damage done by concessions to Japan in 1996. The challenge is to recognize those downsides in advance, and negotiate accordingly. In this regard the economic analyses of Booz Allen and of the Economic Strategy Institute have armed the Government with the knowledge it requires.

What is needed now is the political will to act to avoid the dominance of another successful U.S. industry by Japan. In our view, and we hope in yours, the responsible course requires that the U.S. first reconcile its well-crafted International Aviation Policy with its negotiating objectives. That Policy states that:

> carriers wishing to establish global networks require a higher quality and quantity of supporting route authority than they have sought in the past. Airlines will become increasingly concerned with every market that enables them to flow passengers over any part of their system network. These airlines will be looking for broad, flexible authority to operate beyond and behind hub points, in addition to the hub-to-hub market between two countries. At present, governments operating in a bilateral context naturally focus on opportunities for their respective carriers to serve the local market between their two countries. In a bilateral context, services destined for or coming from third countries receive less consideration. In the future, governments will have to adjust their focus to bargain for the bundles of rights that will permit airlines to develop global networks. (Emphasis added.)

We cannot continue to proceed by committing the same mistakes in the 90's as we did in the '80's. As the International Policy recognizes, adjusting our focus should mean that integrating domestic and international hubs has to have the highest priority. Specifically, it means that undoing the damage of the '80's must be undertaken so that those carriers that can still hub in Japan can once again have the ability to integrate those hubs with their domestic systems. Japan recognizes this need for its carriers. We can do no less for ours.

In addition, as indicated in Chart 7, we should approach negotiations with the following framework in mind:

- Insist that Japan honor its current agreements;
- Steadfastly refuse to fall into the Japanese trap of accepting restrictions on existing rights as a way to secure other opportunities; and
- Set as our negotiating goals objectives which are first determined by economic analysis to be in the best interests of the U.S. as a whole.

United has committed itself to supporting the results of negotiations conducted in accord with these principles, and we firmly believe that they are an absolute prerequisite to the success of our industry in the fastest growing and soon to be the largest international market in the world.

g:\jb\005b\126\martest

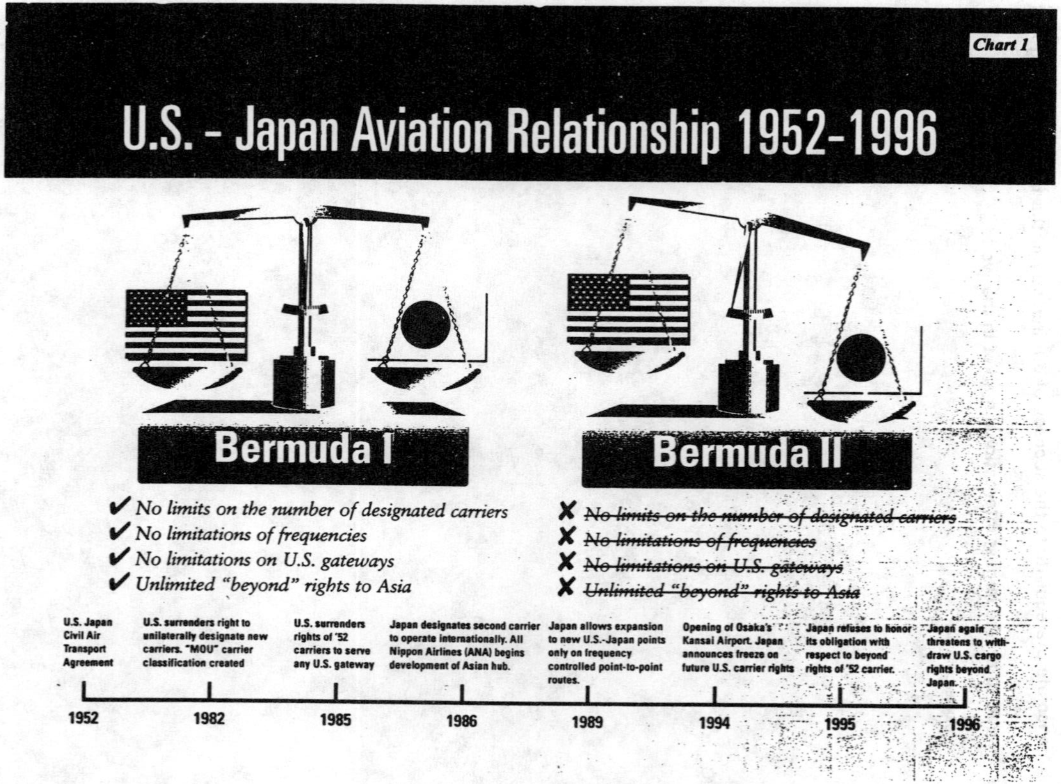
Chart 1
U.S. - Japan Aviation Relationship 1952-1996
Bermuda I
✔ No limits on the number of designated carriers
✔ No limitations of frequencies
✔ No limitations on U.S. gateways
✔ Unlimited "beyond" rights to Asia
Bermuda II
✘ ~~No limits on the number of designated carriers~~
✘ ~~No limitations of frequencies~~
✘ ~~No limitations on U.S. gateways~~
✘ ~~Unlimited "beyond" rights to Asia~~
1952 U.S. Japan Civil Air Transport Agreement
1982 U.S. surrenders right to unilaterally designate new carriers. "MOU" carrier classification created
1985 U.S. surrenders rights of '52 carriers to serve any U.S. gateway
1986 Japan designates second carrier to operate internationally. All Nippon Airlines (ANA) begins development of Asian hub.
1989 Japan allows expansion to new U.S.-Japan points only on frequency controlled point-to-point routes.
1994 Opening of Osaka's Kansai Airport. Japan announces freeze on future U.S. carrier rights
1995 Japan refuses to honor its obligation with respect to beyond rights of '52 carrier.
1996 Japan again threatens to withdraw U.S. cargo rights beyond Japan.

Chart 2

Access: U.S.-Japan — Japan's Trojan Horse

Japan Times

AIR PACT AT ISSUE — February 15, 1996

Group to lobby White House

By SAYURI DAIMON

[illegible] its aviation negotiations with Japan.

ACCESS Japan will be made up of official from U.S. [illegible] the countries and the 1952 bilateral civil aviation agreement.

American Airlines and Del-ta Airlines, which have eliminated rights under the 1952 civil aviation agreement between U.S. and Japan, as [illegible] group, sources said.

Its main objective is to rectify the inequality in the current bilateral treaty that exists between three U.S. airlines known as "incumbent carriers" — United Airlines, Northwest Airlines and Federal Express Corp. — and other U.S. [illegible]

The group is likely to become a strong supporter of Japan, which has been urging the U.S. government to renegotiate the pact.

[illegible] three U.S. carriers [illegible] almost unlimited [illegible] requires separate bilateral negotiations.

These other airlines are call MOU carriers because they obtained their rights to fly between the two nations from the memorandums of understanding reached during the 1980s.

[illegible] u to [illegible] the U.S. and in beyond rights, the rights to fly to and then beyond the U.S.

It is the first time for U.S. MOU carriers to form a coalition, though they have repeatedly asked Washington to renegotiate the treaty.

By forming the group, the airlines could influence the U.S. government in its negotiations with Japan.

[illegible] both sides [illegible] an agreement [illegible] Washington is [illegible] liberalization while Japan is seeking to remove what deems to be the inequality in the 1952 accord.

Once they wrap up the cargo talks, Tokyo hopes to begin negotiations on passenger service, but Washington has not agreed to such a proposal.

A senior Japanese Transport Ministry official said Tokyo welcomes the efforts of the U.S. MOU carriers, and expressed hope that it will lead to an early start of passenger service talks.

The MOU coalition is not inviting United, Northwest and FedEx, claiming that their aviation policy is inconsistent with the new group's, the sources said.

Since the incumbent carriers enjoy wide rights under the current agreement, they are reportedly against starting the bilateral aviation talks in the areas of passenger service.

The group's members reportedly talked with officials from All Nippon Airways, a Japanese MOU carrier seeking to expand its business opportunities in the Asia-Pacific market, to seek the Japanese carrier's cooperation.

During a Wednesday news conference in Tokyo, Rex McClelland, senior vice president of Delta Airlines, said the two governments should start passenger talks as soon as possible to create a competitive structure that eliminates the dominance of the two U.S. incumbent carriers.

He said United and Northwest control 80 percent of the U.S. industry's passenger traffic between the U.S. and Japan, and because of that airfares in between the two countries are excessively high, often more than 20 percent more than fares for other major international routes.

"We think it is time for a new agreement that opens the market to increased competition," McClelland said.

"The group is likely to become a strong supporter of Japan, which has been urging the U.S. government to renegotiate the pact."

"By forming the group, the airlines could influence the U.S. government in its negotiations with Japan."

"A senior Japanese Transport Ministry official said Tokyo welcomes the efforts of the U.S. MOU carriers, and expressed hope that it will lead to an early start of passenger service talks."

Chart 3

Asia - Pacific Markets

(Millions Passengers)

1993	COUNTRY	2010
35	Japan	91
24	Hong Kong	72
8	China	62
19	Singapore	60
14	Taiwan	57
13	Thailand	54
11	Australia	43
11	South Korea	43
6	Indonesia	26
8	Malaysia	25
6	Philippines	22
7	India	21
4	New Zealand	10
3	Pakistan	7

By 2010

10 Asian markets will match or surpass the two largest '93 markets – Tokyo and Hong Kong

Source: IATA

Chart 4

U.S. Marketshare Correlates Directly with Cost Efficiency of U.S. Carriers

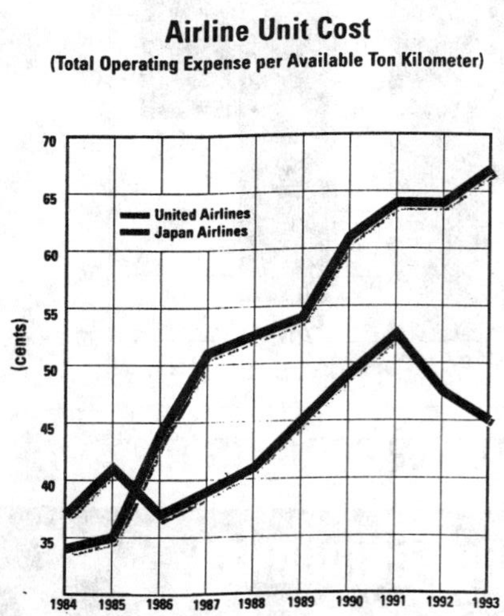

Source: ICAO Financial Data

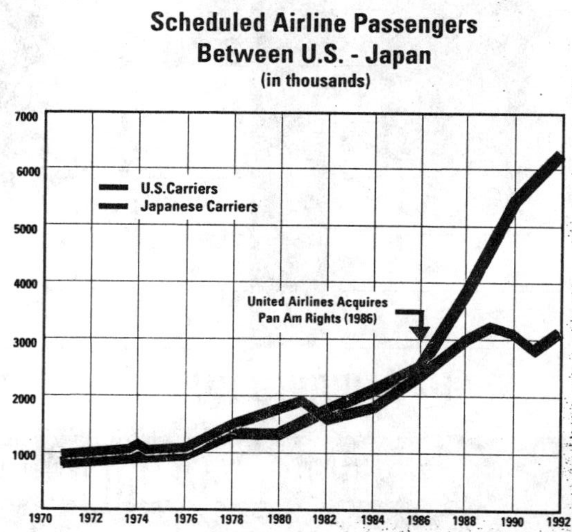

Source: Japan Economic Institute

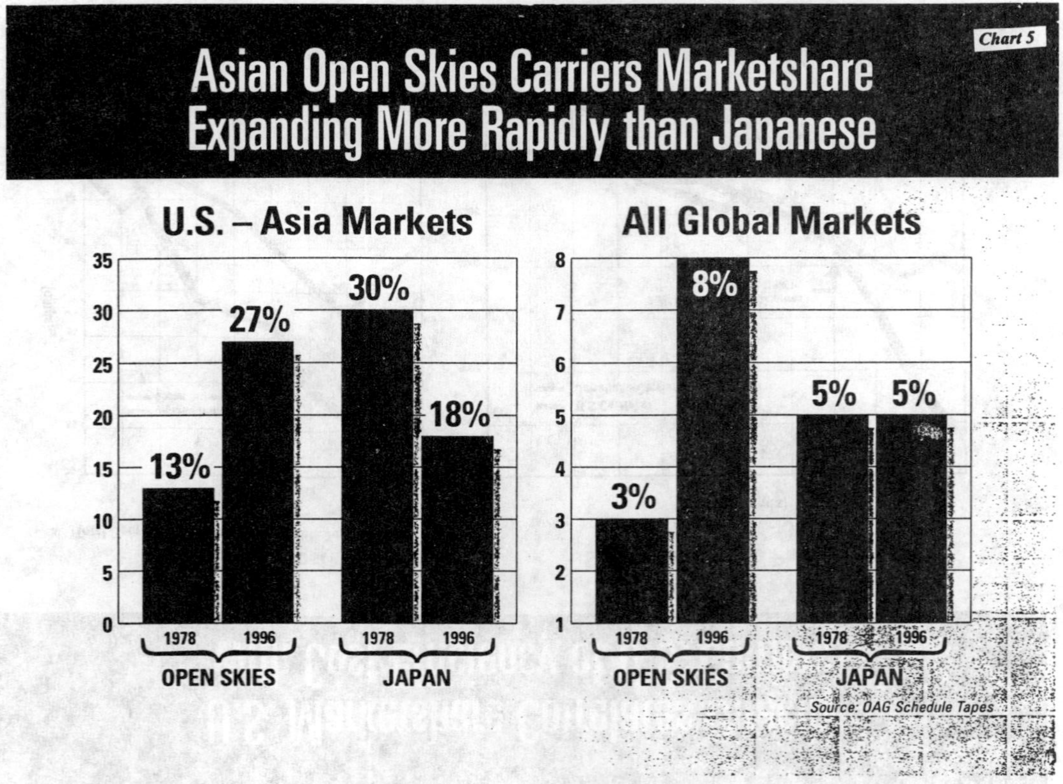
Chart 5
Asian Open Skies Carriers Marketshare Expanding More Rapidly than Japanese
U.S. – Asia Markets
35
30
25
20
15
10
5
0
13%
27%
30%
18%
1978
1996
1978
1996
OPEN SKIES
JAPAN
All Global Markets
8
7
6
5
4
3
2
1
3%
8%
5%
5%
1978
1996
1978
1996
OPEN SKIES
JAPAN
Source: OAG Schedule Tapes

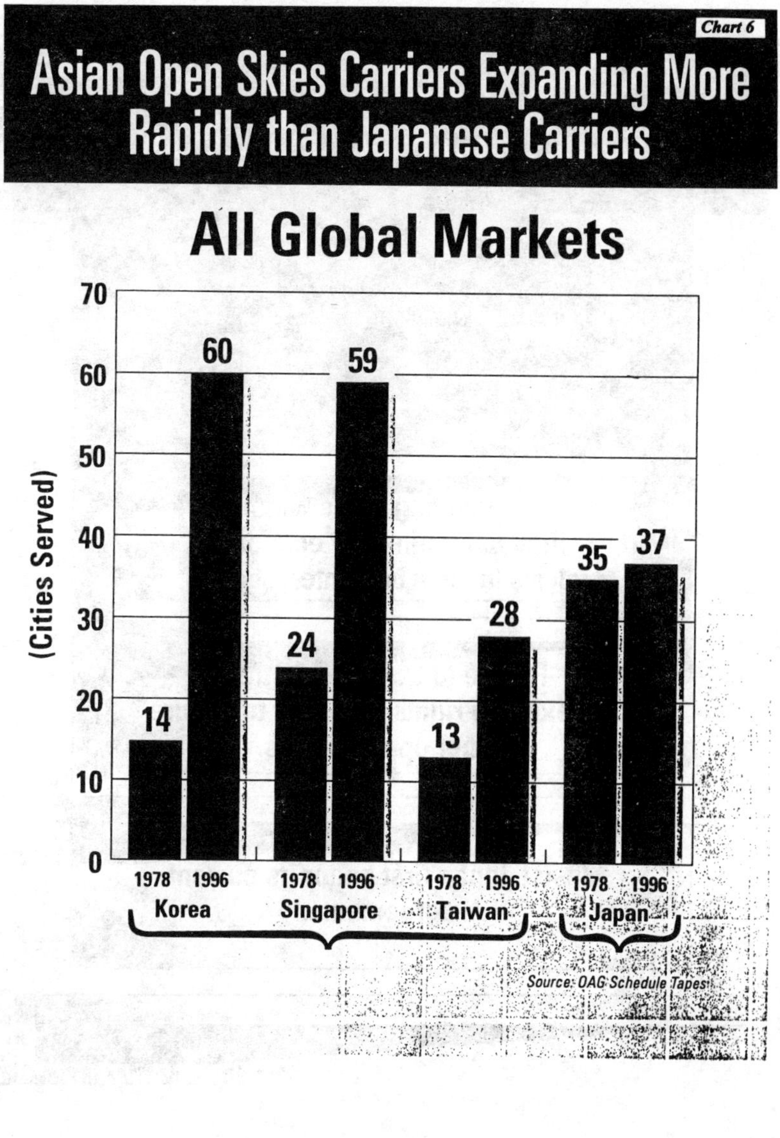
Chart 6
Asian Open Skies Carriers Expanding More Rapidly than Japanese Carriers
All Global Markets
(Cities Served)
70
60
50
40
30
20
10
0
14
60
24
59
13
28
35
37
1978
1996
1978
1996
1978
1996
1978
1996
Korea
Singapore
Taiwan
Japan
Source: OAG Schedule Tapes

Chart 7
A Framework
for Successful U.S.-Japan Negotiations
Set negotiating goals which are first determined by economic analysis to be in best interests of U.S.
Refuse to trade restrictions on existing rights as a way to secure other opportunities.
Insist Japan first honor its current agreements.

The Subcommittee on Aviation
Committee on Transportation and Infrastructure
U.S. House of Representatives

Hearing:
"Problems in the U.S. Aviation Relationship
with the United Kingdom & Japan"
March 27, 1996

Testimony presented by:
Clyde V. Prestowitz, Jr.
President
Economic Strategy Institute
1401 H Street, N.W. #750
Washington, D.C. 20005
202-289-1288

Executive Summary

A new round of aviation negotiations is currently underway between the United States and Japan. These talks are extremely important because of the large impact the U.S. airline industry has on the health and growth of the American economy, and because aviation has become one of the United States' most competitive international industries.

I. Importance of the Aviation Industry

The aviation services industry has become so large and so linked to all other industries that it must be considered one of the fundamental industries of any economy. As shown below, its direct output of $54 billion constitutes about one percent of U.S. GDP and generates one million jobs.

GDP for Selected Industries
In billion dollars

	1993
Food and kindred products	$106
Motor vehicles and equipment	$68
Transportation by air	$54
Petroleum and coal products	$48
Textile mill products	$25

Source: U.S. Department of Commerce

Beyond the direct impact of its own spending and employment, the aviation industry also contributes significantly to the creation of earnings and jobs in virtually all major sectors of the U.S. economy. Through the indirect impact of the off-airport activities of passengers and shippers (such as spending at hotels, restaurants, and tourist attractions) and the induced impact of successive rounds of spending, generated on everything from new cars to groceries, by those who receive direct or indirect payments (the so-called multiplier effect), the U.S. aviation industry, according to one estimate, generated nearly six percent of U.S. GDP in 1993, as shown below.

Air Transport Contribution to the U.S. Economy
Summary

	1993
Economic Impact	
Aviation spending, plus ripple effect	$771 Billion
Earnings of affected industries	$230 Billion
Employment effect	8.8 Million Jobs
Contribution to GDP	5.9 Percent
Impact on Trade Balance	
Passenger air fares	$5.3 Billion

Source: Wilbur Smith Associates, U.S. Department of Commerce

On a global basis, the industry generates over $1 trillion in economic activity and more than 22 million jobs.

Estimates of Worldwide Air Transport Benefits, 1992

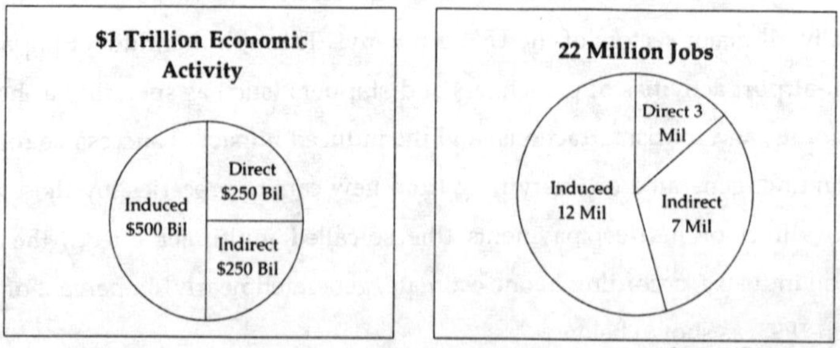

Source: ATAG, IATA

Even more important than the size of the aviation industry is its growth rate and, in particular, the location of most of the growth. As shown below, the volume of passengers and freight carried by the world's airlines has risen at twice the rate of real growth in the world economy over the past ten years and is expected to continue growing at about a six-percent annual rate over the next fifteen years.

Growth Rate Comparison

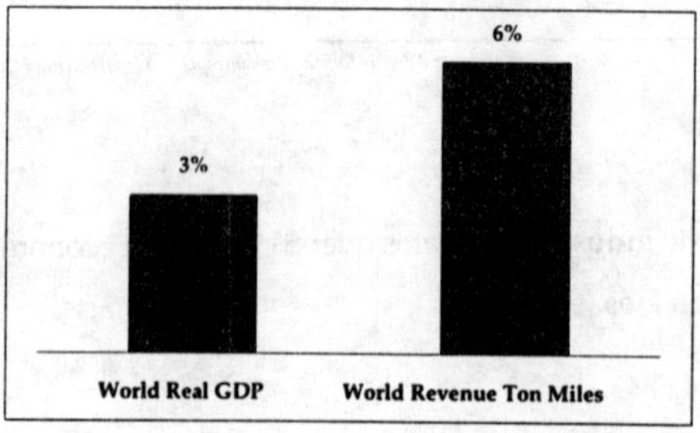

Source: IMF,ICAO

Of great significance for the future shape of the industry is the fact that the bulk of the growth has been, and will continue to be, in international skies, particularly the skies over the Asia-Pacific region. In the ten years between 1984 and 1994, world scheduled airline traffic shifted from being about half domestic and half international to being nearly two-thirds international. This trend is expected to continue, largely because of the explosive growth in Asia-Pacific skies (see exhibits below).

World Scheduled Airline Traffic

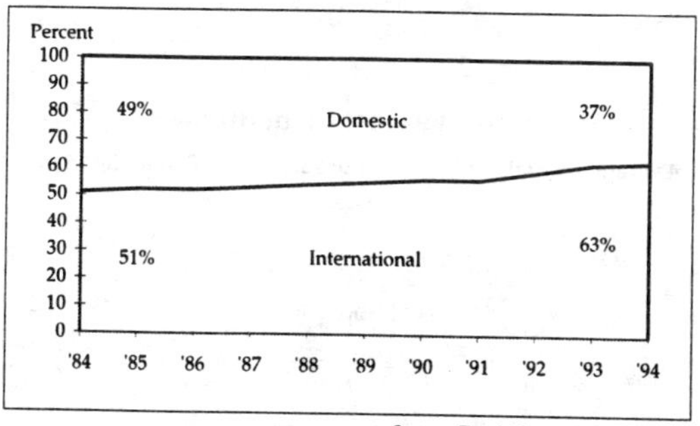

Source: Ton-Miles Performed, ICAO

International Scheduled Passenger Traffic

Annual Rates of Growth

	Actual	Estimates	
	1985-1993	1993-2000	2000-2010
Rest-of-World	5%	4%	3%
Asia-Pacific	10	9	7
World Total	7%	6%	5%

Source: IATA

Thus, it seems clear that a strong and growing U.S. airline industry is necessary for the U.S. economy to grow at an acceptable rate in the future, and anything that would hurt the U.S. airline industry would be a major impediment to overall U.S. economic growth.

II. The United States is Competitive

As a result of having a large domestic airline services market, and of having faced the competitive pressures created by airline deregulation, U.S. carriers now enjoy a strong comparative advantage in airline services, as shown in the figure below.

Relative Cost Structures

Average Operating Expenses per Revenue Ton Mile, 1993

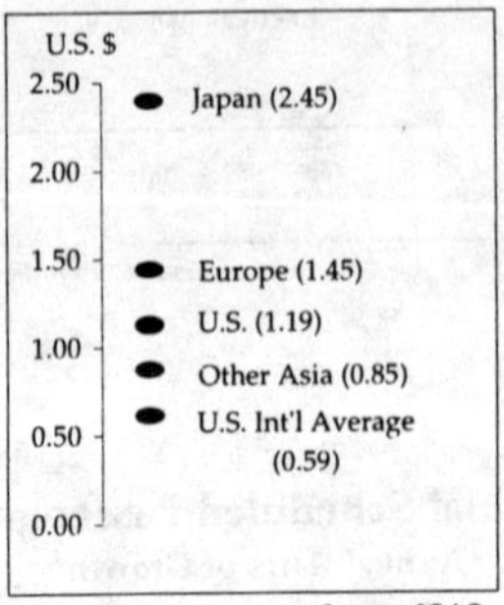

Source: ICAO

The implications of this superior competitiveness are enormous. When the Japanese consumer-electronics industry gained a similar, competitive superiority it was able to use that advantage to gain absolute dominance of most world markets. Indeed, the U.S. consumer-electronics industry was virtually driven out of business. U.S. airlines are in a position to do the same thing in the world's aviation markets. Aviation service, even under today's restricted conditions, is one of the few industries in which the United States has a trade surplus. Based on U.S. carrier experience in key international markets when restrictions were relatively few, American carriers could easily achieve two-thirds of total market share, with a gain of billions of dollars in airline revenue and profits, as well as thousands of new jobs for U.S. residents.

III. Liberalization Efforts

The U.S. government has been negotiating to liberalize international skies and has, in fact, concluded "open skies" deals with a number of European countries, including, most recently, Germany, Europe's largest economy. Progress in the Pacific has been much slower, largely reflecting Japan's reluctance to liberalize.

As shown below, Japan is by far the largest transpacific air traffic market in the region. This, in addition to its location as the gateway to Asia, make it the only practical hub for aviation service between North America and the Asia-Pacific region.

Transpacific Traffic, 1993

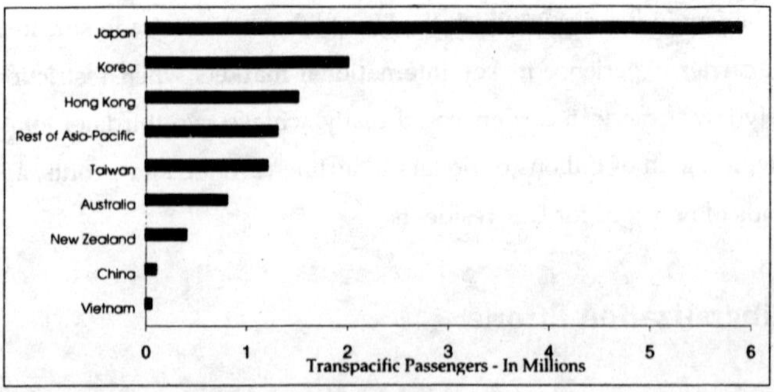

Source: IATA

Just as the hub-and-spoke system of air service has proven to be most efficient domestically, so it is proving to be internationally, and the world's carriers are racing to establish strong footholds at key hubs around the globe. With inefficient carriers, but a crucial hub location, Japan's Ministry of Transportation has used regulation to protect its airlines and has attempted to give them the immense leverage entailed in the control of Asia's key hub. This has led to significant constriction of traffic through Tokyo. While transpacific service has been maintained at a level comparable to that over the Atlantic, intra-Asian load factors and fares are sky high. This constriction, and Japan's manipulation of the agreement, has led to clashes with U.S. carriers and difficult U.S.-Japan negotiations.

Comparison of Retail Air Fares Between the United States and International Locations

(Lowest advertised fares, first calendar quarter)

		Round-Trip Fares		Nonstop	Fares per Mile		Fares per Mile Index: Tokyo City Pairs = 100	
		1987	1996	Miles	1987	1996	1987	1996
Chicago -	Tokyo	$525	$550	6,273	$0.0418	$0.0438	100	100
	Paris	449	509	4,152	0.0541	0.0613	129	140
	Frankfurt	430	519	4,343	0.0495	0.0598	118	137
	London	439	469	3,953	0.0555	0.0593	133	135
Los Angeles -	Tokyo	$529	$530	5,450	$0.0485	$0.0486	100	100
	Hong Kong	599	569	7,247	0.0413	0.0393	85	81
	Taipei	599	569	6,799	0.0441	0.0418	91	86
	Frankfurt	469	549	5,805	0.0404	0.0473	83	97
	Paris	459	549	5,668	0.0405	0.0484	84	100
	London	569	499	5,455	0.0522	0.0457	108	94
Seattle -	Tokyo	$549	$570	4,768	$0.0576	$0.0598	100	100
	Taipei	579	549	6,073	0.0477	0.0452	83	76
	Hong Kong	579	569	6,488	0.0446	0.0439	77	73
	London	469	499	4,799	0.0489	0.0520	85	87

Source: 1987 fares: *American Airlines Exhibit AA-R-235-237, U.S. DOT Docket 44380, Seattle/Porland-Japan Service Review Case*

1996 fares: *Hayward Travel, Hayward, California*

Comparison of Retail Air Fares Between Japan and the United States and Japan and Beyond Locations

(Lowest advertised fares, March 1996)

	Round-Trip Fare	Nonstop Miles	Fares Per Mile	Index: Tokyo-Seattle=100
Japan-U.S.				
Tokyo- Chicago	$550	6,273	$0.0438	73
Los Angeles	530	5,450	0.0486	81
Seattle	570	4,768	0.0598	100
Japan-Beyond				
Tokyo- Bangkok	$800	2,886	$0.1386	232
Hong Kong	700	1,826	0.1917	321

Source: Hayward Travel, Hayward California

Load Factor Comparison Atlantic versus Pacific Operations

	Atlantic	Pacific	Memo: Atlantic vs. Pacific
	(In Percent)		(Percentage Points)
Northwest	78%	72%	+6
United	77	74	+3
American	74	72	+2
Delta	73	67	+6
USAir	70	-	na
Continental	67	67	0
TWA	66	-	na
Industry	73%	72%	+1

Source: BACK Associates

Current operating authority in the U.S.-Japan market is governed by the U.S.-Japan Civil Air Services Agreement of 1952, and by numerous memorandums, consultations, minutes, and amendments negotiated since that time. These permit the designated, so-called "1952 carriers" to provide service from the United States to-and-from Tokyo, Osaka, Okinawa, and beyond, and permit the so-called "MOU carriers" to fly to-and-from Japan, but with more frequency, with capacity and gateway limitations, and with no beyond rights. All traffic moves within this governing framework, which over the years has become increasingly ambiguous and subject to the whim of bureaucratic interpretation. Disputes have multiplied and risen in intensity.

IV. Scenarios

To assist U.S. negotiators, the Economic Strategy Institute projected total U.S. carrier revenues, as well as the impact of the Asia-Pacific operations of U.S. carriers on U.S. trade receipts, frequency and cost of aviation service, and total spending and total employment in the United States, for several scenarios that, in one form or another, are being considered in the negotiating process. These scenarios are (a) completely open skies, in which all airlines are free to establish whatever frequencies, routes, and prices they wish, in response to market forces; (b) an extension of the 1952 Agreement; (c) a capped beyond rights scenario in which the 1952 Carriers continue to fly the same number of beyond flights as they do now, and MOU frequencies to and from Japan are increased; and (d) a capped beyond rights scenario in which substantial attrition of current beyond flights is assumed.

Summary Impact of the Scenarios: All U.S. Carriers

In 1995 Dollars

Scenarios	Impact in the United States			
	Revenue of U.S. Carriers ($ Bil)	Economic Activity ($ Bil)	Employment (Thous)	U.S. Trade Receipts ($ Bil)
TOTAL IMPACT				
Impact in 1995	$8.3	$29.3	647	$7.6
Impact in 2010				
Open Skies	$21.0	$97.8	2,150	$18.4
1952 Extension	19.8	68.3	1,502	17.4
Capped Beyonds	16.6	64.4	1,391	14.6
Capped Beyonds with Attrition	14.6	59.8	1,289	12.3
DIFFERENCE FROM 1952 EXTENSION				
Impact in 2010				
Open Skies	$1.2	$29.5	648	$1.0
Capped Beyonds	-3.2	-3.9	-111	-2.9
Capped Beyonds with Attrition	-5.4	-8.5	-213	-5.1

Summary Impact of the Scenarios: Passenger Carriers

In 1995 Dollars

Scenarios	Impact in the United States			
	Revenue of U.S. Carriers ($ Bil)	Economic Activity ($ Bil)	Employment (Thous)	U.S. Trade Receipts ($ Bil)
TOTAL IMPACT				
Impact in 1995	$7.4	$27.3	602	$6.8
Impact in 2010				
Open Skies	$17.7	$90.0	1,980	$15.5
1952 Extension	17.0	62.2	1,369	14.9
Capped Beyonds	14.9	59.8	1,291	13.0
Capped Beyonds with Attrition	13.1	55.8	1,201	11.2
DIFFERENCE FROM 1952 EXTENSION				
Impact in 2010				
Open Skies	$0.7	$27.8	611	$0.6
Capped Beyonds	-2.1	-2.4	-78	-1.9
Capped Beyonds with Attrition	-3.9	-6.4	-168	-3.7

Summary Impact of the Scenarios: All-Cargo Carriers

In 1995 Dollars

Scenarios	Impact in the United States			
	Revenue of U.S. Carriers ($ Bil)	Economic Activity ($ Bil)	Employment (Thous)	U.S. Trade Receipts ($ Bil)
TOTAL IMPACT				
Impact in 1995	$0.9	$2.0	45	$0.8
Impact in 2010				
Open Skies	$3.3	$7.8	170	$2.9
1952 Extension	2.8	6.1	133	2.5
Capped Beyonds	1.7	4.6	100	1.5
Capped Beyonds with Attrition	1.3	4.0	88	1.1
DIFFERENCE FROM 1952 EXTENSION				
Impact in 2010				
Open Skies	$0.5	$1.7	37	$0.4
Capped Beyonds	-1.1	-1.5	-33	-1.0
Capped Beyonds with Attrition	-1.5	-2.1	-45	-1.4

Summary Impact of the Scenarios: Flight Availability

	B747-400 Equivalents				Implied Actual			
		Japan-Beyond		U.S.-		Japan-Beyond		U.S.-
	U.S.-Japan	Direct	Code-Share	Other Asia	U.S.-Japan	Direct	Code-Share	Other Asia
1952 Carriers								
Available in 1995	169	80	-	62	217	102	-	62
Available in 2010								
Open Skies	473	312	-	298	609	398	-	298
1952 Extension	326	216	-	206	419	275	-	206
Capped Beyonds	228	80	-	206	299	102	-	206
Capped Beyonds with Attrition	212	8	-	206	279	10	-	206
MOU Carriers								
Available in 1995	78	-	-	14	126	-	-	27
Available in 2010								
Open Skies	224	-	-	67	363	-	-	129
1952 Extension	156	-	-	46	252	-	-	89
Capped Beyonds	211	-	136	46	333	-	173	89
Capped Beyonds with Attrition	172	-	104	46	290	-	132	89
Total: All U.S. Carriers								
Available in 1995	247	80	-	76	343	102	-	89
Available in 2010								
Open Skies	697	312	-	365	972	398	-	427
1952 Extension	482	216	-	252	671	275	-	295
Capped Beyonds	439	80	136	252	632	102	173	295
Capped Beyonds with Attrition	394	8	104	252	569	10	132	295

As the summary charts make clear, this analysis indicates that the open-skies scenario is by far the most favorable for the United States, on all measures of performance. Such a conclusion is not surprising, because an open-skies arrangement would enable U.S. carriers fully to exploit their competitive strength in both the U.S.-Japan market and the beyond-Japan market.

The analysis indicates that extension of the 1952 Agreement is the second-best scenario. By maintaining market share across the board, it allows all U.S. carriers to benefit from the rapid growth in Asia-Pacific air traffic while keeping a U.S. carrier presence in all segments of the market. Although it does not add additional U.S. gateways, this scenario actually provides more U.S.-Japan frequencies than all except the Open Skies Scenario.

Surprisingly, the best case of the Capped Beyonds Plus More MOU Frequencies Scenario, comes in only third best. This is striking because the assumptions are unrealistically favorable for the Capped Beyonds Case. For example, it is most unlikely that any U.S.-Japan agreement would result in eight new U.S. gateway cities. It is also extremely unlikely that the 1952 Carriers would be able to maintain current levels of beyond service in a market in which they were rapidly losing share. Nor is it probable that the Japanese will code-share as many of their own flights in the beyond markets as were lost by the 1952 Carriers under this scenario.

There are several reasons, however, why the best capped beyonds scenario would not result in a net gain for the United States.

- First, capping beyond-rights for the 1952 carriers not only would cause their loss of participation in the explosive growth of the intra-Asian market, but, because almost one-half of beyond passengers and cargo travel to and from the United States, would also cause a reduction in their U.S.-Japan service. Furthermore, by sacrificing fifth freedom rights, American carriers would be prevented from establishing networks in the Asia-Pacific market, while unimpeded carriers would be free to build strategic route structures.

- Second, future direct service to Japan from even eight new U.S. cities would generate 15 percent net new traffic from these cities, but this is a relatively small increment for the U.S. system as a whole after substitution is taken into account. This gain is not enough to offset the impact, on the U.S. airline industry and the U.S. economy, of the loss of beyond-Japan traffic.

- Third, while code sharing arrangements may prevent some leakage of beyond passengers from U.S. carriers on the U.S.-Japan leg of their journey, this, too, will offset only a small portion of the 1952 carriers' losses.

That Japan is attempting to constrain U.S. beyond flights is easily understandable. A cap on U.S. rights would transfer more than 200 weekly high-fare, intra-Asia flights from U.S. to Japanese airlines over the next several years and, at the same time, divert a large number of beyond passengers from U.S. to Japanese carriers in the U.S.-Japan leg of their flights. This would be good for the Japanese carriers, but it would not be good for the United States. Ironically, it would not be good for Japan either, because it leaves Japan with less service, higher fares, and lower economic growth.

Capping the current beyond rights for U.S. all-cargo and express-package carriers would also result in a sizable revenue loss, amounting to $1.1 to $1.5 billion, in 1995 prices, in the year 2010. This would translate into a $1.5 to $2.1 billion loss of total spending in the United States in 2010. Furthermore, it would jeopardize the very existence of the express-cargo business, an industry first developed in the United States and not existing anywhere else in its current form.

Recent U.S. aviation policy has been marked by some serious shortcomings. The United States has simply failed to put airline services in their appropriate global context, or to assign them sufficient priority. Over the last five decades the United States has been the primary moving force behind global efforts to expand trade and commerce, and the United States has lost hundreds of thousands of jobs in sectors where other countries had the comparative advantage, such as the textile-and-apparel industry. Yet, in airline services, a sector where the United States has a major competitive advantage, U.S. negotiators have pursued U.S. interests in a less than aggressive manner.

Above all else, the situation calls for a significant change in mindset and priorities. The United States should be aggressive about seeking free trade in airline services, even if that means ruffling the feathers of trading partners.

The Economic Strategy Institute therefore recommends the following strategy for U.S. negotiators:

Recommendation 1: Insist on open skies for both cargo and passenger carriers. A transitional arrangement like those with Canada and Germany should be possible.

As noted earlier, U.S. carriers now enjoy a strong comparative advantage in airline services as a result of having a large domestic airline-services market and having faced the competitive pressures created by airline deregulation.[1] Two other sectors where the United States enjoys a substantial comparative advantage -- agriculture and intellectual property -- have been made priorities of the U.S. government in international trade negotiations. It was sensible to do so. Similarly, it is also sensible to make open skies for the U.S. airline industry a top priority in U.S. trade negotiations. If necessary, the United States can make transitional arrangements, as it did in the case of Canada and Germany, but there should be an agreement on open skies by a time certain.

Recommendation 2: At a minimum, insist that the access and expansion of third, fourth, and fifth freedom rights for both cargo and passenger operations be guaranteed as set forth in

---

[1] See also Clyde V. Prestowitz, Jr., Scott C. Gibson, Paul Willen, and Saul Goldstein, *The Future of the Airline Industry* (Washington, D.C.: Economic Strategy Institute, 1993).

the 1952 Agreement and that additional frequencies, gateways, and code-share opportunities be added for both 1952 and MOU Carriers, including All Nippon Airways and Nippon Cargo Airlines.

The United States must make it clear that current rights under the 1952 Agreement are not subject to negotiation. It is important that an agenda be established prior to any negotiations, making clear what is to be discussed and what is off the table. At the same time, it is entirely understandable that the MOU Carriers are anxious to play a larger role in the market and it is imperative that they do so. The United States cannot fully capitalize on its competitiveness in aviation without obtaining greater access for its airlines. Trading beyond rights to gain increased access for MOU Carriers is not in the interest of the United States, but there is no reason why additional access for MOU Carriers cannot be negotiated.

There is no good, economic rationale for the United States to agree with Japan's MOT and accept the position that the only way to add new services is to trade beyond-rights. When the United States seeks market access for semiconductors or auto parts in Japan, it does not do so by offering to give away its market access in grain. Why shouldn't the United States act in aviation precisely as it does in other areas and demand open markets without some *quid pro quo*?

Recommendation 3: U.S. officials should make it clear that Japan's sixth freedom operations to the United States will be restricted if the Japanese MOT attempts to restrict the fifth freedom rights of U.S. carriers.

In the event of restrictions on U.S. beyond rights, the United States, of course, would also have to study the U.S.-bound operations of other Asian carriers who might cooperate with MOT's protectionist schemes.

Recommendation 4. The United States should seek clear reaffirmation of the APEC (Asia Pacific Economic Cooperation Forum) agreement with regard to achieving free trade in aviation services in Asia-Pacific skies and should add no new restrictions on aviation services.

Frederick W. Smith
Chairman of the Board and
Chief Executive Officer

Federal Express Corporation
2005 Corporate Avenue
Memphis, TN 38132

US Mail: PO Box 727
Memphis, TN 38194-1841

Telephone 901 395-3377
Fax 901 398-1111

Federal Express

TESTIMONY
OF
FREDERICK W. SMITH
CHAIRMAN AND CHIEF EXECUTIVE OFFICER
FEDERAL EXPRESS CORPORATION
BEFORE THE
U.S. HOUSE OF REPRESENTATIVES
SUBCOMMITTEE ON AVIATION

MARCH 27, 1996

24-087 97 - 6

TESTIMONY OF FREDERICK W. SMITH
CHAIRMAN AND CHIEF EXECUTIVE OFFICER
FEDERAL EXPRESS CORPORATION

For a second time in less than a year, the Japanese government has blatantly ignored the provisions of the Japan-U.S. Aviation Agreement by threatening in writing to cancel existing operations of FedEx conducted clearly under the provisions of the existing treaty. Both Japanese carriers and U.S. carriers have operated freely under this agreement for approximately fifty years until late 1993 when Japan unilaterally refused to accept schedule filings made by FedEx with the GOJ. While Japanese carriers continued to operate freely transporting U.S. trade between points in Asia on one hand and the U.S. on the other, the GOJ successfully delayed for over two years implementation of FedEx's schedule filings to participate in Japanese trade to and from other Asian countries. It is clear that the strategy of the GOJ was to maintain its carriers' openness in transporting U.S. trade while requiring a new regulated regime for our competition in Japanese trade requiring the U.S. to negotiate for each and every operational change.

The written threat by Japan clearly illustrates the lack of respect for the recent positions submitted by the United States government in the on going negotiations with Japan and the lack of respect for the commitment of the United States government to protect the rights of FedEx and other cargo carriers who have invested hundreds of millions of dollars to become successful competitors in the Japan market.

One can only imagine the long term impact of a U.S. negotiating strategy so timid that the GOJ feels free to threaten the shut down of an existing U.S. cargo operation in Asia if the U.S. does not accept the restrictions demanded by the GOJ.

It is critical that the United States government as a policy equate sixth freedom (Asia-U.S.) opportunities for Japanese carriers, which is U.S. trade, with the reciprocal fifth freedom opportunities (Asia-Japan) for U.S. carriers, which is Japanese trade. Though very timid in its approach, the U.S. took the first step in that direction prior to the interim agreement some six months ago by threatening countermeasures directed at Japanese carriers' sixth freedom operations. Not only does the 40 year history of the treaty include openness for U.S. and Japanese carriers, it is obvious the negotiators involved in those early days clearly understood and included open markets for their respective carriers. On what basis should the GOJ be allowed to unilaterally alter that understanding?

Appendix A depicts the U.S. trade where Japanese carriers now compete. That U.S. trade is a market of 5,077 million ton miles. Appendix B reflects the Japanese trade where FedEx now competes in a market of 548 million ton miles. As reflected in Appendix C, Japanese flag carriers maintain an advantage over the U.S. flag carriers in competing for U.S. trade by a ratio of 9.3:1. Because of a very weak negotiating stance and the lack of a negotiating strategy to protect U.S. cargo carriers' interest, Japan now asserts that their 9.3:1 advantage in third country markets must be significantly enhanced, or they threaten to shut down FedEx's existing operations in Asia at our new hub in Subic Bay.

I have attached as Appendix D the chronology of events and a copy of the "threat" tabled by Japan. The U.S. negotiators have recently failed to address the initial objective so clearly understood between Dan Tarullo, Department of State, Steve Kaplan with DOT, and FedEx - to aggressively defend the U.S. government's position concerning open access for incumbent cargo carriers, while hopefully liberalizing the entire U.S.-Japan bilateral relationship. Prior to the threat from the GOJ the U.S. negotiators, in discussions with FedEx, clearly signaled that they had given up their attempt to assure a level playing field with Japanese competitors and admitted that no negotiating strategy existed which could result in protecting U.S. cargo carriers' traditional rights under the U.S.-Japan agreement. We hope that, in preparation for the round of cargo talks taking place in Tokyo this week, the U.S. has developed a clear strategy to protect our rights.

The Japanese carriers' access to U.S. trade (the sixth freedom markets) has remained totally open and flexible during these negotiations while the flexibility and openness for U.S. cargo carriers has been unilaterally restricted. The status quo is a clear victory for Japan and is precisely what was contemplated when the GOJ initiated this scheme. It is not the elimination of a particular point or points which is evidence of the GOJ's victory, but rather the increase in capacity by Japanese carriers in our sixth freedom markets by 50%. During the same period, FedEx has been stymied by a two year delay in its attempt to add a small increment of capacity in that same market. Our U.S. negotiators have in effect surrendered and unless there is intervention at the highest levels in this Administration, the only question left is how far will we retreat.

Retreat now will clearly marginalize U.S. aviation's interest in Asia creating a very dangerous situation as we move into a worldwide economy where early in the next century transportation by air will accommodate approximately 60% of the total value of goods moving between the U.S. and Asia. The GOJ will establish Japan as the control point between 2 billion Asian citizens and the U.S., the most productive nation in the world. I believe that acquiescing in such a regime is tremendously shortsighted from an economic, political or military perspective.

The U.S. government must promptly notify the GOJ that if: (1) it follows through on its threat tabled in these negotiations; or (2) it continues in any fashion to unilaterally frustrate FedEx's fifth freedom operations contrary to the agreement there will be a sure and swift response as follows: any beyond country affected by such unilateral action will immediately be precluded by Japanese carriers from sixth freedom access until the U.S. carriers' rights are affirmed.

No longer should the U.S. tolerate the unilateral exclusion of U.S. cargo carriers from Japanese markets *while* Japan continues to operate and expand its sixth freedom services transporting U.S. trade in those same markets. Japan must be denied access to sixth freedom markets until it recognizes the existing fifth freedom rights of U.S. carriers. Additionally, the U.S. government must develop a strategy to deal with the threat of abrogation. That strategy should assure that the GOJ does not misinterpret the resolve of the U.S. government to assure that the aviation services of U.S. carriers in Asia will not be decimated by Japan's unilateral act of abrogation.

I greatly appreciate your interest in this matter and hope you can help others in the administration understand the seriousness of this issue.

LLWASH 1452.1 03/20/96 02:46 PM

Appendix A

JAPANESE AIRLINES PARTICIPATE FREELY IN U.S. TRADE IN THE U.S.-ASIA MARKETS

(Japanese Sixth Freedom Markets)

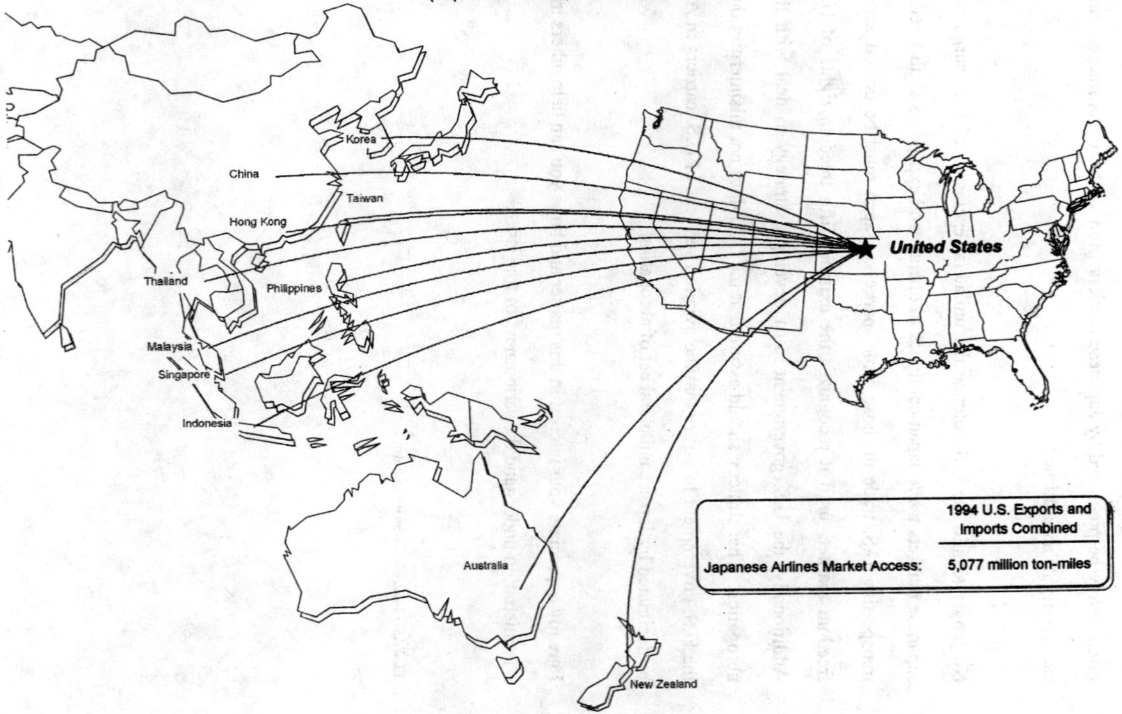

Appendix B

THE U.S. AIRLINES OPERATE A HIGHLY RESTRICTED SCHEDULE BETWEEN JAPAN AND OTHER ASIA

(U.S. Fifth Freedom Markets)

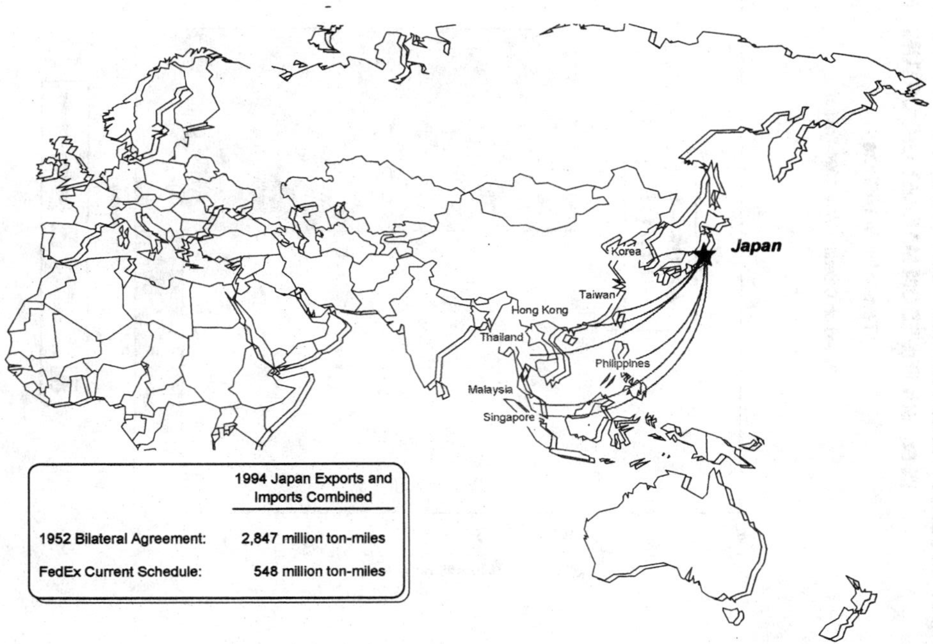

	1994 Japan Exports and Imports Combined
1952 Bilateral Agreement:	2,847 million ton-miles
FedEx Current Schedule:	548 million ton-miles

Appendix C

UNDER THE CURRENT JAPANESE RESTRICTIONS ON U.S. AIRLINE SCHEDULES, THE JAPANESE AIRLINES HAVE A 9.3 TO 1.0 ADVANTAGE IN 5th/6th FREEDOM MARKET OPPORTUNITIES

Ton-Miles in Millions

(Based on Calendar Year 1994 Traffic)

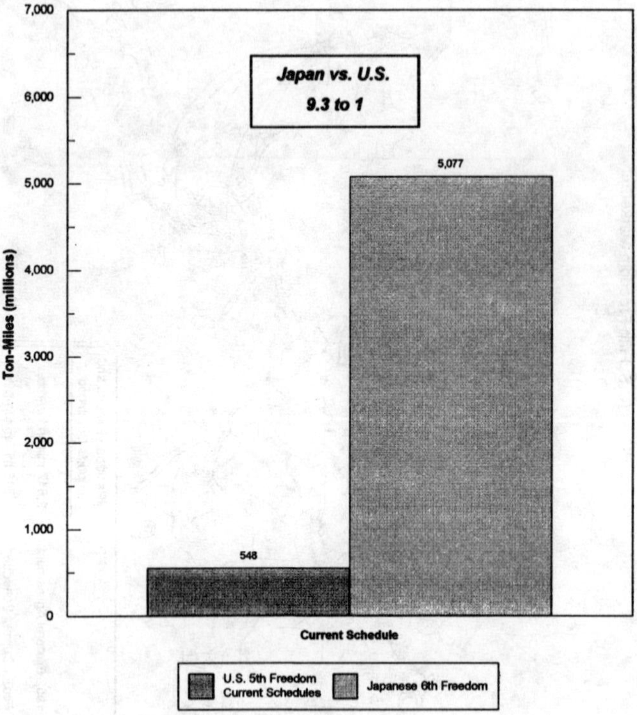

APPENDIX D

FEBRUARY 1996 UPDATE ON FEDEX'S POSITION ON U.S.-JAPAN NEGOTIATIONS FOR A LIBERAL ALL-CARGO AVIATION REGIME

- In July 1993, the Japanese government (GOJ) refused to approve FedEx's filed schedule to operate beyond Japan to Cebu, clearly authorized under the existing U.S.-Japan aviation agreement. The GOJ, subjected FedEx's application for Japan-Cebu service and subsequent schedule filings to a new and more rigorous unilateral approval process, which had not been the case for 40+ years. This action by the GOJ is in violation of the Air Transport Services Agreement between the U.S. and Japan.

- The USG announced proposed counter-measures concluding that 6th freedom opportunities - (between other Asia and the United States) for Japanese carriers, were reciprocal opportunities of fifth freedom (between other Asia and Japan) opportunities which were threatened by GOJ and would be restricted if GOJ refused to allow FedEx to operate as it had traditionally operated.

- After protracted and difficult negotiations to redress this violation of the Air Transport Services agreement, and the threat of counter measures, the U.S. government obtained limited concessions from the GOJ in July 1995. The GOJ accepted the schedule for FedEx to operate 7 of the 13 requested operations beyond Japan. This limited acceptance of our schedule allowed us to begin service at Subic Bay, our Asian regional hub in the Philippines.

- The counter-measures proposed were highly successful because under current operating conditions, the Japanese airlines' sixth freedom markets, in the aggregate, are 9.3 times the size of the U.S. carriers' fifth freedom markets, yet Japan's demand would significantly increase the imbalance in Japan's favor beyond 9.3:1.

- A copy of the GOJ's most recent proposal (threat) is attached. It clearly is a restriction of existing market opportunities for U.S. and greatly expanded opportunities for Japan, and a clear rejection of U.S. incumbent carriers' rights to operate in the same free and unrestricted fashion as Japanese carriers.

- FedEx believes that the U.S. government must act immediately and aggressively to regain control of these negotiations. The primary aim for more than two years was; (1) to assure that U.S. cargo carriers' flexibility which has been in place for 40+ years was restored; and (2) to establish a more liberal all-cargo framework with increased opportunities for both countries' airlines. While the Japanese government is moving toward this goal for its carriers, the U.S. can only do the same for its carriers if it does not permit the Japanese to institutionalize its current process and codify the disparity in market access which it has unilaterally gained.

- In light of the foregoing, the U.S. should make it unequivocally clear that the most recent proposal is unacceptable. Furthermore, if the Japanese insist on using the new proposals as the basis for ongoing discussions, our government should abandon its efforts to obtain a new agreement by March absent a demonstrable willingness on the part of the Japanese to liberalize the existing agreement. The U.S. must table a document which outlines a specific, swift response to any further action which unilaterally eliminates operations by U.S. cargo carriers as set forth in the existing treaty. Since the GOJ has already taken unilateral action against U.S. carriers. The U.S. must forcefully communicate a plan to protect existing U.S. carriers as is set forth in the attached cover letter.

It is understood that if no agreement at the third cascade is concluded by the end of March, 1996, the whole arrangements under the three cascade approach which consists of JCAB's approval of FM's seven beyond sectors operations from Japan and 1995 Record of Consultations which is composed of Japanese new rights and all-cargo services negotiations by the end of March, 1996 shall be canceled.

Japanese Proposal

The following arrangements shall enter into force upon signature.

Japan and the US shall commence consultations between the aeronautical authorities of the two countries three years after the entry into force of this agreement, aiming at further equalization of opportunity between Japanese and US carriers and further liberalization.

Nothing herein shall be considered to alter or shall prejudice each side's interpretation of the rights and obligations under the 1952 Air Transport Agreement, as amended, or other agreements or understandings between the two countries.

With respect to fifth freedom traffic rights except those provided for below, each side's interpretation of the rights and obligations under the 1952 Air Transport Agreement, as amended, or other agreements or understandings between the two countries shall not be considered to be altered.

Japanese Side	US Side
1. JAL JAPAN-US ① Any points in Japan. ② Additional 5 new points in the US. ③ Full coterminalization rights in both countries. ④ Unlimited frequencies on every point served. Beyond ① The same number of points beyond the US as the number of points beyond Japan served by US all-cargo incumbent carriers. ② The same number of frequencies on beyond-the-US sector as the number of US carriers' frequencies on beyond-Japan sector. 2. NCA JAPAN-US ① Any points in Japan. ② Additional 5 new points in the US. ③ Full coterminalization rights in both countries. ④ Unlimited frequencies on every point served. Beyond ① A total of 6 weekly frequencies beyond the US to one point with full traffic rights on a code-share basis with a US all-cargo service carrier. ② A total of 6 weekly frequencies beyond the US to one point on a blind basis.	1. UPS JAPAN-US ① Any points in the US. ② One new point in Japan (Kansai). ③ Full coterminalization rights in both countries. ④ Additional 12 weekly frequencies. Beyond ① A total of 6 weekly frequencies beyond Kansai to one point with full traffic rights on a code-share basis with a Japanese all-cargo service carrier. ② A total of 6 weekly frequencies beyond Kansai to one point on a blind basis. 2. FM 2 weekly frequencies beyond Tokyo to Beijing and Shanghai, respectively. 3. UA 3 weekly frequencies from Anchorage beyond Kansai to Taipei and Manila, respectively. 4. New Entrants ① Any points in the US. ② 3 weekly frequencies for an additional US all-cargo service carrier, to a point in Japan other than Tokyo and Osaka after April 1, 1997.
○ Code-sharing arrangements for third and fourth freedom operations between designated carriers of the two countries subject to a commercial agreement between the carriers concerned, which shall be approved by the aeronautical authorities of the two countries. ○ No limitations on change of gauge for third and fourth freedom operations. ○ 600 one-way charter flights per year for carriage of passengers, mail or cargo in accordance with country of origin rule.	

Before the Aviation Subcommittee of the
House Transportation and Infrastructure Committee

Testimony of Thomas H. Weidemeyer
President
United Parcel Service Co.

March 27, 1996

Good afternoon, Mr. Chairman and distinguished members of this Subcommittee. My name is Thomas H. Weidemeyer and I am the President and Chief Operating Officer of United Parcel Service Co., the airline subsidiary of UPS. I am grateful for this opportunity to appear before you to talk about our government's international aviation policy as it applies to the United Kingdom and Japan. Given the importance of these two trading partners, and the all-cargo talks being conducted in Tokyo this week, this hearing is especially timely.

The world is rapidly changing. Borders -- both political and economic -- are coming down. The international marketplace is changing at a blistering pace. The individuals and businesses involved in this change know it and live it every day. In spite of this, there seems to be a disconnect between the nations of this world wanting free trade on the one hand, as evidenced by GATT and NAFTA, and, on the other hand, wanting to continue to restrict perhaps the most important means of facilitating free trade -- namely, transportation. International air transportation is perhaps the primary facilitator because it allows businesses around the world to participate in the global economy faster and more efficiently.

It is time for governments to recognize this and react in ways that help, rather than hinder, global development. Information and financial resources already flow freely around the world, while the movement of people and goods that support them are too often restricted by archaic and protectionist rules and regulations. Both the United Kingdom and Japan present major challenges to changing the old way of thinking.

I will first speak briefly about the United Kingdom and then turn my attention to the present situation with Japan.

I. <u>The U.S. - U.K. Bilateral</u>

Although our current operations are running smoothly in the U.K., it has not always been that way, due in large part to the bilateral relationship between the U.S. and the U.K. You may notice that I did not refer to the bilateral agreement, but rather the bilateral relationship. I did this to point out the fact that it is the bilateral system, not necessarily the aviation agreements themselves, that are the problem. Let me give you an example to illustrate this point.

Three years ago, UPS decided to move its U.K. operations from the Stansted airport north of London (where very few airlines seem to want to operate from) to the East Midlands airport about 150 miles northwest of London (which very few people have ever heard of). Under the U.S - U.K. aviation agreement, known as Bermuda II, UPS was one of only three U.S. carriers designated to serve the U.K. with fifth freedom beyond rights. This is very important to UPS because our U.K. flight operates to our primary European air hub in Cologne, Germany.

In 1980, Bermuda II was amended and liberalized by what is known as Annex 5, which basically allowed more than three all-cargo carriers to be designated for service to the U.K. (although only the first three could utilize fifth freedom rights). Annex 5 also removed the limitations on what point or points an all-cargo carrier could serve in the U.S. or U.K.

Our fifth-freedom designation was central to our decision to move to East Midlands. However, when we notified the U.K. DoT about our planned schedule change, they informed us that we would have to be redesignated by the U.S. in order to serve East Midlands and that would cause us to lose our fifth-freedom rights to Germany. They said that East Midlands was not one of the points designated for those services under Bermuda II. We did not understand their interpretation of the agreement because Annex 5 had clearly done away with any limitations on which cities or points all-cargo carriers could serve.

We approached our own U.S. DOT to help us solve this misinterpretation of the agreement. To our amazement, our DOT told us that the U.K. was right and that they had always interpreted the agreement this way. They further told us that they would be happy to redesignate us as directed by the U.K. DoT, but that they would not pursue the matter with the U.K. DoT.

Imagine our surprise to have two English speaking government agencies unable to read what was, in our opinion, very plain English. Is it any wonder why we have so many problems interpreting the 1952 U.S.- Japan Agreement?

As it turned out, using the East Midlands airport director and some back-home Members of Parliament contacts, UPS - not the U.S. DOT - was able to convince the U.K. DoT that our interpretation was indeed correct. We were then allowed to move our operations to the East Midlands airport with no restrictions on our fifth-freedom rights. Even after we had the letter in hand, the U.S. DOT did not understand how we were able to accomplish this.

This example underscores the fact that it is often the relationship, not just the agreement, that causes the problems. The U.S. - U.K. relationship is an old one, with a well-defined choreography. The negotiating parties to this bilateral dance seem to be very comfortable with the music being played and very familiar with the steps being taken by the other partner. And that's the problem. We would not have a NAFTA or GATT if we were following the same old dance steps. Why, then, do we allow this to continue for international air transportation?

In last year's bilateral negotiations with the U.K., the U.S. government developed a strategy that separated a potential agreement into a short-term "mini-deal" and medium and long-term priorities that could be dealt with in subsequent negotiations. The U.S. government's belief was that by agreeing to a short-term "mini-deal," we would be in a better position to resolve the medium and long-term issues.

In 1994, the U.K. House of Commons Transport Committee made the following recommendation for resumption of talks with the U.S.:

"Our principal recommendation is that the U.K. Government should offer an immediate deal, with no strings attached, involving total liberalization of access to U.K. regional airports and, *in respect of freight-only services, the removal of all restrictions on fifth freedom rights*, so that both sides can reap the benefits these measures would produce; *these proposals would be decoupled from the main negotiations and should be considered on their own merits, irrespective of the prospects for agreement on the remaining issues.*"

As opposed to the U.S. strategy of dealing with the short-term problems first, this seemed to be a more common-sense approach: *don't let the easier issues get bogged down in the discussion of the difficult ones*. Interestingly, this U.K. Parliament strategy is now the U.S. strategy in the Japan talks, although the "easy stuff" has not proven to be that easy up to this point.

The U.S. DOT did not place the U.K. Parliament cargo liberalization recommendations on the short-term list of priorities for the U.S. - U.K. talks. However, regional airport liberalization did make it to the U.S. DOT short list. Cargo carriers were reassured at a February 1995 meeting where this strategy was first unveiled that a final decision had not been made. However, with regards to cargo, a final decision apparently had been made because we never did make it off the second list -- even in a situation where a U.K. Parliament panel had recommended that cargo be liberalized completely before talks begin on the rest of the issues.

I think that I can safely predict that if your Subcommittee were to make a significant recommendation that supported a U.K. priority, the U.K. negotiators would have that on *their* short list. As a result, I can only conclude that cargo was not a U.S. priority at the time the "mini-deal" was discussed.

Last May, I testified before the Senate Aviation Subcommittee and predicted that it was unlikely that the U.K. would move to liberalize cargo services in a second phase of negotiations once the "mini-deal" was concluded. The reason for this is quite simple: the primary desires of the U.K. were fulfilled in the "mini-deal." Secretary Peña testified at the same hearing and predicted that once the "mini-deal" was done, cargo liberalization would be realized in a matter of days. It is now nearly nine-months since we finalized the "mini-deal" and further cargo liberalization has not been achieved. Recent informal discussions with the U.K. give some hope that we will get back to the table soon, but we are not holding our breath.

II. The U.S. - Japan Bilateral Relationship

Last summer, in negotiations to resolve a dispute over FedEx's Japan beyond rights to its Subic Bay hub in the Philippines, the U.S. and Japanese governments agreed to negotiate a new, more liberalized cargo agreement. The primary desire on the part of the Japanese government for entering into these talks was to address their belief that the Japanese cargo carriers - JAL and NCA - were not on the same footing as the U.S. "Incumbent Carriers" - FedEx and Northwest. Since UPS is one of the 1989 Memorandum of Understanding (MOU) carriers that cannot fully participate in the market, this also signaled a significant opportunity to finally address the competitive balance between MOU and "Incumbent" carriers.

During the first round of talks in Tokyo in September, it became quickly apparent that we were going to spend an inordinate amount of time discussing and debating the respective government positions regarding both the actual and hypothetical beyond operations of U.S. incumbent carriers under the 1952 Agreement. After listening to this on-going debate, only one thing is certain: short of an international legal proceeding of some type, neither of our two governments is going to capitulate to the other's interpretation of the 1952 Agreement. As a result, if the U.S. government's goal is to reach a new agreement that vindicates our interpretation of the 1952 Agreement, we will not get a new agreement. There have been some that have suggested that no agreement would be better than a bad agreement. In our mind, not reaching a new agreement is the worst of all options.

Let me explain that in another way. First, whether one supports an open skies arrangement or simply more liberalization, the only way that can happen is through a new agreement. Maintaining the status quo does not achieve any form of liberalization. Exhibit #1 is a graph that depicts the current weekly operations of the U.S. carriers in the U.S.-Japan and beyond market. As you can see from that graph, FedEx enjoys a 10:1 advantage over UPS and Northwest enjoys a 5:1 advantage. This is a tremendous disparity that only a new agreement can address. To UPS, the status quo is an untenable situation.

Second, even in a status quo situation, we predict that the incumbent carriers would remain successful in getting the U.S. government to protect their rights. Exhibit #2 shows an increase in the operations of FedEx and United in a "no agreement" scenario. This takes into account the present schedule filings of FedEx and United. We would expect the U.S. government to protect those rights as it protected FedEx's Subic Bay rights last summer. If FedEx, Northwest or United had additional route plans in the future that our government acknowledged were within their rights under the 1952 Agreement, we know our government would protect those as well. Consequently, the net result of not reaching an agreement would be that the incumbents would still have an opportunity for growth while UPS would not.

By contrast, Exhibit #3 shows what a new agreement might look like. It shows a markedly different competitive landscape. You will note that the incumbent operations are the same as in a "no agreement" scenario, which means that, for incumbents, any scenario gives increased new opportunities. What is noticeably different are the operations attributed to UPS. For discussion purposes, we have used those services offered by the Japanese government in its latest proposal. It is very clear from this graph that FedEx's advantage over UPS in numbers of operations would be 2:1 and UPS would be nearly even with Northwest. Also, it is very clear that no one has given up or traded anything. Put simply, we now have a bigger pie.

Exhibit #3 points out the dilemma in which UPS finds itself. The only way for UPS to be competitive in Asia is to achieve some level of service parity to FedEx in Japan. The only way to do that is to reach a new agreement. While we do not expect the same level of flexibility (although ultimately under open skies, that should be the case), we do feel that we should not be kept out of the market because the opportunity to negotiate new services is stalled by unresolvable legal battles. UPS is not asking that any incumbent rights be traded off or taken away. UPS is merely urging our government to keep an open mind and find a solution that protects the rights of our carriers but also allows for new competitive services in the U.S.-Japan market. We know that this is not an easy task for our negotiators. However, if our government refocuses its efforts on protecting existing and planned operations of the incumbents -- we have a chance at a new agreement.

Thank you.

EXHIBIT #1

Current Weekly Operations: Japan & Beyond*

Cargo Only

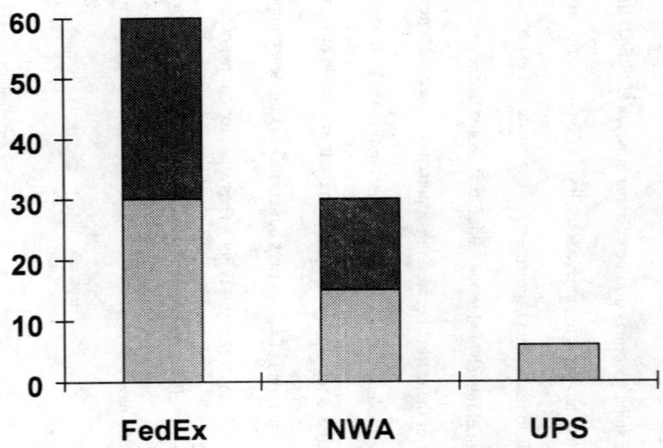

** Assumptions:*

1. Based on OAG schedules

2. Operations by FedEx and NWA may actually exceed those shown

EXHIBIT #2

Estimated Weekly Operations with No Agreement:*

Cargo Only

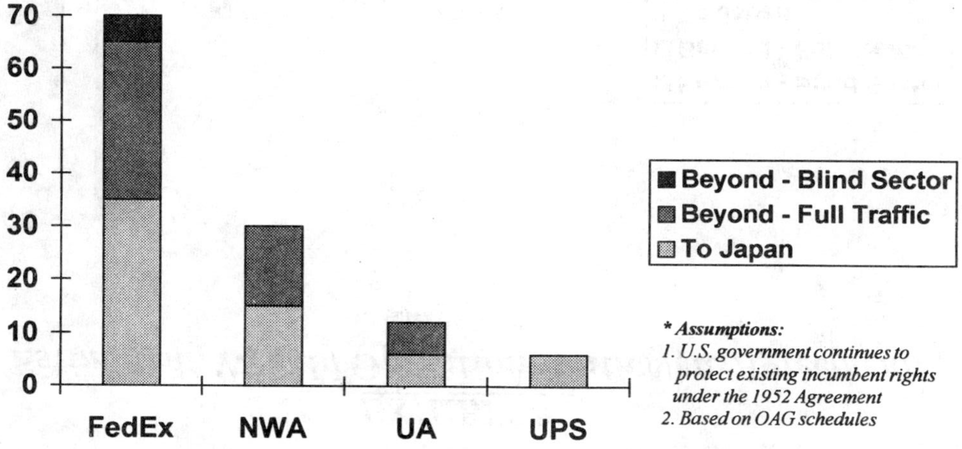

** Assumptions:*

1. U.S. government continues to protect existing incumbent rights under the 1952 Agreement

2. Based on OAG schedules

EXHIBIT #3

Estimated Weekly Operations with New Agreement:*

Cargo Only

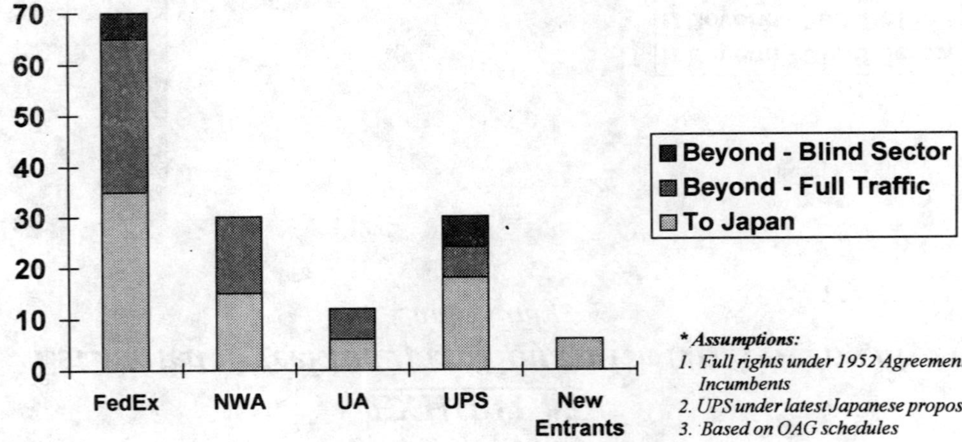

** Assumptions:*

1. *Full rights under 1952 Agreement for Incumbents*
2. *UPS under latest Japanese proposal*
3. *Based on OAG schedules*

ADDITION TO THE RECORD

Congress of the United States
House of Representatives
Washington, DC 20515

March 26, 1996

The Honorable William J. Clinton
President of the United States
The White House
1600 Pennsylvania Avenue, N.W.
Washington, D.C. 20500

Dear Mr. President:

You are scheduled to meet in Tokyo with the Prime Minister of Japan on April 16-17, 1996. A recently formed lobbying group called "Access U.S.-Japan" is urging that you ask the Prime Minister to open talks on a new aviation agreement. Our position is that, prior to any agreement on "talks," Japan must first agree to an agenda which makes it crystal clear that curtailment of existing rights is not on the agenda, and that Japan has, prior to talks, honored all pending applications for Asia expansion. Talks are not now appropriate, because the circumstances are not favorable for a successful outcome. Accordingly, we urge that you not raise this issue at the summit. Moreover, should Prime Minister Hashimoto raise this issue on his own, we respectfully urge that you either decline or set forth the conditions we have stated above.

The current Aviation Agreement with Japan has been enormously beneficial for U.S. interests. Our airlines capture over sixty percent of the market and earn a $4.8 billion annual trade surplus with Japan. The key to this impressive achievement is that the Aviation Agreement allows three U.S. airlines -- Northwest, United and Federal Express -- to establish hub and spoke networks in Japan. These hubs permit them to carry traffic not only between U.S. cities like Minneapolis/St. Paul and Tokyo, but also (1) between Tokyo and cities in Asia, and (2) between U.S. cities and Asia via Japan. A Report issued on March 20, 1996 by the Economic Strategy Institute studied the economic value of these hub networks to our economy, and concluded that they are the source of enormous economic value. Given the importance of these rights, the Report concluded:

> "The United States must make it clear that the current rights under the 1952 Agreement are not subject to negotiation."

Since 1977, Japan's central objective has been to curtail or even eliminate these rights. Japan wants to place its inefficient carriers in a position to dominate the market between Asia and the United States. This would undermine the ability of our carriers to sustain existing levels of service, and cripple their ability to expand. Northwest Airlines, for example, has just announced that it is expanding its Twin Cities to Tokyo service from once per week to four times per week. Minnesota communities and businesses have been urging Northwest to increase its service to Japan, and we are excited it is at hand. Without the traffic support provided by Northwest's Tokyo hub, however, this expanded service would not be possible. Losing this service would inflict great damage on Minnesota's aspirations for increased trade with Japan and Asia. It would harm Minnesota exporters, and foreclose creation of thousands of high paying jobs.

The ESI Study correctly concludes that the best aviation policy is open skies. It is naive to believe, however, that open skies is acheivable with Japan, at least in the foreseeable future. Japan has made it clear that it wants less competition in aviation, not more. Its conduct in the current cargo negotiations, first seeking to curtail expansion rights of U.S. cargo carriers, and even threatening to terminate existing services of Federal Express, leaves no doubt of its objectives.

We should not agree to hold passenger talks with Japan when Japan is seeking to ensnare the United States in a negotiation designed to convert a trade surplus into a trade deficit. This is what happened when we renegotiated our aviation agreement with the United Kingdom, producing the infamous Bermuda II agreement. This mistake must not be repeated with Japan.

When Northwest announced its expanded service from Tokyo to the Twin cities, it also announced the first U.S. service to Guangzhou, China and Jakarta, Indonesia via Japan. U.S. carrier access to these Asian cities -- and the other seven Asian cities Northwest serves -- is no less important to our commercial interests than access to Japan itself. It is obvious to us, however, that if the Aviation Agreement is opened up while these route applications are pending, Japan will hold them up as leverage to obtain an unfair agreement.

This is the strategy Japan has followed in the current air cargo negotiations, where it has held hostage Federal Express' China route. Japan has refused to acknowledge that the plain language of the Agreement gives U.S. carriers the right, without government-to-government negotiations, to add new beyond points and frequencies at will.

If the United States opens up the Agreement under these circumstances, there are two likely results, neither of which is acceptable to our country: (1) Japan will force us to negotiate to obtain approval of pending applications, in spite of the fact that we already have these rights; and (2) Japan will seek to restrict future beyond operations in exchange for new point-to-point routes between the U.S. and Japan.

This is a negotiation we should not enter. The Agreement should not be opened up.

The Honorable William J. Clinton
March 26, 1996
Page Three

Thank you for your consideration of our views. We look forward to working closely with you and your Administration on these important issues.

Sincerely,

Paul Wellstone
U.S. Senate

Rod Grams
U.S. Senate

James L. Oberstar, M.C.

Gil Gutknecht, M.C.

David Minge, M.C.

Jim Ramstad, M.C.

Bruce F. Vento, M.C.

Martin Olav Sabo, M.C.

Bill Luther, M.C.

Collin Peterson, M.C.

PROBLEMS IN THE U.S. AVIATION RELATIONSHIP WITH THE UNITED KINGDOM AND JAPAN

TUESDAY, APRIL 30, 1996

U.S. HOUSE OF REPRESENTATIVES,
SUBCOMMITTEE ON AVIATION,
COMMITTEE ON TRANSPORTATION AND INFRASTRUCTURE,
Washington, DC.

The subcommittee met, pursuant to recess, at 2:03 p.m. in room 2167, Rayburn House Office Building, Hon. John J. Duncan, Jr. (chairman of the subcommittee) presiding.

Mr. DUNCAN. The subcommittee will come to order.

We will go ahead and get started with our hearing this afternoon on our Nation's aviation relations with the United Kingdom and with Japan. This is actually our third hearing involving various aviation-related matters concerning the United States and Japan. We held a hearing on July 20th last year, and on the following day an agreement between the U.S. and Japan was reached. And just last month we held a second hearing which focused on additional passenger and cargo disputes between the two countries.

I hope that we helped, at least in some way, to send a message to the Japanese government that our Government and the U.S. air carrier industry are united in seeking open and fair resolutions to our aviation-related disputes.

First, let me welcome everyone here today and thank our distinguished witnesses for taking time out of what I know are very busy schedules to be with us this afternoon. I believe this is Assistant Secretary Hunnicutt's first time before this subcommittee, so, sir, we welcome you here today.

Mr. Jeff Fegan, executive director of the Dallas-Fort Worth Airport is with us, and we appreciate his presence; and Mr. Gerald Greenwald, who is the chairman of United Airlines, who has been with us before and has provided us excellent testimony in the past, is here with us, as well. We appreciate their presence also.

Japan is our second largest international passenger market, with 12,141,000 passengers in 1995, an increase of 12.7 percent from 1994.

Again, I think this hearing is particularly timely in that the Japanese government seems intent upon making progress in the aviation area very difficult.

In addition, the Japanese have now threatened to refuse United Airlines a second flight between Los Angeles and Tokyo. It is my understanding that Japan has indicated it will not approve this flight in retaliation for the U.S. refusal to approve Japan Airline flights between Tokyo and Hawaii. Apparently, the Department of Transportation has refused to approve this flight in retaliation for Japan's refusal to approve the United Airlines fifth freedom flight between Osaka and Korea.

The subcommittee will be most interested to hear from Mr. Hunnicutt and Mr. Greenwald as to their evaluation of this situation. I think this subcommittee would be even more interested in hearing how we can resolve this dispute favorably, and hopefully without starting an all-out trade war.

Meanwhile, the market share of U.S. airlines between the United States and the United Kingdom continues to decline. Currently, British Airlines—British Airways and Virgin Atlantic—fly 59.5 percent of the passengers between the U.S. and the United Kingdom, while U.S. airlines carry only 40.5 percent.

I think it is general knowledge that the major point of contention between the U.S. and the U.K. involves access to Heathrow Airport.

The United Kingdom is our third-largest international passenger market, with a little over 12 million passengers in 1995, an increase of 3.4 percent from the previous year.

I believe Mr. Fegan will speak to the U.S.-U.K situation and, in particular, the economic impact on the State of Texas should a route be approved from Dallas-Fort Worth to Heathrow.

The subcommittee would very much like to see talks with the U.K resumed as soon as possible.

Again, we look forward to today's testimony from our outstanding witnesses.

I now recognize the ranking member of the subcommittee, Mr. Lipinski.

Mr. LIPINSKI. Thank you, Mr. Chairman.

Mr. Chairman, this afternoon the subcommittee continues its study of the aviation relationship between the United States and United Kingdom and the United States and Japan. I want to thank you for scheduling another hearing on this very, very important subject.

Today we will hear from witnesses from the Department of Transportation, United Airlines, and the Dallas-Fort Worth International Airport.

Unfortunately, some of the other witnesses scheduled to appear at the second hearing were not able to adjust their schedules to be here this afternoon. These witnesses will be submitting testimony for the record that I look forward to reading.

Our first witness this afternoon will be the new assistant secretary of aviation and international affairs. I gave a speech in January right before Mr. Hunnicutt assumed his new position in which I was critical of the Department of Transportation and Department of State's ability to negotiate bilateral agreements which provide U.S. carriers the rights that they deserve.

There are quite a few cases, I will concede, in which DOT and State have been successful in opening markets to U.S. carriers and negotiating open skies agreements. I commend the negotiators for their hard work and success with these nations. The problem, unfortunately, is that we have not had the same level of success with the two most critical nations—the United Kingdom and Japan.

I'd like to mention at this particular time, too, that when I gave my speech, the gentleman who was probably mostly responsible for this particular department, Mr. Pat Murphy, who is here today—and I want to set the record straight now. When I gave that speech, it was not meant as criticism of Mr. Murphy. I think he is a very dedicated, hard-working individual, and I think that if he had gotten more cooperation from some of the powers that be, maybe we could have negotiated some better agreements for the United States of America.

Now, back to my prepared remarks.

Mr. Chairman, these two hearings will focus on the U.K. and Japan because they are the real problem. I encourage our negotiators to continue pushing for open skies in every country in the world, including Japan and the U.K. Open skies is good for American carriers and good for America and good for the world.

But in the cases where open skies cannot happen, where the traditional approaches of negotiating bilaterals go nowhere, we need to be willing to consider alternative approaches. Thinking or acting the same way because that's the way we have always done it is simply not acceptable.

Because of the inherent conflict between carriers on this issue, it is impossible to find a solution which provides every U.S. airline with what it wants. What we must strive towards is creating increased opportunities for U.S. carriers in every market around the world. Our priority should be expanding markets for all U.S. carriers to use their competitiveness against foreign competitors rather than pitting them one against the other to trade the rights we already have.

Mr. Chairman, I want to thank you for working with me to schedule this hearing. We have a full slate ahead of us, so at this point I'd like to yield back the balance of my time.

Mr. DUNCAN. Thank you very much, Mr. Lipinski.

I'd now like to recognize the vice chairman, Mr. Weller.

Mr. WELLER. Thank you, Mr. Chairman. Good afternoon to my friend from Illinois, Mr. Lipinski, the ranking member. I, of course, want to thank each of you for arranging this very important hearing on U.S. aviation relations with the United Kingdom and Japan.

International aviation travel has doubled in the last decade, and this trend is expected to continue on course. In order for the United States to be competitive in the global economy, we must have access to our foreign markets. And while we've worked to deregulate the aviation industry here at home, the international aviation industry remains heavily regulated.

As we continue to work towards open skies, there are issues surrounding our current bilateral agreements that are of great concern.

Today we're going to look at the current state of our relations with Japan and the United Kingdom, two countries that continue to remain highly restrictive.

Mr. Chairman, I want to commend you for having this hearing, particularly as we work to improve transportation, because as we work to improve transportation, as we work to improve aviation opportunities, we create jobs for working Americans. That's always our bottom line and the goals that we have.

Mr. Chairman, I again commend you for holding this important hearing.

Mr. DUNCAN. Thank you very much, Mr. Weller.

Mr. Ewing will be next? Do you have a statement, Mr. Ewing?

Mr. EWING. Mr. Chairman, I am not going to make a statement now except to say that I commend you for holding this hearing. It's very important to some Illinois business constituents that we solve this problem, and I look forward to the testimony today.

Mr. DUNCAN. Thank you very much, Mr. Ewing.

Mr. LaHood?

Mr. LAHOOD. Mr. Chairman, do you have the feeling that this particular hearing is of interest to Illinois?

Mr. DUNCAN. I have noticed that. In fact, I said something to Mr. Schaffer about it. Until Mr. Ehlers got here——

Mr. LAHOOD. Vern, you're welcome to our hearing. We're glad to have you.

[Laughter.]

Mr. DUNCAN. Thank you very much.

Mr. Ehlers?

Mr. EHLERS. Thank you, Mr. Chairman.

I'm happy to join you as one of the two impartial people here to hear testimony and comment on it.

I just have one brief comment to make in beginning, and I think as we approach this issue, whether it's with the U.K. or with Japan, it's very important for us to remember the history of Bermuda 2, and how that particular agreement, I think, put us at a severe disadvantage and continues to do so. I think it's extremely important that we avoid making the same mistake twice.

With that statement, I will proceed to give up my time, or yield it back, and look forward to the rest of the testimony.

Thank you.

Mr. DUNCAN. All right. Thank you very much.

We'll go ahead and start now with the witnesses. We have first Mr. Charles A. Hunnicutt, who is Assistant Secretary for Aviation and International Affairs of the Department of Transportation.

Secretary Hunnicutt, thank you for being with us today. You are accompanied by Mr. Patrick Murphy also. Welcome to the hearing today.

TESTIMONY OF CHARLES A. HUNNICUTT, ASSISTANT SECRETARY FOR AVIATION AND INTERNATIONAL AFFAIRS, U.S. DEPARTMENT OF TRANSPORTATION, ACCOMPANIED BY PATRICK MURPHY, DEPUTY ASSISTANT SECRETARY FOR AVIATION AND INTERNATIONAL AFFAIRS

Mr. HUNNICUTT. Thank you, Mr. Chairman and members of the subcommittee. I appreciate this first opportunity to discuss the important subject of international civil aviation with you before this very important subcommittee. I'm also pleased, as you and Mr. Lipinski have noticed, to have Patrick Murphy, the Deputy Assistant Secretary for Aviation and International Affairs, accompanying me, and would like to associate myself with Mr. Lipinski's remarks regarding his great abilities.

I know that you are primarily interested in hearing today the current status of our aviation relationships with the U.K. and Japan, but I would also like to take this opportunity to briefly update you on the substantial progress the airline industry has made under the Clinton Administration.

The major passenger and cargo airlines reported combined net profits of $2.2 billion and operating profits of $5.46 billion for 1995. International operations, alone, generated combined operating profits of $929 million. The financial community and airline industry experts are predicting that 1996 will be another solid year for the airlines, with operating revenues growing as much as 4 percent.

In fact, despite severe weather conditions in the mid-Atlantic and northeast earlier this year, the major airlines may report a combined net profit for the first quarter of 1996. The major airlines have not shown a first-quarter profit since 1979.

Against the backdrop of a recovering aviation industry and a growing movement toward global liberalization, we continue to be very disappointed by the narrow tit-for-tat approach to liberalization taken by the British. Their position stands in stark contrast to the progressive approach to trans-atlantic liberalization shown by many of our European aviation partners, as well as to the market-oriented approach taken by the United Kingdom to many other trade matters.

British airlines are not struggling to restructure and achieve profitability. The reverse is the case. For its most recent financial year, Virgin Atlantic posted over a $60 million profit. For the 9 months ending December 31, 1995, British Airways had profits of over $1 billion, up 16.6 percent. These airlines are indeed formidable competitors.

Some of you may be wondering about the recent assertion by the British Airways chairman that the fairness of the Bermuda 2 agreement is demonstrated by the fact that U.S. and U.K. airlines offer nearly the same number of flights between the United States and the United Kingdom. He went on to attribute the current market share differential solely to the larger aircraft and consequent higher number of seats flown by the British carriers.

What he failed to mention is that, in an unrestricted market, U.S. carriers could offer a comparable number of seats by increasing the number of flights that they operate, particularly at their U.S. hubs. However, U.K authorities have intervened traffic season after traffic season to restrict U.S. airline proposals to increase flights from their primary U.S. gateways to London, even though their existing flights were nearly full.

It is also extraordinary and unacceptable that at this time, the U.S. and U.K. have an agreement that limits the U.S. passenger carriers at Heathrow Airport to only two.

Some U.K. interests try to justify that restriction by asserting that slot constraints at Heathrow prevent commercially-viable new entry at the airport. However, our analysis indicates that, in addition to American and United replacing TWA and PanAm, 24 of the airlines operating at Heathrow in July 1995, did not have any services there in July 1990.

24-087 97 - 7

In that time, departures from Heathrow have increased over 16 percent, and the airlines and airport authorities continue to work together to use the available capacity more efficiently.

So my answer to the congestion argument is, Get rid of the Bermuda 2 barriers to Heathrow access and let U.S. carriers compete for the slots with everyone else.

I can assure you that U.S. aviation authorities recognize the importance to U.S. airlines and cities of expanding opportunities in the U.K. market. An immediate, full-scale liberalization is our preferred option. Because the British were simply unwilling to expand their focus beyond the immediate needs of their airlines or to allow market forces to shape the development of aviation services, an incremental approach to liberalization appeared to be the only effective way to make progress.

In adopting a step-by-step approach, Secretary Peña emphasized that each incremental increase in opportunities must bring benefits to U.S. airlines and consumers and must be defensible on its own merits.

The June 1995, deal met those tests. American Airlines, Continental, Northwest, and United are all using new opportunities that were secured last year.

This first-stage agreement was also a prerequisite from the British perspective for moving on to discuss further liberalizations.

I recognize and share your concern that a second-stage agreement has not yet been reached; however, we will not accept proposals that do not meet the standards set out by Secretary Peña.

Consequently, we suspended the second stage negotiations because the British proposals on Heathrow were not sufficient to form a basis for discussion. They were structured to prevent certain U.S. cities and airlines from even competing for limited new Heathrow opportunities.

Despite the suspension of formal negotiations, contacts between the U.S. and U.K. continue. I had an informal discussion with my U.K. counterpart last month and a follow-up conversation just last week. I confirmed to the U.K. officials that the Department's goal remains the negotiation of the best possible liberalized bilateral relationship based on competitive considerations in the marketplace.

I also communicated the increasing U.S. frustration that, despite a healthy and growing U.K. carrier presence in the market, U.K. authorities have been unwilling to loosen the constraints of the Bermuda 2 regime even sufficiently for us to move forward on a small, incremental phase two deal.

Although we do not quite yet have a basis for resuming talks, these contacts allow us to explore possible ways of moving the process forward, and we are evaluating what we have learned. We have not closed the door on any options and are continuing to assess all possible ways to make progress.

I would like to turn now to Japan, our largest air market in terms of revenues.

Although there are a few other Asian destinations, such as Korea, Taiwan, and Hong Kong, that can support direct, nonstop service from the United States mainland, Japan is easily the primary gateway to Asia, due to its geographic location and the size of its aviation market.

Japan, where U.S. carriers do very well, will remain a key market for U.S. carriers operating trans-Pacific services for the foreseeable future.

In the last 2 or 3 years, the Japanese have focused increasing attention on U.S. airline operations beyond Japan. It is clear from statements of Japanese officials that one of Japan's primary objectives is to impose constraints on U.S. carrier operations beyond Japan to other Asian points.

We have repeatedly advised the Japanese that any actions to deny our carriers' rights to operate beyond Japan would be viewed as a serious violation of the U.S.-Japan air services agreement.

We did successfully complete cargo talks and are now considering how to move the relationship forward in the passenger area.

Some are reluctant to engage Japan in passenger talks now. They see that Japan's primary objective is to curtail existing U.S. rights to operate beyond Japan. They believe that Japan will use the U.S.' desire for additional U.S.-Japan routes as leverage to achieve this objective. They note that Japan has not indicated much interest in obtaining substantial new opportunities for its own carriers to serve the United States.

Others have a different view. They believe that it would be in the overall interest of the United States to negotiate for new U.S.-Japan routes, even if the cost of obtaining such use is acceptance of constraints on U.S. beyond Japan services. They believe that an agreement could be struck that would preserve all existing beyond operations of U.S. carriers and that constraints would apply only to the rate of future growth of such services. In their view, this would be a reasonable price to pay for opening up the Japanese market to more service.

We are continuing to evaluate both sides of this question. My written testimony describes our work with the economic studies that we have received on this issue.

I would like to note that, despite the ongoing debate about whether the U.S. should accept constraints on future growth of beyond operations to obtain additional U.S.-Japan routes, we are not prepared to subscribe to an either/or philosophy on this issue. Rather, our goal is to mutually expand opportunities. We achieved this in air cargo.

It is vital that our carriers be able to compete effectively for Asian traffic. It is also desirable that we increase opportunities for additional services in this rapidly-growing market.

Our job is to develop a strategy that best serves the overall interests of the United States; however, before any strategy can be pursued, we have several outstanding route applications, which you mentioned, Mr. Chairman, which first must be resolved.

We began yesterday and are continuing today meeting with Japanese officials here in Washington to seek to reach an accord on the resolution for these services.

If the several outstanding issues in the passenger area are resolved, we believe it would be appropriate to meet with the Japanese this summer in government-to-government meetings to agree on a possible framework for passenger negotiations. If an acceptable approach for passenger talks can be worked out, then I would anticipate the two sides would begin formal talks with Japan soon thereafter.

In conclusion, I appreciate your support during my first months as assistant secretary. I recognize that the backing of this admirable, bipartisan forum has been an important contributing factor to the success of the Administration and Secretary Peña in achieving our national goals in international aviation, and I look forward to your continuing input as we work together to address 1996's international aviation challenges.

Thank you, Mr. Chairman.

Mr. DUNCAN. Thank you very much, Mr. Hunnicutt.

I've got just a couple of questions before I turn it over to Mr. Lipinski.

Does the Department feel that the Japanese—that there is a serious threat that the Japanese will block United's second flight between Los Angeles and Tokyo at this time?

Mr. HUNNICUTT. I'm sorry, Mr. Chairman. Is your question whether we believe the Japanese are serious in their denial of the application for United to fly the additional——

Mr. DUNCAN. What's the latest on that?

Mr. HUNNICUTT. The Japanese denial of those applications are still extant and we expect it to be enforced unless we can negotiate their removal today.

Our response, if we are unable to remove them, would be ultimately to prepare for a proportional response against Japanese service in the same city pair market.

Mr. DUNCAN. Let me just ask you, in the other area, as far as our relationship with the United Kingdom, is the Department of Transportation—has it given any consideration to a renunciation of the British bilateral agreement?

Mr. HUNNICUTT. Mr. Chairman, I understand—I more than understand—I know from reading the files that there was some consideration to renunciation earlier in this Administration, and it was tabled for the time being. We hope to examine other possibilities and a less-disruptive means of moving forward, but all policy options will remain open in resolving the aviation relationship with the United Kingdom.

Mr. DUNCAN. I'm going to have some more questions in a few minutes, but I'm going to go at this time to Mr. Lipinski.

Mr. LIPINSKI. Thank you, Mr. Chairman.

Since there is a delegation from Japan here today and we're discussing somewhat this situation, I'm going to go very lightly in regards to the Far East situation, simply to say that I hope we can drive the best possible bargain for the United States, the U.S. carriers, and the world in our negotiations with the Japanese.

In regards to Great Britain, I've had the dubious honor of leading a CODEL to Great Britain and sitting down and actually talking to the transport minister in regards to Heathrow, and I know what a brick wall that can be. I'm hoping that you have much greater success in the near future with the United Kingdom.

But I was just reading in "Aviation Week" magazine where Charles DeGaulle Airport and Orly Airport in Paris have really lost a number of flights over the course of the last year and a half, 2 years or so, because of the—number one was the strike situation there. I forget what the other reason was. But the point I want to make is that there must be a lot of places to land at Orly and Charles DeGaulle, and with the Chunnel now open, perhaps American carriers in the United States ought to look more towards flying in to Paris and bypassing England and London altogether, and people can fly in there, get on the very fast train, go through the Chunnel, and get back to London if they really want to get to London.

My point is that I would like to see an extremely hard line taken with the United Kingdom in regards to this particular situation, because I think they have been enormously unfair to us, and if I was sitting in your position—I'm not asking you to do what I'm going to say, but if I was sitting in your position, I would simply renounce the agreement that we have with them at the present time. I would move towards restricting the access of British Air and Virgin Air to the United States, and I'd try to have the American carriers fly right around London and right around England into the Continent, perhaps into Orly, as I say, or Charles DeGaulle, and see what the British would like to negotiate at that particular point.

I don't think we can take too hard a line against them.

And if you want to comment upon my statement, you're more than welcome to do so. If you don't choose to do so, I can also understand that.

Mr. HUNNICUTT. Congressman, I would like to comment, and I respect and will take your advice under advisement as to how we should proceed, but I do want to comment on the issue of over-flying London.

I think there are issues. Obviously, it's not the U.S. Department of Transportation's desire to tell travelers or shippers how they should respond to the market in the ways most appropriate to them, but what we are finding is that those areas of the north Atlantic market which are already benefiting from open skies arrangements are seeing a growth rate of approximately 9 percent a year in the passengers that are flying through those markets to gateways and to Europe, whereas there is no growth in the U.S.-London element of gateways to Europe.

So I think we're seeing the market response to liberalization in the aviation market for North America already, and it doesn't take us to encourage that. The market forces, alone, will demonstrate to the British that, over the medium-to long-term, they will have a problem sustaining Heathrow as a gateway into Europe from the United States.

Mr. LIPINSKI. Well, you seem to have a strategy, which apparently, by what you just said, is working in regards to surrounding these countries that have such a protective environment for aviation to the advantage of their own home carriers. It appears you're surrounding them with countries that have open skies policy, where there are no restrictions for us, no restrictions for them.

As I say, it seems like it's working, but my question is: do you have any estimate of how long it's going to take for that particular strategy to work until these people are willing to sit down and be reasonable at the table?

Mr. HUNNICUTT. Congressman, I can't give you a specific time estimate at this point.

Mr. LIPINSKI. I understand that.

Mr. HUNNICUTT. We're hoping in the nearest future to be able to re-enter negotiations with particularly the British and hopes of reaching a second stage interim liberalization to re-establish a good aviation relationship between our two countries.

And, as a strategy, I think it may make sense to view our open skies initiative in Europe as an attempt to encircle and capture, but I don't really think that's the intent.

I really think the effort was to gain a critical mass of the European market participating with the United States in an open aviation arrangement which could demonstrate the benefits of bringing more market forces to bear in the aviation arena, and that hopefully the demonstration of those benefits would educate and bring along those countries which we more reluctant to enter into liberalizing market-oriented aviation relationships.

I think we are seeing the effect of it. I think that if we wait for the economic pressure, alone, to force a change in government perspectives, we might wait longer than we want to in order to achieve the efficiencies that we know would be possible.

It will require us to engage in government-to-government activities to try to bring these trading partners into a better aviation relationship with us.

Mr. LIPINSKI. I mis-spoke there. I didn't mean that it was your plan, your strategy, your tactic; it was my interpretation of what was occurring. Perhaps my interpretation is not the correct interpretation, but, nevertheless, that was my interpretation. If it's working, I'm very happy about that.

I had another question I wanted to follow up here on, and now it seems to have escaped me momentarily. Since there are many other wonderful Members from the State of Illinois here who I want to give an opportunity to speak, Mr. Chairman, for now that's all the questioning I want to do.

Mr. DUNCAN. All right. Thank you very much, Mr. Lipinski.

I'm going to interrupt the questioning here at this point because we have Congressman Martin Frost, our colleague from Texas, who has come. He has a very busy schedule, but he wanted to at least introduce to the subcommittee, I believe, one of his constituents who will be testifying in the next panel.

Congressman Frost, it's always good to have you with us. We'll just turn it over to you.

Mr. FROST. Thank you, Mr. Chairman.

I'd like to just make a brief statement, if I may, and introduce one of the witnesses.

Mr. DUNCAN. Yes, sir. Go right ahead.

Mr. FROST. Thank you, because Jeff Fegan, executive director of the Dallas-Fort Worth International Airport will be testifying shortly, and I appreciate your having him testify on this important matter and permitting me to appear today.

Mr. Chairman, I just wanted to say a few words about the United States-United Kingdom aviation negotiations.

We need to do all we can to allow U.S. airlines more access to United Kingdom airports. The halt of the U.S.-U.K. negotiations is a major concern for the Dallas-Fort Worth Airport, the city of Dallas, the city of Fort Worth, and the entire north Texas area.

As you know, no Texas city has access to Heathrow. This is particularly troubling to the north Texas region, given that D/FW Airport is the second-busiest airport in the world in terms of operations and the third-busiest airport in terms of passengers.

Lack of Heathrow service means fewer opportunities for D/FW to attract foreign tourists and business visitors from the U.K., Europe, and the Middle East. It makes it more difficult for the Dallas-Fort Worth area business travelers to reach these destinations.

In addition, export trade by the D/FW area firms is restricted because it is more difficult to ship goods to these destinations.

Mr. Chairman, I have met and corresponded with Secretary Peña on this issue on several occasions. The Secretary has assured the Texas delegation that he is committed to expand opportunities in the U.S.-U.K. market.

It is my hope that somehow talks will resume and that a liberalized air agreement with the U.K. will be achieved, specifically one which will provide D/FW Airport access.

Thank you very much.

Jeff Fegan will be testifying shortly on this issue, which is of critical importance to our part of the country.

Thank you.

Mr. DUNCAN. Thank you very much, Congressman Frost. The concerns that you have mentioned in your statement are some of the very reasons why this is the third hearing that we have held on our aviation relationship with Japan and with U.K.—two extremely important aviation partners with us. We need to look into the whole gamut of our aviation relationship with those two very important countries.

We thank you for being with us. Because we all have a chance to discuss these matters with you privately, I don't ever have any questions of fellow Members. I'll let you just get on with your schedule and we'll go back to Secretary Hunnicutt.

Mr. FROST. Thank you very much. I appreciate it.

Mr. DUNCAN. Thank you very much for being with us today.

Next, we'll go for questioning now to Mr. Weller.

Mr. WELLER. Thank you, Mr. Chairman.

Mr. Secretary, glad to have you with us this afternoon. Of course, you have a tough job. As you can see, there is great interest. Those of us from Illinois and, of course, I represent the Chicago region, and Chicago O'Hare, of course, being not only a major employer but the world's busiest airport, aviation and the opportunity to take advantage of ever-expanding aviation markets is very important for the economy of the Chicago region.

Of course, you have a tough job because we're looking to you to create more opportunity in your negotiations, as well the fact we're always looking over your shoulder to help you along the way.

I appreciate your taking time to be with us today.

I've just got a few questions I'd like to ask of you, Mr. Hunnicutt.

Less than 2 weeks ago your colleague, Pat Murphy, testified for the U.S. Department of Transportation before the Senate Aviation Subcommittee, and he was pretty explicit in warning Japan that if they acted to ground United's Los Angeles-Tokyo flight, United States would be forced to respond accordingly.

From your perspective, do you think that Japan believes that the Department's warning is serious, or do you think they just take that as a bluff?

Mr. HUNNICUTT. Mr. Congressman, first I would like to thank you and say we're always glad to have the Members of Congress looking over our shoulders and giving us input in what we're doing in aviation policy, despite the fact that it is a tough job and we're not always getting kudos for what we're doing at that particular moment.

In answer to your question, of course, Mr. Murphy, it turns out, is sitting next to me, and I will let him comment further after I make a brief response for you.

I think that the Japanese realized last summer that the Department of Transportation was prepared to follow through on its order that would have curtailed Japanese air cargo services sixth freedom rights into the United States if they had not granted the Federal Express fifth freedom applications that were pending and that were covered by the bilateral arrangement.

I think that went a long way to setting the stage for the successful conclusion of the cargo talks.

I don't believe that the Japanese think we are a paper tiger or that we are bluffing in discussing what our reactions would be to denial of existing rights of our air carriers. If they are of the impression that we would not follow through, they're making a serious political miscalculation which will further complicate resolving the issues in this relationship.

Mr. WELLER. Just kind of following up with that, since Mr. Murphy made the statement regarding warning Japan that if they acted to ground that United's L.A.-to-Tokyo flight that, of course, United States would respond, what type of response have you gotten from the Japanese since then? Have you seen any change or any indication of communication?

Mr. HUNNICUTT. Well, the discussions with the Japanese that we're engaged in today—and, of course, you'll understand that I'm reluctant to get into any great detail, since they are ongoing and we will be going further this afternoon—involved more than just the LAX-Narita United frequencies. And while that was the most immediate in terms of urgency because of the timing—they were to come into effect this week—there were a broader range of existing passenger disputes, passenger issues that needed to be resolved, and it was the context of resolving a broader range of passenger issues, not just the LAX-Narita, that was on the table.

So we haven't had a specific response to our saying, on that particular issue, we would respond; however, the response would be proportional and related to the services that we're being denied under our rights under the bilateral.

Mr. WELLER. Mr. Murphy, can you follow up on that?

Mr. MURPHY. Yes, Congressman.

Following my statement to the Senate committee, I met with the chief Japanese negotiator in Washington. He came to Washington. He had a copy of my testimony in his briefcase. He told me he had read it. He understood what we were saying.

I pointed out to him that that testimony, as all of our testimony, had been circulated in the Administration, so I think he understood what we were saying and he understood how serious we were about that.

It was following that testimony and several discussions with him that it was agreed that the Japanese would come to Washington, and talks began yesterday.

Mr. WELLER. So he understood there is no backing down from that statement that you made, that you were dead serious?

Mr. MURPHY. That's my understanding. Yes, sir.

Mr. WELLER. Okay.

Mr. Hunnicutt, just another question I'd like to follow up with you on. If Japan succeeds in its plan to eliminate or restrict U.S. carrier operations beyond Japan, does the Department have a projection of the size of the loss in the U.S. carriers' share of the Pacific air transportation market that could result if the Japanese are successful?

Mr. HUNNICUTT. The short answer to that question is, No, we don't have a specific calculation.

As you know, we have received several studies comparing the value of beyond Japan rights for U.S. carriers to U.S.-Japan market rights. We're in the process of really assessing, as you'll see in my written testimony, a lot of the assumptions that underlie the analysis that goes into those four studies.

We have asked the authors of the studies several questions. We've met with the authors of two of the studies to date to go over their assumptions and their analysis. We have not been preparing an independent analysis of the trans-Pacific economic issues, but intended really to refine our understanding based on a better understanding of the assumptions within the analysis of those four studies.

So while the simple answer to your question is no, that doesn't mean that we don't understand that that's an important question and we aren't trying to grapple with how we get a handle on the relative value and what that should mean for U.S. policy.

Mr. WELLER. In following up on that, if you are analyzing these studies that have been done independently, what's your time table for where you would expect to have some data that you would be able to state as an official answer to the question I've asked?

Mr. HUNNICUTT. I'm not sure. I guess it's—when we met with the authors of the two studies we've met with, which were the access Japan study and the Economic Strategies Institute study, we went over a way of refining and assessing the qualitative assessment of the numbers they've come up with. We were not trying to rerun their data series to come up with new numbers.

We are waiting and hope to meet soon with the authors of the United study to do the same evaluation, as well as the Roberts Roche study that was done for Northwest.

I'm not sure that at this time we plan to calculate an actual number. I'm not sure if I'm understanding your question right, but if you're looking for whether we are going to tag a number, we have not been moving in that direction. We were really moving in terms of getting an understanding of what these four studies collectively show us in terms of the policy options that are out there.

Mr. WELLER. Do you feel, though, from your personal perspective, Mr. Hunnicutt, that if Japan was successful eliminating or restricting U.S. carriers' ability to operate beyond Japan, that it would have a negative impact, from your own personal perspective——

Mr. HUNNICUTT. Yes.

Mr. WELLER.——on our market share?

Mr. HUNNICUTT. Congressman, I am convinced, from the information and the analysis I've read, it would have a very significant negative impact not only on market share but on U.S. economic interest.

Mr. WELLER. And, of course, creating jobs is the bottom line.

Mr. Chairman, I do have additional questions. I realize I've run out of time. Are we going to come around a second time?

Mr. DUNCAN. Yes. If you need to, that will be fine.

Mr. WELLER. Thank you, Mr. Chairman.

Mr. DUNCAN. We'll give Mr. Hutchinson a few minutes to collect his bearings, since he just got here, and go to Mr. Ewing for questions that he has at this time.

Mr. EWING. Thank you, Mr. Chairman.

Mr. Secretary, if you look at the history of the contact between Japan and the United States, it appears there has been a pattern of—at least from our point of view—violations of agreements, or failure to abide by agreements. Even last year with FedEx there were problems. There are problems now. Very recently, according to information I have, Japan has backed away from a commitment to include aviation within the free trade regime for the Asian/Pacific Economic Cooperation members.

What's our response going to be to that? Are we going to enter into negotiations with Japan under that kind of current behavior if it is, in fact, as filled with failures to comply with these agreements?

If we do, how can we be sure that agreements we make are going to be followed out?

Mr. HUNNICUTT. You've asked a very difficult question, and I'll begin——

Mr. EWING. Well this is a difficult situation. We're playing with real marbles here today.

Mr. HUNNICUTT. Yes, sir. And I think what we have found is, of course, some of the things in your question you said "from our perspective." Some of these violations have evolved from disagreements over interpretation of the agreement, itself, which have not been resolved. Some of them have resulted from what we would consider violations, regardless of how one would interpret the agreement, but were engaged in during periods of disputes between the two sides.

I guess what I would say is, having had experience in negotiations with the Japanese in other trade areas at the International Trade Commission over the years, I find that often the negotiations are very difficult, and sometimes reaching agreement on what is the basic understanding that you have agreed to is sometimes very difficult.

We would expect that any agreement that succeeds the current aviation bilateral with Japan would be negotiated in a way that would be enforceable and that it would be clear to the Japanese that the U.S. Government intended to enforce the terms of that agreement that are agreed to if we engage in a broader round of aviation negotiations now.

I think that part of the answer to this complicated situation is to make clear in the new agreements that are reached what the rights and responsibilities are and to make clear that the United States is not hesitant to enforce the rights of its carriers under the agreements that have been reached.

Mr. EWING. What are some of our options in enforcing the rights of our carriers?

Mr. HUNNICUTT. The most obvious and the best example is the one I cited earlier of looking to Japanese economic interests in the aviation relationship that are in some ways equivalent to the rights that we're trying to enforce.

For example, in the Federal Express disputes, to look at sixth freedom cargo coming into the United States on Japanese carriers and to assess and take down a similar amount of economic activity against the Japanese side that's occurring—being denied to the U.S. carriers under their rights.

Another would be, in a dispute like the LAX-Narita to respond in a proportional manner in the same market against the Japanese carrier in that market.

Mr. EWING. Would you assess that it is really to both sides' advantage to have a workable agreement?

Mr. HUNNICUTT. Yes, sir. Undoubtedly. It's to both sides' advantage to have a workable agreement for the economic development of both countries. The lack of cargo and passenger services is a bottleneck in developing the greater efficiencies and economic integrations of the two economies.

Mr. EWING. Would you feel that we have workable agreements now between the two countries?

Mr. HUNNICUTT. My assessment of the agreement, as it exists now, is that it is—I want to say "muddling through," but that's not even the—it's limping along. I don't think that it's an adequate agreement for moving into the future, based on the economies that we have in Japan and the United States.

Mr. EWING. The Japanese have major access to our markets and our airports?

Mr. HUNNICUTT. Yes, sir. I guess the interpretation is what is "major." We have—there is major access on both sides.

Mr. EWING. But we're not trying to restrict their access at this time. The restrictions come——

Mr. HUNNICUTT. No.

Mr. EWING.——on a one-sided basis.

Mr. HUNNICUTT. The only restrictions we're interested in are restrictions that are reciprocal because they're restricting the relationship on their side of the equation.

Mr. EWING. Well, it just appears to me that if it is indeed beneficial to the Japanese economic community to have access here, that they need to understand that access to Japan is important to us. I guess maybe we need to make that very clear that we intend to enforce the bilateral part of those agreements. I would hope your

Department and your agency would take that as part of their responsibility.

Mr. HUNNICUTT. Yes, sir.

Mr. DUNCAN. Thank you very much, Mr. Ewing.

Mr. LaHood?

Mr. LAHOOD. Mr. Hunnicutt, did you read Mr. Greenwald's testimony?

Mr. HUNNICUTT. For today?

Mr. LAHOOD. Yes, sir.

Mr. HUNNICUTT. No, sir, I haven't seen it.

Mr. LAHOOD. Do you believe that United is being discriminated against by the Japanese government or by Japan on their ability to engage flights into that country?

Mr. HUNNICUTT. Do I believe that——

Mr. LAHOOD. Do you believe that United Airlines is being discriminated against by the Japanese government on their ability to engage flights into Japan?

Mr. HUNNICUTT. I believe that United Airlines is being denied their bilateral rights by the Japanese government to enter into the Japanese market under the agreement we have. I'm hung up on the word "discriminated against" because there are also other U.S. carriers that are being denied those rights.

Mr. LAHOOD. Like who?

Mr. HUNNICUTT. Like Northwest, for their beyond rights; until the cargo agreement, Federal Express.

Mr. LAHOOD. So there are actually three then?

Mr. HUNNICUTT. I'm not sure that I would call it "discrimination," but several U.S. carriers are being denied their rights.

Mr. LAHOOD. Three. There are three U.S. carriers then? United, Northwest, and——

Mr. HUNNICUTT. Bilateral.

Mr. LAHOOD. Pardon me?

Mr. HUNNICUTT. Under the bilateral, Federal Express.

Mr. LAHOOD. What do you think that you should be doing about that? What do you think that our government should be doing about that?

Mr. HUNNICUTT. Our Government's role should be to enforce the rights that exist under the bilateral.

Mr. LAHOOD. Are we doing that?

Mr. HUNNICUTT. The Government—the reason we are in discussions with the Japanese today is an attempt to move forward in doing that. Yes, sir.

Mr. LAHOOD. But are we doing it?

Mr. HUNNICUTT. I guess my answer would be that it's never 100 percent perfectly achieved, but in the example of Federal Express and cargo, all of the requests for bilateral rights that existed were taken care of in the agreement that we achieved. So yes. And what are we trying to do in passengers? That's achieve at least a similar resolution of those outstanding issues before we move forward to try to achieve a better bilateral relationship.

Mr. LAHOOD. Is Japan in any violation of any agreements that we have with them?

Mr. HUNNICUTT. I would say that they are in violation of the aviation bilateral now in applications that have not been approved, particularly the United application for Osaka. Yes, sir.

Mr. LAHOOD. So what is our recourse as a government?

Mr. HUNNICUTT. We have not acted on the application for Japan Airlines to serve Kona, Hawaii.

Mr. LAHOOD. Is there a provision in the agreement or the treaty that allows for anything other than not acting on their request?

Mr. HUNNICUTT. There are no dispute resolution mechanisms, but there are provisions for consultations, required consultations; there are provisions for arbitration; and there is a potential for renunciation of the agreement, itself, as an ultimate.

Mr. LAHOOD. So you've only really taken one small, minute step; is that correct? I mean, you really haven't done anything except you have not agreed to look at whatever Japan's request is to the United States. You've taken none of the other steps.

Mr. HUNNICUTT. That's correct. We have not taken——

Mr. LAHOOD. Why is that?

Mr. HUNNICUTT. We have not engaged in consultations or—because at the current time—we didn't assess that the possibility of achieving our goals, our objectives of getting the U.S. carriers' rights implemented were possible through consultations or arbitration.

Mr. LAHOOD. But they're not. It's very apparent that they are not. Would you agree with that?

Mr. HUNNICUTT. They have not yet been—those applications have not yet been approved. That's correct.

Mr. LAHOOD. Well, you know, with all due respect—Mr. Murphy, would you like to comment on this?

Mr. MURPHY. I was just going to suggest, Congressman, that when we ran into our problems with Federal Express last summer, we solved those immediate problems with a meeting between the two ministers last July. The ministers then agreed to work on cargo problems until this March, and just a few weeks ago we were successful in resolving the problems our cargo carriers were having. So both governments agreed to focus on cargo issues.

Now we have passenger issues that are coming to the fore.

Mr. LAHOOD. Well, I would say this: with all due respect, I think to this point you folks have defaulted on your responsibility to offer an even playing field with respect to United Airlines. Now, maybe you've resolved the freight issue. I don't know. I assume—I'll take your word for that. But you have not resolved this issue, and I hope that at some point it—you can get with the program here and get it resolved.

I assume that at some point you'll read this testimony, which is an astounding indictment against one particular airline. If half of this stuff is true, which I assume that all of it is, United is getting hosed in the process here. And it doesn't look like our Government is doing anything about it, or at least following the agreements and the steps that should be taken here.

I hope you get with the program here.

Thank you, Mr. Chairman.

Mr. DUNCAN. Thank you, Mr. LaHood.

Mr. Hutchinson?

Mr. HUTCHINSON. Thank you, Mr. Chairman.

I'd like to follow up on what Mr. Ewing and Mr. LaHood both have pointed out.

Just since I have been here you have pointed out that we are muddling through, limping along. You have said that United Airlines, FedEx, and Northwest have been denied their bilateral rights under existing agreements and that Japan is in violation of the aviation bilateral. That's since I've been here.

It seems to me—I am increasingly concerned and disturbed over the problems that our industry is encountering in the markets of the United Kingdom and Japan.

This is the third—if I'm correct, this is the third hearing the Aviation Subcommittee has held on this issue in the past year, and I want to thank our chairman for calling these hearings, for bringing these issues to light, and for airing them. But it's also quite frustrating that, in the course of these three Aviation Subcommittee hearings on the subject, that instead of our trading partners becoming more cooperative, they have become more intransigent.

And I am wondering, Mr. Secretary, that, while historically these international aviation agreements have been negotiated between Department of Transportation and the State Department and individual foreign countries, is there a role, as you see it, for us here in Congress? What can we do to assist you in these negotiations and the enforcement of these agreements? And if there is no dispute resolution or any mechanism beyond what you have said, what do you propose to do and what can we do to assist you?

Mr. HUNNICUTT. Congressman, I think, one, my words that you have just quoted I think are very accurate, because obviously we were not here to tell you we have resolved this issue or that it's taken care of. We're here to tell you that there is still a problem, but to inform you on how we've been working on it and where we're trying to go with it.

I believe that the—there are two issues you've raised. One is the issue of enforceability, dispute settlement mechanisms, whether it makes sense to have these relationships on a bilateral basis, and I think there has been some thought about that in the aviation community and a look at it, and really a view that at the present time we're in this bilateral world in terms of aviation agreements, and the best we can do in terms of providing market access for our carriers, and therefore improved economic efficiencies for global aviation, is to have better bilateral agreements with those countries with which we can negotiate them, and to negotiate with those countries that are reluctant to move to liberalize, to market-oriented aviation relationships as far as possible.

With that, it means being consistent and going back to the Japanese and the U.K. with our objectives, being willing to be pragmatic in making issues—in resolving issues like the cargo agreement, accepting that the cargo agreement wasn't everything we wanted it to be.

When the cargo negotiations were launched, our goal was a completely liberalized cargo regime, and we ended up with a cargo agreement which greatly improved market access for the U.S. carriers, but did not take us all the way to the liberalized regime that we were hoping to achieve.

I think that part of the goal here has to be a unified U.S. consensus on what we want from these countries in terms of an open aviation relationship and an ability to have the staying power in these negotiations to continue to insist on movement in that direction.

I don't know if that——

Mr. HUTCHINSON. That addressed one of the issues I raised. The other one was what role do we have. Beyond oversight hearings, do you see Congress in any way being able to strengthen your position?

Mr. HUNNICUTT. Well, we're certainly interested always in Congressional input into ideas, concepts, thoughts of moving forward. In terms of proposed legislative changes, in terms of the structure of how the U.S. Government deals with these issues, or the legal authority we have to take actions, I'm not today prepared to give you any clear answers on that because I haven't really given that a great deal of thought to prepare for this hearing, but I would be glad to do that.

Mr. HUTCHINSON. I would appreciate that.

[The information received follows:]

Considering the various ways that the Congress conveys its concerns, there seems now to be a pretty effective mix of communications tools that can be tailored to the different issues that engage both the Congress and the Administration. When it comes to specific, difficult, high-profile negotiations like those with Japan, hearings such as these, and the other public statements made by Members of Congress, can exert a very positive influence. Earlier in this hearing, it was noted that the chief Japanese negotiator was carrying a copy of Mr. Murphy's prior Congressional testimony in his briefcase. Foreign embassies here pay close attention to the level of your interest in these issues. Our major aviation partners understand the U.S. political system and recognize that our policy and positions must take into account the strongly-held, bipartisan views of this Subcommittee and Committee and of your counterparts in the Senate. So Members' public statements effectively reinforce our negotiating stance. When we tell a foreign negotiator that his proposal is, politically, a non-starter, our credibility is strengthened by the questions Members ask and the statements they make, in these hearings and elsewhere.

When it comes to legislation, the existing fair competitive practices law has proven to be an excellent tool for the Department to use in resolving problems with other governments. In cases where new legislation might be considered, probably informal, staff-level consultation early in the process will be the most efficient way to proceed. Sometimes there can be pitfalls in terms of integrating new legislation with existing statutory mandates. Also there may be unintended effects on rules that have been refined over the years in response to industry concerns. A potentially serious possibility could be inconsistency with specific negotiating situations that may be evolving even as new bills are being drafted. So we would welcome the opportunity to touch base with you informally, early in the course of legislative initiatives, and then to continue to work with you throughout the process.

Mr. HUTCHINSON. Are you optimistic that we're going to see greater cooperation and see these issues resolved in the relatively near future?

Mr. HUNNICUTT. I am cautiously optimistic that we can make at least incremental improvements in the very near future, and that we can make genuine aviation liberalization at least in the near to medium term for both of these major trading partners.

Mr. HUTCHINSON. Thank you, Mr. Chairman.

Mr. DUNCAN. Thank you, Mr. Hutchinson.

If these issues are not resolved to your satisfaction and the satisfaction of the majority in the Congress, we can come up with legislation that would take some action in that regard.

I'll go back to Mr. Lipinski at this time.

Mr. LIPINSKI. Thank you, Mr. Chairman.

I would certainly support the chairman's remarks in regards to legislation. If we don't get the desired results out of the negotiations, I think it's only right that we members of the Aviation Subcommittee and the full Committee on Transportation and Infrastructure in the House of Representatives wind up weighing in on this particular issue, and I would say that our patience probably is not too extensive on this, so I would recommend we move as quickly as possible in regards to achieving some of the goals we want to achieve with the U.K. and with Japan.

I'd like to get back to a point that was raised over here by my very good friend, Congressman LaHood, about discrimination against United Airlines by the Japanese government.

It seems to me that United is a wonderful airline. It's my home town airline. I fly it back and forth all the time. They're magnificent. But I think that every U.S. carrier could take the same position, and probably they do take the same position, that Japan is discriminating against them. I'm talking about Northwest, FedEx, UPS, American, Delta, just to name a few. I could probably go on, but those are the only ones I'm aware of being interested in going to Japan and going on. I'd like to hear you or Mr. Murphy comment on the expansion of the discrimination.

Mr. MURPHY. Congressman, I think you're right; that is, each of those carriers, and we could probably name a few more, feel that they are not receiving the rights to serve Japan, either that the agreement sets forth or which they ought to be entitled to, especially at a time when we're talking about a country where we have a huge trade imbalance and they're denying more access by our airlines, one sector where we do extremely well. Where we can outcompete the Japanese is in the aviation sector, yet they keep our airlines out of the market. So I agree. From that standpoint, I think our carriers would feel it is discrimination.

Mr. LIPINSKI. Yes. And certainly there are different cases to be made. As far as United goes and Northwest and FedEx, they have an agreement that at one time apparently this country and Japan agreed upon what that agreement meant. That has not been fulfilled as far as U.S. carriers are concerned, the U.S. Government is concerned, and I'm sure the members of this subcommittee are concerned.

Then there are other carriers here who, for their own benefit, for the benefit of this country, for the benefit of consumers, want to get more access to Japan and even beyond rights of Japan.

As I say, they have a different argument to be made. I happen to agree with both arguments, and I think that we should press both causes very strenuously.

I'd like to get back to the agreement on cargo. That agreement was announced shortly before one of our hearings here, and I'll only speak for myself, but I think it was universally supported that we were—I was in a state of euphoria because of the agreement that we were told was reached with the Japanese in regards to cargo, but a gentleman who's sitting behind you, slightly to your left, that particular day—a different Murphy. Those Irish are all over the place. A Cyril Murphy from United Airlines was the only voice of real reason that particular day, and he was not carried away by the euphoria by any means whatsoever.

He said at that time that all we got really was what they had promised us a long, long time ago in an agreement, plus a few routes for UPS.

I have ultimately come to the same conclusion as Mr. Murphy, but he's much more knowledgeable in this area than I, so he came to it very quickly.

But really that agreement in regards to UPS and FedEx, we almost got—we got very little, really, out of that other than what, by agreement, we were entitled to.

Now, I know United Parcel was very happy about it because they finally got some access to Japan, but I don't think that we should give the Japanese any particular points in regards to that agreement.

If you'd like to comment on it, go right ahead and comment on it. If not—

Mr. HUNNICUTT. Well, Mr. Congressman, I would only start by commenting that I've never seen Mr. Cyril Murphy euphoric, but I'm looking forward to the day——

[Laughter.]

Mr. HUNNICUTT.——when I can observe that for myself.

Mr. LIPINSKI. Well, when LaHood was talking about United being discriminated against by Japan he was euphoric at that time.

Mr. HUNNICUTT. But I do want to say that, as I said earlier in my testimony, we were looking for, in the beginning of those negotiations, a cargo liberalization agreement much broader in scope than where we ended up.

On the other hand, we were really pleased that we did have for United and Northwest and FedEx the ability to serve from all points in the United States and to additional points in Japan, and for UPS this was a major agreement to have beyond rights from Japan for their services, and we will select an additional cargo carrier to serve Japan, which was a new element of the cargo deal, as well.

So, while I don't want to say that I disagree with you in that we shouldn't think that the cargo deal was all that it should have been or that we would have hoped for, we do believe it was a useful deal.

Mr. LIPINSKI. But you wouldn't get euphoric over it?

Mr. HUNNICUTT. I would not be euphoric.

Mr. LIPINSKI. For a man who said he wasn't going to get into Japan, I certainly have managed to slide into that. But some of my fellow Illinoisans have led me down that path.

I just have one last question for you two gentlemen.

I am interested in your thoughts on having the U.S. trade representative handle negotiations for the United States in regards to international aviation. Now, I know a lot of people are opposed to that because they say you don't want to talk about aviation and soybeans and things like that, but I counter to say that if the international trade representative handled the negotiations for the United States with Japan and the United Kingdom, particularly in Japan we might not want to talk about soybeans—although, on the other hand, we might want to talk about soybeans. But what we could talk about was automobiles, and I think that that would give us a very significant talking point when it came to automobiles and access to the American market by Japanese automobile manufacturers. Even though they do have a number of transplants here, we still do import a number of automobiles from Japan.

Do either one of you gentlemen have any comments on having the U.S. trade representative taking over our negotiations?

Mr. HUNNICUTT. Congressman, I think maybe both of us can give a quick response, because I bring "no baggage of history" in terms of dealing with this current arrangement of the Department of State other than the last 3 months, and a great deal of history working with the U.S. Trade Representative's office over the years in trade negotiations.

My first reaction to being asked that—and I've been asked once before in front of the Senate subcommittee—was to say that the current structure of having the negotiators operate out of the Department of State versus a structure which would have the negotiations done at the U.S. Trade Representative's office really is a choice between whether you want aviation to be potentially traded off or traded to benefit from or be penalized for geopolitical purposes in terms of the objectives of the negotiators, or do you want it to benefit from or be traded off for potential trade and commercial benefits of the United States.

That's something that I haven't resolved in my own mind in terms of where the greater benefits for aviation come, because there is some protection being somewhat separate, and that protection is it doesn't get traded off for other, less-competitive American industries in the international marketplaces.

On the other hand, the down side is exactly what you've pointed out and exactly what some of your fellow majority members have pointed out by indirection, which is: what leverage do you have for achieving greater good in the aviation world when your only ability to respond is against aviation services and you're really cutting shippers' and passengers' potential choice of services down every time you do that?

So I guess that's somewhat of a non-response, but I hope it gives you the flavor of where my thinking is, because I haven't resolved it.

I will say that, having arrived at the Department now almost 3 months ago, the working relationship between the current team of negotiators at the State Department and the aviation specialists at the Department of Transportation is very good and working very smoothly.

Mr. LIPINSKI. Thank you.

Mr. Murphy, you want to add anything?

Mr. MURPHY. No, sir.

Mr. LIPINSKI. Okay. I want to thank very much Mr. Hunnicutt and Mr. Murphy for their testimony here today. I look forward to working with these gentlemen in the future, and I'm very happy that I got to ask that question before Mr. Aviation, Mr. Oberstar, arrived because I happen to support using the trade representative and Mr. Oberstar is opposed to it.

Have a good day, gentlemen.

Mr. HUNNICUTT. Thank you.

Mr. DUNCAN. All right. Thank you, Mr. Lipinski.

Mr. Hunnicutt, let me ask you—I assume you're familiar with this group headed up by former Governor Baliles, Access: U.S.-Japan, and do you—what do you think about their objectives and really, going from that, does it cause any problems for your Department that there seem to be some divisions between U.S. airlines? Does that cause problems for you in negotiating with some of these other countries?

Mr. HUNNICUTT. I think historically and currently there have been serious divisions within the industry over major issues, and obviously, from someone trying to put a negotiating policy together and a strategy for negotiators to work on, it's very much complicated when you have varying interests in the industry, but that's not unlike many other industries in the United States where some members of the industry import components and other members don't, so that interests end up really being varied, and the role of the government is to discern the greatest national interest.

In terms of Access: U.S.-Japan, we have met with them. As I said earlier, we're working with their study. I've met with the governor to discuss their proposals, and I have found them to be responsible and making responsible arguments. Whether they will prevail in the end in their arguments is another question, but I don't think it's necessarily, at this point, disruptive to have different points of view over an issue that's as important as the U.S.-Japanese aviation relationship and its future development and those views of all of the industry, as well as cities, consumers, shippers, labor, to be taken into account as the Federal Government decides what the policy going forward ought to be.

So yes, it complicates matters to have clear elements within an industry taking different positions. It also complicates it to have some elements of the industry on one position closer to where your negotiating partner may be in terms of their arguments. But I don't see that as irresponsible or an unreasonable position for them to be in.

Mr. DUNCAN. Well, I assume you've been told what we've been told—that they have at least 500 members in all of the 50 States. Have they told you that?

Mr. HUNNICUTT. Congressman, I think the latest figure I heard was at a speech by Governor Baliles to the Aero Club, and it was considerably more than 500.

Mr. DUNCAN. Is it fair to sort of summarize our relationship with Japan by saying that they seem to want free trade in automobiles and other areas, but in one of the few areas where we lead the world, aviation, they want to manage trade and restrictions and capacity limits? Is that accurate?

Mr. HUNNICUTT. Yes, sir. And, I think, as Mr. Murphy tried to indicate, it's particularly galling that they would pick the one area in our economic relationships where we clearly are competitive and succeeding as the one where they want to restrict trade, while continuing to argue for open markets in other areas.

Mr. DUNCAN. All right.

We'll go now to Mr. Weller.

Mr. WELLER. Thank you, Mr. Chairman. I just have one more question I'd direct to Mr. Hunnicutt.

It's my understanding you've had extensive experience with the ITC, been involved in trade issues with the Japanese prior to your current role as an assistant secretary and bring a breadth of experience to this issue.

We're fortunate, with our current situation, as I understand it, we do have a trade balance in our favor, a surplus, when it comes to aviation, with the Japanese. What is that amount right now, the estimated balance in the United States' favor with Japanese?

Mr. HUNNICUTT. Congressman, we know the market share, which is about 62 percent, but I can't give you the current trade balance in dollars, but it's substantial and I will get that to you precisely for 1995.

Mr. WELLER. I'd appreciate that.

[The information received follows:]

Overall, taking into account both passengers and freight, on both scheduled and charter services, United States-Japan represents a $10 billion aviation revenue market. The United States had over a $2 billion revenue advantage in 1995 and in each of the preceding 2 years. During this period, the United States airlines realized a passenger share of over 60 percent and a freight share of well over 50 percent.

Mr. WELLER. I was wondering, what is, overall, just to compare where we've been and where we are now, with the trade balance with the Japanese, where are we today? What's the balance? Whose favor is it in and what's the estimated difference.

Mr. HUNNICUTT. The overall trade balance—I can't give you numbers, but it is still substantially in Japan's favor. It has been declining somewhat and continues to appear to be declining in terms of the overall trade balance, including manufactured goods and services.

Mr. WELLER. Do you know the dollar figure?

Mr. HUNNICUTT. I can't give you the dollar figure, but I can certainly get that for you.

Mr. WELLER. You're saying it's declined over the last 3 years?

Mr. HUNNICUTT. It has declined in most recent periods. I don't know about 1995 over 1994.

Mr. WELLER. Well, what's—from your experience in trade, what was the trade balance 3 years—how long have you been assistant secretary now?

Mr. HUNNICUTT. Three months.

Mr. WELLER. Three months. Prior to that you were with the ITC?

Mr. HUNNICUTT. No. I left the ITC in 1987.

Mr. WELLER. All right. Okay. But 3 years ago what was the trade balance with the Japanese? Do you remember that figure?

Mr. HUNNICUTT. I'll have to get you those numbers.

Mr. WELLER. So you're not sure of that figure and you're not sure of it now, but you think that it's gotten better.

Mr. HUNNICUTT. It has been reduced.

Mr. WELLER. I'm very interested in——

Mr. HUNNICUTT. I will give you the specifics.

Mr. WELLER. I would like to see those specific figures to compare where we've been, where we are now, and also with the aviation sector to see what that trade balance—those would be very helpful.

Mr. HUNNICUTT. I'll be glad to get that. I'm sorry. I didn't know you'd be interested.

Mr. WELLER. Obviously, rooting for the home team, I'd like to see it in our favor.

[The information received follows:]

If one looks at the overall transactions balance with Japan, we had a $60.2 billion deficit in 1995, down from $64.5 billion in 1994, but still more than the $53.3 billion recorded in 1993. Referring specifically to the *trade* balance, if we net out investment income so as to include only trade in goods and services, the deficits are $43.3 billion last year, $52.6 billion in 1994, and $46.7 billion in 1993, so it is indeed the case that the 1995 deficit was lower than either of the preceding 2 years.

Mr. WELLER. From your experience on these issues—and, of course, it's become a real bone of contention with the folks back home in my District. My District is very dependent on international trade. Of course, major manufacturers such as Caterpillar and petrochemicals and plastics in my District, but also agriculture, so trade issues, in general, are very, very important to me, and particularly our trade opportunities with the Japanese.

Just from your experience, looking back to your experience prior to being assistant secretary before 3 months ago, and also going back to your ITC days experience, do you think that the Japanese government believes the United States lacks the political will to defend the rights of its air carriers today?

Mr. HUNNICUTT. Congressman, I'll say I got a similar question related earlier and feel that they shouldn't. I think, based on the Federal Express cargo order that was issued last summer, in preparation for taking down Japanese service in order to defend Federal Express' rights; I think the response that we've given most recently in not approving Japanese applications for increased service based on their denial of pending U.S. applications for services that U.S. carriers are entitled to; that the signal is out there for the Japanese to read pretty clearly that we intend to vigorously defend the rights of our carriers.

As I said earlier, I think that they're making a serious political miscalculation if they are looking at the United States as a paper tiger in terms of defending aviation rights.

Mr. WELLER. Mr. Murphy, do you want to add to that?

Mr. MURPHY. No, sir.

Mr. WELLER. All right. So, as I understand from your testimony, you're standing firm, and that the Japanese should not expect you to back down from your position?

Mr. HUNNICUTT. That's correct.

Mr. WELLER. Okay. Thank you, Mr. Hunnicutt. Mr. Chairman, thanks for the courtesy of a second go-round.

Mr. DUNCAN. Well, thank you. And I might say that the trade deficit last year with Japan was $60 billion, which most economists say conservatively translates into a loss of 20,000 jobs per billion, which would—that was with just Japan. I don't know what it was 3 years ago, but it was $60 billion last year.

Mr. WELLER. And, if the chairman would yield, how many jobs?

Mr. DUNCAN. Conservatively, most economists say a minimum of 20,000 jobs per billion, so that would be 1,200,000 jobs lost just last year in that trade imbalance.

Mr. WELLER. Thank you, Mr. Chairman.

Mr. DUNCAN. Thank you.

We're always pleased to have with us the former chairman of this subcommittee and the ranking member of the full committee, and a man whom all of us consider to be the real aviation expert in the Congress, Mr. Oberstar.

Mr. OBERSTAR. Thank you very much, Mr. Chairman, again for your very kind and thoughtful words. Let me return the compliment by appreciating the work that you have done and the diligence you have invested in the issue of aviation in all of its aspects and the quick study you have done in your very judicious manner in conducting the hearings.

I very much appreciate and strongly support your continuation of hearings on international aviation trade policy. These hearings and—this subject matter is of great importance not just to the airlines, to the communities they serve, to the airports out of which they operate, to the employees of the airlines, to the traveling public. And the policies we develop are important to our international trading partners, as well.

I'm not going to repeat, because I've said it earlier at the outset of these hearings, my overall view on U.S. policy in international aviation trade, on cargo and passengers.

I just want to say that I am very pleased with the statement that you prepared, Mr. Hunnicutt, for today's hearings. If you continue to take the sound advice of Mr. Murphy you'll do very well in this position.

I also am very pleased with Secretary Peña's continuing support of movement toward international liberalization of aviation trade, and especially that we not put aviation trade rights on the bargaining table with other trade issues. If ever aviation trade becomes a part of a broader negotiating scheme in which we are thrown in with crackers, hotel rooms, automobiles, eucalyptus oil, all of which are part of the broad U.S. trade talks that we've undergone in the general agreement of tariffs and trades of the World Trade Organization, aviation will be swallowed up and spit out like little pieces.

Valuable rights which we have worked and negotiated to build a U.S. preeminence in virtually every market but two in the world will quickly be traded away for beads and blankets, as we did with the Native Americans 100 years ago.

Mr. LIPINSKI. Would the gentleman yield for one second?

Mr. OBERSTAR. I'd be happy to yield to my good friend.

Mr. LIPINSKI. I was talking to the chairman over there. I assume you're talking about the U.S. trade representative.

Mr. OBERSTAR. I didn't say anything about him yet.

[Laughter.]

Mr. LIPINSKI. I just felt it was coming. I wanted to make sure that it was coming, because I wanted to listen intently. Thank you, sir, for yielding.

Mr. OBERSTAR. To throw our international aviation trade to the tender and uninformed mercies and untrained disposal of the U.S. trade representative would be a serious mistake.

Mr. LIPINSKI. Would the gentleman yield for just one moment?

Mr. OBERSTAR. I'd be happy to yield.

Mr. LIPINSKI. But my complete plan here is, after we get aviation into that position, I'm going to speak to the President to appoint you to it, and then we'll have no problems whatsoever.

[Laughter.]

Mr. LIPINSKI. On top of that, there will be one less person ahead of me on this full committee.

[Laughter.]

Mr. OBERSTAR. You know, years ago when Eisenhower was President he was looking around for a Secretary of Defense and he looked at Carl Vincent, who was chairman of the House Armed Services Committee, and he called Mr. Vincent and pleaded with him to take over the position of Secretary of Defense.

Vincent thought about it over the weekend and he called Eisenhower back on Monday and he said, "Thank you, Mr. President, but I'd rather run the Pentagon from the Hill."

[Laughter.]

Mr. OBERSTAR. I'd rather run U.S. trade policy from here, if you don't mind.

Restrictive aviation trade agreements always mean foregone economic opportunities. You've concluded a study of what the effects have been of liberalizing our agreement with Canada—a role in which this subcommittee played a very significant part 5 years ago in getting those talks started, and then they slacked and went back again, but we've supported that liberalization agreement.

Has the Department done an analysis of the dollar value on foregone opportunities because of our restrictive agreements with the U.K. and Japan?

Mr. HUNNICUTT. Congressman, we have, as you'll see in my prepared statement, we are looking at the studies that have been prepared on the value of the rights under the bilateral agreement, fifth freedoms, and third and fourth, with Japan, but to my knowledge I have not seen and am not aware of any particular Department of Transportation analysis of the cost incurred by the restrictive nature of the agreements. No, sir.

Mr. OBERSTAR. I think that would be a useful study and one that would be well worth considering and undertaking. I think it strengthens our hand in dealing—in pushing for more open liberalized trade agreements.

One of your policies is to, in effect, surround protectionist countries with open skies agreements. That was something I advocated in a talk that I gave in Brussels in 1991, that the way to penetrate the European cartel mentality is to not necessarily surround, but to select a partner with which, in the European Community, to negotiate a liberalized agreement. Once that would be done, it would be difficult for other countries to resist negotiating, particularly the U.K., a more liberalized agreement.

We picked out a very small partner, the Netherlands, and that worked to a very small degree, but didn't have much effect at all on the British.

Now we've negotiated under this Administration an agreement with a much bigger partner, Germany. It still hasn't had much effect on the British.

Maybe that policy doesn't work with a major economic force with Japan, but it's something that we need to consider and we need to develop a strategy for dealing with a force such as Japan that you can't easily circumvent and can't go around. You can't, in cargo trade, for example, just go to Singapore and pick up enough business on a 747 freighter to make that service valuable. You have to top that trade off in Japan.

So the beyond rights that we own with Japan are extremely valuable, and opening up that market beyond Japan is extremely important to us. And developing strategies that lead to opening that market without sacrificing existing rights, certainly without sacrificing the 1952 treaty right carriers, has to be a central part of our trading strategy.

Mr. Hunnicutt, would you like to respond to that?

Mr. HUNNICUTT. Congressman, I guess I could respond by saying, "Yes, sir."

Mr. OBERSTAR. That's sufficient. Thank you.

[Laughter.]

Mr. OBERSTAR. I think the chairman wants to go on with other witnesses, and I very much appreciate and wish you well in your endeavors. Welcome to the committee. We hope you'll spend a lot of time here.

Mr. HUNNICUTT. Thank you, sir.

Mr. DUNCAN. Thank you very much, Mr. Oberstar.

We're always pleased to have the chairman of the full committee, Mr. Shuster, with us. He is certainly one of the most active and involved chairmen in this entire Congress, and I think even in the history of the Congress.

Mr. Shuster, do you have any statement or comments or questions at this time?

Mr. SHUSTER. Thank you, Mr. Chairman. I just want to congratulate you and the ranking member for proceeding with what I think are extremely vital hearings. I am deeply distressed by what I believe to be an abrogation of agreements by our Japanese trading partners, and I believe that, unless we can get a comfort level that agreements are going to be adhered to, then this Congress is going to have to consider taking legislative action.

Thank you.

Mr. DUNCAN. Well, thank you. That backs up something I said just a few minutes ago. I know that when Chairman Shuster speaks on transportation and infrastructure issues, not only this country listens but people throughout the world listen, as well, so I appreciate that.

Mr. Geren?

Mr. GEREN. Thank you, Mr. Chairman. I apologize for missing the testimony earlier. I'm in between two markups. I had one that started at 1:30 and one that's just now starting at 3:30, so I hope

I'm not going to be repeating some of the questions that have already been asked, Mr. Hunnicutt.

I know you all talked at some length about the Japan issue, as well as the U.S.-U.K., and I guess just kind of an overview question: Mr. Hunnicutt, what progress would you say that DOT has made since last June on United States-U.K. aviation relations? What's been happening since June when things started coming apart?

Mr. HUNNICUTT. I guess I would say that I can't report any concrete success or advances. What I can say is we have re-engaged following the implementation of the first interim agreement, which had some liberalizing and goodwill gestures in it.

Since the breakdown of the discussions in October, really there hasn't been a great deal of activity. Since I've come into the job I have re-engaged the British in some informal discussions, going to London once and telephonically, to explore parameters of where we may be able to find flexibility that would allow us to go forward with a second interim arrangement of liberalizations.

We're not yet ready to engage in formal discussions based on those conversations, but I'm cautiously optimistic that we'll make some headway.

Mr. GEREN. Is it still a top priority for DOT?

Mr. HUNNICUTT. The U.S.-U.K. and U.S.-Japan aviation relationships are the highest priority for the Department of Transportation.

Mr. GEREN. You say you've had some discussions and nothing tangible or nothing concrete. Do you have any kind of a time table that we could look towards that you expect something happening?

Mr. HUNNICUTT. No, sir. I don't have a specific time table, although, as I said earlier, I'm hoping that in the shorter term we will be able to make some progress on an interim arrangement, short of a full-scale liberalization, and hopefully to move forward toward larger liberalization measures in the medium term.

Mr. GEREN. I know it's impossible to answer a question like this with any certainty, but on the shorter term are we talking about by the end of this year? What kind of—it just seems like negotiations that don't have any time limits imposed upon them just seem to drift and drift and drift, and time is not on our side. Time is on their side.

Mr. HUNNICUTT. Right. I think that the issue of the drift is unrelated to not having a date certain for completion; it's more related to the ability of the British to talk to us about the issues of liberalization that have to be on the table.

I'm hopeful that the commercial realities not only of the changing North Atlantic market, based on the open skies arrangements that are beginning to really change the marketing structure, and the positions of the British carriers in terms of what they hope to achieve commercially, will, within the matter of months, lead to agreement on at least interim measures for liberalization.

Mr. GEREN. And that's as specific as you feel like you can get at the present time?

Mr. HUNNICUTT. Yes. I'm sorry. I don't want to be evasive, but I just don't have any indication at this point of timing.

Mr. GEREN. But it's specific as far as specific measures, too, as well, that you all are pushing or negotiating angles that you feel like you might have? Is there——

Mr. HUNNICUTT. Well, I wouldn't want to talk about any negotiating angles, but the issues that were on the table at the time of the breakdown of discussions in October were, of course, Heathrow access for U.S. carriers, cargo liberalization, fly America provisions that the British were interested in, dispute settlement mechanisms that the British were interested in. Those were the areas of discussion that——

Mr. GEREN. Yes. I'm very well aware of the areas of discussion, but I'm thinking more in terms of what things you all are doing specifically to advance the American position in the negotiations in regard to those issues.

Mr. HUNNICUTT. Obviously, I don't want to get into specifics. What we have done is tried to find where we thought there was more flexibility on those issues than we had at the time the discussions broke down and tried to help the British find more flexibility on their side on those issues at the time the discussions broke down.

Mr. GEREN. All right. Thank you, Mr. Chairman.

Mr. DUNCAN. Thank you, Mr. Geren.

Mr. Ehlers?

Mr. EHLERS. No questions, Mr. Chairman.

Mr. DUNCAN. All right. Well, thank you very much, Secretary Hunnicutt, Secretary Murphy. We appreciate very much your being with us today.

We'll move on to the second panel at this time and ask those panel members to come forward, please.

The second panel—and we're very pleased to have this very distinguished panel before us—consists of: Mr. Gerald Greenwald, chairman and chief executive officer of United Airlines; Mr. Cyrus F. Freidheim, Jr., vice chairman of Booze Allen & Hamilton; Mr. Jeffrey Fegan, who is the executive director of Dallas-Fort Worth International Airport, accompanied by Kevin Cox, the deputy executive director of the Dallas-Fort Worth International Airport.

I want to welcome all of you here today.

Mr. Geren, I believe you have a statement you want to make at this time.

Mr. GEREN. Thank you, Mr. Chairman. I appreciate your letting me proceed out of order. As I mentioned, we're in the middle of markup on the authorization bill for the National Security Committee, and I'm going to have to go back to the markup, but I wanted to welcome Jeff Fegan and Kevin Cox to the committee today and thank them for their excellent work. I've had a chance to review the testimony, and just once again want to express our appreciation to you for the great work you do for the aviation community in this country and the help you've given this committee.

Welcome to Washington. I look forward to continuing to work with you.

Thank you, Mr. Chairman.

Mr. DUNCAN. Thank you, Mr. Geren.

I suppose what we'll do is we'll just go right down the table, and so, Mr. Freidheim, we'll start with you and then go to Mr. Greenwald and then Mr. Fegan and proceed in that manner.

Mr. Freidheim.

TESTIMONY OF GERALD GREENWALD, CHAIRMAN AND CEO, UNITED AIRLINES, INC.; CYRUS F. FREIDHEIM, JR., VICE CHAIRMAN, BOOZ ALLEN & HAMILTON, INC.; AND JEFFREY P. FEGAN, EXECUTIVE DIRECTOR, DALLAS-FORT WORTH INTERNATIONAL AIRPORT, ACCOMPANIED BY KEVIN COX, DEPUTY EXECUTIVE DIRECTOR

Mr. FREIDHEIM. Thank you, Mr. Chairman and Representative Lipinski and members of the subcommittee. It's always an honor to be invited to appear before the committees of our Congress.

As indicated, I am Cyrus Freidheim. I'm a vice chairman of Booz Allen & Hamilton, which is a management and technology consulting firm. We have over 6,000 employees and 100 offices worldwide and we work in a number of industries, and particularly extensively in the airline industry, both the United States and abroad.

Mr. Chairman, I would like to place this report dated today into the record. My comments will summarize the conclusions that are in the report.

Mr. DUNCAN. That report will be placed in the record. Thank you.

Mr. FREIDHEIM. Thank you.

Last summer we were asked by United Airlines to analyze the value of the beyond rights that U.S. passenger airlines were accorded by the air service agreement of 1952 between the United States and Japan.

We did this by estimating and projecting the revenue and profits for the U.S. carriers and the impact on the U.S.-Japan trade balance under three scenarios: first, full utilization of beyond rights, which is the ability of carriers to use Japanese cities as hubs to serve other Asian cities; second, elimination of those rights; and, third, limiting the beyond rights to those Asian cities served by U.S. carriers today through Japan.

Our overall conclusions were the following:

First, that beyond rights have great value to the two U.S. carriers, United and Northwest Airlines, that had these rights. We estimated the value at between $4 and $5.5 billion, based on the discounted value of the earning stream from these routes.

We included, of course, only the routes affected by beyond rights, so that is those that used the Japanese cities as hubs.

The value loss by limiting these rights to Asian cities currently served is computed at about $2.5 to $4 billion. It is important to recognize that, long-term, the cities currently served will have less need for the Japanese hub since the markets will merit direct flights from the U.S.; hence, the value of beyond rights is greater for cities net yet served than for cities currently being served through the Japanese hubs.

The impact on the U.S. balance of trade we estimated to be about $100 billion cumulatively over the next 20 years. This reflects the lost revenues by United and Northwest caused by the elimination of those beyond rights.

Now, it's important to understand how we arrived at these numbers. We used passenger forecasts by Iota and modified them only slightly through our own analysis and some other sources. Passenger growth between the United States and Japan is projected at 6 percent. Growth from the U.S. to other Asian cities varies from 6 percent for cities like Singapore to 15 percent for cities like Beijing, Shanghai, and Ho Chi Minh. The average for the U.S.-non-Japan cities from the United States is to grow at about 9 percent. We ought to remark that this is the highest growth rate of any area in the world.

We project yields or prices to decline in real terms at the rate of about 3.5 percent per year for the U.S.-Japan routes over the next 10 years and 3 percent thereafter, and yields for the U.S.-Asian routes to decline at about 3 percent annually. These projections are in line with the experience that we've seen over the last 10 years on the heavily-competitive routes between U.S. and Europe.

We concluded that the best solution for the consumer, the countries involved, and the carriers is open skies. We also concluded that trading beyond rights for added flights between U.S. and Japan is a very bad deal for consumers, for the U.S., and in net, in total, for the U.S. airline industry.

The group, Access: U.S.-Japan, questioned our conclusions. They claimed the following:

One, that additional flights between U.S. and Japan had substantial value, much greater than the unexercised beyond rights of the two carriers, United and Northwest.

Secondly, that U.S. communities would benefit by $9 billion annually.

Third, that prices between the U.S. and Japan are artificially high, 20 to 60 percent over the U.S. European routes, and that added competition would cause prices between U.S. and Japan to drop substantially.

They concluded that the U.S.-Japan market is grossly underserved compared with the U.S.-European market, and that passenger traffic would be stimulated by a large amount if more competition and prices were allowed to decline.

And that we've vastly overstated the value of the unexercised beyond rights. Why, they ask, don't United and Northwest serve these beyond cities now if they're so valuable.

Finally, that the impact on the balance of trade was not a traditional way of valuing air transportation rights and therefore shouldn't be included in the analysis.

Well, if only Access: U.S.-Japan were right, we could immediately accede to the Japanese demands to stop granting the rights guaranteed by the 1952 air service agreement and ultimately stop U.S. carriers from using Japanese cities as hubs to Asia, and we'd all be better off, and what a terrific win/win solution.

Unfortunately, this is not the case. Let me discuss each of these issues.

First, the core of the argument is that U.S.-Japan routes are under-served and over-priced. They claim that U.S.-Japan should have many more passengers, based on a comparison if U.S.-U.K. passenger travel. They compared populations and GNPs among the two countries with available seat capacity and, since Japan is larger and has a higher GNP than the U.K., they should have, therefore, more air service, but, in fact, the answer is the reverse.

Using this argument, the U.S. should have 10 times its current service with Spain and 50 to 300 times as many flights to China today. We don't believe that argument holds.

Secondly, the best measure of adequacy of service is what is called the "load factor." That's the percentage of seats that are actually occupied on average over time at a comparable price.

The U.S.-Japan load factors are, in fact, lower than the U.S.-European load factors—73 percent for U.S.-Japan and 76 to 78 percent for the United States to Europe. We'll demonstrate in a moment the prices, in fact, are comparable.

Access: U.S.-Japan claims that the additional competition will cause prices to drop by 25 to 40 percent, which will unleash large, pent-up demand across the Pacific.

We certainly agree that a 40 percent real price reduction would stimulate plenty of tourism in Japan and the U.S.; unfortunately, it would bankrupt any carrier which added substantial capacity at those fares.

Access: U.S.-Japan's argument is based on the assumption that U.S.-Japan prices are artificially high; that they are 25 to 60 percent higher on a per mile basis than the U.S.-European fares. This is partly true for published fares. Fortunately for consumers, they actually pay far less than published fares.

In fact, our data shows that actual fares paid—again, on a per mile basis—for discounted travelers are 15 percent lower for U.S.-Japan than for the U.S. and Europe in season, and about 15 percent higher off-season. Business class fares, in fact, are lower for the U.S.-Japan than the U.S.-Europe in all seasons.

Interestingly, the same round trip purchased in Japan is substantially higher than purchased in the U.S. JAL sets the pricing in Japan. JAL has a substantially higher cost than U.S. carriers—somewhere between 50 and 100 percent—and hence charge higher fares.

This is important to note, because without U.S. competition consumers can rightfully expect higher fares from Japanese carriers, and JAL, in particular.

We have projected a real decline in the average fares between the U.S. and Europe of 3.5 percent, as I indicated earlier, for the next 10 years, which will result in fares in the year 2005 30 percent lower than they are today, and 10 years from now, that's 1 year later, it would be 40 percent.

These projections follow the experience of the tightly-competitive U.S.-European routes. There is plenty of challenge for U.S. carriers to continually improve their productivity to be profitable with declining prices of that magnitude.

We also believe that our projection of 6 percent growth in passengers between the U.S. and Japan is realistic and further stimulation probably will not result in significantly higher growth rates. The bulk of the growth will come from vacation travel, business opportunities, rather than low fares to determine how often people travel for business.

Hence, we stand by our projections of volume growth and price declines.

Now let us examine the value of unexercised rights. Japan, as I think we all know, is a natural hub to Asia. It's on the great circle route to most Asian cities from the United States. It has a large population which travels—the largest in Asia. It is an excellent location to consolidate passengers from Asian cities headed for the U.S. and U.S. passengers headed for Asia. Tokyo and Osaka, in fact, rate number one and number two as Asian destinations and hubs from the U.S.

U.S. carriers add service to Asian cities, when potential traffic volume permits, three flights per week. This is the basis on which they decide which city is next—from that city to the Asian hub, Tokyo or Osaka. These passengers then board the U.S. flights that are already there to the United States to the city of their choice.

The U.S. carriers add direct nonstop service to Asian cities when the potential traffic merits three round trips from the United States to that city per week.

Markets are built first by serving a city through a hub, and later providing direct service as the market grows. Even when direct nonstop service is provided, carriers continue to serve the city through the hub to offer more options to the consumer; that is, if they continue that they'll have—when they get the three times per week direct service, they'll continue three or four times a week through the hub city and you'll wind up with daily service.

It's interesting to note that no U.S. carriers provide direct service to Asian cities—other than Japan and one to Korea—without accompanying hub service through Japan. The economics, the market, and the customer service just don't work without the hub.

The cities not now served—take Pusan as an example—do not yet have sufficient traffic to provide service through Japan to the U.S. Now, in the case of Pusan, in 2005 it will, and in 2010 it will merit direct service to the U.S., along with the hub service from Japan.

The vast Asian market is coming to fruition in the next 15 years. Projections call for Asia to become the largest international air transport market in the next 20 to 25 years.

U.S. carriers must be well-positioned to capture their share of that market. Japanese hubs are key to U.S. competitiveness, and that is why the unexercised beyond rights are so valuable—more valuable than the currently-exercised rights.

Much of the travel to cities currently being served through Japan will be provided directly from U.S. cities in the next 10 years.

Finally, the impact on U.S. communities and the economy—Access: U.S.-Japan projects a $9 billion economic advantage for U.S. communities by adding more U.S.-Japan flights. Their estimate is based on a multiplier of $7,000 per added passenger and 1.3 million additional passengers.

Our research has concluded that most economists believe that multiplier to be closer to $4,000 or $5,000, and we use the ESI—the Economic Strategy Institute—number of $4,300 in computing our impact.

Secondly, the Access: U.S.-Japan assumed that a high incremental volume—that's the 1.3 million passengers with no offset. We computed that about 700,000 incremental passengers would be stimulated if you dropped prices by an additional 10 percent beyond the—as I said, in 10 years—36 percent that we've already got—in other words, a 45 to 47 percent price reduction—would give us about 10 percent additional passengers, and that would be about 700,000.

On that basis, and using our $4,300 multiplier, we get a net positive impact of about $3 billion. That is if there is no offset. If all that happens is the Japanese allow us a whole bunch of additional flights between the United States and Japan. The likelihood of that happening is, frankly, not high.

If, however, U.S. beyond rights were limited in trade for those added U.S.-Japan flights, the loss of passengers from the U.S.-Japan to Japanese carriers and the consequent drop in U.S. employment would more than offset the benefit of added passengers to U.S. communities. Our report documents those conclusions.

I don't know how to respond to the Access: U.S.-Japan's comment that balance of trade has no role in these discussions. We do, and the numbers, as I indicated earlier, are very, very large.

Two other points are relevant. First, what is the impact of code sharing on these results? Secondly, in our view, what is Japan's strategy and what is in the best interest of the United States?

First, code sharing—code sharing is good for consumers, for countries, for the industry. Code sharing enables one reservation, more-convenient connections, more-reliable baggage service, broader use of frequent flier miles, more options. It enables carriers to serve more cities without supporting low-yield routes or battling for positions in tough markets.

Code sharing, however, is not a replacement for economic on-line service through a hub—not for the consumer, not for the carrier, not for the countries involved.

Pricing on the leg controlled by the other airline—in this case the Japanese carrier—can and probably will be much higher. The U.S. carriers in those cases lose the revenue on the code-shared leg, and the country of the carrier loses in balance of trade and employment—big losses and, as we indicated with our numbers, far overshadowing any value that we get by additional flights between U.S. and Japan.

We support market development through code sharing, as does the Department of Transportation, but not in trade for on-line service.

Finally, Japan's position—in our view, to determine what the U.S. posture should be in negotiations with Japan on air transportation rights, it's important to understand Japan's position.

We believe their interests are clear and well-documented publicly: first, to gain greater control over its most-rapidly-growing market—Asia, Japan—and to benefit fully from the growth and provide Japanese airlines a basis of profitability.

Japan's solution: to limit low cost—that is, U.S. carrier competition in that market—as much as possible.

Secondly, to maximize the value of its natural Asian hub, which they view, quite correctly, as a national asset to Japan, and to use that hub to capture a significant share of the rapidly-growing U.S.-Asian market.

Japan's solution: limit or eliminate the right of U.S. carriers to use Japanese cities as hubs.

Third, limit the losses across the Pacific where Japanese carriers are reportedly losing money. As I indicated, their costs are somewhere between 50 and 100 percent higher than the efficient U.S. carriers.

Japan's solution: limit open skies competition with substantially lower-cost U.S. carriers.

Japan's strategy: argue that the U.S. 1952 agreement is unbalanced and should be equalized. Curtail United and Northwest rights to use Japanese hubs to serve Asian cities, which will also result in the reduction of U.S.-Japan flights for those carriers because they don't have the passengers going beyond. And additional MOU rights—those carriers other than United and Northwest—would be granted between the U.S. and Japan, along with added Japanese rights which would, in effect, replace United and Northwest flights and substantially weaken their two strongest competitors, especially if code sharing arrangements can assure that a high proportion of the remaining U.S.-Asian market connects through Japan.

So their solution is quite clear and, frankly, it's in their best interest to pursue this in a very, very hard fashion. They are, as was indicated earlier, now in a balance of trade deficit position with the United States. I believe it's one of the only major—it may be the largest deficit position they have in any industry. Our numbers tell us—to answer the question that somebody asked earlier—it was $4.8 billion last year and growing.

The United States should equally understand its interests. Air transportation is one of the few industries in which the U.S. enjoys a trade surplus with Japan. This surplus will grow if the 1952 agreement is followed. Simply, it will decline or be eliminated if hub rights in Japan are restricted or eliminated and jobs follow. In our estimate, by the year 2015 some 80,000 to 100,000 jobs would be lost if these rights were curtailed.

U.S. carriers currently have a major share of the U.S.-Japan and U.S.-Asian market, somewhere between 60 and 70 percent. These markets are the fastest-growing markets in the world. That share advantage is routed in the hub rights in Japan and U.S. carriers that are substantially more efficient than their Japanese competitors, the reverse of many other industries in which our countries compete.

Third, the U.S. business and vacation travelers are, in fact, well served to Japan and Asia, fares and load factors, as travelers are to Europe. U.S. carriers must aggressively add flights and reduce costs to maintain that share and profitability in those markets which are growing, as we indicated, at 6 percent for Japan and 9 percent for elsewhere, and prices are expected to decline at the rate of 3 percent.

Finally, the best solution, in our view, for the U.S. across the Pacific is open skies. Unlimited rights to serve any market by any airline and build hubs wherever economically justified would enable U.S. carriers to utilize their substantial competitive advantages. Elimination or limitation to the use of the Japan hubs by U.S. car-

24-087 97 - 8

riers is a step in the opposite direction and plays directly into the strategy to alter the competitive field to their advantage.

Thank you.

Mr. DUNCAN. Thank you very much, Mr. Freidheim.

Mr. DUNCAN. We'll go next to Mr. Greenwald.

Let me just say first of all, though, there apparently is some sort of misunderstanding, or at least a misimpression, that the subcommittee rescheduled this hearing just to accommodate Mr. Greenwald and to disadvantage certain other carriers, and that did not happen. I would always be pleased to have anybody who wants to testify in front of this committee to testify. At all the hearings we've held, we've had far more people who have wanted to testify than we've been able to accommodate, but we've always made sure that all viewpoints and all sides are well-represented.

Mr. Menendez, who is a good friend of mine and who has been an outstanding member of this subcommittee, but who is not here at this time, sent a statement in which he said that—he says, "I am wondering why an entire facet of this issue is being excluded from the chance to testify. It appears that American, Continental, Delta, and Access: U.S.-Japan have been scheduled out of appearing. I think this is grossly unfair, and I hope that they will have another hearing opportunity."

I can say publicly that if we have enough interest to have another hearing, then we will schedule another hearing at an appropriate time. This subcommittee has held, I'm told, more hearings than any other subcommittee in the entire Congress, I believe, over the last year and 4 months. And we'll hold another hearing if it seems appropriate to do so. These are important issues.

But we certainly did not exclude anybody from testifying.

Mr. SHUSTER. Would the chairman yield?

Mr. DUNCAN. Yes, sir.

Mr. SHUSTER. It's my understanding that other carriers were invited to testify this morning.

Mr. DUNCAN. That's correct.

Mr. SHUSTER. Is that right?

Mr. DUNCAN. That's correct.

Mr. SHUSTER. And they chose not to appear. Thank you.

Mr. LIPINSKI. Mr. Chairman?

Mr. DUNCAN. Yes?

Mr. LIPINSKI. I would simply like to state that the chairman of this subcommittee has always gone out of his way to accommodate any requests that people have made to testify before this subcommittee. I am very disappointed that some other people who had expressed an interest in testifying were not able to adjust their schedule to come and testify here today. I hope that maybe at some time in the future, if we have a window of opportunity, they might be able to have another opportunity to testify.

But I want to state very, very strongly that the chairman of this subcommittee has always gone out of his way to accommodate people, and I don't think that a great deal of weight should be given to a statement by anyone saying that people were somehow deliberately prevented from testifying.

As many people probably know, I am a very good friend of the chairman of one of America's great airlines, Mr. Bob Crandall. He wanted to testify. We tried to accommodate him. Unfortunately, the scheduling just did not work out for him. But he does stand ready if we schedule another hearing to come and testify once again, Mr. Chairman, and I'm sure if we have that opportunity that you will see to it that it is worked out.

Mr. DUNCAN. Well, thank you, Mr. Lipinski. I'm not upset with anyone. All I was trying to do was—I think that I have a very good relationship with all of the airlines, and certainly we're not attempting to exclude people. We want to have a good airing of views on all of these issues. But we'll proceed at this time now with Mr. Greenwald.

Mr. Greenwald, thank you very much for being patient and being here with us today.

Mr. GREENWALD. Thank you very much, Chairman Duncan and Representative Lipinski and members of the subcommittee.

I'll make my comments brief, I hope to the point.

In my view, today the subcommittee is addressing a very, very major issue. In my view, the outcome of this issue will set a pattern in a number of ways: first, for air travel between the U.S. and many Asian nations; second, air travel to and from Japan; third, trade relations with a major economic impact well beyond air travel between Japan and the U.S.

As you've heard, the fastest-growing and largest air travel market in the world is developing before our eyes. For U.S. carriers, the geography is too far for nonstops as of now, and for some markets is too thin for nonstops.

Service hubs in Japan are essential to U.S. entry into Asia.

The Ministry of Transport—MOT—of Japan would have us believe the deep Asian market should be reserved for Japanese carriers. Would you believe the U.K. if they laid claim to the Russian-U.S. market as theirs? Why should we surrender the Asian market because Japan claims the right to Shanghai or Seoul or Singapore or Jakarta?

United, Northwest, and in the cargo sector FedEx, have existing rights based on an agreement between the U.S. and Japan to fly deep into Asia, take passengers or cargo, land in Japan, and go on to the United States.

Now, over the years the agreements, like I suppose most subjective of this kind, tend to use language that is best understood by those who write the agreements. We talk of beyond rights and third freedoms and fifth freedoms and so on. But I tend to bring it down to an example.

Picture one Indonesian citizen in Jakarta, the capital. Picture another, who is a U.S. citizen. And picture a third, who is a Japanese citizen. Why should the Japanese carriers lay unique claim to transporting those three people from Indonesia to Japan and on to the United States? It makes no sense.

Why should they choose to unilaterally refuse to comply the existing agreements? Well, my suspicion is they want to protect their Japanese carriers from competition. In my view, this is not good relations with our country, it is not good for the U.S. consumers nor the Japanese consumers, and peculiarly not even good for the Japanese carriers.

Other Asian carriers are growing and prospering under the heat of competition—in fact, because of competition. Simply put, Japan is trying to win through regulation the advantage that they are losing in the competitive marketplace.

Japan is unilaterally not complying with an agreement. The implications are: first, a severe rupture in basic international relations. I state the obvious. If two countries sign an agreement and one ignores it, then international agreements, themselves, are in jeopardy.

Second, the U.S. will lose, by the year 2010, about $5 billion a year in trade and about 100,000 jobs. Booz Allen, as you've heard, and Clyde Prestowitz of the Economic Strategy Institute, have both completed studies with similar conclusions.

There are those in the U.S., particularly American and Delta and former Virginia Governor Baliles, who think differently on this subject than I do. American and Delta argue they want to fly from the U.S. to Japan. Their view goes, "Let's have talks with Japan and agree to trade off some of United or Northwest deep Asia routes, the beyond rights, for some additional U.S.-to-Japan rights for American and Delta."

In other words, American and Delta are ready to reward Japan's intransigence by trading away rights that belong to their chief U.S. competitors, and they cloak this travesty in the red, white, and blue rhetoric of free trade.

How do we get in this situation? Our U.S. competitors, in my view, are playing right into Japan's hands. A route from the U.S. to Japan is worth less for the U.S. than beyond rights. The Japanese would love that swap. Most of the passenger traffic from deep Asia would come into Japan on Japanese carriers and conveniently continue on Japanese carriers to the U.S. Only United and Northwest, as of today, have rights to compete on an equal footing head-to-head out of Asia with the Japanese carriers.

Governor Baliles argues, "Let's all speak with one voice in the U.S. and be good guys and start talking with the Japanese and ignore that they, the Japanese, are unilaterally violating existing international agreements."

Mr. Chairman, I ask you: how can the U.S. ignore this violation and expect to negotiate a fair agreement after that? How can the U.S. cave in on airline issues and then expect Japan not to press for concessions in literally every other trade sector?

I'm told some of our opponents argue that United and Northwest are using the Japanese violation as an excuse to avoid opening the market. First, that is dead wrong. Second, it is a distraction.

The Japanese are refusing United the right to fly tomorrow from Los Angeles to Narita. And why not, if there is no penalty for them doing so?

Tell me about trade relations of any type between our nations in that kind of climate. Can we count on them?

I want to take a couple of minutes more and take you through a couple of charts, and then I'll sum up.

The first chart is my way of describing to you how successfully Japan—and I might add, the U.K.—historically have been in micromanaging our trade relations in the airline industry, and what this chart shows is that, as a result of regulatory constraints, Chicago, which is our major international city, our largest hub—international I mean for international flying—does not offer very many international flights. Compare United's 14 percent in Chicago to American's 81 percent in Dallas or TWA's 100 percent from St. Louis.

Similarly, of the top 15 international carriers outside the U.S., all are the leading international operators out of their largest domestic hub. Through the—well, I was about to say "unpleasant," but, nevertheless, through some history that for me isn't very pleasant, we are restricted in the frequencies we can fly out of O'Hare/Chicago both to the U.K. and to Japan today.

Let me move on for a moment to the next chart.

Mr. DUNCAN. Mr. Greenwald, let me interrupt you just for a second. Does this mean the percentage of international flights that each of the airlines has out of these hub cities? What is the—I'm not clear.

Mr. GREENWALD. Thank you, Mr. Chairman. I need to be clearer about it. It says that, of all the international flying out of O'Hare, United does 14 percent of it, though we are by far the largest carrier out of O'Hare. That is not our preference, it is our restriction. That was the point I was trying to make.

The second chart is to emphasize again with a chart the point I made earlier—that since 1978 the Asian carriers in countries that have liberal aviation policies with the United States and other countries—Korea and Taiwan and Singapore- have more than doubled their share of the U.S.-Asia market and nearly tripled their share of the global market.

During this same period, the Japanese carriers, with their restrictive policies, have lost nearly half of their share of the U.S.-Asia market and have not grown at all in the global market over the past 18 years.

If I've ever seen a vote for open competition, there it is.

The third point I want to make is: from a study that has been done in Japan, United commissioned Mitsubishi Research Institute, a leading economic research institute in Japan, to study the impact of U.S. carriers' competition on Japanese consumers.

Their study shows that, with U.S. carriers competing beyond Japan, fares are reduced by 10 to 20 percent, passenger demand is stimulated by 1 to 10 percent, and travelers save up to $530 million annually in reduced travel costs. That's a study from Mitsubishi Research Institute in Japan.

The most telling of all these charts—and that's why I saved them for last—describe the effectiveness to date of the Japanese stopping United and Northwest from building their systems in Asia while they go on to build their own.

While the Japanese are busy expanding their networks out of the new airport, Osaka, U.S. carrier efforts to start a hub at Osaka have been held hostage by the Japanese government since December of 1994.

This chart shows the extensive hub the Japanese carriers have set up at Osaka while U.S. carrier services have been restricted.

Chart five shows the only city, Manila, that U.S. carriers—happens to be Northwest—can now serve beyond Osaka. Just as the Japanese have succeeded in constraining the use of our largest

U.S. hub, Chicago, since 1985, they are now seeking to create the same constraints on our use of Japanese hubs.

So what do we do about it all?

The Congress and the airlines should support the Administration's efforts to: one, refuse to open discussions on future agreements with Japan until existing agreements are complied with; two, refuse to trade away existing rights, any or all of them; three, offer to negotiate additional rights for U.S. carriers and the Japanese carriers, but test the deal based on the economic benefit to the United States. I did not say United. As a whole, I do not see any other rational alternative.

Thank you.

Mr. DUNCAN. Thank you very much, Mr. Greenwald.

Mr. DUNCAN. Now we'll go to Mr. Jeffrey P. Fegan, who is the executive director of the Dallas-Fort Worth International Airport.

Mr. Fegan, thank you very much for being here.

Mr. FEGAN. Thank you, Mr. Chairman. I appreciate the opportunity to come out today.

I do have the pleasure of serving as the executive director of the Dallas-Fort Worth International Airport. With me today is Kevin Cox, who is our deputy executive director for governmental affairs and is responsible for air service development for the airport.

At the outset, I would like to express my sincere appreciation for allowing D/FW to testify here today and provide our perspective, which is really a local/regional perspective, on the opportunities which exist for expanding the aviation market between the United States and the United Kingdom, as well as between the U.S. and Japan.

As you know, D/FW International Airport, the second-busiest airport in the world, has been trying for years to obtain access to London Heathrow. Unfortunately, the bilateral aviation agreement between the United States and the United Kingdom, commonly known as Bermuda 2, restricts the access to two U.S. airlines and a limited number of airports. Except for Chicago, only east coast and west coast cities have access to London Heathrow.

In effect, the southwest and southeast regions of the U.S. have no direct access to London Heathrow. As a result, one in seven D/FW passengers traveling to London must either stop at an east coast city with London Heathrow access or incur the additional time and expense of taking an hour-long train ride from London Gatwick Airport to Heathrow.

London Heathrow is the principal London airport, with the greatest array of connecting flights to the rest of Europe, the Middle East, and Africa. It is the most convenient way for Texas business and exports to move beyond London.

Based on a recent economic impact study, it is estimated that a route from D/FW to London Heathrow would equate to $60 million in new economic opportunities for the State of Texas. It was also estimated to bring annually 50,000 new passengers to the State of Texas. These estimates do not include the additional revenues that would be earned by airlines serving the new D/FW-Heathrow route.

As this subcommittee well knows, the U.S. and U.K. were in negotiations over several months in 1995 to expand access to London Heathrow. Unfortunately, the U.S. suspended these negotiations in

October, 1995. In doing so, the United States walked away from a United Kingdom offer which would have permitted two new London Heathrow routes and two new London Gatwick routes. One of these new Heathrow routes could have been used for D/FW-Heathrow.

This United Kingdom offer was consistent with the United States' position of obtaining a very limited exchange of new London Heathrow routes.

Acceptance of the United Kingdom proposal was supported by D/FW airport and virtually every other city, as well as by American Airlines, Continental Airlines, United, and Northwest. In fact, only Delta Airlines and TWA opposed the U.K. proposal.

With U.S. carriers losing market share, U.S. airlines carry about 42 percent of the U.S.-U.K. market in 1995 versus 58 percent for U.K. airlines. The Administration's rejection of the British offer only perpetuates this disadvantage.

In short, D/FW seeks this subcommittee's help in urging Secretary Peña to gain the White House support for resumption of talks this year. The U.K. has already signaled its willingness to resume talks in a recent speech by foreign Secretary Malcolm Rifkin.

With your permission, I'd also like to focus on aviation issues from the U.S. to Japan.

D/FW recognizes that Japan is a particularly important market for many of the most important export-oriented growth industries, including high-technology. In this country, affiliates of Japanese companies employ literally hundreds of thousands of Americans and invest billions in the U.S. economy.

As you know, passenger aviation between the U.S. and Japan is covered by the 1952 treaty that significantly restricts the number of flights, the cities served, and the carriers that can fly between the two countries.

Only 11 mainland U.S. cities have nonstop service to Japan, less than half the number of cities with London flights. Major cities, such as Houston, Orlando, Cincinnati, Miami, St. Louis, Phoenix, and Boston are shut out entirely. D/FW is limited to 7 weekly flights to Tokyo.

Efforts to expand U.S.-Japan air service should open new gateways, including new service to Osaka, seek to increase existing flights, and include new air carriers.

The U.S. national interest, as well as the interests of D/FW, is served by expanding market access. D/FW's specific interests are nonstop access to Osaka through Kansi Airport and additional flights to Tokyo. Load factors on American Airlines' current Tokyo flights are extremely high, which is inhibiting growth of business travel, exports, and inward investments.

North Texas is home to a number of high-tech export-oriented companies in the computer, telecommunications, and electronics fields. Texas Instruments, EDS, Dell Computer, and Motorola are household names in both countries and account for the fact that Japan is the D/FW area's biggest trading partner, despite the restricted access into Japan.

The lack of adequate D/FW-Japan air service is retarding growth trade in both countries. According to a study by Coopers & Lybrand, based on an analysis done by U.S. Bias in its pioneering

1990 study, one more flight a day departing D/FW for Tokyo or Osaka could lead to a potential increased economic benefit of more than $500 million a year for the area and the Nation. This figure reflects jobs resulting from increased exports, inward investment, and Japanese visitor spending in the area.

Competition would mean expanded choice and lower fares for customers. For too many cities, U.S.-Japan passenger service is extremely limited or does not exist at all.

More flights mean more jobs. U.S. economic activity will grow by an estimated $9 billion a year because of increases in tourism and the expansion of trade and investment.

The successful conclusion of the cargo talks is a model for passenger talks. A new cargo agreement preserved rights and expanded the market. It will generate thousands of U.S. jobs in aircraft maintenance, cargo handling, shipping, and other related businesses. We are confident that we can duplicate this success in passenger talks.

I might point out that D/FW Airport has never advocated negotiating away any beyond rights.

The economic marketplace of the future is the Pacific Rim. U.S. business must increase their access to the region. Forty States have already realized the importance of this area and have established offices in Japan.

A grassroots coalition commonly known as Access Japan is comprised of over 2,000 communities, organizations, and businesses who are urging the Administration to immediately commence passenger negotiations with Japan. D/FW seeks this subcommittee's help in urging the administration to begin negotiations now with Japan in an effort to expand the passenger service agreements, thereby providing opportunities for more U.S. cities to receive service to Japan.

In closing, D/FW strongly supports a broader U.S.-Japan passenger agreement that will open up more access to Japan from the U.S.

And, regarding the U.S.-U.K. aviation talks, let me say that D/FW also only seeks the right to compete for a London Heathrow route, but unless the Administration gets back to the negotiating table we will not be offered that opportunity.

Whether it's Japan access or London Heathrow routes, the issue is simple: no U.S. negotiations equals no new U.S. aviation opportunities.

Thank you very much.

Mr. DUNCAN. Well, thank you very much, Mr. Fegan.

I'm going to yield my time at this point to Vice Chairman Weller.

Mr. WELLER. Thank you, Mr. Chairman.

Before I begin my question, I do want to thank you for the courtesy you extended Mr. Greenwald of United Airlines in accommodating his schedule so that he could participate in today's hearing. I know they greatly appreciate that. Considering the fact United is a major employer in my home State of Illinois, we appreciate that.

I'd like to direct my first question to Mr. Greenwald. Again, I want to thank you for taking time to be here, as well.

As I now understand it, the position of Access: U.S.-Japan is that the United States should negotiate new access to Japan while at the same time preserving all the rights U.S. carriers such as United now hold. This sounds pretty similar to what I've heard United urge in the past, and I was wondering, do you and Access: U.S.-Japan now agree on negotiating objectives?

Mr. GREENWALD. The situation is a bit unclear, in my mind. My schedule and Governor Baliles have been missing each other, and my hope is—I tried to sit with him this morning, but I hope we will be able to have a chance to get together. Over a several-month period, he and I have been on the phone together.

I think the clearest answer I can give today is that Governor Baliles, in his statements, does take that position. What I want to raise with the governor is: how can what he represents be called a coalition if some of the primary members of that coalition—in particular, American Airlines—does take an opposite position? What is a coalition if it isn't one spokesman representing a common view of its members?

So, to be as clear as I can, I believe the governor is making the same statement that we are; that there should be no bending on existing rights of any form, rights being used or rights not being used today, but rights.

I have not had a chance to explore with the governor the next question, however, which I do feel very strongly about: would the coalition support a view that United has, which is that there should be no talks until Japan complies with the existing agreements? I suspect we differ on that view.

Mr. WELLER. Do you anticipate the two of you getting together in the near future?

Mr. GREENWALD. Yes. I'd very much like to do that.

Mr. WELLER. Earlier, when Mr. Hunnicutt was testifying—I know you were present for quite a bit of his testimony—I made reference to some comments that Mr. Murphy had made 2 weeks ago before the Senate Aviation Subcommittee regarding Japan's threat to shut down a daily United Los Angeles-Tokyo flight beginning tomorrow, and I was wondering, from your perspective, if Japan followed through on its threat to shut down that particular flight, do you have any projection what the economic loss might be as a result of Japan's action?

Mr. GREENWALD. Well, it is in the range of about $7 million a month, and I don't—I mean, I have stated this to folks who are in the midst of the negotiations in the Administration that this issue is big enough, wide enough, and deep enough that if the Japanese take a step like that don't bend. We'll take the initial profit loss, but the matter needs to get resolved.

I would guess—maybe I should say it more strongly—I would expect that if we are refused the right to fly from Los Angeles tomorrow by the Japanese government, that at least an appropriate step would be that they would be refused a similar right to fly into Los Angeles.

Mr. WELLER. Tell me again what that estimated economic impact is? Was it $7 million a day or a month?

Mr. GREENWALD. A month.

Mr. WELLER. A month. So that's about $84 million a year in lost economic opportunity.

Mr. GREENWALD. Yes. I'm sure it wouldn't go on that long.

Mr. WELLER. Pardon me?

Mr. GREENWALD. We sure hope it wouldn't go on that long.

Mr. WELLER. I certainly hope not, too. Twelve months is a long time, let alone 1 month. Hopefully we'll hold firm.

I do have a question for Mr. Freidheim with Booz Allen.

It's clear from your testimony and what you've said today that you've spent a great deal of time immersed in this issue—aviation issues, particularly between Japan and the United States. I was wondering, in your view, your personal view as a result of that, what policy should the United States be pursuing with Japan in the area of aviation?

Mr. FREIDHEIM. As I indicated, open skies is clearly the right long-term policy. The question is: how do you get there?

Number one on the list would be to retain the rights that currently exist to go, as Mr. Greenwald calls it, deep into Asia, because the growth of the Asian market is going to be extremely important to the United States well beyond the U.S. Airlines' interests.

Secondly would be to increase flights across the Pacific to all places, which would include to Japan. We certainly believe that the long-term interest in the country is to open more cities to have more flights from a variety of different places.

But the market, which we believe is very robust and growing—the first and foremost issue is to retain the rights and enable the United States to exercise the rights that it has in Asia, because that's really the lynch pin for the U.S. aviation industry to participate in that extraordinarily high-growth market and to enable U.S. companies to participate more readily, as well.

Mr. WELLER. Following up with that, of course a lot of us believe that whenever you improve transportation opportunities you create jobs, and of course what we're trying to do is not only protect American jobs but create more American jobs.

Mr. FREIDHEIM. Right.

Mr. WELLER. You know, we've heard a lot about hubs and beyonds and point-to-point routes. I was wondering, could you just lay out for us, in plain terms, from your perspective with Booz Allen, what you believe Japan hubs and beyond rights are worth in economic terms and job creation for the United States?

Mr. FREIDHEIM. Well, the value we put on it is in trade, about $100 billion over the next 20 years. That grows over the period of time. That's additional balance of trade benefits that being able to serve cities beyond Japan through Japan would result in.

Now, the multiplier on that is something like 15,000 or 20,000 jobs per billion dollars of trade, so you can do the arithmetic there and you'd come up with, at the end of a 15-year period, something like 200,000 jobs. So it's quite considerable.

Now, to the U.S. consumer there's a major benefit and, as others pointed out, there's a benefit to the Asian consumer, as well, that the U.S. carriers have a significantly lower cost position. And it's not just United and Northwest; it's American and Delta, as well. Enabling those airlines to compete freely will give the consumers a significant benefit.

As we indicated, if you buy a round-trip ticket to Tokyo in the United States you pay substantially less than if you buy that same ticket from JAL in Tokyo. It reflects the difference in economics of the airlines. So there is a tremendous consumer benefit there, as well.

We believe, as a result of that, there will be higher trade, more travel with the lower fares.

Mr. WELLER. Well, thank you.

Mr. Chairman, I do have some additional questions. Will we have a second go-round?

Mr. DUNCAN. Yes.

Mr. WELLER. Okay. Thank you. I appreciate my time. I recognize I went over. Thank you.

Mr. DUNCAN. All right. We'll go next to Ranking Member Lipinski. Mr. Lipinski?

Mr. LIPINSKI. Thank you, Mr. Chairman.

I welcome all you gentleman here today. This is an enormously important issue. I'm very happy that you could come and testify.

Mr. Freidheim, I found your study enormously interesting. I've read it over once. After I read it over two or three more times I'll understand it hopefully 80 percent, not because it's confusing, it's just that I have a difficult time sometimes digesting all that information. It is very, very good study.

Of course, there are a couple of other studies out which are very good, also. But, as I say, I compliment you on that.

The chairman of the board of the airline that I fly back and forth between Chicago and Washington, D.C., probably 45 weeks a year—always received excellent service. It's always nice to have the plane at B–7 because I get out of my car about 100 feet from B–7, and if it could always be there it would be ideal. About 8:15 would be perfect. Of course, there is one at 8:15 now.

I welcome you.

I'd like to go over what you had to say here about our negotiations with Japan and make sure I understand clearly what you're talking about here.

Insisting that the Japanese honor their current agreement? What do you mean? Could you amplify on that? What is their current agreement as far as you are concerned in this statement?

Mr. GREENWALD. I am talking about the written agreements between the United States and Japan. In particular, United had on application for over a year now the plan to fly from Osaka to Seoul, Korea, and more recently we have added to that an application to fly from Osaka to Jakarta.

The Japanese government is supposed to, according to these agreements, respond favorably within 45 days or give reasons why not. We have yet to hear. It's been over a year. That is the most important step.

Incidentally, Northwest has some other applications pending of the same sort.

The second issue, of course, is that the Japanese may tomorrow refuse United the right to fly from Los Angeles to Japan, and that needs to get resolved.

By the way, the Japanese have an application with the U.S. Government to fly from Japan to Hawaii to Kona, and presumably, as part of all this straightening out, that should be settled on their behalf.

Second, we need to have a very clear understanding with Japan that both United and Northwest are now free to go on and add more flying, more than the two applications, from Osaka into Asia.

That's what I mean by existing agreement.

Mr. LIPINSKI. And you believe that you have the right to do this based on the 1952 agreement or any subsequent agreements?

Mr. GREENWALD. That is correct.

Mr. LIPINSKI. Do you believe you have the right to do so on the 1952 agreement, alone, or are there subsequent agreements that give you the rights to do that?

Mr. GREENWALD. The 1952 agreements have been amended over time, but I would answer your question by saying the 1952 agreements as amended. Yes.

Mr. LIPINSKI. Because it seems to me that you have the right to do that based upon the 1952 agreement, and it seems to me that amendments to that really have somewhat liberalized other carriers' access to Japan.

Mr. GREENWALD. I believe that to be true—that over the years both—all of the airlines on the U.S. side and on the Japanese side have incrementally received additional flying rights to fly between the U.S. and Japan, but none of those additional agreements—I think I'm right in saying this—have added to the unique, if I could describe them that way, beyond rights to fly deeper into Asia.

Mr. LIPINSKI. That was my understanding based upon about a three-and-a-half or four-hour seminar I had for myself conducted at Archer Avenue in Chicago by Mr. Murphy over there. I just wanted to make sure United was united in their agreement on the 1952 agreements.

Mr. GREENWALD. I should point out that Mr. Murphy has asked me to step aside for 30 seconds to stand up and show that he can be euphoric.

[Laughter.]

Mr. GREENWALD. I suppose we won't take that time.

Mr. LIPINSKI. I know he can be embarrassed. His face is getting redder and redder every time I refer to him here.

Refusing to trade existing rights or to accept restriction on those rights in exchange for the promise of other opportunities—I think this is perfectly clear. You don't want to give up any of your beyond rights or anyone else, including yourself, to get additional access simply into Japan?

Mr. GREENWALD. That is exactly our position, sir.

Mr. LIPINSKI. Setting our goals on the basis of economic analysis that identifies the best interests of the United States. Now, are you talking about Mr. Freidheim's study over here on economic analysis, or are you talking about something we're going to do in the future?

Mr. GREENWALD. No. I was actually repeating a plank in the policy statement—I think that goes back to late 1993 even, or 1994—from the Administration, from DOT, that states a policy under which bilateral negotiations should be conducted.

Basically what it says is that when a negotiation is pending, that they or someone for them should do an economic analysis of that particular pending deal. And if the answer comes out favorable for the United States, do it. If it doesn't, pause. That's what I was referring to.

Mr. LIPINSKI. Let me ask you the $64 million question here: you, Northwest, Federal Express have certain rights given to you in agreements between the United States and Japan. I think that you should keep those rights. I don't think that you should have to give up any of those rights. You either negotiated for them or you purchased them. In your case you bought PanAm's. There are other airlines that had the opportunity to buy those routes at the same time that United did.

I don't want to see you lose anything. I don't want to see Northwest lose anything. I don't want to see FedEx lose anything.

By the same token, we know absolutely that American, Delta, United Parcel, and perhaps other American carriers want to gain access to Japan.

I want to see them gain access to Japan. I want to see them have that opportunity.

Now, to the best of my knowledge, none of them have said at the present time that they want beyond rights, because the situation gets a little confusing here, because at times the—let us say the outs don't advocate giving up any beyond rights in order for them to get additional access to Japan; at other times it appears as though some elements of that coalition are advocating giving up your beyond rights, Northwest's beyond rights. So right now they're just advocating getting that access to Japan. I would like to see them get the access to Japan and also beyond rights.

Now for the $64 million question: what would you recommend a person such as myself, and hopefully the United States Government, do to preserve your rights and to obtain additional rights for other carriers that are interested in flying into Japan?

Now, I know you stated your position over here, but I would like to have you elaborate on how you think we might be able to achieve that goal.

Mr. GREENWALD. Well, I think I should first state that, as we do with the U.K. or Germany or any other sovereign nation, we are trade partners, and they have the right—they have their rights and we have ours, so we cannot unilaterally take a position and insist on it.

But it seems to me that, at the very beginning, we have got to find a means by which to insist that once an agreement is struck that it's complied with.

That, to me, has to be plank number one.

It is our impression—and I am not certain of this—that the Japanese government would like to open new discussions on—bilateral discussions, also. I would hope that once existing agreements have been complied with, that those new discussions could be opened and at that point the U.S. Government would insist on simply getting more rights for U.S. carriers and that the Japanese would insist, in exchange, on getting more rights for their carriers. And that's fine.

Mr. LIPINSKI. Are you concerned about opening negotiations without having a reaffirmation of your existing rights under treaties that we have signed with Japan?

Mr. GREENWALD. I am absolutely very concerned about that. I think it would send a—first, it would expose—selfishly, it would expose United and Northwest to losing rights.

Mr. LIPINSKI. And I can understand that.

Mr. GREENWALD. But, beyond that, it would, in my view, set a terrible precedent with Japan. It would reward them for unilaterally violating existing agreements.

Mr. LIPINSKI. Well, what would have to be done by Japan and this country to reassure you and Northwest—and I'm sure Northwest feels the same way that you feel, and I'll even put in Federal Express. What would have to be done to assure you by Japan and the United States that they were not going to negotiate away any of your rights for you to fully support the real hard negotiations for additional access for other American carriers?

Mr. GREENWALD. The primary—this is not primarily a question of assurances for the future; it is an absolute demonstration we are seeking today that Japan would free us to use our existing rights.

Mr. LIPINSKI. And if I said future, I didn't mean to infer anything for the future. What I'm asking you is: what does Japan have to do for you to support negotiations that would give greater access to all American carriers simply to Japan?

Mr. GREENWALD. I believe that what Japan needs to do is this afternoon say, "We're freeing you to fly from Los Angeles to Narita and—

Mr. LIPINSKI. And the Osaka one?

Mr. GREENWALD. It's Narita. And, second, that they would sign off on this longstanding application and the newer ones to have us start flying from Osaka to Seoul and from Osaka to Jakarta, and whatever the pending requests are that Northwest has—that they would sign off on them and we'd start.

And they would also state that it is their expectation—or we would state and they wouldn't disagree—that we have a plan, a business plan, to continue to add more routes out of Osaka deeper in Asia.

Once done, open negotiations.

Mr. LIPINSKI. Okay. I thank you very much. My time is up and we have to move on.

Thank you very much, Mr. Chairman.

Mr. DUNCAN. Thank you, Mr. Lipinski.

Mr. Ewing?

Mr. EWING. Thank you, Mr. Chairman.

Welcome, Mr. Greenwald. I, like Bill Lipinski and Jerry Weller, fly your airline most of the time back and forth. I like gate B–5, just so that we don't have agreement on either side.

Would you be able—I know you can—explain to me just a little more about your chart "on international agreements constrain Chicago's growth."

Why is that affecting your airline in Chicago and its growth?

Mr. GREENWALD. It is an unfortunate result of some bad decisions in recent history. There are two primary international markets that we would love to fly from O'Hare that we are not permitted to do so. One is the U.K.

We, after 4 years of effort, did get approval to fly daily—limited for the moment to a 767 until January 1997, but that compares with American's rights to fly three times a day and British Air's rights to fly three times a day from O'Hare. We'd love to add flying from O'Hare to the U.K.

Second, we are even more restricted in our flying from O'Hare to Japan. We are limited to six times a week. We would love to fly much more frequently from O'Hare to Japan.

There are a few other examples of that kind, but that's essentially the reason why we have this—as do other airlines. Their primary hub brings in so much of our passengers from various places into Chicago, and we could serve those international passengers out of Chicago if we were free to do that.

Mr. EWING. The agreements that you purchased for United with Japan, they don't govern the number of flights, they govern the beyond? Or do they cover both?

Mr. GREENWALD. The agreements that we've been talking about have no limits on beyond Japan into Asia flying. That is the issue. We want to be able to freely add flights as those markets become attractive.

Mr. EWING. I'd like to ask a couple questions to Mr. Freidheim.

Number one, as a result of your study of the U.S.-Japan aviation situation, why do you think that Japan is so interested in capping or restricting the beyond rights of U.S. carriers?

Mr. FREIDHEIM. Well, I think there are two very significant reasons.

One, the U.S. carriers are competing on the Japan-Asia leg of those routes, and they want to—they recognize those are very substantial growth routes, and so they do not wish to have that competition. The U.S. carriers are lower cost, and therefore keep pressure down on prices.

Secondly, they do not want to have the competition on the Asia-U.S. routes. As was explained, the best way to get to an Asian city until it grows to the point where it can take direct service is through the Japanese hub. And by eliminating those routes, you eliminate your primary competition between that Asian city and the United States.

So the Japanese interests are very clear.

Mr. EWING. If the U.S. were to surrender some of these beyond authorities of its carriers and receive in return more authority for U.S. carriers to fly in between the U.S. and Japan, would the U.S. consumer be better off?

Mr. FREIDHEIM. No, for a couple of reasons. We think it's a very bad trade. We do believe that there should be more flying between the United States and Japan, but we believe it's a very bad trade for consumers to trade that for the beyond rights for two reasons: one, they will pay more on the U.S.-to-the-Asian-city flights through Japan than they would if the U.S. carriers had those beyond rights; and, secondly, we see the U.S.-Japan market as competitive, and there are now 12 carriers serving that marketplace, so there is a lot of competition.

There will be continued price reductions over that market as a result of that competition, but the U.S. consumer would not benefit significantly by a lot of additional flights early on. They'll benefit over time, and we think that they are continuing to benefit.

But the big issue is the Asian flights. And today I think the total of flights from the United States to Asia is about half for Japan and the rest for the other Asian cities, and that balance is going to shift. The Asian cities are growing faster than the U.S.-Japan routes and will pass them significantly in the future.

Mr. EWING. Thank you.

Finally, Mr. Greenwald, it appears to me that, as we continue these very sensitive negotiations with both Japan and England, it is extremely important for the Congress and for the Administration not to take an inflexible stand, but to take a very firm stand that we must have open markets for our carriers just like we provide to their carriers. Would you agree that's the bottom line?

Mr. GREENWALD. To paraphrase a comment made earlier, all I can say is, "yes, sir."

Mr. EWING. Thank you. My time is up.

Mr. DUNCAN. Thank you very much, Mr. Ewing.

Mr. Ehlers?

Mr. EHLERS. Thank you, Mr. Chairman.

I would just like to make a brief statement, then I will yield the remainder of my time to Mr. Weller.

I'm very concerned about this issue, and in my opening statement I referred to Bermuda 2 and what had happened as a result of that. I hope that we, as a Nation, learn from that and don't make the same mistake twice.

I happen to represent the State of Michigan. We have a lot of experience in dealing with issues of international trade, particularly in the automobile business, and I can assure you it's been very frustrating dealing with a number of nations who, on paper, say that they will provide equal opportunity in their countries but, in fact, they don't, through a whole host of practices that inhibit or occasionally prohibit business activity by the U.S.

I believe the situation that you are in and that the other American airlines are in is, again, typical of that practice. I believe that it's absolutely essential for the United States to be not only firm but tough.

I certainly agree with Mr. Ewing on his comments on that.

It's just unconscionable, I think, to not act on the applications that you and other airlines have pending, just to hold them in abeyance, in contradiction to the international agreements we have. I don't believe it's something that we, as a Nation, should put up with. I hope that this committee, through its influence on the Federal Government, and you, in turn, using your influence, can make sure that we come up with a fair and proper solution that benefits all parties.

I believe that the closer we can come to free and open trade in this area, as well as other areas, the better we are. But we have to ensure that it is free and open, and that has to be our prime goal.

Having said that, I will yield the remainder of my time to Mr. Weller.

Mr. WELLER. Thank you, Mr. Ehlers. Thank you so much for sharing some of your time with me.

I have a couple remaining questions I'd like to ask our panel here, and the first one I'd direct to Mr. Freidheim, just to follow up on some of the questions I was asking earlier, as well as Mr. Ewing's question.

If Japan were to cap the beyond rights of U.S. carriers, couldn't our airlines gain the same type of hub advantages through code sharing agreements with Japanese carriers?

Mr. FREIDHEIM. No. Code sharing is good, but, as I indicated in my prepared remarks, it's no replacement for direct, on-line service. And the biggest reasons for that are, number one, the—in this case, Japan Airlines, assuming that's the code share partner, would control the Asian leg and would be able to price that independently of the U.S. leg. So the U.S.-to-Asia fare would go up, and possibly substantially, and we believe that would have a dampening effect on U.S.-Asian travel through Japan.

Secondly, that gives the Asian carrier—and assuming now that we are where we are, which is we have those rights now—that would give the Asian carrier the revenue and the employment that relates to it, so the U.S. carriers would lose both of those, which would have significant balance of trade impacts and employment impacts.

Mr. WELLER. Thank you.

My last question I want to direct to the gentlemen from Dallas-Fort Worth Airport. I know most of the attention has been paid to the other two guys. You fellows are important and I'd give you a question, too.

I appreciate your desire for service to London's Heathrow Airport, as you had indicated in your statement, but am I not correct that as things stand now that Texas and California are the only states that have two cities serving as gateways to London?

Mr. FEGAN. Right now there are no cities in Texas that provide nonstop service to London Heathrow. We do have service to Gatwick, but not Heathrow.

And Heathrow is critical, I think, for our regional economic development, mainly because of all the connections it does provide to other parts of the Middle East, Africa, and Eastern Europe, and those connections simply aren't as convenient through London Gatwick.

Mr. WELLER. You say you do not have nonstop service. Where is the stop that you have that goes out of Dallas-Fort Worth?

Mr. FEGAN. Well, if a passenger wants to go to London Heathrow, they would either have to go through New York or maybe one of the other east coast cities before going on to London Heathrow, and that does have an impact on convenience, not only for the passenger, but the cargo trade really does get impacted quite a bit with that one-stop activity, change of planes activity.

Mr. WELLER. Thank you. I've enjoyed actually using your facility a few times, and you've got a well-run airport.

Mr. FEGAN. I appreciate that.

Mr. WELLER. Of course, we feel O'Hare is better.

[Laughter.]

Mr. WELLER. And, of course, statistics show we are a busier airport there in the Chicago area, but we're glad to have you here.

Mr. FEGAN. Thank you.

Mr. WELLER. Mr. Chairman, I want to commend you for conducting today's hearing. I think this has been extremely helpful, and also I think a very important hearing as we discuss particularly U.S.-Japan and also U.S.-U.K. aviation agreements. This has been particularly helpful in making sure that people know the facts. I want to thank you for conducting the hearing and accommodating all of our witnesses.

Mr. DUNCAN. Well, thank you very much, Mr. Weller.

Gentleman, let me just ask just a couple question in conclusion.

Once this year and once last year Fred Smith of Federal Express has been before this subcommittee and has been very outspoken in his criticism of U.S. negotiating policies in regard to cargo rights. What I would ask you is: how would you describe the U.S. negotiating policies in regard to air passenger travel? Would you say it's been tough or timid, or do you agree with a lot of what Mr. Smith has said?

Mr. GREENWALD. I think first, in fairness, we should not forget the home runs while we talk about the strike-outs.

I think the Administration has completely succeeded in negotiations with Canada, in negotiations with nine smaller countries in Europe, is on its way, we hope, to a successful full open skies agreement with Germany. And there are a number of other improvements. Thailand now is on its way to having a bilateral agreement with the United States, and so forth.

The two most difficult countries that we all tend to come back and talk about at hearings are the U.K. and Japan. And I don't know that I would describe those as failures. I would describe them as tough nuts to crack.

I think that certainly with regard to Japan, if, in fact, the Administration stays firm today and going forward, we will see some acceleration in progress with Japan.

I think that with the U.K. my own view is that what the Administration needs to do and what we airlines need to do is that the Administration needs to make their decisions on an economic basis, and the airlines need to get out of the way and let them do that and not try to politicize those issues.

I might say, I share the view expressed from my friend to the right here that we were, as a Nation, close to the second mini-forward step with the U.K., and though United had nothing to gain from it, we had said, "Fine. Here are some other airlines that look like they can get something in the way of liberalized trade with the U.K. We ought to get out of the way." But there were a couple of airlines who chose not to do that, got in the way, and the end result was that nobody got anything.

So, to summarize, I do think the Administration needs to stay firm and go forward with Japan and with the U.K. I think all the airlines need to get out of the way and the Administration needs to make their decisions on an economic basis.

Mr. DUNCAN. Is that why you think the trend lines have been so pronounced? You know, in the last 15 years we talked about getting tough with the Japanese, and I think we do need to be tough in negotiating all of these aviation agreements, but our market share of traffic between the U.S. and Japan has gone way up in the last 15 years or so, and yet our share of the traffic between the United States and the U.K. is now about 40 percent and has trended in a different direction. Is it because the airlines have gotten in the way, as you say, or what reasons? What do you think the reasons are for that?

Mr. GREENWALD. I think that there is a lesson to watch with regard to the U.K. as it would apply to Japan. What I mean by that is, Bermuda 2 got negotiated on an argument that BA was a weak airline and needed help. Well, that's all well and good to provide some temporary help, but to provide permanent help in the form of Bermuda 2, and then watch that airline become strong, that is the reason for their higher market share. Now we're trying to get back to balance that the U.K. and it's taking a long time.

Now, to shift over to Japan, we ought to listen carefully to what the Japanese are saying to us: "The Japanese airlines are weak, so give us, the Japanese, permanently all of the flying deeper into Asia, the fastest-growing market in the world." We should not come close to accepting anything like that, because if we do, at some point JAL and ANA will strengthen again and we'll be having meetings on the same subject about their strength and market share and not knowing what to do about it, and we shouldn't let that happen.

Mr. DUNCAN. We've got to—I've got to bring this to a close because we're going to have some votes here in just a minute, but, Mr. Fegan, I assume—are you a member of Access: U.S.-Japan?

Mr. FEGAN. Yes, sir, we are.

Mr. DUNCAN. What did you think when Mr. Greenwald said that his view of the goal or the main goal of Access Japan is to—the end result would be for us to give up more-valuable deep Asia routes in return for less-valuable routes between the United States and Japan? Do you think that was an accurate statement about the goal of your group?

Mr. FEGAN. Mr. Chairman, when we were approached by Access Japan about joining that coalition, there were a number of questions, a number of discussions held related to why D/FW would be interested in that. Throughout those discussions it was always stated that there was no interest by this group, the coalition, to eliminate any fifth freedom rights that any existing carriers might have. The real issue was to grow the pie, expand access to other major cities of the United States to Japan.

I've seen statements and I've seen speeches that the governor has provided, and all the documentation that we signed up for does not include any negotiations of fifth freedom rights by existing carriers.

Mr. DUNCAN. Well, I mentioned this earlier, but Governor Baliles has testified in front of this subcommittee before and certainly is welcome here again.

Thank you, gentlemen. You've been outstanding witnesses, and we appreciate very much your testimony here today.

That will conclude this hearing.

[Whereupon, at 5:07 p.m., the subcommittee was adjourned, to reconvene at 1:00 p.m. on Wednesday, May 1, 1996.]

Testimony before the House Transportation and Infrastructure Subcommittee on Aviation
April 30, 1996

Jeffrey P. Fegan
Executive Director,
Dallas-Fort Worth International Airport

Mr. Chairman,

On behalf of Dallas-Fort Worth International Airport, I want to introduce myself, I am the Executive Director of the DFW International Airport and with me today is Kevin Cox, the Deputy Executive Director of the Airport responsible for Government Affairs and Air Service Development. At the outset, I want to express my sincere appreciation for allowing DFW to testify here today and provide our perspective on the opportunities which exist for expanding the aviation market between the United States and the United Kingdom as well as between the U.S. and Japan.

As you know, DFW International Airport -- the second busiest airport in the world -- has been trying for years to obtain access into London-Heathrow Airport. Unfortunately, the bilateral aviation agreement between the United States and the United Kingdom, commonly known as Bermuda 2, restricts the access to two U.S. airlines and a limited number of airports.

Except for Chicago, only East Coast and West Coast cities have access to London-Heathrow. In effect, the Southwest and Southeast regions of the U.S. has no direct access to London-Heathrow. As a result, one in seven DFW passengers traveling to London, must either stop in an East Coast city with London-Heathrow access or incur the additional time and expense of taking an hour-long train ride from London-Gatwick Airport to Heathrow. London-Heathrow is the principal London airport with the greatest array of connecting flights to the rest of Europe, the Middle East and Africa. It is the most convenient way for Texas Business and Exports to move beyond London.

Based on a recent economic impact study, it is estimated that a route from DFW to London-Heathrow would equate to $60 million in new economic opportunities for the State of Texas. It is also estimated to bring annually 50,000 new passengers to the State of Texas. These estimates do not include the additional revenues that would be earned by airlines serving the new DFW-Heathrow route.

As this Subcommittee wells knows, the U.S. and the U.K. were in negotiations over several months in 1995 to expand access into London-Heathrow. Unfortunately, the U.S. suspended these negotiations in October 1995. In doing so, the United States walked away from a United Kingdom offer which would have permitted two new London-Heathrow routes and two new London-Gatwick routes. (One of these new Heathrow routes could have been used for DFW-Heathrow.) This United Kingdom offer was consistent with the United States' position of obtaining a "very limited" exchange of new London-Heathrow routes. Acceptance of the United Kingdom proposal was supported by DFW Airport and virtually every other city, as well as, by American Airlines, Continental Airlines, United Airlines, and Northwest Airlines. In fact, only Delta Air Lines and TWA opposed the U.K. proposal. With U.S. carriers losing market share -- U.S. airlines carried only 42% of U.S./U.K. traffic in 1995 versus 58% for U.K. airlines -- the Administration's rejection of the British offer only perpetuates this disadvantage.

In short, DFW seeks this Subcommittee's help in urging Secretary Peña to gain the White House's support for a resumption of these talks this year. The U.K. has already signaled its willingness to resume talks in a recent speech by Foreign Secretary Malcolm Rifkind.

With your permission, I would now like to focus on aviation access from the U.S. to Japan. DFW recognizes that Japan is a particularly important market for many of our most important export-oriented growth industries, including high technology. In this country, affiliates of Japanese companies employ literally hundreds of thousands of Americans, and invest billions in the U.S. economy.

As you know, passenger aviation between the U.S. and Japan is governed by a 1952 treaty that significantly restricts the number of flights, the cities served, and the carriers that can fly between the two countries. Only 11 mainland U.S. cities have nonstop service to Japan, less than half the number of cities with London flights. Major cities such as Houston, Orlando, Cincinnati, Miami, St. Louis, Phoenix and Boston are shut out entirely. DFW is limited to 7 weekly flights to Tokyo.

Efforts to expand U.S.-Japan Air service should:

1.) open new gateways, including new service to Osaka;
2.) seek to increase existing flights; and
3.) include new air carriers.

The U.S. national interest, as well as the interest of DFW is served by expanding market access.

Dallas-Fort Worth's specific interests are nonstop access to Japan's second city Osaka, through Kansai Airport and additional flights to Tokyo. Load factors on American Airlines' current Tokyo flights are extremely high, which is inhibiting growth of business travel, exports and inward investments. North Texas is home to a number of high tech, export-oriented companies in the computer, telecommunications, and electronics fields. Texas Instruments, EDS, Dell Computer and Motorola are household names in both countries and account for the fact that Japan is the DFW area's biggest trading partner despite the restricted access into Japan. The lack of adequate DFW-Japan air service is retarding trade growth in both countries.

According to a study by Coopers & Lybrand, based on analysis done by USA-BIAS in its pioneering 1990 study, one more flight a day departing DFW for Tokyo or Osaka would lead to a potential increased economic benefit of more than $500 million a year for the area. This figure reflects jobs resulting from increased exports, inward investment and Japanese visitors spending in the area.

Competition would mean expanded choice and lower fares for consumers. For too many cities, U.S.-Japan passenger service is extremely limited or does not exist at all. More flights mean more jobs. U.S. economic activity will grow by an estimated $9 billion a year because of increases in tourism and the expansion of trade and investment.

The successful conclusion of the cargo talks is a model for passenger talks. **The new cargo agreement preserved rights and expanded the market.** It will generate thousands of U.S. jobs in aircraft maintenance, cargo handling, shipping and other related businesses. We are confident that we can duplicate this success in passenger talks.

The economic marketplace of the future is the Pacific Rim. U.S. business must increase their access to that region. Forty states have already realized the importance of this area and have established offices in Japan.

A grassroots coalition, commonly known as Access-Japan, is comprised of over 2000 Communities; organizations and business who are urging the Administration to immediately commence passenger negotiations with Japan. DFW seeks this Subcommittee's help in urging the Administration to begin negotiations now with Japan in an effort to expand the passenger service agreement, thereby providing opportunities for more U.S. cities to receive service to Japan.

In closing, DFW strongly supports a broader U.S.-Japan passenger agreement that will open up more access to Japan from the U.S. And regarding the U.S.-U.K. aviation talks, let me say that DFW only seeks the right to compete for a London-Heathrow route, but unless the Administration gets back to the negotiating table, we will not be offered that opportunity. Whether it is Japan access or London-Heathrow routes: the issue is simple -- no U.S. negotiations equals no new U.S. aviation opportunities.

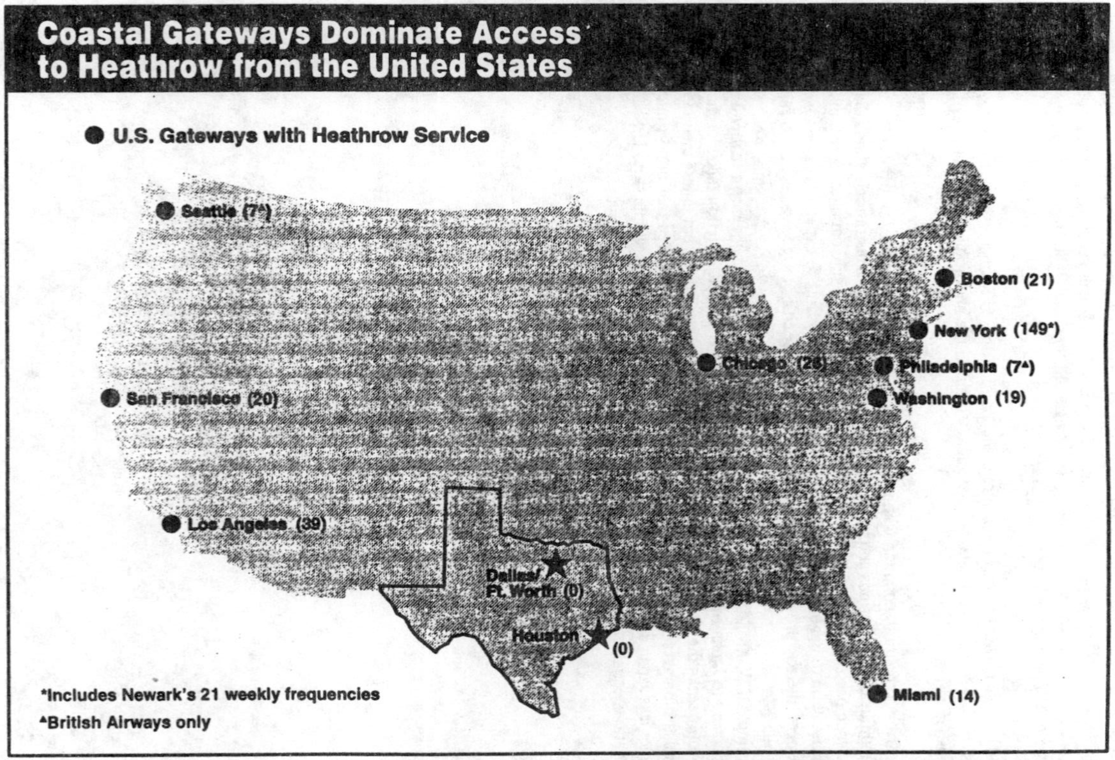

Source: Published airline schedules, effective November 1995

Estimated Economic Impact of Incremental Air Service Between

Dallas/Fort-Worth International Airport and Oska International Airport

	RANGE OF ESTIMATES	
	Lower	Upper
Flights Departing DFW International Airport Each Week	7	7
Annual Increase in Passengers:[1]	59,150	70,980
U.S. ECONOMIC IMPACT[2]	**$419 million**	**$503 million**
Including:		
Increased Local Tourism Spending:	*$ 66 million*	*$ 80 million*
Higher Local Payrolls from Foreign Investment:	*$ 33 million*	*$ 40 million*
Greater Local Manufacturing Production from Expanded Export Opportunities:	*$100 million*	*$120 million*

---

[1] Lower estimate is based on 250-seat plane while upper estimate is based on 300-seat plane. Both estimates assume 65 percent of seats would be filled.

[2] Based on USA-BIAS report (*Economic Impact of International Air Services*, USA-BIAS, October 14, 1992) that estimated the economic impact of an additional international passenger to be $7,082.

TESTIMONY

Chairman Duncan, Representative Lupinski, members of the subcommittee. It is always an honor to be invited to appear before committees of our Congress.

I am Cyrus Freidheim, Vice Chairman of Booz Allen & Hamilton, a management and technology consulting firm with over 6,000 employees and over 100 offices worldwide. We advise major corporations and governments on a variety of top level management and technology issues. We were founded in 1914. We work extensively in the airline industry in the U.S. and abroad.

Last summer, we were asked by United Airlines to analyze the value of the beyond rights that U.S. passenger airlines were accorded by the Air Service Agreement of 1952 between the United States and Japan. We did this by computing the revenue and profits for the U.S. carriers and the impact on the U.S.-Japan trade balance under three scenarios: First, full utilization of beyond rights the ability of carriers to use Japanese cities as hubs to serve other Asian cities). Second, the elimination of beyond rights and third, limiting the beyond rights to those Asian cities served today.

Our overall conclusions were that:

- The beyond rights had great value to the two U.S. carriers - United Airlines and Northwest Airlines -- that had these rights. We estimated the value at $4-5.6 billion based on the discounted value of the earning stream from those routes. We included only the routes affected by beyond rights -- i.e., with the right to use Japanese cities as hubs to serve Asia.

The value lost by limiting this rights to Asian cities currently served is computed at $2.3-$4 billion. It is important to recognize that long term, the cities currently served will have less need for the Japanese hub since their markets will merit direct flights from the U.S. Hence, the value of beyond rights is greater for cities not yet served than for cities currently being served through the Japanese hubs.

- The impact on the U.S. balance of trade is estimated at about $100 billion cumulatively over the next 2 years. This number is an estimate of the lost revenues by United and Northwest caused by the elimination of beyond rights.

It is important to understand how we arrived at these numbers.

- We used the passenger forecasts by IATA (International Air Transport Association) and United Airlines. Passenger growth between the U.S. and Japan is projected at 6%. Traffic growth from the U.S. to other Asian cities varies from 6% for ______ to 15% for ________. The average is projected at 8%.

- We projected yields (or prices) to decline in real terms at 3-5% per year for U.S. Japan for the next 10 years and 3% thereafter. We projected yields at 3% annually. These projections are in line with the heavily competitive routes between the U.S. and Europe over the past 10 years.

We concluded that the best solution for the consumer, the countries involved, and the carriers was open skies. We also concluded that trading beyond rights for added flights between the U.S. and Japan

____

_for consumers, for the U.S. and net for the U.S. airline industry.

A group called Access-U.S. Japan questioned our conclusions. They claimed:

- That additional flights between the U.S. and Japan had substantial value -- much more than the unexercised beyond rights of the '52 carriers, United and Northwest.

- That communities would benefit by $9 billion annually

- That prices between the U.S. and Japan are artificially high (___% over U.S.-Europe) and that added competition would cause prices between the U.S. and Japan would drop by 25% to 40%

- That the U.S.-Japan market is grossly underserved compared with the U.S.-European market and that passenger traffic would be stimulated by the drop in prices by ____%

- That we vastly overstated the value of only unexercised beyond rights. Why, they ask, don't United and Northwest serve these beyond cities now if they are so valuable?

- That the impact on the balance of trade was not a traditional way of valuing air transport rights

If only Access U.S.-Japan were right. We could immediately accede to the Japanese ______________________________ guaranteed by the 1952 Air Service Agreement and ultimately stop U.S. carriers from using Japanese cities as hubs to Asia. And we would all be better off. What a terrific win-win solution.

Unfortunately, this is not the case. Let me discuss each of these issues:

- Core to the argument is that U.S.-Japan routes are underserved

- They claim that U.S.-Japan should have —— times the passengers based on a comparison of U.S.-U.K. passenger travel. They compared populations and GNPs with available seat capacity; i.e., Japan is twice as big as the U.K. and therefore should have twice the air service with the U.S. In fact, U.S.-Japan has fewer passengers. Using this argument, the U.S. should have 10 times its current service with Spain and 50-300 times as many flights to China as today.

- The best measure of adequacy of service is load factor at a comparable price. U.S. Japan load factors are in fact lower than U.S.-U.K. (____% vs ____%). As we will demonstrate in a moment, price

____

• Access U.S. Japan claims that added competition will cause prices to drop by 25-40% which will unleash large pent-up demand across the Pacific. We certainly agree that a 40% real price reduction would stimulate plenty of tour groups in Japan and the U.S. Unfortunately, it would bankrupt any carrier which added substantial capacity at those fares.

The Access U.S. Japan argument is based on the assumption that U.S.-Japan prices are artificially high -- that they are ___% higher on a per mile basis than U.S. Europe. This is true for "published fares." Fortunately for consumers, they actually pay far less than the published fares. In fact, our data shows that actual fares paid (again on a per mile basis) for discounted travellers are 15% lower for U.S. Japan than for U.S. UK in season and 10-15% higher off season. Business class fares are lower for U.S. Japan than U.S.-UK in all seasons.

Interestingly, the same round trip ticket purchased in Japan is substantially higher

____

______________________ JAL sets pricing in Japan. JAL is substantially higher cost than U.S. carriers (50%-100%) and hence, changes higher fares. This is important to note because without U.S. competition, consumers can rightfully expect higher fares from JAL.

We have projected a real decline in fares between the U.S. and Japan of 3.5% per year for the next 10 years which results in fares in 2006 of ___% lower than today. These projections follow the experience of the tightly competitive U.S.-European routes.

There is plenty of challenge to U.S. carriers to continually improve their productivity to be profitable with declining prices of that magnitude.

We also believe our projection of 6% growth in passengers between the U.S. and Japan is realistic. The bulk of the growth will come from vacation travel. Business opportunities rather than low fares determine business travel.

Hence, we stand by our projections of volume growth and price declines.

Next, let us examine the value of unexercised rights

- Japan is a natural hub to Asia. It is on a great circle route to most Asian cities from the U.S. It has a large population which travels. It is an excellent location to consolidate passengers from Asian cities headed for the U.S. and U.S. passengers headed for Asia.

- U.S. carriers add service to Asian cities when potential traffic volume permits three flights per week from that city to the Asian hub, i.e., Tokyo or Osaka. These passengers then board the Japan U.S. flights to the cities of their choice.

- U.S. carriers add direct, non-stop service to Asian cities when the potential traffic merits three round trip flights per week

- Markets are built by first serving a city through the hub and later providing direct service as the market grows. Even when direct, non-stop service is provided, carriers continue to serve ______________________________ more options to the customer -- i.e., daily service to the U.S. vs. three times per week on direct flight.

- It is interesting to note that no U.S. carriers provide direct service to Asian cities (other than Japan and one to Korea) without accompanying hub service through Japan. The economics and market and customer service just don't work.

- The cities not now served - take Tiajin as an example -- do not yet have sufficient traffic to provide service through Japan to the U.S. In 2000, it will ... and in 2010 it will merit direct service to the U.S. along with hub service through Japan. The vast Asian market will come to fruition in the next 15 years. Projections call for Asia to become the largest international air passenger market in the next 20-25 years.

- The U.S. carriers must be well positioned to capture that market. Japanese hubs are key to U.S. competitiveness -- and that is why the unexercised beyond rights are so valuable.

- Much of the travel to cities currently being served through Japan will be provided directly from U.S. cities by 2010.

24-087 97 - 9

Finally, the impact on U.S. communities and the economy:

- **Access U.S. Japan projects a $9 billion economic disadvantage for U.S. communities by adding more U.S.-Japan flights. Their estimate is based on a multiplier of $7000 per added passenger. Our research concludes that most economists believe the multiplier to be $4000 to $5000. We used $4300 from the ______ study.**

- **Secondly, Access U.S. Japan assumed a high incremental volume, 700,000 passengers, with no offset. We computed the number of passengers stimulated by an additional 10% price decline in 2005 on top of the 36% we had projected. On that basis and using $4300 multiplier, we get a net positive impact of $____ billion with no offset.**

- **If, however, U.S. beyond rights were limited in trade for added U.S.-Japan flights, the loss of passengers to Japan and the consequent drop in U.S. employment would more than offset the benefit of added passengers to U.S. communities. Our report documents that conclusion.**

Two other points are relevant:

- **What is the impact of code sharing on these results?**

- **In our view, what is Japan's strategy and what is in the best interests of the United States?**

Code Sharing

Code sharing is good -- for consumers, countries, and the industry. Code sharing enables one reservation, more convenient connections, more reliable baggage services, broader use of frequent flyer miles. It enables carriers to serve more cities without supporting low yield routes or battling for positions in tough markets.

Code sharing is not a replacement for economic on line service through a hub -- not for the consumer, not for the carrier and not for the countries' carrier. Pricing on the leg controlled by the other airline (in this case, a Japanese carrier) can/would be much higher, carriers lose the revenue on the code-shared leg, and the country of the carrier losses in balance of trade and employment.

We support market development through code sharing as does DOT but not in trade for on line service.

Japan's Strategy

- **To gain greater control over its most rapidly growing market -- Japan-Asia -- and to benefit fully from that growth and provide Japanese airlines a basis for profitability.**

Japan's solution: to limit low cost (i.e., U.S.) competitor participation in that market as much as possible

- To maximize the value of its natural Asian hub (a national asset) to Japan, and to use that hub to capture a significant share of the rapidly growing U.S.-Asian market. Japan's solution: to limit or eliminate the right of U.S. carriers to use Japanese cities as hubs.

- To limit losses across the Pacific where Japanese carriers are reportedly losing money. Japan's solution: to limit open skies competition with substantially (50%) lower cost U.S. carriers

- Japan's strategy: Argue that the 1952 agreement is unbalanced and should be equalized. Curtail United and Northwest rights to use Japanese hubs to serve Asian cities which will also result in a reduction of U.S.-Japan flights for those carriers. Additional MOU flights between U.S.-Japan can be granted (along with added Japanese carrier rights) which would in effect replace the United and Northwest flights, especially if code sharing arrangements ensure that a high proportion of the remaining U.S.-Asian market connects through Japan.

<u>U.S. Interests</u>

- Air passenger transportation is one of the few industries in which the U.S. enjoys a trade surplus with Japan. This surplus will grow if the 1952 agreement is followed. It will decline or be eliminated if hub rights in Japan are restricted or eliminated.

- The U.S. carriers currently have a major share advantage in the U.S.-Japan and U.S.-Asian markets, i.e., 60-70%. These markets are the fastest growing markets in the world. That share advantage is rooted in hub rights in Japan and U.S. carriers that are substantially more efficient than their Japanese competitors ... the reverse of many other industries in which our countries compete.

- U.S. businesses and vacation travelers are as well served to Japan and Asia (fares and load factors) as U.S. travelers to Europe. U.S. carriers must aggressively add flights and reduce costs to maintain share and profitability in markets growing at 8% on average with prices expected to decline at 3%.

- The best solution for the U.S. across the Pacific is Open Skies. Unlimited rights to serve any market by any airline and build hubs wherever economically justified would enable U.S. carriers to utilize their substantial competitive advantages. Elimination or limitation to the use of the Japan hubs by U.S. carriers is a step in the opposite

direction, and plays directly into the Japanese strategy to alter the competitive field to their advantage.

SHAPING PACIFIC AVIATION IN THE 21ST CENTURY

RESPONSE: HUNNICUTT-ORAN MARCH 5
ACCESS: U.S.-JAPAN

BOOZ·ALLEN & HAMILTON INC.

April 30, 1996

A STUDY PREPARED FOR UNITED AIRLINES

TABLE OF CONTENTS

I. EXECUTIVE SUMMARY

Access U.S. Japan, a coalition of businesses interested in expanding air service between the U.S. and Japan, published a report supporting substantially increased flights from additional U.S. cities in trade for limitations on beyond rights of United and Northwest Airlines. The report took exception with Booz•Allen's analysis and report dated September 24, 1995.

Booz•Allen and Access U.S. Japan support the same goal: free market access in air transportation. We agree that expanded competition, broader service, and high growth are good for everyone. The objective of our report and this paper is to shed light on the facts. We have focused on the costs and benefits of alternative arrangements and air transportation relationships with Japan. Our yardstick for measuring has been the overall interest of the United States, its consumers and its airline industry. We believe a strong U.S. participation in the Pacific market is in the best interest of the United States.

Both Access U.S. Japan and the September Booz•Allen report argue that eliminating hub (beyond) rights for the U.S. '52 carriers in Japan would be very detrimental to the United States. Both support the addition of flights and city-pairs between the U.S. and Japan. The issue is whether or not it is in the U.S. interest to trade away unexercised beyond rights of the U.S. 1952 carriers for additional U.S. flights between the U.S. and Japan. To understand this issue, the following questions need to be answered:

- To what degree will traffic between the U.S. and Japan be stimulated by added flights between the U.S. and Japan? What would be the impact on traffic volume and airline profitability of major reductions in Pacific fares and of major increases in U.S.-Japan flights? To what extent are the U.S.-Japan actual fares paid substantially higher than the U.S.-European fares paid?

- How much revenue will U.S. carriers and cities lose if their hub rights were limited to cities currently served? Which cities not now served through the Japan hubs would realistically be served by 2005 and by 2015? What is the value of unexercised beyond rights?

- How much revenue might U.S. carriers gain through additional U.S.-Japan flights -- net of the lost revenue by the U.S. '52 carriers and gains by MOU and Japanese carriers? What would be the impact of code sharing on these results?

- What would be the impact on the efficiency and competitiveness of the U.S. air transportation system under each scenario?
  - Unconstrained U.S. carrier hubs in Japan vs. additional U.S.-Japan access?
  - Currently and in the future when Asian markets have grown?

- What would be the impact on consumers (prices and options)?

- What would be the impact on U.S. communities?

This summary and the attached report deal with these questions.

Traffic Between U.S. And Japan

Access U.S. Japan argues that the U.S.-Japan market is seriously under-served based on a comparison to the U.S.-U.K. and U.S.-European markets. Access U.S. Japan relates the number of flights/seats to the relative populations and GNPs. We believe this comparison is meaningless. Making similar comparisons with the U.S. and other countries leads to ludicrous results. For example, their analysis would argue for ten fold increase in flights from the U.S. to Spain and 50-300 times the flights from the U.S. to China.

Clearly, other factors are at play. The cultural, language, business, and historical closeness of the U.S. and U.K. have led to a large transportation market between the countries. No similar closeness exists except possibly with Canada. The U.S.-Japan relationship is important and growing -- i.e.,. Japan is the second largest trading partner with the U.S. -- . but does not approach the U.S.-U.K. relationship. We should also mention that New York-London is a six-seven hour flight compared to 13-14 hours from New York to Tokyo.

A market is under-served if demand exceeds capacity under reasonable pricing scenarios. Load factors between the U.S. and Japan are lower than those between the U.S. and the U.K. (73% vs. 76-78%).

Access U.S. Japan argues that U.S.-Japan fares are 25%-60% higher than U.S.-European fares on a per mile basis. Access U.S. Japan uses published fares which are significantly different than actual fares paid between the U.S. and Japan. Actual discounted fares to Japan are 7-14% lower in season than U.S.-European fares, even during the "shoulder" and 15% higher off season. Actual business class fares to Japan are somewhat lower in all seasons. Pricing is different, however, for tickets purchased in Japan where JAL heavily influences market prices. Discount tickets purchased in Japan are higher than the comparable flights purchased in the U.S. Peak season discount fares "when all of Japan goes on holiday" can be more than twice U.S.-Japan fares purchased in the U.S. In the shoulder and off-season the data are less clear. Quotes from Japanese discount stores are much closer to realized U.S.-Japan fares. Actual realized fares to Europe and Japan were obtained from United Airlines.

U.S. CARRIERS PASSENGER GROWTH TRENDS

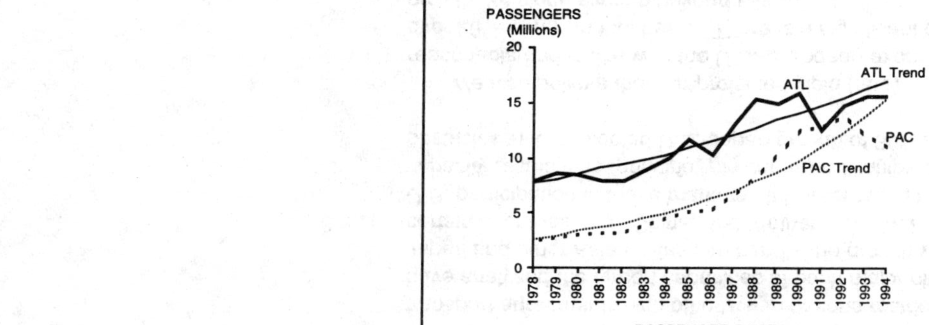

YIELD** 1978–1994 (U.S. GDP Deflator 1994 = 100)

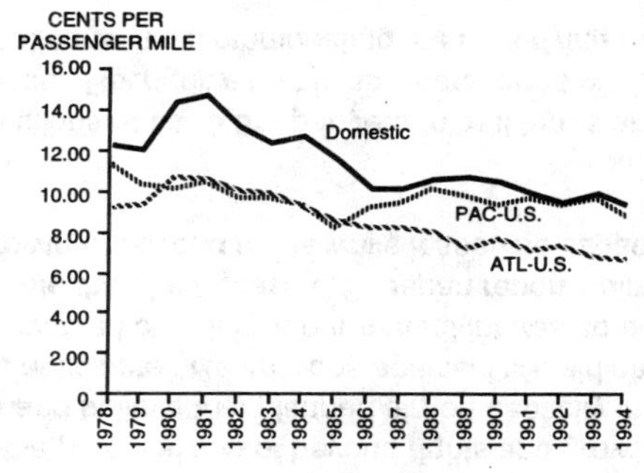

PASSENGER CAGR*

	U.S.-ATL	U.S.-PAC
1978–1994	4.9%	11.1%

YIELD** CAGR*

	U.S.-ATL	U.S.-PAC	Domestic
1978–1994	(2.8%)	(0.8%)	(2.4%)
1984–1994	(2.9%)	0.2%	(2.2%)
1978–1985	(1.1%)	(3.4%)	(0.8%)

* *CAGR: Compounded annual growth rate (best fit-trend line)*

** *Yield: Revenue per passenger mile*

Source: U.S. Dept. of Transportation Form 41 Database; International Financial Statistics Yearbook 1995; BA&H analysis

RPCH247-005-002LLa

The "reductions" proposed by Access U.S. are unrealistic. If the MOU carriers did reduce prices by 25% from current actual fares, their losses would be huge regardless of the volume stimulated by those fares.

We believe that our assumptions on market growth and fare reductions over time are reasonable. Passenger traffic growth is estimated at 6% per year for U.S.-Japan and a range from 6% to 15% for various U.S.-Asian cities with an average overall growth of the U.S.-Asian market (excluding Japan) of 8%. Our projections are based on IATA forecasts and the relationship between airline usage and GDP/capita which projects the increases in trade and tourism between the U.S. and the Asian countries. Details are included in our September 1995 report.

Access U.S. Japan argues that capacity constraints in Japan and elsewhere in Asia and air transport agreements with other Asian nations restrict the potential use of beyond rights and growth. We have analyzed the airport capacities of each major city and believe that planned airport capacity in Japan and other Asian cities can handle the growth we anticipate. Restrictions against U.S. airlines in certain countries, e.g., China, and Vietnam, can/will be worked out. It is in our mutual interest to enable U.S. participation in these markets. It is interesting to note that the Access U.S. Japan report claims that capacity restrictions (principally in Japan) will inhibit growth of beyond rights while it sees no capacity obstacles in its projected U.S.-Japan growth of 30%+.

We also believe that our projected yield (fare) reductions of 3%-3.5% per year in real terms are reasonable and in line with the U.S.-European experience. Recognize that in six years, fares will be over 20% lower on that basis. There is a significant challenge in accommodating the underlying market growth, let alone expand beyond this.

Revenue From Beyond Cities Not Now Served

United and Northwest currently serve eight Asian cities through the Japan hub. Three of these cities, Hong Kong, Seoul and Taipei, are also served directly from the U.S. In our analysis, nine additional cities would merit service through the Japan hub by 2005 and an additional two cities would be served by 2015.

If the U.S. '52 carriers were limited to serving the current cities through the Japan hub, the U.S. would lose 100% of all potential revenues from Japan to these nine cities, because there would be no U.S. carriers. Based on our growth and yield projections, the U.S. would lose about $900 million in Japan-Asia revenues in 2005. The Japanese carriers would get most but not all of those revenues. Third country carriers would get the remainder.

In addition, the U.S. carriers would lose a large share of the U.S.-Asia traffic to these nine cities, which includes the U.S.-Japan leg because of the overwhelming attractiveness of on line service. None of these nine cities would support nonstop service from the U.S. by 2005. Again based on our growth and yield projections, the U.S. '52 carriers would lose approximately $1.5 BN in revenue in 2005. An additional $200 million would likely be lost on the U.S.-Japan O&D market as U.S. carriers become less competitive

Code sharing between U.S. and Japanese carriers could revert some of that lost revenue back to U.S. carriers. A good code share agreement might result in a 50/50 split of the U.S.-Japan leg of U.S.-Asian passenger business originating in the U.S. Because of lack of presence in the Asian cities, U.S. carriers would get little if any of the business originating in those cities. Hence, the amount of revenue lost to the U.S. compared with uncapped Japan hub rights might be reduced by $300-500 million in 2005.

Consequently, the total lost revenues to U.S. carriers in 2005 would be in the range of $2.1-2.6 BN, which would result in a reduction in the balance of trade with Japan of almost an equal amount.

These estimates are for nine currently unserved cities in 2005. In 2015, these markets would have grown robustly (6% to 15% annually) and two additional cities would have been served by the U.S. '52 carriers through Japan under current agreements. Some of these Asian cities would be served directly from the U.S. The total lost revenues for 2015 would be in the range of $5-5.5 billion, virtually all of which would go to reducing the overall U.S. balance of trade with Japan.

<u>Gain In U.S. Revenues From Added MOU Flights</u>

Access U.S. Japan argues that the addition of MOU carrier flights between U.S. and Japan would more than offset the lost revenue of the U.S. '52 carriers from Asian cities not currently served through Japan. Hence, there would be a net benefit to the United States.

The addition of flights from new cities in the U.S. to Japan (whether by MOU or U.S. '52 carriers) would add to competition, cause some reduction in fares beyond our assumption of 3% to 3 1/2% per year, and result in somewhat higher volumes (provided capacity additions are over and above the underlying growth rate of 6% p.a.). We believe these actions would be beneficial to the U.S., the consumer and the airline industry.

We do not believe additional real price reductions of 25%-40% as suggested in Access U.S. Japan are realistic. The Japanese are not interested in dramatic price reductions on the U.S.-Japan routes because they are losing money. Note their pricing behavior on Pacific flights originating in Japan compared with those originating in the U.S. Similarly, major cuts would put U.S. carriers in the red on the Pacific routes. In our judgment, competitively induced price reductions would be less than 10%. Yields on the U.S.-European routes have declined an average of 3% per year in real terms over the past decade with heavy competition. We see no reason that Pacific fares would behave substantially differently.

Any additional U.S. carrier routes to Japan would have to be negotiated with Japan and would likely result in added Japanese carrier flights. New U.S. cities would benefit from direct service, but many cities do not appear to have adequate markets to Japan to merit daily service from one, much less, two carriers.

Consequently, we do not foresee a major increase in demand on the U.S.-Japan O&D routes, well less than projected in the Access U.S. Japan report. If demand does not rise substantially, then major increases in MOU carrier rights will simply transfer revenue among U.S. carriers (to those operating without the efficiencies of a Japan hub) and lower industry load factors and profitability. Clearly the net gain in U.S. revenue on the U.S.-Japan routes would be far less than the $2.1-2.6 billion revenue lost in 2005 by capping U.S. beyond rights in Japan or the $5-5.5 billion lost in 2015.

Impact On Consumers

Access U.S. Japan argues that consumers would benefit from increased frequencies, direct U.S.-Japan service to additional U.S. cities, and lower fares. All of these could be partially true but we should examine the three sets of customers impacted:

- Japan-Asia: For the passengers to/from the nine cities that would not be served by U.S. carriers from Japan by 2005, their options would be reduced and they would be limited to carriers with substantially higher costs. Hence, prices would likely rise.

- U.S.-Asia: For the passengers traveling between the U.S. and the nine unserved (by U.S. carriers) Asian cities through Japan, the Japan-Asian leg would have less competition and would be served by carriers with substantially higher costs. The Japanese airlines could strongly influence the total fare because they would have a virtual monopoly on the Japan-Asia leg and compete only with Korean Airlines (and other secondary Asian carriers) in the O&D markets. The passenger would likely face higher fares than with a U.S. competitor with rights to serve those cities through Japan. When direct service from the U.S. to those cities becomes economical, the fares through Tokyo will likely drop to market rates. These U.S.-Asian markets are growing faster than the U.S.-Japan market and should approximate 60% of the U.S.-Tokyo market by 2005.

- U.S.-Japan: Additional competition on U.S.-Japan routes will likely result in reduced fares and added U.S. cities with direct flights to Japan. If, however, the additional MOU flights simply replace flights from the U.S. '52 carriers, and the total capacity remains the same, fares and frequencies would probably not change. We believe the market will grow at 6% per year with a yield decline of 3%-3 1/2% per year. A greater reduction in price will likely result in a higher growth rate of the lowest fare passengers. Business travel will probably not be impacted because the cost of executive time on such an extended trip outweighs most price reductions in the decision to travel.

Consequently, the addition of a number of MOU flights suggested in the Access U.S. Japan report would result in some stimulation of discount vacation travel, added convenience to people in new U.S. cities with direct service to Japan, and huge losses to all carriers on the U.S.-Japan routes.

Impact On Communities

We fully understand the major economic benefit that a robust air passenger market brings to a community. The multiplier effect on jobs and trade is large. The question is which U.S. policy would result in the maximum benefit to U.S. communities. U.S. communities which gain direct service to Japan would benefit. Communities which lose frequencies to Japan would lose. Service on U.S. carriers benefits communities significantly more than service on foreign carriers because U.S. carriers employ residents of the communities who spend their earnings locally. Employment costs total about 30-35% of airline revenues.

In our judgment, the incremental growth in the market caused by the added MOU flights will not be great enough to offset the lost revenue. This is especially true if additional MOU rights are traded for beyond services. The impact of reduced competition on these routes could more than offset any stimulation through additional MOUs. We do not see a $9 billion benefit by adopting the Access U.S. Japan policy.

Japan's Position

To determine what the U.S. posture should be in its negotiations with Japan on air passenger rights, it is important to understand Japan's position. Japan's interest is clear and well documented publicly:

- To gain greater control over its most rapidly growing market -- Japan-Asia -- and to benefit fully from that growth and provide Japanese airlines a basis for profitability. Japan's solution: to limit low cost (i.e., U.S.) competitor participation in that market as much as possible

- To maximize the value of its natural Asian hub (a national asset) to Japan, and to use that hub to capture a significant share of the rapidly growing U.S.-Asian market. Japan's solution: to limit or eliminate the right of U.S. carriers to use Japanese cities as hubs.

- To limit losses across the Pacific where Japanese carriers are reportedly losing money. Japan's solution: to limit open skies competition with substantially (50%) lower cost U.S. carriers

- Japan's strategy: Argue that the 1952 agreement is unbalanced and should be equalized. Curtail United and Northwest rights to use Japanese hubs to serve Asian cities which will also result in a reduction of U.S.-Japan flights for those carriers. Additional MOU flights between U.S.-Japan can be granted (along with added Japanese carrier rights) which would in effect replace the United and Northwest flights, especially if code sharing arrangements ensure that a high proportion of the remaining U.S.-Asian market connects through Japan.

The United States should equally understand its interests.

- Air passenger transportation is one of the few industries in which the U.S. enjoys a trade surplus with Japan. This surplus will grow if the 1952 agreement is followed. It will decline or be eliminated if hub rights in Japan are restricted or eliminated.

- The U.S. carriers currently have a major share advantage in the U.S.-Japan and U.S.-Asian markets, i.e., 60-70%. These markets are the fastest growing markets in the world. That share advantage is rooted in hub rights in Japan and U.S. carriers that are substantially more efficient than their Japanese competitors ... the reverse of many other industries in which our countries compete.

- U.S. businesses and vacation travelers are as well served to Japan and Asia (fares and load factors) as U.S. travelers to Europe. U.S. carriers must aggressively add flights and reduce costs to maintain share and profitability in markets growing at 8% on average with prices expected to decline at 3%.

- The best solution for the U.S. across the Pacific is Open Skies. Unlimited rights to serve any market by any airline and build hubs wherever economically justified would enable U.S. carriers to utilize their substantial competitive advantages. Elimination or limitation to the use of the Japan hubs by U.S. carriers is a step in the opposite direction, and plays directly into the Japanese strategy to alter the competitive field to their advantage.

II. VALUE OF JAPANESE HUBS

The right to operate hubs in Japan is critical to the '52 carriers' ability to compete in Asia.

As is recognized by U.S. International Air Transportation policy, capping or eliminating these rights would severely restrict U.S. carrier abilities to participate in the expanding Asian markets. Eliminating these rights would reduce the U.S. '52 carriers' air revenues by an estimated $4.8 BN in 2005 and profitability by $630M. Restricting the U.S. '52 carriers to current beyond destinations (without frequency limitations) would reduce air revenues by $2.6 BN and profits by $380 MN in 2005 (before considering the impact of code sharing, which might "return" $300-500 million to the U.S.)

These rights can be exercised. While Narita will always be constrained, existing expansion plans should allow the U.S. '52 carriers to expand as forecast without increasing their share of slots until 2010-2015 — when additional airport capacity in the Tokyo area will be required to serve the local Japanese market. Osaka, the alternate hub to Narita, has substantial capacity which is being doubled.

Similarly, third country access should not prove an insurmountable obstacle. The U.S. DOT needs to be vigilant in negotiating appropriate access to China and Vietnam in particular.

U.S. AIR TRANSPORTATION POLICY RECOGNIZES THE IMPORTANCE OF INTERNATIONAL HUB AND SPOKES

"To meet demand and to improve their efficiency, many carriers are developing international hub-and-spoke systems that permit them to combine traffic flows from many routes (the "spokes") at a central point (the "hub") ...Internationally, an even larger portion [than domestically] of traffic moving over hub-and-spoke systems will require the use of at least two hubs (e.g., a hub in both the U.S. and Europe...)

"[Carriers] require a higher quality and quantity of supporting route authority than they have sought in the past. Airlines will become increasingly concerned with every market that enables them to flow passengers over any part of their system network. These airlines will be looking for broad, flexible authority to operate beyond and behind hub points, in addition to the hub-to-hub market between two countries. ...In the future, governments will have to adjust their focus to bargain for the bundles of rights that will permit airlines to develop global networks."

Source: U.S. International Air Transportation Policy Statement, April 1995

THE VALUE OF A HUB TO CUSTOMERS AND CARRIERS

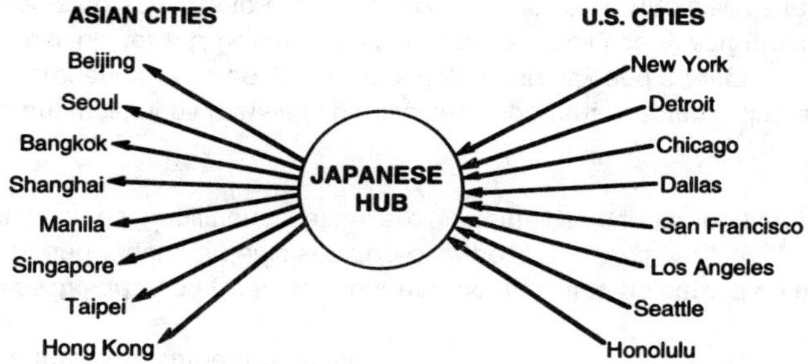

EXAMPLE:

- Passengers on the Los Angeles–Tokyo flight are traveling to Tokyo, Beijing, Seoul, Bangkok, Shanghai, Singapore and Hong Kong
- The Los Angeles passengers to Shanghai join with Shanghai destined passengers from other U.S. cities in Tokyo and fly together to Shanghai
- These U.S.–Shanghai passengers are joined by passengers originating in Tokyo

AS A RESULT:

- Consumers have frequent service options from several U.S. cities to several Asian cities
- Carriers can deploy the optimum aircraft on each leg of the route

RPCH247-005-008F

United 4/30 VA

THE JAPAN HUBS ARE CRITICAL TO THE U.S. '52 CARRIERS' ABILITY TO COMPETE EFFECTIVELY IN ASIA

As recognized by U.S. air transportation policy, the beyond rights make it possible for the U.S. '52 carriers to capitalize on the economic benefits of a hub in serving Asia: a broad set of Asian destinations can be reached economically by concentrating passengers through the Japan hubs and augmenting trans-Pacific traffic with Japanese passengers to Asia. Conversely, the broad set of Asian markets served makes non-stop services to a broader set of U.S. airports from Japan economical.

These hub economics will allow the U.S. '52 carriers to serve a number of Asian destinations which could otherwise not afford U.S. carrier presence.

- Cities such as Jakarta and Kuala Lumpur are too distant to be served on a non-stop basis from the U.S. and require an efficient stop-over point
- Other cities, such as Tianjin and Pusan, are 'too small' to support non-stop U.S. service at this time

The right to operate local hubs in Asia is particularly important in establishing an Asian market position and building presence. The ability to serve Japan directly and a range of Asian cities on a one-stop basis makes it possible for a U.S. carrier to enter an Asian city early and grow its market until it can eventually support non-stop services to U.S. gateways. In fact, following Delta's recent withdrawal from Asia, **no U.S. airline serves Asia on a non-stop basis without a hub in Japan** (except for Seoul, which Delta still serves from Portland).

UNITED NETWORK 2005
UNLIMITED BEYOND RIGHTS

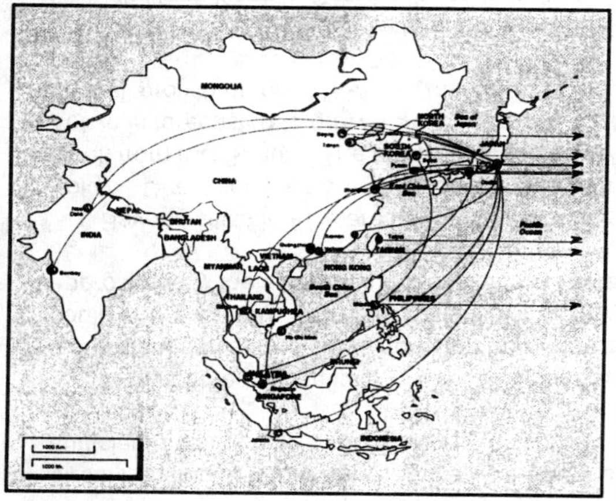

UNITED NETWORK 2005
NO BEYOND RIGHTS

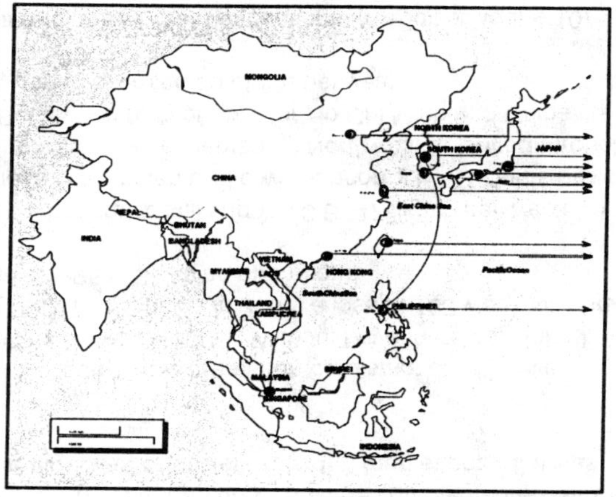

RPCH247-005-005Maps 2

AS DEMONSTRATED IN BOOZ·ALLEN & HAMILTON'S SEPTEMBER 1995 REPORT, THE JAPAN HUB ALLOWS THE U.S. CARRIERS TO ESTABLISH EXTENSIVE ASIAN NETWORKS

Unrestricted use of the 1952 rights should allow United Airlines to establish an extensive Asian system serving some 19 cities with a total of 401 weekly frequencies by the year 2005, compared to 10 cities and 178 weekly frequencies currently. Services via the Japan hub would be complemented with direct nonstop services between the U.S. and the main Asian cities wherever the market potential was sufficient and the city is in range.

Many of the destinations which can be served through Tokyo are either too distant or will have insufficient demand to serve non-stop from the United States by 2005. Without beyond rights, United could only serve 10 Asian destinations with 238 weekly frequencies in 2005, a loss of 163 weekly flights, approximately the same number of flights in United's 1995 U.S.-Asian operations.

Beyond cities in Asia are added through Tokyo when traffic will support 3 B747 flights per week from Tokyo. Direct service from the U.S. is added to these cities when traffic will support 3 B777 flights per week from a U.S. hub. The annual market for Asian cities not yet served by Northwest or United through Tokyo is forecasted to grow from a low of 6% for Pusan to a high of 15% for Ho Chi Minh and China. Overall growth of the U.S.-Asian market excluding Japan is projected at 8% per year.

United would (probably) attempt to serve India and a few other destinations (in addition to the 10) through Hong Kong or Seoul if Japan hub right were capped. The economics of such services would, however, likely be marginal since they are dependent on a much weaker local traffic base and since United would be disadvantaged by using alternative gateways versus Japanese carriers.

JAPAN IS BY FAR THE BEST HUB IN ASIA - IN FACT, THE ONLY REALISTIC OPPORTUNITY FOR U.S. CARRIERS TO ESTABLISH A SIGNIFICANT ASIAN PRESENCE

- Japan is a natural place to establish a hub since:
  - It is in range of all major U.S. gateways with current aircraft technology
  - It is situated on the great circle route between the U.S. and most Asian cities
  - It is in range of many Asian cities which cannot be reached from the U.S. with current long-range aircraft such as the Boeing 747 - 400
  - U.S.-Japan is by far the largest Asian origin/destination (O&D) market - currently 50% of total U.S.- Asian market

- In order to operate economically, a hub needs a sizable local passenger base
  - Tokyo has a larger metropolitan area population of 27 million
  - Osaka has a greater metropolitan population of 17 million and is a very useful complement to Tokyo
  - Seoul has a population base of 16 million
  - Taipei is a third-best choice with a population base of 6 million

- U.S. beyond rights have allowed United and Northwest to establish strong market presence in Japan that supports the operation of a hub. If beyond rights were limited or eliminated, the presence of both carriers would be reduced substantially.

- In addition to the advantages of a Japanese hub noted above, establishing an alternative hub is difficult if a well-established incumbent is present, which is the case for Seoul (Korean Air, Asiana), and Taipei (China Airlines, EVA)
  - Incumbents' breadth of destinations limits the yield potential of an entrant
  - Large investment needed both in infrastructure and marketing

CAPPING OR ELIMINATING THESE HUB RIGHTS WOULD SERIOUSLY REDUCE UNITED'S AND NORTHWEST'S ABILITY TO COMPETE IN ASIA

Without beyond rights and the hubbing opportunities provided, the two carriers' ability to compete would be severely limited

(1) Need to serve Asia without the efficiencies of a hub (which no U.S. carriers without an Asian hub does)

(2) Need to reduce U.S.-Japan frequencies by a third

(3) Would offer far fewer options to customers traveling between the U.S. and other Asian cities. For example, each U.S. carrier would have to concentrate passengers flying to/from Asia in one or two U.S. cities to provide adequate volume to support flights to Asian cities ... and fewer Asian cities would qualify.

(4) Could not participate in developing new markets as effectively, but would be relegated to entering those in which Asian competitors had developed and established a presence

Similarly, capping beyond rights would be highly damaging since it would freeze the U.S. carrier hubs in Tokyo, allowing its chief Japanese competitors to develop and strengthen their positions. This would be analogous to freezing American Airlines operations in Chicago in 1981 (940 daily departures) while allowing United to grow (1,391 daily departures in 1981, 2,849 in 1995) and 'dominate' the market. **Ultimately the capped operations would cease to be a competitive factor.**

ESTIMATED IMPACT OF ELIMINATING/CAPPING BEYOND
DOLLARS IN BILLIONS

MARKET (O&D)	CURRENT REVENUE (UA/NW)	PASSENGER GROWTH (P.A.)	YIELD DECLINE (REAL P.A.)	UA/NW REVENUE PROJECTED IN 2005			SHIFT IN REVENUE FROM U.S. IN 2005 (1)	
				UNFETTERED BEYOND RIGHTS	NO NEW BEYOND DESTINATIONS	ELIMINATING BEYOND	NO NEW BEYOND DESTINATIONS	ELIMINATING BEYOND
U.S.-Asia	$3.3 BN	9%	3%	$8.6	$7.1	$6.1	($1.5)	($2.5)
Japan-Asia	$0.7 BN	7%	3%	$2.0	$1.1	$0.0	($0.9)	($2.0)
U.S.-Japan	$2.0 BN	6%	3.5% (1995-2005) 3% (2005+)	$4.3	$4.1	$4.0	($0.2)	($0.3)
Total	$6.0 BN	8%	3%	$14.9	$12.3	$10.1	($2.6)	($4.8)

Note (1) Most would go to Japanese airlines

IMPACT ON UA/NW PROFITABILITY IN 2005	
Capped	($376 Million)
No Beyond	($635 Million)

UA 4/30 VA

THE PRIMARY BENEFICIARY OF SUCH ACTIONS WOULD BE JAL

Eliminating or restructuring United and Northwest's' Japanese hub rights would strengthen JAL substantially

- JAL would obtain dominant or exclusive use of Tokyo and Osaka as hubs (with ANA) and consequently would have a near monopoly on U.S.-Asian traffic through Japan. Without restrictions in 2005, the U.S. '52 carriers would have U.S.-Asian revenues of $2.5 BN to destinations which are either too distant or too small to serve on a nonstop basis from the U.S. A strong Asian hub is required to serve these markets effectively

- JAL would have no U.S. competition in Japan-Asia. United and Northwest revenues for Japan-Asia are projected to be $2.0 billion in 2005 with full beyond rights.

- JAL would become more competitive on U.S.-Japan since JAL's Tokyo hub economies would improve while UA and NW would have to reduce frequencies by a third with the loss of hub rights and economies in Tokyo. The additional shift in revenue from U.S. to Japanese carriers in the U.S.-Japan market could be substantial. We have been conservative and assumed that Northwest and United would choose to discount fares to limit frequency reductions to those induced by the loss of connecting passengers. This might entail a net revenue loss of $200-300 million in 2005. JAL and ANA would be best placed to benefit from the loss of loyalty to the U.S. carriers

Korean Air and other Asian operators would clearly also benefit, but would stand to gain much less since only a component of their traffic would be affected and Tokyo is a far superior hub (for example, the U.S.-Tokyo O&D market is an estimated 3.5 times larger than U.S.-Seoul).

The impact of capping United and Northwest's Tokyo hub rights would be similar longer term as United and Northwest would be increasingly disadvantaged over time. In 2005, for example, United and Northwest revenues would be reduced by at least $2.6 BN by capping beyond rights to today's destination.

CURRENT SITUATION	ASSUMPTIONS ON CAPACITY	CONCLUSIONS
<u>Narita</u> • One runway today (second runway by 2000) • Noise cap (360 movements per day) • Currently operated at max. 28 movements per hour • IATA believes that max. 36 movements per hour are feasible -- indicating 25% extra capacity currently unused	<u>Narita</u> • 2nd runway will double current capacity by 2000 • Utilization level of both runways will go up by 15% by 2005 • Utilization level goes up to the 25% limit by 2010	<u>Implied UA's Slot Share in Narita</u> (Unrestricted Expansion Scenario) Current: 8.4% 2000: 6.3% 2005: 7.6% 2010: 8.0% 2015: 12.8%
<u>Osaka</u> • One runway today (second runway after '2005) • Currently operating at max. 24 movements per hour, soon to be 26 movements, and eventually can go up to 32 movements per hour • Hard to define "capacity" for US carriers because the airport has a lot of domestic traffic	<u>Osaka</u> • Capacity will be expanded significantly by the 2nd runway and increased utilization level of the runways • Assume that UA can obtain one additional slot per year (current 6 slots)	This assumes United can obtain one additional slot per year at Osaka.

United 4/30 VA

JAPANESE AIRPORT CAPACITY SHOULD NOT LIMIT THE USE OF TOKYO AND OSAKA AS HUBS

Although Narita is currently "constrained" there are plans to add a second runway (expected some time before the year 2000), and IATA believes that Narita can be utilized more efficiently (another 25%). In addition, Kansai (Osaka) is not yet capacity constrained, and there are plans for a second runway. These Narita capacity additions and incremental use of Kansai should allow United and Northwest to expand their Asian networks without needing to gain more than their current share of Narita slots until 2010, when additional Japanese airport capacity will be needed.

It is reasonable to assume that Japan will increase Narita capacity utilization and eventually invest in additional capacity since this will be necessary to accommodate the underlying market growth and allow the Japanese carriers to capitalize on this growth.

ASIAN COUNTRIES AVIATION POLICY AND INFRASTRUCTURE

	CURRENT AGREEMENT	HISTORY	INFRASTRUCTURE
KOREA	• Unlimited frequencies, capacity, intermediate and beyond rights	• Has been receptive to US carrier competition.	• A new airport in Seoul is planned, to accommodate 100 million passengers per year
TAIWAN	• Unlimited frequencies, capacity, intermediate and beyond rights	• Has been receptive to US carrier competition	• Planning a major expansion for Taipei to meet the demand
SINGAPORE	• Unlimited frequencies, capacity, intermediate and beyond rights	• Excellent aviation relationship with US. Reportedly interested in negotiating "open skies"	• Added the second terminal to Changi in '90, enhancing the engineering facilities
PHILIPPINES	• Multiple (but limited) destinations permitted. No restrictions on frequencies. Unlimited intermediate rights for US	• Several negotiations in which Philippines has sought to postpone full effectiveness of the agreement	• US $3 billion expansion planned of the second passenger and cargo facility at Manila
MALAYSIA	• No restrictions on frequencies, and capacity. Unlimited intermediate and beyond rights for US	• Despite liberal agreement, currently no US carrier passenger service to Malaysia	• Plans to complete new airport in Kuala Lumpur in '98
THAILAND	• Relatively liberal agreement reached last year which allows increase in US carrier opportunities to Thailand	• Discontinued its liberal post deregulation agreement in 1990 to protect Thai Air, but caused damage to tourist industry	• New airport is proposed -- to handle 25 million passengers quadrupling the capacity
INDONESIA	• Fifth freedom service via Japan and other named points are permitted without limit	• Recently, indicated a hesitancy on US carriers' 5th freedom rights, but not been tested	• Preparing to construct three new airports over the next couple of years
CHINA	• Relatively restrictive agreement that limits destinations and frequencies. But, UA is able to operate a daily service to Beijing and Shanghai via Tokyo	• Tend to refuse to allow the US carriers to increase frequencies as scheduled in the agreement. Last year, two sides agreed to slow down US carriers' growth	• 17 new airports are under construction. Guangzhou -- will open in '99 Beijing and Shanghai: ATC rather than slot constrained
HONG KONG	• Bermuda II type. 14 weekly fifth freedom flights via Tokyo permitted. UA /NW have 7 each	• Agreement with Hong Kong established in '1995, intended to continue after '97 integration	• New airport is under construction-- 2 runways, 24-hour operation
VIETNAM	• No air service agreement today	• Early indications are that Vietnam is not yet interested in a liberal agreement.	• Plan to improve the existing Hanoi and Ho Chi Minh airport. Plan to build a new airport in Danang

ACCESS TO THE THIRD COUNTRIES SHOULD NOT BE A PROBLEM SINCE MANY OF ASIAN COUNTRIES ARE MOVING TOWARDS MORE LIBERAL AVIATION AGREEMENTS WITH THE U.S.

Protectionist sentiments in air transportation in Asia appear to have crested in the early '90s with Thailand's renunciation of its agreement with the U.S.

- The Thai government terminated the bilateral agreement in 1990 due to the imbalance in the market share
- The resulting traffic decline negatively impacted local tourism
- Thailand re-established bilateral agreements in early 1996 to revitalize traffic -- U.S. carriers were allowed to regain the frequencies they had when the old bilateral was terminated

Recent agreements with the Philippines, Hong Kong, Macao, and Thailand, have expanded opportunities and allowed services via Japan.

The U.S. already have arrangements for services via Japan to Korea, Taiwan, Malaysia, and Singapore.

The primary obstacles are China, where aviation policy is evolving, and Vietnam, where there are no bilateral agreements.

Considering their need for economic growth, these countries should find it in their interest to negotiate new bilateral arrangements as their markets evolve. Most are also members of APEC and have just committed to free trade, including air transportation for the first time.

THE PRIMARY OBSTACLE TO EXERCISING BEYOND RIGHTS IS RESISTANCE BY THE JAPANESE GOVERNMENT

Beyond rights can only be exercised when a market becomes large enough to support U.S. carrier presence via Japan. A number of unserved destinations are expected to reach such a threshold in the next few years, and UA and NW have a number of applications pending.

The biggest obstacle to expanding their hub operations in Japan is resistance by the Japanese government

- In the last 15 years, the Japanese government has imposed restrictions on the rights of the U.S. carriers
  - 1982: U.S. surrenders right to unilaterally designate new carriers ("MOU")
  - 1985: U.S. surrenders rights of '52 carriers to serve any U.S. gateway
  - 1994: Japan announces freeze on the future U.S. carrier rights (Having refused a number of applications to exercise these rights in 1992)
  - 1995: Japan refuses to honor its obligation with respect to beyond rights
- Japan has been trying to impose a maximum limit of 50% local traffic beyond Japan
- It is apparent from the recent cargo negotiations that the Japanese government is prepared to take beyond rights "hostage" to pressure the U.S. government in renegotiating the '52 bilateral agreement

Access to some Asian countries, such as Thailand, China, and Hong Kong, has also been a challenge in the past due to their restrictive aviation policy. But, as discussed, such access should not be the major constraint going forward.

III. VALUE OF ADDITIONAL MOU RIGHTS

Additional capacity will be required to accommodate the expected growth in the U.S.-Japan market. We estimate that U.S. carriers will need an additional 28 daily frequencies to Japan by 2005 to maintain the U.S. market shares based on the 6% growth projection. Under the '52 agreement, Northwest and United can add frequencies without approval; 23 frequencies would be required to maintain their market share. Hence, an additional 5 daily rights would be necessary to maintain the overall market share for U.S. carriers.

Additional rights above the 28 frequencies to maintain share are clearly valuable in stimulating the market further, although the potential appears more limited than ACCESS U.S.-Japan has argued. Specifically:

- Actual fares per mile are not substantially higher across the Pacific than across the Atlantic
- The Japanese government has little incentive to free the U.S.-Japan market given the losses being sustained by Japanese carriers across the Pacific and their stated objective to "manage the market"
- An additional fare decline of 25-40% (as suggested by ACCESS U.S.-Japan) associated with substantial increases in trans-Pacific capacity would, in fact, make it virtually impossible for U.S. carriers, let alone Japanese, to operate the Pacific profitably

Any trade of beyond rights for additional MOUs would be highly detrimental to the U.S. airline industry and balance of trade.

- A loss of access to new beyond destinations would cost the U.S. '52 carriers an estimated $2.6 BN in lost revenue potential by 2005
- Additional MOU flights (above those required to maintain share) might raise MOU revenues by $500-600M. This would be offset by a U.S. '52 carrier revenue loss of $200-400 on the U.S.-Japan market

DISCOUNT FARE DIFFERENTIAL OF SELECT U.S. TO EUROPEAN CITIES VS. SELECT U.S. TO TOKYO

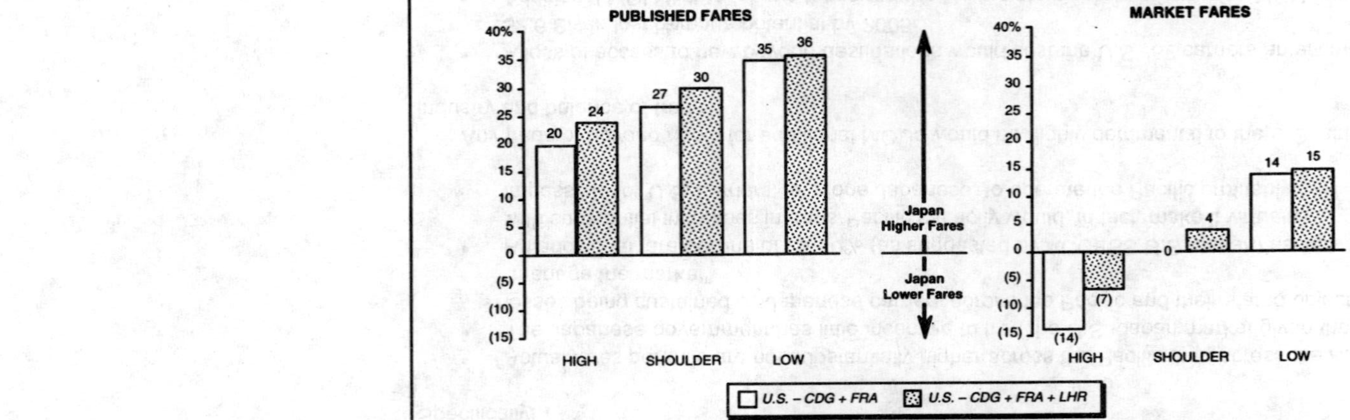

This chart provides a comparison of lowest "meaningful" fares – those a reasonable proportion of travelers can take advantage of. A comparison was made for the high season (August 1, 1995 chosen as a representative date), low season (January 15, 1995) and shoulder season (October 2, 1995). The comparisons are from Chicago, Los Angeles, San Francisco, and Seattle to Tokyo, Frankfurt, Paris, and London

Note: All fares are U.S. point of sale
Source: Published fares: ATP CO database; Market fares: United Airlines best estimate of selling fares through discount distribution channels

RPCH247-005-001BB

III-2F

United 4/4 VA

ACTUAL U.S.-JAPAN FARES ARE NOT SUBSTANTIALLY HIGHER THAN FARES ACROSS THE ATLANTIC

A recent document published by ACCESS U.S.-Japan claims that routes between the U.S. and other major international destinations are generally more than 50% lower on a per mile basis than fares to Japan because of greater competition. That study concludes that higher fares to Japan have led to pent up demand and that the introduction of competition among commercial carriers on U.S.-Japan routes would lead to 20-45% reduced fares.

Published discount economy fares can range from 20% to 35% higher from the U.S. to Tokyo than to some European cities. However, a comparison of actual economy fares paid during similar seasonal periods shows that actual discounted fares to Japan are actually 7-14% lower in season than U.S.-European fares and 14-15% higher off-season (see opposite).

Economy fares from Japan to the U.S. are typically higher than U.S. to Japan. Actual economy fares paid originating in Japan to the U.S. can be double (or slightly more) the U.S. purchased fares during the peak August season on a U.S. $ per mile basis. This is fully understandable given the dramatic seasonal spike during August in Japan ("everybody travels during this month"). By virtue of its market position in Japan, United obtains typical economy fares from Japan to the USA which are 30-40% higher than U.S.-Japan in the shoulder and off season. A simple check on market fares through Japanese discount houses however reveals Japan-U.S. fares which are very similar to U.S.-Japan fares

Published full fare business class tickets to Japan by contrast are some <u>15-20% lower</u> on a per mile basis than to Paris, and substantially lower than to London.

Net-net, actual economy fares paid to Japan are similar to those to Europe, business class fares to Japan are lower while economy fares from Japan to the U.S. are higher. Price differences vary with seasonality and city pair. Given this picture, we consider an annual yield decline of 3.5% per annum reasonable

HOWEVER, U.S.-JAPAN IS ONE OF THE MORE ATTRACTIVE INTERNATIONAL O&D MARKETS

U.S.-Japan is a large, high growth market. Asia/Pacific comprises more than 35% of the total world aviation market (IATA). The U.S.-Japan market makes up just over 50% of the total U.S.-Asia market. Historically, the annual passenger growth rate across the Pacific has been more than 11% which is consistent with an expected demand growth of 6% between the U.S. and Japan and 8-15% between the U.S. and Asia.

U.S.-Japan is also one of the richer markets, with a substantially higher proportion of business travel than most other international routes. This is why United Airlines U.S.-Japan yields are about 25% higher than its Atlantic yields. Average costs per passenger are also higher to Japan than Europe since the aircraft serving these markets have very high proportions of business class seats and because of Japanese cost factors (cost of local presence, landing fees, etc.).

This also explains why Tokyo is, and will remain, the critical hub to serve Asia from the U.S.

It is also why we were conservative in our previous evaluation and assumed that U.S.-Japan prices would fall by 3.5% per annum (1995-2005) as leisure traffic gains in importance and competition intensifies. Other Asian yields were assumed to fall 3% per annum, consistent with U.S.-Atlantic experience (the lower rate of U.S.-Pacific yield declines 1984-1994 was likely in part a consequence of rapid growth and rapidly changing Yen-U.S. exchange rates).

JAPAN'S NATIONAL INTEREST IS CLEAR AND PUBLICLY ARTICULATED

- To gain greater control over its most rapidly growing market -- Japan-Asia -- and to benefit fully from that growth and provide Japanese airlines a basis for profitability. Japan's solution: to limit low cost (i.e., U.S.) competitor participation in that market as much as possible

- To maximize the value of its natural Asian hub (a national asset) to Japan, and to use that hub to capture a significant share of the rapidly growing U.S.-Asian market. Japan's solution: to limit or eliminate U.S. carriers' use of Japanese cities as hubs.

- To limit losses across the Pacific where Japanese carriers are reportedly losing money. Japan's solution: to limit open skies competition with substantially (50%) lower cost U.S. carriers

- Japan's strategy: Argue that the 1952 agreement is unbalanced and should be equalized. Curtail United and Northwest rights to use Japanese hubs to serve Asian cities which will also result in a reduction of U.S.-Japan flights for those carriers. Additional MOU flights between U.S.-Japan can be granted (along with added Japanese carrier rights) which would in effect replace the United and Northwest flights, especially if code sharing arrangements ensure that a high proportion of the remaining U.S.-Asian market connects through Japan.

STAGE-LENGTH ADJUSTED COST COMPARISON

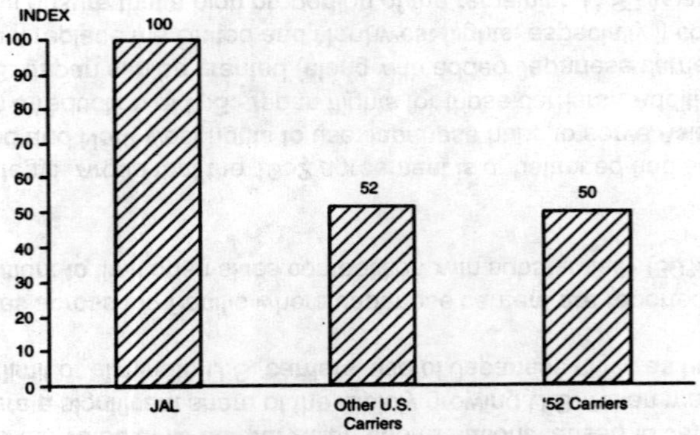

Note: Data based on ¢/ATK for 1993 and are stage-length adjusted using carrier route frequencies and United's cost and stage length curve
Source: Airline Business, November 1994, BA&H analysis

RPCH247-005-007B

IT IS UNLIKELY THAT ADDITIONAL MOU RIGHTS WOULD LEAD TO SUBSTANTIALLY EXPANDED TRAFFIC ABOVE THE UNDERLYING GROWTH OF THE U.S.-JAPAN MARKET

As we have seen, fares across the Pacific are not substantially higher than across the Atlantic.

The U.S.-Japan market has been growing steadily and is expected to continue to grow at 6% per annum as leisure and business traffic develops. It would take substantial capacity additions to stimulate the market over this rate.

The Japanese government has little incentive to free the U.S.-Japan market given the losses being sustained by Japanese carriers across the Pacific and their stated objective to "manage the market".

An additional fare decline of 25-40% (as suggested by ACCESS U.S.-Japan) associated with substantial increases in trans-Pacific capacity would, in fact, make it virtually impossible for U.S. carriers, let alone Japanese, to operate the Pacific profitably.

2005 SCENARIOS

	US MOU FLIGHTS (Daily)	LIKELY ANNUAL FARE DECLINE 1995-2005 (Real Terms)	INCREMENTAL FARE DECLINE VS ALTERNATIVE IN 2005	RATIONALE
BA&H Base Case No Trade MOU For Beyond	Memo: 1995=7 12	-3.5%	–	• Market shares assumed constant, full use of beyond rights
Access 1: Beyond Rights Traded for Sufficient MOU's to Lower Prices 10% in 2005	17	-4.2%	-10%	• Additional US MOUs are granted in exchange for restrictions on new beyond destinations. Japanese MOU carriers are also granted additional rights. It is assumed that US MOU carriers take up 50% of additional capacity, Japanese carriers pick up 30%, US '52 carriers add the final 20%
Access 2: Beyond Rights Traded for Sufficient MOU's to Lower Prices 25% in 2005	29	-5.2%	-25%	• Two thirds of capacity additions are US MOU carriers. Japanese cannot afford any capacity increase at these prices, US '52 carrier add one third to defend their positions

RPCH247-005-006F

III-6F

United 4/4 VA

THREE SCENARIOS WERE DEVELOPED TO COMPARE THE VALUE OF ADDITIONAL MOU RIGHTS TO CAPPING BEYOND RIGHTS

The base case scenario assumes that the U.S. '52 carriers are allowed to exercise their beyond rights freely and that sufficient additional MOU rights are obtained to allow the MOU carriers to maintain their U.S.-Japan shares as the market grows (an additional 5 daily MOU's by 2005).

The other two scenarios explore the Access U.S.-Japan proposition that additional MOU's be traded for the right to fly to new beyond destinations (frequencies to existing destinations can be increased).

- "Access 1" assumes that the number of daily MOU carrier flights is raised from 7 in 1995 to 17 in 2005 and that Japanese and U.S. carriers respond sufficiently to lower fares 10% over and above the underlying price decline (see opposite)

- "Access 2" makes the unrealistic assumption that sufficient capacity is added to allow prices to drop 25% over and above the trend decline. In this case, it is assumed that no Japanese carrier can afford to add capacity and that the U.S. '52 carriers would add one-third of the total additional capacity addition (over and above the base case) to protect their positions.

2005 PROJECTIONS BY SCENARIOS

	PASSENGERS (RETURN TRIPS)		REVENUE (PACIFIC TOTAL)		PROFIT CHANGE FROM BASE CASE		IMPACT ON THE BALANCE OF TRADE VS BASE CASE
	USA-ASIA	USA-JAPAN	'52	MOU	'52	MOU	
BA&H Base Case No Trade MOU For Beyond	8.7 MM	6.8 MM	$14.9 BN	$1.6 BN	–	–	–
	$15.5 MM		$16.5 BN				
Access 1: Beyond Rights Traded for Sufficient MOU's to Lower Prices 10%	8.2 MM	7.5 MM	$12.2BN	$2.1 BN	($1.0) BN	($0.1) BN	($2.2) BN
	$15.7 MM		$14.3 BN		$(1.1) BN		
Access 2: Beyond Rights Traded for Sufficient MOU's to Lower Prices 25%	8.2 MM	8.5 MM	$12.3 BN	$3.3 BN	($2.2) BN	($0.5) BN	($1.0) BN
	$16.7 MM		$15.6 BN		$(2.7) BN		

RPCH247-005-007F

United 4/4 VA

IT IS CLEAR THAT ANY TRADE OF BEYOND RIGHTS FOR ADDITIONAL MOU RIGHTS WOULD BE HIGHLY DETRIMENTAL TO THE U.S. AIRLINE INDUSTRY AND BALANCE OF TRADE

Preventing the U.S. '52 carriers from participating in the new beyond markets would involve a loss of $2.6BN in U.S. airline revenues in 2005 (a complete loss of beyond rights would result in a loss of $4.8BN).

Five additional daily MOU rights, by contrast, might increase MOU carrier revenues by some $500-$600M in 2005 over and above the BA&H base case. Additional competition would, however, reduce the revenues of the U.S. '52 carriers by some $400M, some of which could be regained through additional services ($200M).

The net trade of "Access 1" is a net gain of $300-$400M in U.S. airline revenues on the U.S.-Japan market (and hence balance of trade) for a loss of $2.6BN to Asia. In addition, the U.S. airline industry would have been substantially weakened through the restrictions on U.S.-Japan hubs. The net profit reduction to the U.S. airline industry would be in the range of $1BN, which would come from the U.S. '52 carriers.

Sufficient capacity addition to cause a 25% average price reduction over and above the trend price decline would lead to a U.S. carrier profit decline of $2.7BN. It would lead to a substantial share gain across the Pacific since no foreign carrier could afford to compete at such prices. This scenario is simply not realistic.

THE CONSEQUENCES ARE CLEAR

1) The U.S. government should negotiate for additional access to Japan for the MOU carriers. This will be necessary to allow them to maintain share and allow further direct access from the U.S. to Japan

2) Any trade which involves the loss of beyond rights is, however, disadvantageous to the U.S. airline industry and balance of trade (the impact on consumers and communities will be addressed in Chapter V).
   - Would have a significant impact on the balance of trade (In excess of $2BN in 2005 under realistic scenarios).
   - Would reduce the efficiency of the U.S. airline system by limiting access to the efficiencies of a Japan hub and transferring rights to carriers which are less efficient in serving the Japanese market (Carriers which use smaller gauge aircraft on valuable Narita slots).

The main reasons that these conclusions are so different from those of ACCESS U.S.-Japan are that they chose to compare the NPV of lost earnings to the U.S. '52 carriers (i.e., the value of their profits) to the revenues earned on the additional MOU services. The other factors considered by Access U.S.-Japan -- differences in discount rates, elasticities and even whether one or two individual services can be operated -- are inconsequential when weighed against the erroneous comparison of lost profits with added revenues.

IV. CODE SHARING

Code Sharing ...

Code sharing was not explicitly considered in the original & Hamilton valuation of U.S.-beyond rights.

Code sharing allows U.S. carriers to establish global service networks and provide consumers improved services and choice. The balance of trade improves with the U.S. carriers' ability to leverage some of their comparative advantage.

Direct on-line U.S. participation in foreign markets is superior to code sharing since it allows U.S. carriers to participate more fully in developing high growth international markets and offer lower cost U.S. carriers' service to more destinations.

While open skies with Japan would be the preferred outcome, code sharing and unfettered use of beyond rights would be a second-best solution and help create a level playing field -- a possible precursor to open skies.

Code sharing is, however, a poor substitute to Japan hub rights.

- It would transfer traffic and employment to Japanese (and Asian) carriers with an estimated $2.1-2.6 BN negative impact on the balance of trade
- It would cause upward pressure on prices to interior Asian destinations and hence to U.S.-Asian travel via Japan

CODE SHARING ALLOWS U.S. AIRLINES TO EXTEND THEIR GLOBAL REACH AND OFFER CONSUMERS GREATER CHOICE AND IMPROVED SERVICES

Code sharing is a way for airlines to establish global networks without making huge investments in new hubs and displacing local carriers. It is an effective mechanism to increase traffic and revenues.

- Gives access to a large number of cities through the partner's hub -- both smaller local communities which cannot support direct U.S. service and larger, more distant cities which are out of range

- Allows U.S. carriers to serve larger non-hub destinations directly from the U.S. by leveraging the partners' local market presence and frequent flyer base

Consumers benefit through shorter layover times (as a result of close schedule coordination), more hassle-free connections, one-stop check-in, and a greater choice of carriers and routes between cities.

According to the GAO, it is likely that there is some traffic stimulation from competition among alliances in the short term, but there is insufficient data to determine whether consumers are paying higher or lower fares as a result of alliances and whether alliances will reduce or increase competition in the long term.

ILLUSTRATIVE

ON-LINE SERVICE VS. CODE SHARE

HUB RIGHTS

- U.S. carriers are free to serve and develop beyond geographies via the hub country and directly

NO BEYONDS CODE SHARE

- U.S. carrier "share" U.S.-hub routes
- Code share presence helps U.S. carriers develop direct U.S.-beyond services but less effectively than with hub routes

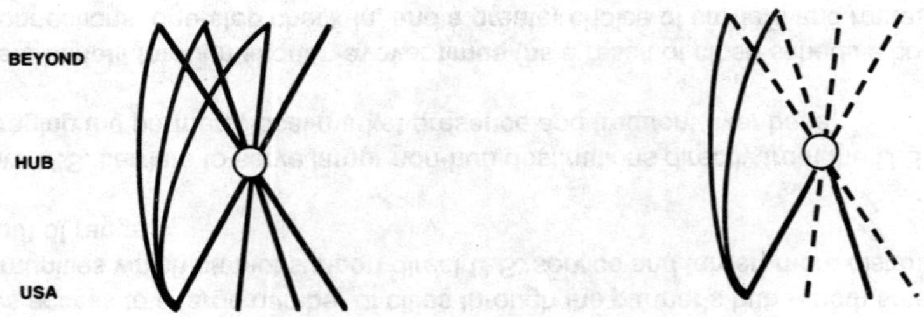

KEY

— *US Carrier Segment* - - *Partner Segment*

RPCH247-005-005F

United 4/30 VA

ON-LINE U.S. CARRIER SERVICE THROUGH A HUB IS MORE BENEFICIAL THAN CODE SHARING

"Seamless" code sharing between two carriers can provide consumers effective connecting services. On-line U.S. carrier service through a 'foreign' hub has significant advantages over code sharing:

- Consumers benefit through lower cost services to a broader range of destinations, especially when an efficient U.S. carrier hub can be operated (constrained or subscale hubs will be less effective)
  - U.S. carrier services can be provided to more destinations (see opposite)
  - A greater number of destinations can be served directly from the U.S. by U.S. carriers

- U.S. airlines have the ability to build their local presence in the beyond cities to leverage their comparative advantage in more foreign growth markets

- The balance of trade is more favorable with free beyond rights, as U.S. carriers can capture a greater share of revenues than with code sharing

- U.S. employment is similarly affected -- more pilot, crew and support jobs are captured in the USA

CODE SHARING AND UNFETTERED BEYONDS

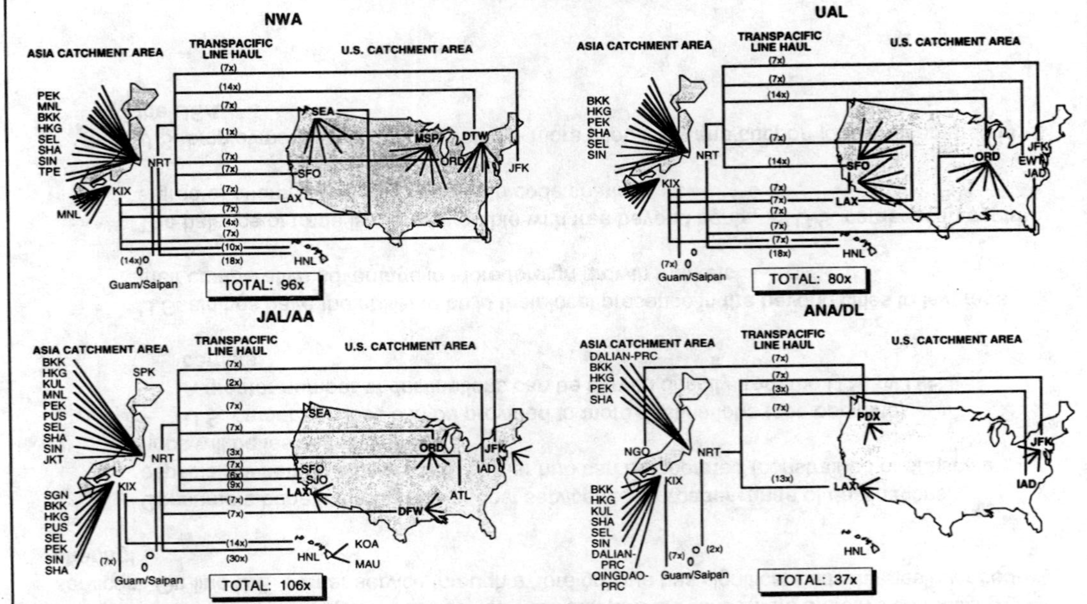

Note: NWA & UAL will need third country code sharing rights to effectively expand their Japan hubs in direct competition with JAL/AA and ANA/DL

RPCH247-005-003Maps4

United 4/30 VA

IN THE CASE OF JAPAN, CODE SHARING AND UNFETTERED USE OF BEYOND RIGHTS WOULD CREATE A "LEVEL PLAYING FIELD" AND COULD BE A PRECURSOR TO OPEN SKIES

Code sharing and the unfettered use of beyond rights would clearly allow four parties (UA, NW, AA/JAL, DL/ANA) the opportunity to develop "unconstrained" Asian and U.S. hub-and-spoke networks. This should serve to redress the "unbalanced relationship" which the Japanese government is concerned about since Japanese carriers would have access to U.S. and Japanese hubs. Competitive parity clearly requires the right for U.S. '52 carriers to develop their Tokyo hub in an unconstrained fashion and the ability to establish third country code sharing relationships (since JAL and ANA can code share in Asia).

The consumer should benefit from competition between stronger participants in the U.S.-Asia market and the U.S. balance of trade should benefit from the U.S. '52 carriers' ability to continue to expand and MOU carriers' ability to leverage their Asian partners' network.

Code sharing and unfettered use of beyond rights could clearly be a step toward an open skies type relationship between Japan and the USA.

ESTIMATED IMPACT OF CAPPING BEYOND RIGHTS VS. IMPACT OF CODE SHARING
(DOLLARS IN BILLIONS)

MARKET (O&D)	PROJECTED REVENUE U.S.'52 CARRIERS 2005	SHIFT IN REVENUE FROM U.S.-NO NEW BEYONDS	POTENTIAL RECAPTURE THROUGH CODE SHARE ALLIANCE	COMMENTS
U.S.-Asia	$8.6	($1.5)	0.5	Maximum Potential • Code sharing partners capture 100% of the lost traffic • U.S.-Japan leg is split 50/50 • U.S.-Japan leg contributes 65% of revenue
Japan-Asia	$2.0	($0.9)	–	No presence in Japan-Asia
U.S.-Japan	$4.3	($0.2)	–	Most likely assumption is that code sharing partners maintain relative shares, U.S. '52 carriers defend share of O&D market. Data reflects a price erosion and small share loss.
Total	$14.9	($2.6)	0.3-0.5	$500M is the maximum recapture. Any additional share gain that the alliance partners obtain will largely be at the expense of U.S. '52 carriers and reduce the net revenue gain to U.S. airlines

Note: The code sharing scenario evaluated is AA/JAL, ANA/DL

United 4/30 VA

CODE SHARING IS IN NO-WAY AN EFFECTIVE SUBSTITUTE FOR JAPAN HUB RIGHTS

Code sharing with frozen or eliminated beyond rights would be detrimental to the consumer and the balance of trade since it would severely weaken the two strongest U.S. competitors in the Pacific, reduce the degree of competition, and lead to a higher proportion of travel on high cost carriers (JAL, ANA). Code sharing with restrictions on Japan hub rights would, in effect, shift traffic and employment to Japanese carriers.

- As we have seen, restrictions on beyond rights to current destinations would shift $2.6 BN of air revenue in 2005 to Asian carriers with the right to serve the destinations (an elimination of hub rights would 'cost' $4.8 BN in air revenue)

- Code sharing might recapture $300-500 million of this in 2005

  – The U.S.-Japan market would be shared between the code sharing partners (the net impact on balance of trade would be small since the carriers would likely broadly maintain their relative shares)
  – Code sharing cannot capture any of the Japan-Asia market
  – U.S. carriers could recapture a proportion of the U.S.-Asian market on the U.S.-Japan leg. The maximum potential in the year 2005 would be $500 million
  – Any additional general share gain by the alliance partners on the U.S.-Japan or U.S.-Asian routes would largely be at the expense of U.S. carriers and would reduce the overall balance of trade (U.S. '52 carriers would have the most to lose)

IN CONCLUSION

- Code sharing is beneficial to the consumer and the economy
- Code sharing is in no way an effective substitute for free Japan hub rights -- a trade would transfer significant revenue and employment to Japan and Asia and raise prices to interior Asian destinations
- The preferred option would be unfettered hub rights and code sharing

V. BENEFITS TO CONSUMERS, ECONOMY AND COMMUNITIES

In September 1995, we concluded that the U.S. would be better off with unrestricted Japan hub rights than additional U.S.-Japan access:

- Consumers lose service alternatives to Asian cities and pay higher fares.

- U.S. carriers lose the ability to grow competitively in Asian markets, lose the efficiencies of operating through an Asian hub, and lose the advantages of a superior cost and service position.

- Restrictions on beyond rights will reduce the U.S. balance of trade surplus in air transportation -- in excess of $100 billion over the next two decades if beyond rights are lost all together. The detrimental impact on U.S. economic activity would be compounded by the multiplier effect on U.S. jobs and economic activity.

This document has expanded on this analysis. We estimate that the impact of trading the right to serve new beyond destinations for additional U.S.-Japan access would not increase total U.S.-Asia travel as traffic gains between the U.S. and Japan are offset by losses to interior Asia. However, there are significant consequences in where the passengers travel and which carriers perform the transportation

- Asian carriers would gain share and jobs would be exported
- The economic benefits of travel would be reduced as employment is shifted abroad
- Fares between the U.S. and Japan would fall somewhat but fares to interior Asia rise more significantly
- U.S. communities and consumers with new direct access to Japan would gain at the expense of communities and consumers elsewhere

COMPONENT OF AIR TRANSPORT BENEFITS

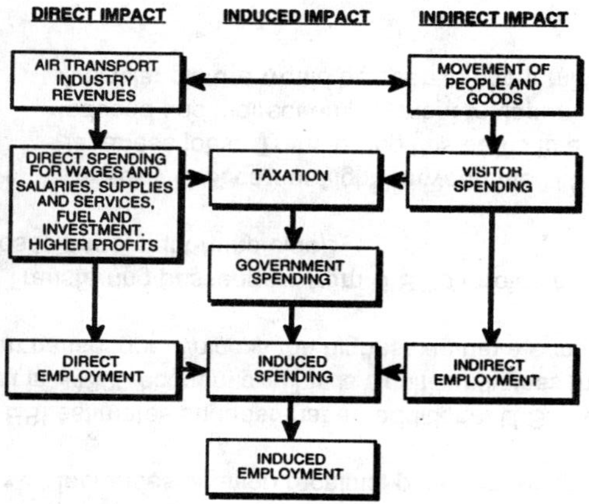

Source: ESI/ATAG

ANNUAL ECONOMIC IMPACT OF A WEEKLY ROUNDTRIP B747-400 AIR SERVICE BY A U.S. CARRIER

	U.S.–JAPAN NON-STOP (Location Of Activity)	
	U.S.	Japan
SPENDING (Dollars In Millions)		
• Direct		
– Airlines	$9.4	$7.7
– Airports	$2.4	$3.0
Total	$11.8	$10.7
• Indirect	$18.0	$4.5
• Induced	$29.8	$15.2
Total	$59.6	$30.4
EMPLOYMENT (Number Of Jobs)		
• Direct	153	13
• Indirect	356	30
• Induced	802	626
Total	1,311	669
REVENUE (Dollars In Millions)	$21.0	—
U.S. TRADE ACCOUNT		
• Passenger Fare		
– Receipts (Dollars In Millions)	$20.5	—

Source: ESI

RPCH247-005-014F

INCREASING TRAFFIC FLOWS AND TRANSFERRING TRAFFIC BETWEEN CARRIERS HAS SIGNIFICANT ECONOMIC IMPACT

As is well known, air transportation has a significant positive impact on a local economy (see opposite page, left-hand side).

- Leads to direct airline and airport employment, investments, and expenditures on supplies and services
- Results in additional trade, visitor spending, and consequential indirect employment
- Increases taxation receipts, government spending, and "induced" employment

ESI estimates suggest that an additional U.S.-Japan return passengers on a U.S. carrier would result in $4300 economic. This is significantly less than Access-U.S. Japan's estimate of over $7000 per return passenger, which is the highest we have encountered.

Transferring passengers from U.S. to foreign carriers will have significant economic impact (see opposite page, right-hand side).

- A weekly U.S. carrier flight between the U.S. and Japan would add 1311 U.S. jobs and 669 Japanese jobs. Transferring this traffic to a Japanese carrier would shift some of the direct, induced and indirect employment to Japan.
- A similar picture would be seen in economic impact.

CONSUMERS WOULD BE BETTER OFF WITH UNFETTERED HUB RIGHTS THAN ADDITIONAL U.S.-JAPAN ACCESS

The U.S.-Japan market is served by twelve carriers. U.S. origin fares are no higher than across the Atlantic and average load factors are in fact lower across the Pacific than the Atlantic. (73% vs. 76-78%)

On line U.S. services to many destinations in Asia are dependent on the U.S. carriers' abilities to operate their Japan hubs in an unconstrained fashion [(1)]. Without such rights, fares to many interior Asian destinations would rise significantly.

U.S. code sharing arrangements to these beyond destinations are unlikely to maintain the same discipline on prices as U.S. carrier access via Japan since at least one leg of the service would be on a higher cost carrier and since the degree of competition between the origin and destination city pairs would be severely reduced with the loss of U.S. '52 carrier presence.

Lastly, consumers in some MOU carrier cities would experience improved Japan services at the expense of reduced services between the whole U.S. and interior Asia. The U.S. government should strive to gain access from these U.S. cities to Japan as the market grows but not at the expense of beyond rights.

Note (1) Including their ability to link their Japanese and U.S. domestic hubs effectively

24-087 97 - 11

ESTIMATED IMPACT OF TRADING RESTRICTIONS ON NEW BEYOND DESTINATIONS FOR ADDITIONAL U.S.-JAPAN SERVICES

Net Impact on Balance of Trade	$2.2 BN	See page 7F
Direct Loss in U.S. Employment in Airlines	10 - 15,000	Assuming that 30-35% of cost is labor related, taking into account U.S. Airline employment shifts with changing geographic focus
Indirect and Induced Impact on Employment	10 - 15,000	Assuming an airline employment multiplier of 2.
Total Employment Loss	20 - 30,000	

Benefits…

TRADING JAPAN HUB RIGHTS FOR ADDITIONAL U.S.-JAPAN SERVICES WOULD SHIFT TRAFFIC AND EMPLOYMENT BETWEEN GEOGRAPHIES AND CARRIERS BUT WOULD NOT INCREASE TOTAL AIR TRAVEL

As discussed, additional U.S.-Japan rights over and above the underlying market growth might stimulate up to 700,000 return passengers in 2005, with a local economic impact of $3-3.5BN where service is added ($4000-5000 per return passenger)

U.S.-Asian traffic (excluding Japan) may well fall by at least this amount if the additional services are at the expense of restrictions on services to new beyond destinations-- an offsetting economic loss of $3-3.5 BN where services are reduced

- The underlying market to the nine cities which would not receive U.S. carrier service would approximate 40% of the U.S.-Japan market by 2005 (2.6-2.7 million return trips)
- It would only take a 25% price increase to reduce travel by 700,000 return trips, which is perfectly feasible since the primary alternative sources of supply are the Japanese carriers (twice as high costs) and other Asian carriers (Such as Korean air, who are also a higher cost operator)

The net effect would be a transfer of $2.2 BN in balance of trade in air transportation and a transfer of 20-30,000 jobs abroad (direct, indirect and induced).

In addition, U.S. jobs would be transferred between U.S. communities as share shifts to the MOU carriers and Japanese carriers add services to alternative US cities

Benefits ...

IN CONCLUSION, WE DO NOT SEE AN ECONOMIC BENEFIT OF $9BN FROM ADDITIONAL U.S.-JAPAN SERVICES AS SUGGESTED BY ACCESS U.S.-JAPAN.

ASSUMPTIONS REQUIRED TO 'GENERATE' $9 BN OF BENEFITS IN 2005 (1)	COMMENTS
• U.S. economic multiplier of $7082 per return passenger	• This is the highest estimate we have come across. $4000-5000 per passenger is more reasonable
• Stimulation of 1.27 million return passenger trips, requiring a price reduction of 17-19% over and above underlying price decline	• Such price reductions would make it impossible for U.S. and Japanese carriers to operate economically
	• Ignores the traffic loss to interior Asia as a result of reduced U.S. carrier presence. We estimate this would completely offset any U.S.-Japan gains in practice
	• Ignores the economic impact of transferring jobs to Japan as U.S. '52 carrier activities are constrained

Note (1): Access U.S.-Japan did not target the year 2005. Any attempt to increase the market by 1.27M return passengers before the year 2005 would require even greater price reductions

STATEMENT OF THE HON. MARTIN FROST
BEFORE THE AVIATION SUBCOMMITTEE
APRIL 30, 1996

Thank you, Mr. Chairman for asking Jeff Fegan, Executive Director of the Dallas/Fort Worth International Airport, to testify here today on this very important issue, and for allowing me to appear as well.

Mr. Chairman, I just want to say a few words about the United States - United Kingdom aviation negotiations. We need to do all we can to allow U.S. airlines more access to United Kingdom airports. The halt to the U.S./U.K. negotiations is a major concern for the DFW Airport, the City of Dallas, the City of Fort Worth, and the entire North Texas area. As you know, no Texas city has access into Heathrow. This is particularly troubling to the North Texas region given that DFW Airport is the second busiest airport in the world in terms of operations and the third busiest airport in terms of passengers.

Lack of Heathrow service means fewer opportunities for DFW to attract foreign tourist and business visitors from the U.K., Europe and the Middle East. It makes it more difficult for DFW area business travelers to reach these destinations. In addition, export trade by DFW area firms is restricted because it is more difficult to ship goods to those destinations.

Mr. Chairman, I have met and corresponded with Secretary Pena on this issue on several occasions. The Secretary has assured the Texas delegation that he is committed to expand opportunities in the U.S./U.K. market. It is my hope, that somehow, talks will resume and that a liberalized air agreement with the U.K will be achieved, specifically, one which will provide DFW Airport access. Thank you.

BEFORE THE

SUBCOMMITTEE ON AVIATION

OF

THE COMMITTEE ON

TRANSPORTATION AND INFRASTRUCTURE

OF THE

UNITED STATES HOUSE OF REPRESENTATIVES

STATEMENT OF

GERALD GREENWALD

CHAIRMAN AND CHIEF EXECUTIVE OFFICER

UNITED AIRLINES, INC.

APRIL 30, 1996

STATEMENT OF

GERALD GREENWALD

CHAIRMAN AND CHIEF EXECUTIVE OFFICER

UNITED AIRLINES, INC.

Chairman Duncan, Congressman Lipinski, Members of the Subcommittee. Thank you for allowing me to appear before you today.

I want to begin my testimony by commending the Committee for allocating the time essential to a careful examination of the state of the U.S.-Japan air services relationship. Your interest reflects a keen awareness that at stake is billions of dollars in trade revenues and the livelihoods of hundreds of thousands of Americans. The policies and actions of the Ministry of Transportation are having a severe impact on business and on consumers both here and in Japan.

Nevertheless, the issues raised by the questions in contention reach far beyond the aviation industry in several important ways. They are indicative of a hardening of Japan's attitude toward bilateral trade negotiations and they betray a reversion to protectionism. They also imply, as I will demonstrate today, that America's willingness to compromise in the past has convinced Japan's trade negotiators that they have an open invitation to renege on treaty obligations and to impose their will on us. That impression is mistaken and, for the sake of every industry for which fair trade and an active presence in Asia are vital, it must be corrected.

Make no mistake about it. Japan's recent behavior represents both a political and an economic threat. Last summer Japan resorted to hostage-taking against FedEx in order to force cargo talks under a virtual ultimatum. That tactic was rewarded in the subsequent agreement. A dangerous precedent was set and the tactic is being repeated. With the not-so-tacit support of several American carriers, tomorrow Japan will impose sanctions on United's daily double flights from Los Angeles to Narita. According to the Japanese, this step is being taken in retaliation for the U.S. refusal to approve Japan Airlines (JAL) service between Tokyo and Kona. In fact, the LA-Narita action marks the second time a U.S. passenger route has been taken hostage by Japan. The first was United's proposed Osaka-Seoul route, which Japan has unilaterally refused to approve for more than a year in direct contravention of the 1952 Air Transport Agreement.

We at United want to move ahead with the additional LA- Narita service, but we believe the time has come to address the real problem, not its fringe symptoms. If the U.S. allows the JAL-Kona request to justify implementation of Japan's LA-Narita sanctions, Japan will have achieved another gain and the basic problem will remain, unsolved and exacerbated. Japan will get more service to the U.S. while further restricting U.S. rights to fly beyond Japan to Asian destinations under an existing treaty. And every day that United is prevented from commencing its legally guaranteed right to Seoul from Osaka, Japan will go on drawing the noose tighter on the economic neck of the U.S., barring us from a growth market and inflicting serious harm.

Your hearings cover aviation relations with two of our biggest trading partners. This is appropriate because the policies of both exemplify protectionism in the extreme and challenge the competitiveness the American industry has been urged to pursue and has worked so hard to achieve. In the case of the U.K. we labor under an agreement -- Bermuda II -- that represents one of the worst bargains we have ever struck. Together, the inequities of Bermuda II and the accumulated distortions of our air agreement with Japan present us with numerous absurdities. None is more egregiously ridiculous than the fact that Chicago is the only major international city where the largest hub carrier does not offer the most international flights. (See Chart 1) From Dallas, its home hub, American operates 81 percent of the international flights; from Houston, Continental operates 77 percent; from St. Louis, TWA operates 100 percent; from Detroit, Northwest operates 91 percent; from Atlanta, Delta operates 73 percent. But from Chicago, its main hub and home city, United operates only 14 percent of all international flights because of restrictions imposed under the current bilaterals. Who operates the most? American Airlines, of course.

Our Government and our carriers are of the uniform belief that we must negotiate a much more liberal regime with the British. In Japan, on the other hand, we have a very liberal basic agreement. Indeed, in the words of Chairman Bud Shuster, that agreement is "extremely liberal; so liberal that Japan has spent decades engrafting restrictions upon its basic terms. It is these restrictions that need to be removed. However, it seems that Japan wants to bring all of the rights granted in 1952 under its tight regulatory control. This should not be permitted."[1] The problem arises from the fact that the 1952 Agreement has been whittled down over the years to the point that it provides for only a fraction of the opportunities originally exchanged. This has produced a regime that is in fact quite similar to what we have with the U.K. By now offering to exchange a few point-to-point routes in return for the surrender of the rights that allow United, Northwest and Federal Express to compete in the Asian market, Japan hopes to duplicate the U.K.'s position under Bermuda II. The irony is that since 1985 it is frequently the loudest U.S. carrier critics of the U.S.-U.K. agreement that are the strongest advocates of its repetition in the Pacific.

The restrictive bent of the U.K. and Japan policies may be similar but there is one fundamental difference in our aviation relationships with them. The United Kingdom (and the United States) scrupulously honor the agreement that they

[1] Letter dated February 27, 1996, from Bud Shuster to Federico Peña.

signed; Japan does not. Japan's actions represent a direct political challenge to the U.S. I trust that this Committee recognizes that this challenge must be met head on.

In December, 1994, Japan unilaterally decided to prevent United, Northwest and Fed Ex from any further exercise of the rights we hold to extend our transpacific flights beyond Japan to other points in Asia. For instance, for over a year now Japan has refused to allow United to operate one of its flights beyond Osaka to Seoul, Korea. This is, as the Department of Transportation acknowledges, a clear violation by Japan of the provisions of the Air Services Agreement. That is, of course, a valid assertion. I want to point out, however, that the MOT's denial of the Osaka-Seoul route is not only a political ploy or a bargaining chip. It has an obvious competitive purpose and can be characterized as a kind of commercial aggression. Since our request was turned down illegally, JAL and ANA have instituted many flights to Asia from the new Kansai airport, as you can see on chart 2, while Japanese authorities present us with excuses regarding the inadequacies of a brand new facility. ANA blatantly attributed its return to profitability to its ability to add international flights from Osaka -- without, let us note, U.S. competition. During this period, MOT has approved only one additional beyond Osaka segment -- Northwest 's flight to Manila, Asia's lowest yielding market. (See Chart 3) Although United and Northwest have the right to extend flights beyond Osaka, we are simply not being allowed to compete for no other reason than that MOT, JAL, and ANA know we cannot keep pace without Osaka. Just to make sure, they have imposed further restrictions on our Tokyo operations.

And, as I've mentioned, Japan is threatening to impose sanctions on United's second daily LA-Narita flight, a violation of the basic U.S.- Japan service as of May 1, tomorrow. Japan earlier threatened to withdraw approval for key beyond rights being exercised by Federal Express and other U.S. cargo carriers unless the U.S. negotiated a new cargo agreement by the end of March. This was avoided only because an agreement was reached. Japan has thus made it plain that it is willing to ignore any provision of its aviation trade agreement that it believes to be working in favor of U.S. air carriers. If we turn a blind eye to that behavior -- as some urge we must do -- we would be ratifying it. We would also be sending a message that U.S. businesses operating under a variety of trade agreements with Japan, do so only at that country's sufferance. The message to U.S. companies would be: "Being too successful will place your rights at risk."

As I said earlier, this transcends aviation issues. It is a matter of international trade principle on which the U.S. must not waiver. The U.S. must expect its trade partners to honor their bilateral obligations and must demand that they do so.

How did we get ourselves in this position with Japan? As Mr. Jiro Hanyu, Deputy Director General of the Civil Aviation Bureau and Chairman of the Japanese aviation negotiating delegation recently pointed out, it began "in the wake of the U.K. government's successful renegotiation of the U.S.-U.K. aviation agreement which introduced a limit on the number of flights that could be operated by the U.S. carriers."[2] (See Charts 4 and 5) It was Bermuda II that prompted Japan in 1977 to seek a similar "comprehensive revision of the bilateral agreement." There can be little doubt about the outcome the Japanese seek from that revision.

Japan and the U.S. have now been "renegotiating" for almost 20 years. Those negotiations have moved step-by-step toward a U.S.-Japan aviation regime which mimics that which we have -- to our serious disadvantage -- with the U.K. At each step in the process, the overall scope of U.S. rights was restricted.

Let us be clear, Japan's tactic of holding the proverbial gun to our heads is not new. Over the years, as they have pushed and we have caved, they have become adept at keeping us guessing as to what will satisfy them. The ritual is like a game of three-card monte in which the rules always seem to change just when the player thinks he has figured out what the dealer is doing. Their artful orchestration of protests, infrastructure excuses and plain refusals to honor obligations have eroded U.S. rights, weakened our resistance, and created a tangle

[2] J. Hanyu, "Japan-U.S. Aviation Negotiations--In Pursuit of Elimination of Inequalities," Transport, Feb. 1996, pp.34-36.

of restrictions subject to their interpretations. And we have stood by watching, much like the tourist mesmerized by the dealer's moves.

In the early 1980's Japan refused to honor its obligation to accept the designation of United Airlines to operate on a route from the Pacific Northwest to Tokyo. In June, 1982, the U.S. Government acquiesced in that violation, accepting an arrangement whereby United became the first "MOU carrier" with its frequencies and beyond rights limited by Japan's insistence. The U.S. accepted the principle that henceforth any new U.S. carrier serving Japan would be precluded from developing a hub in that country. All service by new carriers would be point-to-point, without beyond authority and limited as to the frequency, without a provision for growth.

In 1985, at the urging of Delta and American, the U.S. agreed to cap the rights of the so-called "1952 carriers" to those gateway points already listed in their certificates. In conjunction with what it had surrendered in 1982, this step backwards precluded any U.S. carrier from providing non-stop service to Japan from a large number of cities, including Atlanta, St. Louis, Salt Lake City, Las Vegas, Pittsburgh and Philadelphia unless Japan was willing to agree to it. It also precluded the U.S. carriers from integrating their highly efficient domestic hub structures with international routes to the Pacific. For instance, United, the largest

U.S. carrier to Asia, can fully integrate its Pacific routes only with San Francisco of its principal domestic hubs.

The unwillingness of the U.S. to stand up to Japan at these critical junctures placed us in the position where we are today.

In 1986, Japan authorized ANA as its second international flag carrier, and it began developing Asian hubs and seeking access to them from the U.S.

In 1989, Japan expanded the number of U.S. routes and capacity under the control of Japanese regulators by limiting the expansion of new points to those only subject to MOU conditions.

In 1994, the first opportunity in years for expanded U.S. flag services -- the opening of the new Kansai Airport at Osaka -- took place. Japan immediately moved to block its expanded use by American carriers by announcing a freeze on their airport slots at prior levels. When the U.S. carriers agreed to restraints on the pace of their growth as the price of expansion, Japan accepted it, yet only months later reneged on the understanding and blocked all new beyond services. This left U.S. carriers with a single beyond flight from Osaka; the same number of beyond flights that U.S. carriers now operate at Heathrow.

In 1995, the U.S. believed it had reached an agreement with Japan to honor all of the fifth-freedom rights of Federal Express as well as other U.S. cargo operators, except for the potentially most important -- China. In March 1996,

Japanese officials threatened to renege on that agreement as well. U.S. passenger rights beyond Japan remain both frozen and unaddressed. And, Japan is now threatening direct U.S. - Japan service with sanctions on United's L.A. - Narita route.

To understate the case, the record is abysmal. One can hardly blame MOT officials for leaping at every opening provided and then coming back to demand more. I have cited this record in detail precisely because only a playback of this horror show can generate a true measure of understanding for what our negotiators are up against today. The score has been so one-sided that when the U.S. asks the Japanese to live up to the spirit and the letter of an agreement, they act as if they have never heard of such a thing and accuse us of changing the rules.

The rules, however, are changing -- globally. The World Trade Organization has been formed to smooth the transition from obsolete statism to market economics. And the 18 economies represented in the Asia Pacific Economic Cooperation (APEC) organization have set 2010 as a target date for an open skies regime. United, I am proud to say, has been the only U.S. passenger carrier actively working with the U.S. government to get APEC to set competitive standards for aviation -- and to get Japan to honor the concept in fact and well as oratory.

I ask the Committee to note that this will not be as easy to accomplish as it should be. It is, in fact, becoming increasingly evident that Japan is working within APEC -- using its influence on smaller Asian nations and its all-too-familiar style of obstructive diplomacy -- to divert or derail the process of liberalization.

Recent events provide some cautionary examples. First, some background. As you know, The Bogor Declaration, adopted at the 1994 APEC summit in Indonesia, established "free and open trade and investment" as the organization's primary goal. At the Osaka summit in November of 1995, it was confirmed, in spite of Japan's opposition, that transportation is to be included among the business sectors covered in the multinational effort. This inclusion of the transportation sector reflects the APEC principle of Comprehensives, which recognizes that all key sectors must be addressed. The other key principle endorsed by the APEC economies is that of a Standstill, which, in brief, says each member should refrain from increasing levels of protection.

The Standstill principle is, of course, highly relevant to aviation and to the business of this meeting and presents Japan with a dilemma the MOT will probably ignore. We welcomed it as a significant step in the right direction and were pleased when Mr. Hashimoto, Japan's Deputy Prime Minister and Minister of International Trade and Industry, endorsed the concept in admitting publicly that the "give and take" of bilateral negotiations "is not necessarily the best way to go about liberalization." That, too, seemed like progress.

How, then, has Japan behaved since last November? First, it has worked unilaterally to undermine the liberalization consensus and to strike aviation from the APEC agenda. Then in January, MOT invited 17 Asia-Pacific nations to Kyoto for a conference on aviation issues. Although the guest list paralleled the APEC membership roster, it pointedly excluded the United States, Canada, and Mexico. Hong Kong was also left out, presumably because the MOT believed China's presence would suffice. The United States protested its exclusion because it was seen as indicative of a Japanese attempt to build an Asian consensus against liberalization. An administration official, quoted in the *Journal of Commerce*, said, "Excluding the United States and Canada gives Japan political cover for their own protectionist instincts."

Another example of Japan's true attitude toward multinational liberalization -- and its belief that the U.S. is the enemy -- emerged earlier this month at the Vancouver meeting of APEC's transportation working group. The Japanese delegation not only tried to have air services deleted as a trade liberalization category, but for several hours attempted to keep a member of the U.S. delegation -- from United Airlines -- from delivering a five-minute statement.

I cite these examples of Japan's behavior to illustrate the difficulties the U.S. is going to encounter in the months ahead unless it takes the strongest possible stand.

Those difficulties are multiplied by the fact that, over the years, Japan has gained significant and essentially unilateral regulatory control over what was originally a balanced and very liberal regime. It has created a class of U.S. carriers and a class of U.S. cities which must act as supplicants to the Japanese government if they are to gain even point-to-point access to Japan. It is little wonder then, that, adding arrogance to aggressiveness, Tokyo is encouraging a lobbying group largely funded by American and Delta Airlines -- and almost comically called Access U.S.-Japan -- to actually champion Japan's cause, promote Japanese trade strategy, and to make the promise of a few more point-to-point flights seem like victory instead of another defeat.

It is this control that now allows Japan to dangle the carrot of new service in front of those cities, and new designations for U.S. carriers to serve them. The price is that they support Japan's negotiating objectives before the U.S. government. That is why the *Japan Times* reported that Access U.S.-Japan "is likely to be a strong supporter of Japan" and led an official of Japan's Ministry of Transport to say that Tokyo "welcomes the efforts of the MOU carriers.

Our negotiators often point to the difficulties that they encounter because of the conflicting objectives of our cities and our carriers. In this instance, I hope the Committee will recognize that those "conflicting objectives" could have been avoided entirely if in the 1980's the U.S. had resisted Japan's effort to restrict the 1952 Agreement and demanded that its provisions be honored.

Typical of the disinformation being circulated by the Japanese-American coalition are the comments of JAL president Akira Kondo in an interview published in the *Japan Times* of April 23. Among other things, Mr. Kondo alleges that what he calls the present "disparity" stems from the 1952 agreement. That is totally wrong. The 1952 pact established a virtual open skies regime and, by definition, could not contain disparities. Any problems that may have arisen since then -- with the U.S. by far the loser -- originate with Japan's repeated efforts to twist the agreement to its own favor. And what does Mr. Kondo suggest Japan do to overcome those disparities? Like his allies here, he says our beyond rights should be frozen. Furthermore, he says the current bilateral pact should be terminated if talks do not make what he calls progress.

Mr. Kondo's assertions and thinly-veiled threats are not the key points here. The point is that the problem is Japan's intransigence coupled with the inexplicably short-sighted positions being taken by U.S. airlines and executives supposed to be on the U.S. side.

This may seem like ancient history, but it bears directly on the situation that confronts us now. Contrast, if you will, United's and the U.S. government's efforts to achieve open skies with American Airlines' April 1 Department of Transportation filing in which it is asserted that curtailing fifth freedom rights in exchange for more third and fourth freedom rights is an attractive proposition. The last time anyone fell for a comparable argument, the year was 1938 and the place was Munich. Contrast, also, United's stand on behalf of U.S. economic interests with the Access group's contention that the U. S. should move to negotiate a new treaty even though Japan is refusing to honor the current agreement.

Japan maneuvered the U.S. into accepting the concept of "second tier" rights for certain of our cities and our carriers despite the 1952 Agreement's open designation provision. Japan now hopes to use the frustrated aspirations of those same cities and carriers to eliminate the remaining liberal provisions of the basic agreement: our beyond rights. If that attack is successful all U.S. cities and carriers will become "second tier" when it comes to direct services to much of Asia.

It is this sort of irresponsible behavior that leads Japan to believe it can have its own way with the U.S. It is in the interest of putting an end to the sending of mixed signals that I say it is imperative for U.S. carriers to come together in support of our negotiators and to present a solid front as we contemplate exploratory talks that could, if we hold firm, lead to progress and the kind of liberalization the market demands. It is equally important for the Congress to form a united front on these issues, so that Japan and the policy makers at MOT have no choice but to recognize the era of domination -- the free ride -- is over.

In 1995, the Clinton Administration released its Statement of U.S. International Aviation Policy. Its specific acknowledgment of (i) the necessity of regional networks if U.S. air carriers are to compete on a global basis and (ii) the need for the U.S. to negotiate to secure the bundles of fifth-freedom rights needed to construct those networks, was a rejection of the approach followed with Japan in the 1980's and received widespread, bipartisan support in Congress as well as general support in our industry.

Japan has taken this policy statement to heart and is acting -- with the help of American collaborators -- to subvert its intentions. It is, in effect, moving to nullify U.S. policy on both sides of the fence. It realizes that by unraveling the "bundle of fifth freedom rights" that United, Northwest and Federal Express now hold it can cripple their competitive abilities by emasculating their hubs in Asia, just as they limited U.S. carrier access from their domestic hubs in the 1980's.

At the same time, it is supporting the networks of JAL and ANA by allowing them to develop Asian hubs at the new Osaka Airport as well as at Tokyo, and encouraging them to enter into marketing arrangements with U.S. carriers to assure broad coverage of the U.S. via U.S. domestic hubs, just as British Airways has done with U.S. Air and now, it seems, with America West. In fact, ANA and Delta have recently announced plans to code share and have filed their first application to begin L.A.-Tokyo service. If the sanctions on United's L.A.-Tokyo service stand, United's injury will be compounded since ANA will likely pick up many of those passengers denied service on United by Japan. Japan's hope is that the U.S. will focus its attention on the fringes of the Agreement: gaining some additional point-to-point flying at the expense of the greater U.S. interest in the future growth of Asia.

The stakes, of course, are enormous. Asia is the fastest growing air transportation market in the world. The dimensions of the forecast passenger growth for key cities in that region over the next 14 years are truly amazing. By 2010, ten Asian markets -- China, Singapore, Taiwan, Thailand, Australia, South Korea, Indonesia, Malaysia, Philippines, and India -- will have matched or exceeded in size today's two largest Asian markets, while the Japan market itself will have jumped from 35 to 91 million passengers per year.

Of those countries, six lie well beyond the non-stop range of even the B-747-400 aircraft from Los Angeles (Singapore, Thailand, Indonesia, Malaysia, India and Pakistan). To serve them effectively, a stop in Asia is essential. Agreements that the U.S. has today position us to participate in that growth -- if they are maintained and enforced. Japan is doing its best to see that our participation is minimal and that their carriers alone can make use of Japan's natural geographic and economic position as an Asian hub. To their minds it has worked for the U.K. in Europe; it can work for them in Asia.

Why, with the projected growth in the market, is Japan being so protectionist? Why is Japan so insistent that the "fault" in their carriers' market performance lies not with their carriers' business decisions but with the Agreement?

The answer is that Japan's Ministry of Transport has had the responsibility for regulating the economic health of Japan's aviation industry. The simple, inescapable fact is that it has failed miserably.

That failure is evident even in Asia. The Japanese carriers are rapidly being eclipsed in growth by the more competitive carriers of those Asian countries with which we have essentially an "open skies" agreement: Taiwan, Singapore and Korea.

As you can see from Charts 6 and 7, since 1978 the other Asian carriers have more than doubled their share of the U.S.-Asia market while Japanese carrier share has been almost halved. Also, on a global basis their participation in the global market has nearly tripled, while Japan's carriers show no growth over the past eighteen years.

The reasons the Japanese carriers have fallen behind both U.S. and other Asian carriers lies in relative efficiencies. Since deregulation, U.S. international carriers have become among the most efficient in the world. It is not surprising, therefore, that our carriers' share of the U.S.-Japan market has increased significantly. Rather than acknowledge that our traffic gain is in part of function of MOT policies that protected Japanese carrier inefficiencies, Japan's bureaucrats contended that the underlying agreement was "unbalanced." While this may have served to divert attention from the real problem, there is no question that, factually, the argument is nonsense. Under the same agreement JAL had no problem gaining approximately 50 percent of the total U.S.-Japan traffic, until its costs began to diverge sharply from those of its competitors. See Chart 8. That cost disparity, as measured by ICAO statistics is remarkable. It reflects the cost of regulation by MOT. In 1985, Japan Air Lines was more efficient than was United on a cost per available ton kilometer basis. By 1993 the equation had changed dramatically. United's efficiency edge was enormous and growing. See Chart 4.

Rather than acknowledge its own bureaucratic mistakes, Japan has taken a predictable tack. It blames its carriers' performances on foreigners; in this case foreigners abetted by an "unfair" air services agreement. By characterizing the agreement as unfair, of course, they can rationalize ignoring it. And by ignoring it, they hope to buy time to salvage their own position.

From the U.S. standpoint, however, we are being asked to sacrifice our nation's future in the Asian transportation market to protect the reputation of Japan's bureaucrats and their ill-conceived policies. This is a burden we cannot accept.

Equally important, we must recognize that no U.S. carrier today operates any nonstop service to any Asian point (except Japan) unless that carrier also operates a hub in Japan. These nonstop and hub services are complementary, giving U.S. carriers a presence in an Asian city that is competitive with both Japanese and other Asian carriers. If we lose hub access beyond Japan, all U.S. carriers will be in the same position as a number of U.S. carriers, most recently Delta, which have tried and failed to maintain a system of service to other Asian points without a hub in Japan. It leaves Japan with the only efficient carrier networks in the Pacific.

What should be done?

Just last month, DOT's Assistant Secretary for Aviation and International Affairs, Charles Hunnicutt, stressed the need for U.S. policy makers to concentrate on the long-term: "It is important to underscore that in our dealings with Japan, we ought not settle for short-term gains at the cost of sacrificing long-term needs into the next century."[3] His comments echoed those of Secretary Peña in

---

[3] Response of Assistant Secretary for Aviation and International Affairs, Charles Hunnicutt, to Access U.S.-Japan Announcement, February 21, 1996.

conjunction with his recent extended trip trough Asia.[4] We agree completely. We believe that no policy can be relied upon if it is not based on economic reality. That is why we took the lead in gathering those facts.

A study conducted for us by Booz Allen and Hamilton concluded that over the next two decades the cumulative reduction in U.S.-Asian trade balance from restrictions on the U.S. expansion of passenger transportation in Asia through Japan could exceed $100 billion. Japan, it believes, would be the primary beneficiary.

A study conducted under the supervision of Clyde Prestowitz of the Economic Strategy Institute reached much the same conclusion. In that independent analysis, a cap on U.S. carrier beyond rights would mean that in the year 2010, U.S. carriers as a group would earn almost $3.2 billion less in the best case and $5.4 billion less in the worst. In that same year, the cap would reduce U.S. employment by between 111,000 and 213,000 jobs and reduce U.S. trade receipts by up to $5.1 billion in that year alone. Unfortunately, we believe the worst case is more likely to prevail.

These are real dollars and real jobs that will be lost to the U.S. economy if Japan has its way. And, just as it is now easy to criticize the mistake we made in Bermuda II, it will be easy in 2010 to recognize the damage done by concessions to

---

[4] "Pena Asserts Shift in Focus from Europe to Asia," Aviation Daily, November 1, 1995, p. 179.

Japan in 1996. The challenge is to recognize those downsides in advance, and negotiate accordingly. In this regard the economic analyses of Booz Allen and of the Economic Strategy Institute have armed the Government with the knowledge it requires.

Given these projections, it should come as no surprise that ESI states flatly that the trading away or reduction of U.S. beyond rights is -- and I quote -- unacceptable.

I should point out here that what is unacceptable to the U.S. should also be unacceptable to Japanese consumers and business. A study recently concluded in Japan by the highly-regarded Mitsubishi Research Institute (MRI) found that the presence of U.S. carriers on Japan-Asian routes has benefited the Japanese flying public and industry. By introducing effective competition, U.S. carriers have raised demand, lowered fares, and helped control service costs. Furthermore, as you can see on Chart 9, MRI estimates that the removal of U.S. carriers from these routes would raise air fares by 10 to 20 percent, depress demand by up to 10 percent, and cost Japanese passengers between 44-53 billion yen, or approximately $500 million. Finally, MRI says that the opening of the Osaka-Seoul route, currently denied, would benefit consumers by up to 3.8 billion yen in the form of reduced fares. All of this supports the theory that the MOT is not interested in serving the public, but is in the business of covering its own mistakes and protecting JAL.

What is needed now is the political will to act to avoid the dominance of another successful U.S. industry by Japan. In our view, and we hope in yours, the responsible course requires that the U.S. first reconcile its well-crafted International Aviation Policy with its negotiating objectives. That Policy states that:

> carriers wishing to establish global networks require a higher quality and quantity of supporting route authority than they have sought in the past. Airlines will become increasingly concerned with every market that enables them to flow passengers over any part of their system network. These airlines will be looking for broad, flexible authority to operate beyond and behind hub points, in addition to the hub-to-hub market between two countries. At present, governments operating in a bilateral context naturally focus on opportunities for their respective carriers to serve the local market between their two countries. In a bilateral context, services destined for or coming from third countries receive less consideration. In the future, governments will have to adjust their focus to bargain for the bundles of rights that will permit airlines to develop global networks. (Emphasis added.)

We cannot continue to proceed by committing the same mistakes in the 90's as we did in the '80's. As the International Policy recognizes, adjusting our focus should mean that integrating domestic and international hubs has to have the highest priority. Specifically, it means that undoing the damage of the '80's must be undertaken so that those carriers that can still hub in Japan can once again have the ability to integrate those hubs with their domestic systems. Japan recognizes this need for its carriers. We can do no less for ours.

Japan has made it clear that it will ignore any treaty provisions benefiting the U.S. It has provided us with a clear signal as to what the U.S. must do. In joining the APEC consensus calling for open skies liberalization by 2010, Japan is making a gesture toward long-term acceptance of the international community's course. However, the here and now of U.S.- Japan aviation relations show no such gestures and indicates the messages we have to communicate: No more concessions. No more limitations on our existing agreement. And no more excuses to camouflage protectionist roadblocks.

The question is not whether we should move toward liberalization, open skies, and market competition. No one argues with that idea. The day of the cozy arrangement, the guaranteed route, fixed fares, and subsidies is over. U.S. carriers took too long to do it, but we have learned the lessons of deregulation and today are among the world's most cost efficient airlines. JAL has to learn the same lessons, with or without the help of the MOT, because that is the way things are in the global marketplace.

The question, then, is: How do we help Japan to face facts, step into the 21st century, and embrace the idea that air service is the prime responsibility of an air carrier? The answer is that we do not do it by continuing to indulge the MOT in its bad habits. We do it by:

- Insisting that Japan honor the current agreement;
- Refusing to trade existing rights or to accept restriction on those rights in exchange for the promise of other opportunities; and
- Setting our goals on the basis of economic analyses that identify the best interests of the United States.

United is the only airline that has devoted resources to developing a foundation for reliable economic analysis both in the U.S. and Japan. We have done so because we are totally committed to serving this nation and the customers whose trust and patronage we have earned around the world. The more than 80,000 men and women of United -- our more than 50,000 employee owners -- are ready and eager to compete. We ask the Committee's support -- and that of the entire Congress -- to make that possible.

Chart 1

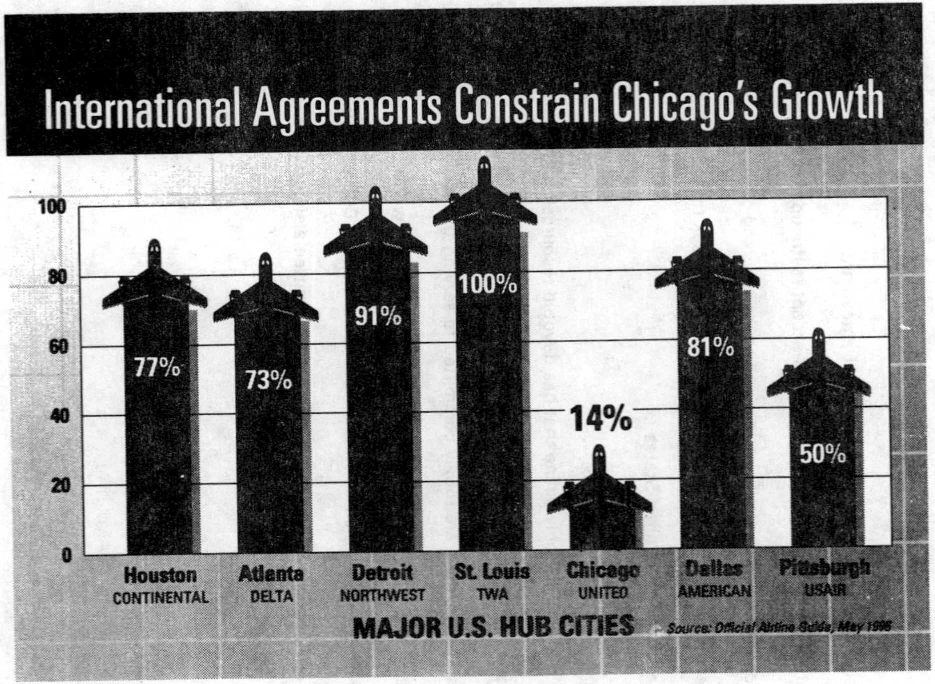
International Agreements Constrain Chicago's Growth
100
80
60
40
20
0
77%
73%
91%
100%
14%
81%
50%
Houston
CONTINENTAL
Atlanta
DELTA
Detroit
NORTHWEST
St. Louis
TWA
Chicago
UNITED
Dallas
AMERICAN
Pittsburgh
USAIR
MAJOR U.S. HUB CITIES
Source: Official Airline Guide, May 1996

Chart 2

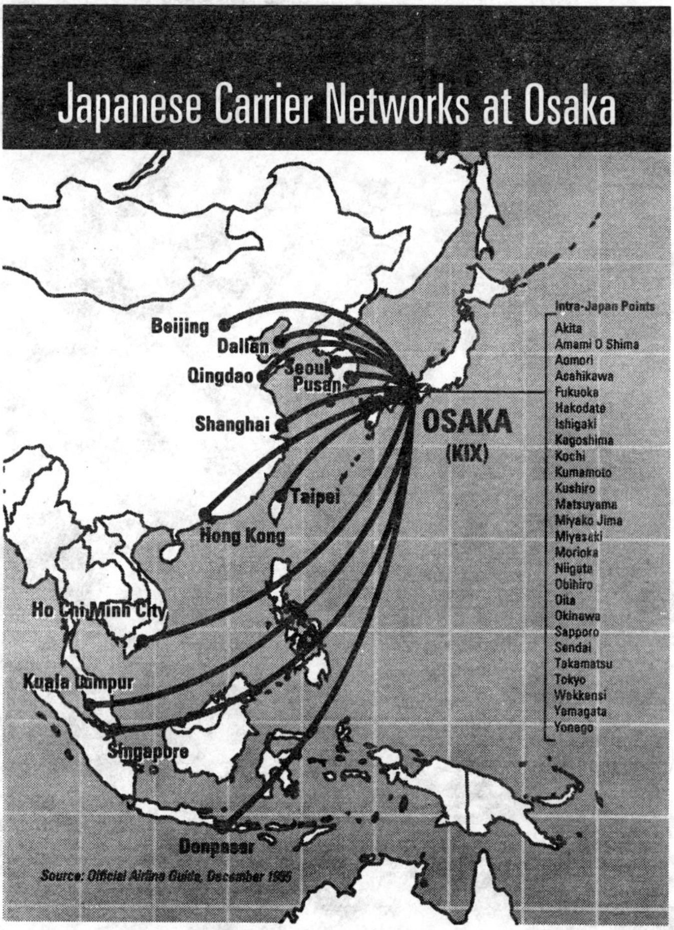

Japanese Carrier Networks at Osaka
Beijing
Dalian
Qingdao
Seoul
Pusan
Shanghai
OSAKA
(KIX)
Taipei
Hong Kong
Ho Chi Minh City
Kuala Lumpur
Singapore
Donpasar
Intra-Japan Points
Akita
Amami O Shima
Aomori
Acahikawa
Fukuoka
Hakodate
Ishigaki
Kagoshima
Kochi
Kumamoto
Kushiro
Matsuyama
Miyako Jima
Miyasaki
Morioka
Niigata
Obihiro
Oita
Okinawa
Sapporo
Sendai
Takamatsu
Tokyo
Wakkensi
Yamagata
Yonago
Source: Official Airline Guide, December 1995

Chart 3

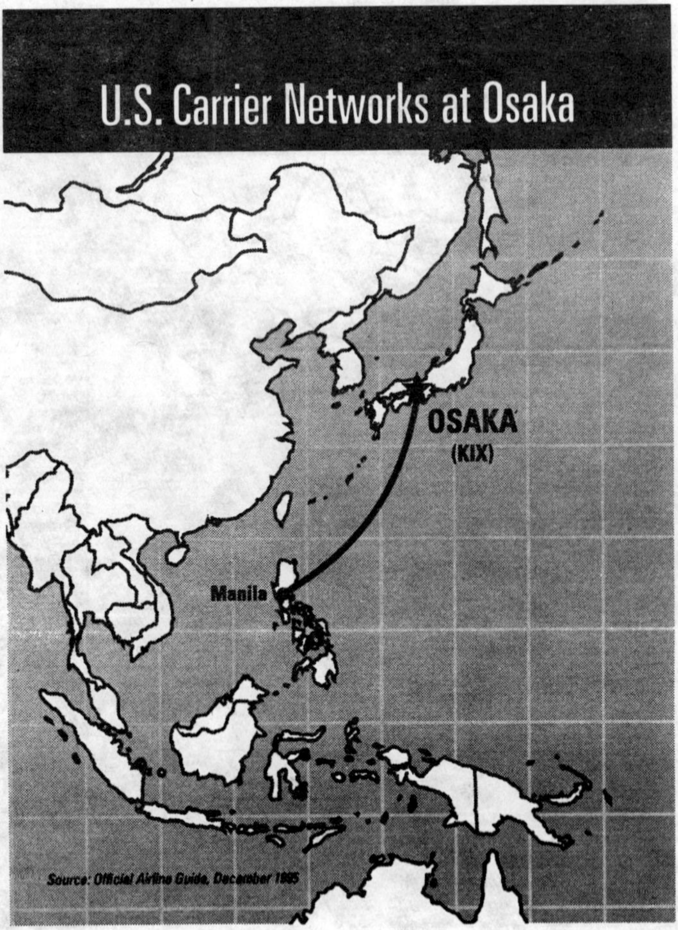
U.S. Carrier Networks at Osaka
OSAKA
(KIX)
Manila
Source: Official Airline Guide, December 1995

Chart 4

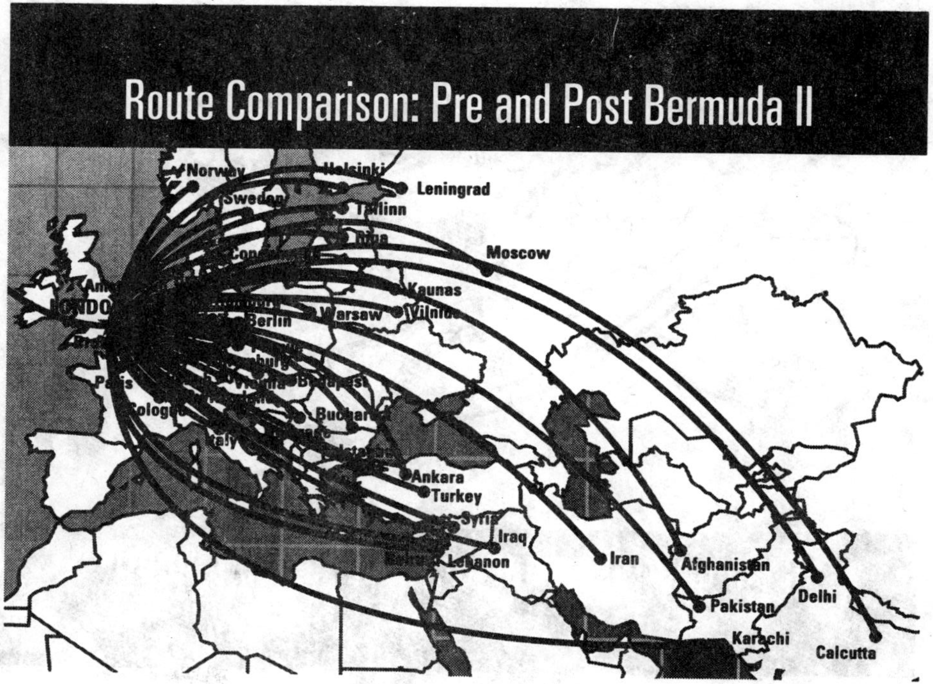
Route Comparison: Pre and Post Bermuda II
Norway
Sweden
Helsinki
Leningrad
Tallinn
Riga
Moscow
Kaunas
Warsaw
Vilnius
Berlin
Paris
Cologne
Vienna
Budapest
Bucharest
Ankara
Turkey
Syria
Iraq
Lebanon
Iran
Afghanistan
Pakistan
Karachi
Delhi
Calcutta

Chart 5

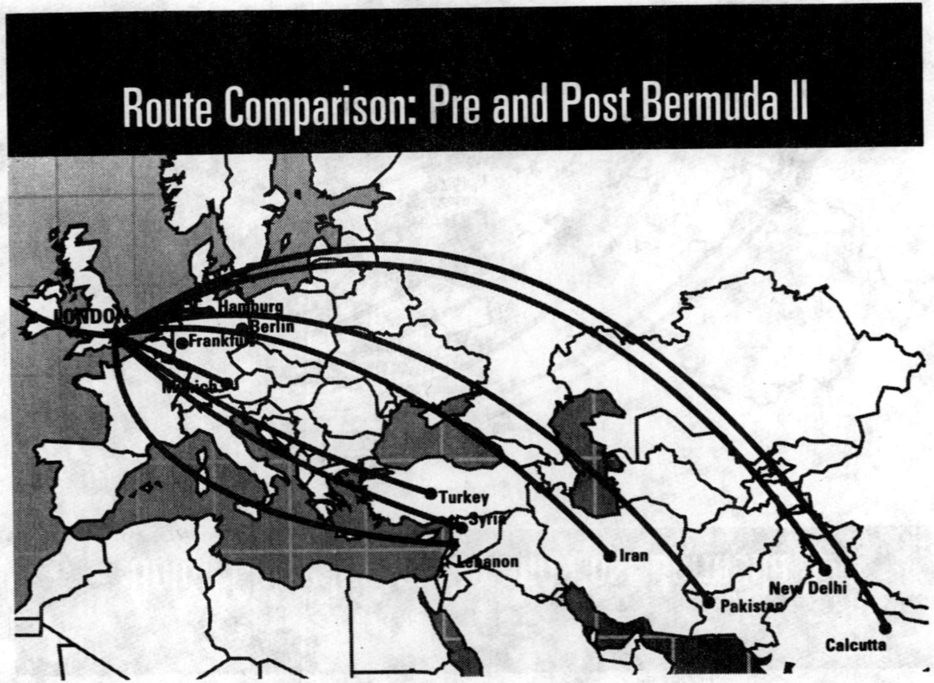

Route Comparison: Pre and Post Bermuda II
Berlin
Turkey
Iran
Pakistan
New Delhi
Calcutta

Chart 6

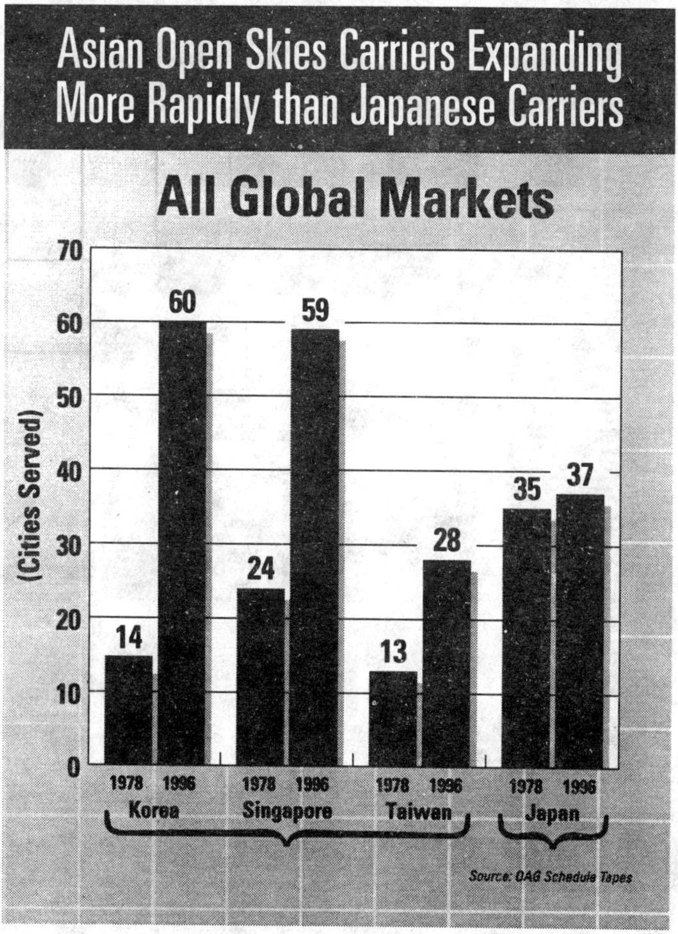
Asian Open Skies Carriers Expanding
More Rapidly than Japanese Carriers
All Global Markets
(Cities Served)
70
60
50
40
30
20
10
0
14
60
24
59
13
28
35
37
1978 1996
Korea
1978 1996
Singapore
1978 1996
Taiwan
1978 1996
Japan
Source: OAG Schedule Tapes

Chart 7

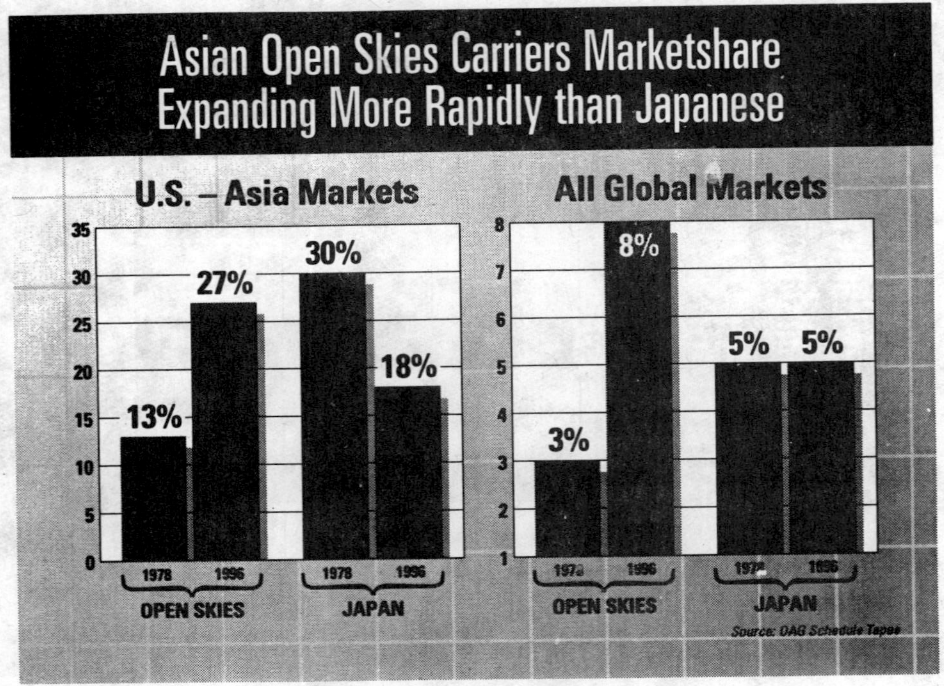
Asian Open Skies Carriers Marketshare
Expanding More Rapidly than Japanese
U.S. – Asia Markets
All Global Markets
13%
27%
30%
18%
3%
8%
5%
5%
1978
1996
OPEN SKIES
JAPAN
Source: OAG Schedule Tapes

Chart 8

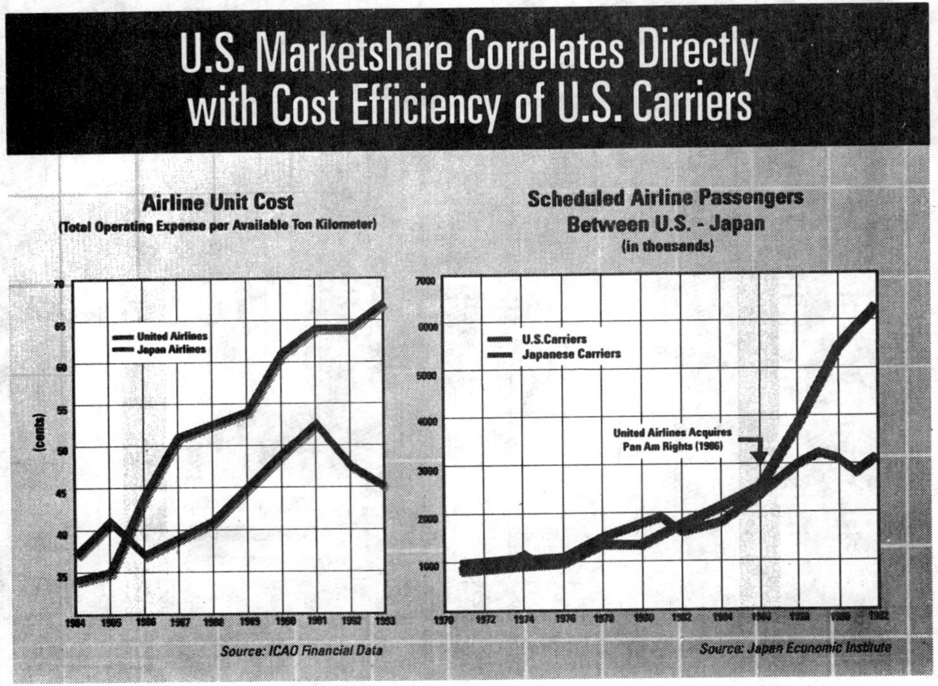
U.S. Marketshare Correlates Directly
with Cost Efficiency of U.S. Carriers
Airline Unit Cost
(Total Operating Expense per Available Ton Kilometer)
(cents)
United Airlines
Japan Airlines
Source: ICAO Financial Data
Scheduled Airline Passengers
Between U.S. - Japan
(in thousands)
U.S.Carriers
Japanese Carriers
United Airlines Acquires
Pan Am Rights (1986)
Source: Japan Economic Institute

Chart 9

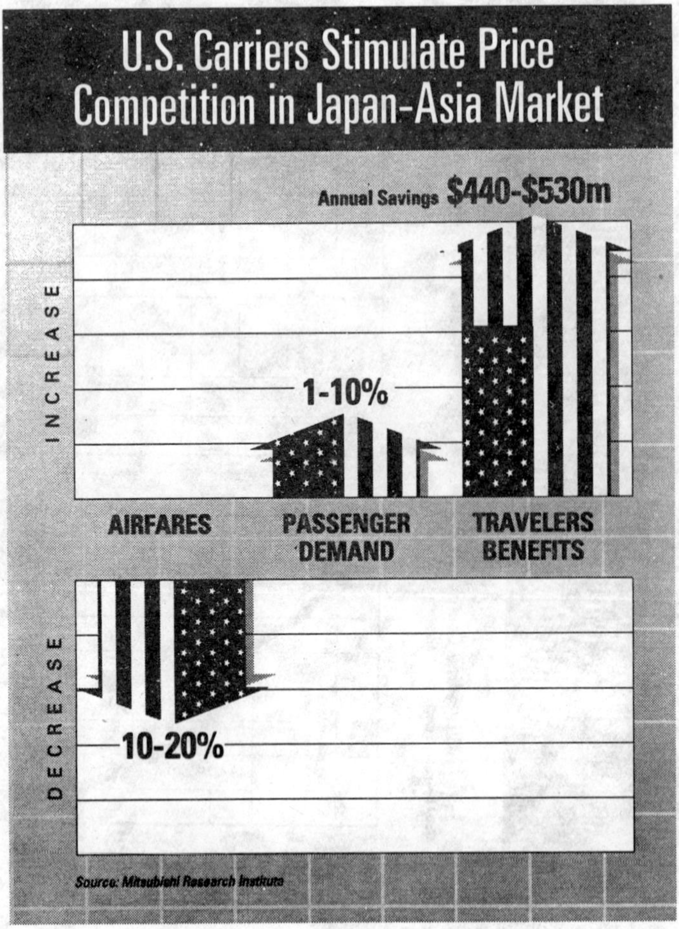
U.S. Carriers Stimulate Price Competition in Japan-Asia Market
Annual Savings $440-$530m
INCREASE
1-10%
AIRFARES
PASSENGER DEMAND
TRAVELERS BENEFITS
DECREASE
10-20%
Source: Mitsubishi Research Institute

STATEMENT OF
CHARLES A. HUNNICUTT
ASSISTANT SECRETARY FOR AVIATION
AND INTERNATIONAL AFFAIRS
DEPARTMENT OF TRANSPORTATION
BEFORE THE
AVIATION SUBCOMMITTEE
OF THE
HOUSE TRANSPORTATION AND INFRASTRUCTURE COMMITTEE
APRIL 30, 1996

Thank you, Mr. Chairman, Members of the Subcommittee. I appreciate the opportunity to discuss the important subject of commercial international aviation with you. Today, I know that you are primarily interested in the current status of our aviation relationships with the United Kingdom and Japan, but I would also like to take the opportunity of my first appearance before this Subcommittee to bring you up to date on the substantial progress the airline industry has made under the Clinton Administration.

I am pleased to report that our airline industry is much better off today than it was during the dark days of the early 1990s when it was facing a financial crisis domestically and a resurgence in protectionism internationally.

The major passenger and cargo airlines reported combined net profits of $2.2 billion and operating profits of $5.46 billion for 1995. International operations alone generated combined operating profits of $929 million. The financial community and airline industry experts are predicting that 1996 will be another solid year for the airlines, with operating revenues growing as much as 4 percent. In fact, despite severe weather conditions in the mid-Atlantic and northeast earlier this year, the major airlines may report a combined net profit for the first quarter of 1996. The major airlines have not shown a first quarter profit since 1979.

Internationally, we have significantly improved our aviation relations with other countries. We have signed liberal aviation agreements with many nations, and as I shall highlight later, we have had tremendous success creating new opportunities for airline services around the world.

Against this backdrop of a recovering aviation industry and a growing number of liberalization successes, we continue to be disappointed by the narrow, tit-for-tat approach to liberalization taken by the British. Their position stands in stark contrast to the progressive approach to transatlantic liberalization shown by most of our European aviation partners, as well as to the market-oriented approach that the United Kingdom itself takes to trade matters in other economic sectors. The U.K.'s attitude towards transatlantic aviation liberalization might be understandable, although still unacceptable, if British airlines were struggling to restructure and achieve profitability. However, the reverse is the case. For its most recent financial year, Virgin Atlantic posted over a $60 million profit. For the nine months ending December 31, 1995, British Airways had profits of over $1 billion, up 16.6%. These airlines are indeed formidable competitors.

Some of you may be wondering about the recent assertion by British Airways' Chairman, Sir Colin Marshall, that the fairness of Bermuda 2 is demonstrated by the fact that U.S. and U.K. airlines offer nearly the same number of flights between the United States and the United Kingdom. He went on to attribute the current market-share differential solely to the larger aircraft, and consequent higher number of seats, flown by British carriers. What he failed to mention is that, in an unrestricted market, U.S. carriers could offer a comparable number of seats by increasing the number of flights that they operate, particularly at their U.S. hubs. However, U.K. authorities have intervened traffic season after traffic season to restrict U.S. airline proposals to increase flights from their primary U.S. gateways to London even though their existing flights were nearly full.

In addition to intervening in U.S. carrier scheduling decisions, U.K. authorities have also consistently disapproved U.S. airline pricing initiatives that would have stimulated traffic by giving more attractive fares to passengers to interior U.S. cities.

It is also extraordinary and unacceptable that the U.S. and the U.K. have an agreement that limits the U.S. passenger carriers at Heathrow to only two. Some U.K. interests try to justify that restriction by asserting that slot constraints at Heathrow prevent commercially viable new entry at the airport. However, our analysis indicates that, in addition to American and United replacing TWA and Pan American at Heathrow, 24 of the airlines operating at Heathrow in July 1995 did not have any services there in July 1990. In that time, departures from Heathrow have increased over 16 percent, and the airlines and airport authorities continue to work together to use the available capacity more efficiently. So, my answer to the congestion argument is: get rid of the Bermuda 2 barriers to Heathrow access and let U.S. carriers compete for slots.

I can assure you that U.S. aviation authorities recognize the importance to U.S. airlines and cities of expanding opportunities in the U.K. market, and immediate full-scale liberalization is our preferred option. Since the British were simply unwilling to expand their focus beyond the immediate needs of their airlines or to allow market forces to shape the development of aviation services, an incremental approach to liberalization appeared to be the only effective way to make progress. In adopting a step-by-step approach, Secretary Peña emphasized that each incremental increase in opportunities must bring benefits to U.S. airlines and consumers and be defensible on its own merits. The June 1995 deal met those tests. American Airlines, Continental Airlines, Northwest Airlines, and United Airlines are all using new opportunities that were secured last year. This first-stage agreement was also a prerequisite, from the British perspective, for moving on to discuss further liberalizations.

I recognize, and share, your concern that a second-stage agreement has not yet been reached. However, we will not accept proposals that do not meet the standard set out by Secretary Peña. Consequently, we suspended the second-phase negotiations because the British proposals on Heathrow were not sufficient to form a basis for agreement. They were structured to prevent certain U.S. airlines and cities from even competing for limited new Heathrow opportunities.

Moreover, despite the recommendations of their own Parliamentary Select Committee that all-cargo services be opened up, the British were not prepared during the second-phase talks to move aggressively to full cargo liberalization. Their approach ignored the broader benefits that flow throughout the economy from an expanded network of cargo services. The U.K. offer was again narrowly focused to satisfy the immediate interests of U.K. carriers. For example, U.K. carriers are not interested in U.S.-Philippines rights and consequently, under the U.K. proposal, Federal Express would have been unable to feed U.K. traffic into its Pacific hub at Subic Bay.

Despite the suspension of formal negotiations, contacts between the U.S. and the U.K. continue. I had an informal discussion with my U.K. counterpart last month and a follow-up conversation last week. I confirmed to the U.K. officials that the Department's goal remains the negotiation of the best possible deal for U.S. airlines and cities, based on competitive considerations in the marketplace. I also communicated the U.S. frustration that, despite a healthy and growing U.K. carrier presence in the market, U.K. authorities have been unwilling to loosen the constraints of the Bermuda 2 regime even sufficiently for us to move forward on a small, incremental deal. Although we still do not have a basis for resuming talks, these contacts allow us to explore possible ways of moving the process forward, and we will be evaluating what we have learned. We have not closed the doors on any options and we are continuing to assess all possible ways to make progress.

Although any optimism for an early resumption of talks must be tempered by the experience of those who have preceded me, commercial pressure is our ally. The European open-skies initiative and competing carrier alliances between U.S. and European airlines are already affecting transatlantic traffic flows. As these alliances mature and the expanded opportunities in the open-skies regimes are exploited, the British will not be able to ignore their impacts if London's preeminence as a gateway to the world is to be maintained. Moreover, with its aspirations to complete a worldwide integrated service network, British Airways will have to take into consideration the possibility that some of its European competitors, such as KLM, will be able to perfect their alliances with antitrust immunity. Thus, the ramifications of our open-skies initiative are far from being played out.

I would like to turn now to Japan, our largest air market in terms of revenues. Although there are a few other Asian destinations, such as Korea, Taiwan and Hong Kong, that can support direct nonstop service from the U.S. mainland, Japan is easily the primary gateway to Asia due to its geographic location and its size as an aviation market. Japan, where U.S. carriers do very well, will remain a key market for U.S. carriers operating transpacific services for the foreseeable future.

As you know, our aviation relationship with Japan in recent years has not always gone smoothly. The United States and Japan have very different aviation policies. While the United States favors a market-based regime and minimal restrictions on entry, routing, pricing and the amount of service that airlines may provide, Japan favors a more regulated approach. Japan favors this protective approach since its airlines are not yet as efficient as the U.S. carriers.

In the last two or three years the Japanese have focused increasing attention on U.S. airline operations beyond Japan. It is clear from statements of Japanese officials that one of Japan's primary objectives is to impose constraints on U.S.

carrier operations beyond Japan to other Asian points. We have repeatedly advised the Japanese that any actions to deny our carriers' rights to operate beyond Japan would be viewed as a serious violation of the U.S.-Japan Air Services Agreement.

An example of Japan's approach toward U.S. carrier beyond services occurred approximately eighteen months ago when the Japanese refused to approve several new routings proposed by Federal Express to Asian points, including Subic Bay in the Philippines where FedEx was establishing a new air cargo hub. Several rounds of talks took place with Japan to address this matter. Finally, in July last year Secretary Peña and his counterpart, Minister Kamei, met in Los Angeles and resolved that cargo dispute. The Japanese agreed to approve the Federal Express flights.

As a consequence of our resolution of the FedEx issue, we agreed to begin broad-scale cargo negotiations in order to liberalize the regime for cargo services. As you may have heard, these negotiations led to the two sides reaching an agreement in the last week of March which permits significant expansion of all-cargo services. The final text of this agreement was negotiated earlier this month.

In the early rounds of our cargo negotiations with Japan, the U.S. side proposed that a liberal regime for cargo services be phased in over five years. We argued that it would serve the interests of both countries to remove restrictions on such services. We indicated that we had considerable flexibility on the time period and the manner in which this would be done. The Japanese rejected this concept. As a result, the agreement we reached is not as expansive as we would have preferred. Nevertheless, it represents a significant step forward. It removes all restrictions on the U.S. gateway points that may be served with all-cargo services by United, Northwest and Federal Express and it permits these carriers to serve three additional points in Japan. It enables UPS to serve the new Kansai International Airport at Osaka and permits the United States to name a new entrant, which will be permitted to serve any one point in Japan except Tokyo six times per week. Although we continue to desire a fully liberal cargo regime, these are welcome improvements to the air cargo regime. The incremental nature of these improvements, however, are instructive of Japan's approach to expanding U.S.-Japan air service opportunities.

With the cargo talks completed, we are now considering how to move the relationship forward in the passenger area.

Some are reluctant to engage Japan in passenger talks now. They believe that Japan's primary objective is to curtail existing U.S. rights to operate beyond Japan. They believe that Japan will use the U.S. desire for additional U.S.-Japan routes as leverage to achieve this objective. They note that Japan has not indicated much interest in obtaining substantial new opportunities for its own carriers to serve the United States.

Others have a different view. They believe that it would be in the overall interest of the United States to negotiate for new U.S.-Japan routes even if the cost of obtaining such routes is acceptance of constraints on U.S. beyond-Japan services. They believe that an agreement could be struck that would preserve all existing beyond operations of U.S. carriers and that constraints would apply only to the rate of future growth of such services. In their view, this would be a reasonable price to pay for opening up the market to more service.

We are continuing to evaluate both sides of this question. In this regard, we have received four studies that relate directly to this subject. We have the Booz Allen & Hamilton study, produced for United Airlines, which focuses on the projected benefits to the U.S. trade balance that would flow from the beyond networks operated by United and Northwest. There is the ACCESS U.S.-Japan study, prepared by Coopers and Lybrand, which emphasizes the benefits that would flow from additional U.S.-Japan services to U.S. cities not now enjoying direct air service to Japan.

A third study, prepared by Roberts, Roach & Associates and

Northwest, attempts to rebut the ACCESS U.S.-Japan study. It underscores the benefits inherent in the existing aviation bilateral which permits carriers like Northwest to operate extensive Asian networks based on their hub operation at Tokyo.

The assumptions made and the methodologies used for each study vary greatly. Each attempts to address the question of the relative value of additional U.S.-Japan operations versus the value of beyond rights.

The fourth study by the Economic Strategy Institute (ESI) lays out an approach to assess the value of the market to the United States in 2010 under four different policy options: open skies, continuation of the existing regime, trading future expansion of beyond operations for additional U.S.-Japan services and trading both future and existing beyond operations for more U.S.-Japan services. Forecasting the U.S.-Japan market at some future point under different policy scenarios, particularly if the point is as far away as 2010, requires major assumptions on a number of complex issues. It is not clear what foundation exists for many of the critical assumptions made in any of these four studies. As part of our evaluation of the four studies, we have asked such questions as: What would be the value of enhanced competition between the United States and Japan for U.S. consumers in terms of service and fare competition? What evidence is there regarding potential demand in the U.S.-Japan market and what overall level of increased service between our two countries could be sustained? What air fare assumptions should apply if new U.S.-Japan routes are added? What assumptions were made regarding the availability of slots at Tokyo in calculating the value of future services?

In order to get a better understanding of what assumptions were made, we have sent follow-up questions to United and the ACCESS U.S.-Japan groups. We have received a response from the later and expect a response from United soon. All of these studies are helpful in that they focus attention on some of the variables that we need to take into account as we develop a strategy for furthering our aviation policy goals with respect to Japan.

I would like to note that despite the ongoing debate about whether the U.S. should accept constraints on future growth of beyond operations to obtain additional U.S.-Japan routes, we are not prepared to subscribe to an "either-or" philosophy on this issue. Rather, our goal is to mutually expand opportunities. We achieved this in air cargo. It is vital that our carriers be able to compete effectively for Asian traffic. It is also desirable that we increase opportunities for additional services in this rapidly growing market. Our job is to develop a strategy that best serves the overall interests of the United States.

Even before such a strategy can be implemented, we have several outstanding issues in the passenger area. One issue concerns a longstanding request by United Airlines to operate beyond the new Kansai International Airport at Osaka to Seoul, Korea. United has also recently filed in Japan to operate beyond Kansai to Jakarta. Neither of these requests have been approved. These proposed services are, in our view, authorized by the existing bilateral agreement. Northwest also seeks to initiate this summer a new service from Osaka to Jakarta, which it is entitled to operate under the U.S.-Japan bilateral. The Japanese have indicated that the approval of this service is in question.

Another issue concerns Japan Airlines' request to operate three weekly flights to Kona, Hawaii from Tokyo. JAL proposed to begin this service on April 1. We have not acted on JAL's request. Since this application is contested and remains pending before the Department, I am not at liberty to talk about its merits. However, I can say that we appreciate the importance of this proposed service to Hawaii. At the same time we must also consider the implications of approving a request of JAL to operate a service authorized by the bilateral while Japan is refusing to approve requests by a U.S. carrier which are also authorized by the bilateral. In response to our inaction on JAL's Kona application, Japan's Ministry of Transport has deferred action on a United proposed increase in frequencies in the Los Angeles-Tokyo market planned for May 2. We began yesterday, and are continuing today, meeting with Japanese officials here in Washington to seek to reach an accord on the initiation of these services.

If the several outstanding issues in the passenger area are resolved, we believe it would be appropriate to meet with the Japanese this summer in government-to-government meetings to agree on a possible framework for passenger negotiations. If an acceptable approach for passenger talks can be worked out, then I would anticipate the two sides would begin formal talks with Japan soon thereafter.

The importance of aviation trade with the U.K. and Japan is undeniable; however, we cannot ignore the commercially significant developments that are continuing to occur throughout the airline industry.

At the beginning of the 1990s, the aviation industry was in the midst of a serious crisis. The United States had just lost two major airlines and three others were in bankruptcy. New entry -- that important spur to competition and innovation -- had almost disappeared. The industry's financial results for 1990, 1991, and 1992 were disastrous. The international sector accounted for more than half of the record $2.4 billion operating loss in 1992.

In addition, not only were we making no significant progress in opening new international markets, even worse, we were facing a resurgence in protectionism in that critical economic sector. France and Thailand had renounced their liberal bilateral aviation agreements with us. Germany was threatening to do the same. And some members of the European Union were urging it to develop a unified, restrictive aviation relationship with us.

The remarkable recovery of our airline industry, which I highlighted at the beginning of my statement, is a success story of which we can be proud, just as we are proud of the bipartisan support for that recovery and the promotion of growth and expansion of international aviation services.

Today, none of our major airlines is in bankruptcy. The industry turn around that became evident in 1994 is continuing into 1996. New entry has increased dramatically -- and successfully. Since the Administration took office over three years ago, the Department has authorized 27 new entrant jet air carriers that have started commercial air service. Today, we have 12 more pending applications for new carrier jet service.

This economic resurgence and growth were complemented by two government initiatives. Domestically, President Clinton and the Congress appointed a talented, bipartisan National Commission to examine the airline industry, and we are implementing the recommendations. In addition, Secretary Peña issued a new international aviation policy statement, the first comprehensive articulation of U.S. policy in nearly two decades, that is guiding us as we move forward internationally.

I would like to emphasize that our aviation policy statement marked the beginning of a dramatically productive era in the history of international aviation relations. Our approach to this subject is based on a number of core principles, including the recognition that it is our responsibility to lead, to create new pathways for commercial activity, and to allow market forces to shape service patterns to the benefit of users and providers of air transportation. With these considerations in mind, we will continue to take a fresh look at aviation issues, fashion innovative strategies for achieving our objectives, and place greater emphasis on economic analysis. We will be pragmatic in dealing with other countries, and engage their leadership personally and professionally so as to enhance our ability to reach mutually satisfactory solutions to problems that have impeded progress towards liberalization.

Over the past year and a half, we have created more new opportunities for international aviation services than during any other comparable period in our aviation history. As a result of our efforts, there are now new U.S. flag services around the globe -- in North America, South America, Europe, and Asia.

In achieving those successes, the Department has been flexible in matching negotiating strategy to individual situations and objectives. In addition, we have recognized that the items of trade in negotiations have altered. Facilitation of alliances has, in more mature markets, assumed more importance than requests for additional gateway cities. This element will be an essential factor as we move increasingly towards a globally integrated air transportation system. Code-share access and the possibility of antitrust immunity are among the tools to complement an aviation system that can be shaped by competitive market forces -- one that has been freed from unnecessary bilateral restrictions. We will depend on extensive, careful, and thorough analysis to ensure that investment and competition policy decisions contribute to the momentum towards open competitive markets.

Putting the new approaches I have outlined into practice has yielded specific, concrete results. Our new transborder aviation agreement with Canada opened the largest single bilateral aviation market in the world. We marked the first anniversary of this agreement last month, with traffic growth exceeding one million passengers. Never in commercial aviation history has a new agreement spurred growth of that level.

As you know, demand for aviation services is now global, and many of our airlines are responding through arrangements such as code sharing, joint marketing agreements, and cross-border investments. Traffic growth over the European gateways of each of the three largest strategic alliances has averaged about nine percent per year, compared with little change in traffic in the balance of the transatlantic market. Our landmark open-skies agreements with ten European countries have provided important public benefits by allowing airlines to respond to this commercial imperative. For the first time, we were able to reach accords with multiple countries, which laid the foundation for providing the industry with the infrastructure it needs to meet the growing demand for worldwide air service. New services between the United States and the open-skies countries are already being put in place. Current and additional new air services will stimulate tourist and other traffic to the United States.

The code-sharing relationship between Northwest and KLM, the flag carrier of our first open-skies partner -- The Netherlands -- has demonstrated the potential of airline alliances. That relationship is continuing to develop, bringing important strategic and economic benefits to both alliance partners and to the market as a whole. Amsterdam has surpassed Paris' Charles De Gaulle Airport as the fourth largest European gateway airport. Despite the presence of the alliance, competition between the United States and Amsterdam has not diminished, and the traffic of U.S. carriers competing with the alliance has increased significantly.

Building on the success of last year's open-skies initiative, we have continued our liberalization efforts in Europe. The United States has reached agreement on an open-skies aviation relationship with Germany, our second largest European aviation market with close to six million passengers. When the German agreement comes into force, nearly 40 percent of the passenger traffic between the United States and Europe will be travelling under open-skies arrangements.

These initiatives collectively represent by far the largest effort to deregulate airline services since domestic deregulation over 15 years ago.

In addition, we reached agreement to phase in an open-skies regime with the Czech Republic, to liberalize operations to Ukraine, and to introduce new opportunities in the U.S.-Poland market. We held exploratory discussions with Hungary two weeks ago. The talks were useful in answering questions that the Hungarians had about our open-skies approach, and we plan future contacts to pursue an agreement. We will work to see that these initiatives lead to liberalization throughout the broader Central European area.

We have not ignored other areas of the world. I would point to successes in securing new rights with our South American partners. In particular, we have provided new opportunities for growth in both the U.S.-Peru and U.S.-Brazil markets, which together represent more than a third of the passenger traffic between the United States and South America. We will be seeking additional progress with Brazil, our largest South American market, in talks this week.

Last month, the United States and South Africa reached a new aviation agreement that significantly expands opportunities for U.S.- South Africa air service. The agreement is the first with an African nation to allow airlines from each country to operate code-share services.

The fastest growing region for aviation services is Asia, with more than half of the world's population and most of the fastest-growing economies. Last June, Secretary Peña hosted a meeting of the Asia-Pacific Economic Cooperation transport ministers, which produced a landmark joint ministerial statement. We agreed to reduce trade barriers, to encourage competition in the transport sector, to improve global transportation systems, and to enhance cooperation in training, safety, and security. The United States has aggressively pursued those objectives, and we have successfully negotiated expanded opportunities for U.S. airlines to participate in the Asian market.

New rights have been introduced in Hong Kong, Macau, India, Fiji, the People's Republic of China, the Philippines, and Thailand.

Hong Kong is our fourth largest market in the Far East. Although the other markets have not reached Hong Kong's maturity, their growth potential is undeniable, and we are working to ensure that U.S. carriers can participate in their development.

Just last week, we met with Singapore, one of our most liberal Asian partners, to discuss possibilities for moving forward with liberalization in Asia.

We are proud of the successes that we have achieved. However, we have not lost sight of what remains to be done. We are continuing our efforts to allow competitive forces to direct the development of international air services so that the full potential contribution of aviation to the global economy can be realized.

In conclusion, I appreciate your support during my first months as Assistant Secretary. I recognize that the backing of this admirable bipartisan forum has been an important contributing factor to the success of the Administration and Secretary Peña in achieving our national goals in international aviation. I look forward to your continuing input as we work together to address 1996's international aviation challenges.

OPENING STATEMENT OF THE HON. ROBERT MENENDEZ
ON
US AVIATION PROBLEMS WITH THE UNITED KINGDOM AND JAPAN

Mr. Chairman, I want to salute you for your continuing efforts in promoting the interests and concerns of US Aviation. However I am disturbed that we are shorting the oversight process. I am wondering why an entire facet of this issue is being excluded from the chance to testify. It appears that American, Continental, Delta and Access-US-Japan have been scheduled out of appearing. I think that this is grossly unfair and I hope that they will have another hearing opportunity. This issue today is extremely important to me, my district, state and region. Newark International Airport is losing its only direct, non-stop service to Tokyo on March 31. Over 85,000 passengers flew between New Jersey and Japan in 1995. There are 300 businesses in New Jersey which deal directly with Japan. These businesses employ 80,000 people. Japan has become the second largest export market for New Jersey products, totalling $1.5 billion. Yet there are only four routes to Tokyo from the New Jersey/New York metropolitan area airports. There are no flights to Osaka, a city nearly as large as Tokyo.

What will be done to replace this critical air service for New Jersey business? I am afraid precious little and I am angry about the posture the federal government is taking on bilateral talks with the Japanese (and also with the British.)

The mere fact that the bilateral agreement between the U.S. and Japan was signed before I was born does not give it the status of the Ten Commandments. If we are

looking for guiding principles of lasting value, then we would be better served by adhering to the "open skies" policy that President Eisenhower enunciated from that same era. I believe that fair trade increases business opportunities and ultimately benefits everyone. It is not fair competition if foreign governments and their air carriers can determine who their competitors will be. If our great cities do not have access to the great market places of the world then we cannot be competitive.

It has been said that we have little leverage in bilateral talks. I disagree. Our policy should always be open skies. If we are to have bilaterals, then they should be dynamic and flexible to reflect the nature of the aviation industry and the national economies. They should not be carved in stone. If we face monolithic opposition,

we should not be reluctant to use renunciation and sanction. The United States market is the market of opportunity. It is the location that foreign carriers would like to serve, therefore we should insist on transparent, market oriented bilaterals. We should never submit to economic mercantilism.

In beginning my statement with reference to the immediacy of the Japanese aviation access problem, I do not want to single out their intractable behavior. Equally odious are the antics of the United Kingdom, which has long touted the "special relationship" which supposedly exists between our nations. If this relationship exists, why shouldn't there be open skies between our nations? It appears to be a special relationship if the British benefit. This is comparable to British policies when they had the

world's largest navy and forced their mercantile version of free trade in the last century. Since signing the last bilateral, the British have allowed 25 new carriers to fly to Heathrow but not one new American carrier. This is clearly prejudicial to the U.S. Sixty percent of the profit of British Airways is made on the North Atlantic route. Opposing new American routes is clearly a bottomline decision to limit competition.

A word for my friends at Transportation: It is important to always remember first principles. Our policy is open skies because our role as the federal government is to promote opportunity by seeking to open markets. We seek to open markets for new carriers and not merely to open new opportunities for incumbents, because the fortunes of airlines are capricious. An international route

maybe lucrative for a company which may fold for entirely different reasons. Each day, the commerce of the United States depends more on international markets. If we cannot get there because of limited airline access, or one of the two incumbents on a route has gone bankrupt and the foreign nation will not allow transfers, then we have harmed our economy and lost jobs. We must insist on robust opportunities for access. This nation must never go hat-in-hand into trade negotiations of any kind. I fully expect our negotiators to get the message that the passenger service talks must begin immediately and to deliver the message that these markets must open or face the consequences.

To my friends in the aviation industry: The issues before us today have been characterized as the "Haves"

versus the Have-nots." I hope that we have greater foresight than to address these issues as factions. It is the obligation of everyone to look beyond the immediate moment for the good of the entire nation. If we work together, then we can open the skies around the world and all share the benefits.

Again, Mr. Chairman, I look forward to working with you on expanding job opportunities for our aviation industry.

STATEMENT OF THE HONORABLE

JAMES A. TRAFICANT, JR.

TRANSPORTATION AND INFRASTRUCTURE

SUBCOMMITTEE ON AVIATION

HEARING ON U.S. AVIATION RELATIONSHIP

WITH UNITED KINGDOM AND JAPAN

APRIL 30, 1996

24-087 97 - 14

Thank you Chairman Duncan for holding a second hearing on this issue. I think it is vitally important for Congress to work closely with the Clinton Administration to aggressively expand passenger and cargo air service between the United States and Japan, as well as the United Kingdom.

I am especially concerned over our aviation relationship with Japan. The Pacific Rim is one of the fastest growing markets in the world. Expanding U.S. airline service -- passenger and cargo -- to the Pacific Rim will depend, on the large part, on the ability of U.S. airlines to expand their hubs and presence in Japan.

Of particular importance is the ability for U.S. airlines to use Japan as an important stopover point to other destinations along the Pacific Rim.

I would like to make a few comments about the U.S.-Japan aviation relationship. The history of the trade relationship between Japan and the United States over the past forty years should teach Congress one thing: unless the United States stands firm in protecting its own interests, Japan will run roughshod over U.S. business.

Page Two

I strongly support expanding access of U.S. airline companies into Japan and other markets in the Pacific Rim. I believe we can -- and should -- achieve such expansion without compromising one inch on the inroads we have already made through the U.S.-Japan Aviation Agreement.

I would caution my colleagues on this panel not to support any proposal that benefits one sector of the U.S. passenger industry at the expense of other sectors.

Congress and the Administration should work together with the airline industry on a plan of action to force Japan to further open up its aviation markets to U.S. competition -- without making any concessions to Japan that would, in the end, result in less access and less competition.

The goal should be a truly open and free market. This overarching goal should be applied to both the U.S.-Japan relationship and the U.S.-UK relationship.

Page Three

The U.S. airline industry has made remarkable strides in recent years. Given the opportunity to compete with interference and roadblocks, I know they will continue to do quite well.

Once again, Mr. Chairman, thank you for holding this hearing. I look forward to working with you and the distinguished ranking member from Illinois, Mr. Lipinski, on this issue in the weeks and months ahead.

###

ADDITION TO THE RECORD

Testimony of Paul B. Gaines
Director of Aviation
City of Houston
before the
U.S. House of Representatives
Subcommittee on Aviation
April 30, 1996

I appreciate this opportunity to submit to the Committee these views on behalf of Houston, Texas and the Greater Houston Partnership. The Partnership is an association of the Chamber of Commerce, World Trade and Economic Development Organizations, all of which have a keen interest in our air service.

Good international air service is, of course, essential to economic development, especially for a city such as Houston with so many worldwide international business interests. Because of its size -- the fourth largest U.S. city -- and unique multicultural character, Houston also has a need for good air transportation to all corners of the globe to satisfy the personal travel needs of our citizens.

I understand that this hearing has been convened to consider problems in the U.S. aviation relationship with the U.K. and Japan. This is a subject of tremendous interest to the City of Houston because of the considerable need for good air transportation to and beyond London and between Houston and Asia, and because the restrictive aviation bilateral agreements between the U.S. and the U.K. and Japan respectively preclude Houston from receiving the service to Heathrow and the nonstop access to Japan that it so badly needs.

As we have expressed before to this Committee, as well as to the U.S. Departments of Transportation and State, Houston typically favors any agreement which will increase opportunities for international air transportation by Americans, and particularly for the businesses and residents of the Houston community. Our primary goal is, of course, to obtain the best possible service for Houston residents and those in the large catchment area our airport serves in the West and Midwest. Generally we think that any move toward liberalization tends to be beneficial in that it adds to the momentum for opening up international air service generally. The sooner the world as a whole moves toward free and open skies, the better served we in Houston, and Americans everywhere, will be. Accordingly, we strongly support efforts by the U.S. Government to liberalize both the U.S. - U.K. and U.S. - Japan aviation agreements.

Let me begin by addressing the issues we deem most important where the U.K. is concerned. We recognize that many countries do not share our vision of full liberalization of international aviation services, and that their reluctance to move speedily towards a more open regime represents considerable difficulties for U.S. negotiators. I believe our Government is genuinely interested in obtaining international air transport arrangements that are as liberal as possible, and that insofar as Heathrow is concerned, our negotiators have been stymied in their efforts by the U.K. Government's ongoing refusal to permit access to Heathrow for Houston and the other U.S. cities that need such access. Meanwhile, the U.K. airlines continue to enjoy a major advantage in Heathrow-U.S. services. The U.K. carriers serve more U.S.-Heathrow gateways than U.S. carriers; they operate more weekly frequencies by a significant margin; and they offer approximately 133% more seat capacity.

Where we differ at times with U.S. negotiators is on how to achieve U.S. liberalization goals, and the issue of Heathrow access is one of the major areas where our views are significantly different. For many years the City of Houston has been pressing for changes in the U.S. - U.K. bilateral agreement that would permit air service between our community and Heathrow airport, the so-called "crown jewel" in the U.K. aviation infrastructure. Despite these efforts, Houston remains economically disadvantaged by the lack of such service, and recent rounds of negotiations with the U.K. appear to have left us as far away from meeting our needs in this respect as we have always been. At the same time the U.S. appears to be moving closer towards opening up U.S. aviation markets for U.K. carriers and providing even more benefits to the few U.S. interests that already enjoy Heathrow access. Accordingly, I believe that the only approach to future bilateral negotiations that will serve the public interest is to begin by addressing the current imbalances in the agreement, and by insisting on creating additional Heathrow opportunities on a phased-in basis over a specific time frame for all those who need Heathrow access.

One simply cannot underestimate the importance of Heathrow services to a city such as Houston. Not only is Heathrow the most convenient London airport in terms of access to London itself, it is especially valuable for connecting services beyond. This is of particular importance to Houston because of its oil business ties with the Middle East, which enjoys far better service from Heathrow than from Gatwick. For these reasons and others, Heathrow is highly favored by passengers, especially higher fare business travellers. For example, British Airways, which serves Gatwick from Houston, has more than twice as many beyond destinations with connections at Heathrow as it does at Gatwick, and studies show that twice as many transatlantic passengers make beyond connections at Heathrow as at Gatwick. Thus Houston passengers are considerably inconvenienced by not being able to fly nonstop to Heathrow.

As the third largest U.S. gateway without Heathrow service, and the largest Texas gateway without Heathrow service based on population and London traffic, no city in Texas deserves Heathrow service more than Houston, the fourth largest city in the United

States. An agreement which so severely disadvantages one of this nation's most important communities through the perpetuation of antiquated, protectionist restrictions has no place in the aviation arena of the 1990s.

The significant imbalances in the U.K. agreement that exist between U.S. and U.K. carriers, and the numerous restrictions that exclude cities such as Houston from the list of communities eligible for Heathrow services, are exacerbated by the fact that, as a carryover from an earlier agreement with the British, the U.S. is limited to only two airlines eligible for Heathrow service, namely United and American, the so-called "duopoly carriers". Instead of insisting on the removal of this two carrier rule, interim agreements that have been reached with the U.K. in recent years have benefitted only United and American among the U.S. carriers, giving them an unreasonable advantage over their U.S. competitors and depriving the U.S. traveling public of additional competition. Although American is one of the most vocal carriers in demanding more Heathrow rights, it is noteworthy that one of its prominent advertisements boasts more nonstops to Heathrow than any other U.S. airline. Meanwhile airlines without Heathrow access -- such as Houston's hub carrier, Continental -- have an extremely difficult time competing with those that serve Heathrow, both in terms of the number of passengers they can attract and their profitability.

Until now, progress towards liberalization of the U.S. - U.K. aviation relationship has come largely by means of limited agreements on a few issues, such as the so-called "mini-deal" agreed to last year which gave United -- one of the existing duopoly carriers at Heathrow -- the right to provide yet more Heathrow service, this time from Chicago. In late 1995 the U.S. seriously considered entering into another mini-deal, which would have had only a limited impact on Heathrow access and which would have continued to exclude most of the U.S. parties seeking such access. As was the case with prior agreements, the proposal made no provision for the long term access to Heathrow that is so badly needed. Fortunately that deal was rejected by the U.S., and rightfully so, but unless the U.S. takes a firm stand and insists on the negotiation of long term access to Heathrow, the pressure to enter into more mini-deals is likely to re-emerge.

Some would argue that whenever the U.K. makes an offer that improves U.K. access for any U.S. carrier or city we should jump at the chance to take what we can while continuing to press for further liberalization. The problem is that this approach has not worked to the advantage of the majority of American consumers. For example, the United States made a major mistake when, in its eagerness to allow American and United to buyout the U.K. authority of Pan American and TWA, it agreed to continue restrictions on its freedom to designate Heathrow carriers and services in a way that would maximize competition and consumer benefits for Americans. The result of this and other agreements has been a steady erosion of the U.S. carrier share of the U.S. - U.K. market.

Moreover, the U.S. has paid dearly for the few crumbs that have been offered by the British in recent years. The Pan Am/TWA buyout is one example, and last year's agreement benefitting United at Chicago is another. Indeed, the United-Chicago situation was particularly egregious: the U.S. - U.K. aviation bilateral already contained a provision that would have allowed the U.S. to designate United for Chicago service once the market reached a certain size, a size which probably would have been reached before the mini-deal (thus making the mini-deal unnecessary) had the existing carriers not limited their capacity in the market. So the U.S. paid twice for those rights, while other interested parties -- such as Houston -- were left out altogether.

Thus these mini-deals have focused primarily on addressing the demands of U.S. incumbent Heathrow carriers without undertaking a more equitable distribution of bilateral benefits among those who really need them, namely the parties who have <u>no</u> Heathrow access. It is this failure to address the inequities of the situation that is the heart of the problem, and it is this issue that in Houston's view <u>must</u> be made the U.S.'s first priority. United, American, and the cities that already enjoy

Heathrow service have every right to continue to press for further liberalization and additional opportunities. But when so many other needy parties, both U.S. carriers and communities, have nothing insofar as Heathrow rights are concerned, there must be an insistence in negotiations on a full range of opportunities for these interests and a fair apportioning of new rights that become available. No existing beneficiary of Heathrow service should be given more new opportunities until those who have long been deprived, such as Houston, receive the Heathrow service that is so vital to their growth and economic well-being.

As a beginning, the U.S. should no longer accept the British stonewalling on Heathrow access that has become an accepted part of every recent negotiation. It has become standard fare for the U.K. to repel U.S. requests for additional Heathrow access by simply stating that Heathrow is "full". Yet at the same time the U.K. presses the U.S. to bestow further benefits on U.K. carriers in U.S. markets. Take Fly America, for example. The proposal by the U.K. to allow their carriers to carry U.S. Government traffic previously reserved for U.S. carriers has been the subject of bilateral negotiations for far too many hours, days, and indeed months. This is an issue that benefits only the U.K., and the U.S. has devoted inordinate amounts of time to addressing U.K. "concerns" about U.K. "needs" in this regard. But when the discussion turns to Heathrow access for the U.S., the U.S. is told by the British that there is no point discussing the subject because there are no slots available at Heathrow! Meanwhile rumors abound that numerous new Heathrow slots become available each year, and carriers from other countries receive new Heathrow rights. We cannot allow this stonewalling on the part of the U.K. to continue further. As each year slips by without Heathrow access, communities such as Houston lose valuable opportunities and economic growth due to the lack of air service to Heathrow. The United States, and individual communities, need and deserve better.

It is not my desire to critique every aspect of prior agreements or the techniques of U.S. negotiators, who face a challenging task. Hindsight is always 20/20. But we can and should learn from past experiences in order to better serve the U.S. public interest in the future. In my opinion there is only one way to address the problem. The U.S. should not continue to accept the U.K.'s refusal to address the Heathrow question, and should make a commitment that nothing less than fairly apportioned, fully competitive access to Heathrow must be found for the consumers, communities and airlines of the United States. I do not believe that we have ever made that commitment or fully communicated it to the U.K., and without it, I believe that the U.K. will continue to do what they have done all along, namely tell us that Heathrow access is an intractable problem.

We in Houston recognize that long term problems usually demand long term solutions, and that instant access to Heathrow cannot be made available overnight to everyone. Much as we would like instant access, we are realistic and rational in our goals, and recognize the legitimate needs of various carriers and communities. Because there are so many competing needs, it makes all the more sense to develop a long term approach that first addresses the airlines and cities without Heathrow access. We must establish and negotiate a plan which assures that all U.S. airlines and cities will have an opportunity to obtain Heathrow service over a reasonable period of time.

Let me now turn to Japan. Although the critical Japan-related issues that affect Houston differ from those applicable in the U.K. situation, there are significant similarities, and, in our opinion, common problems with respect to the attention given U.S. community concerns by the U.S. Government.

Just as service to Heathrow is integrally related to our community's ability to trade effectively with the U.K. and points beyond, so too U.S. - Japan trade is a vital component of the Houston community's economic health and growth. In 1994, for example, the Port of Houston handled $1.2 billion in Houston-Japan trade, and Japan ranked fifth in the dollar value of total trade through the Port. I might add that the Houston Port ranks first in the U.S. in foreign tonnage and third in total tonnage, and so these statistics are particularly impressive. Houston's air cargo growth in 1994 totaled over 2.7 million kilos, 93 percent of which were products exported to Japan.

In addition, we have extensive community ties with Japan and the entire Pacific Region. For example, there are more than 240 Houston companies currently trading goods and services with Japan, nearly 200 other Houston companies that trade with East Asia as a whole -- including Japan -- and nearly 90 subsidiaries of Japanese companies operating in Houston. We also enjoy the largest concentration of Japanese specialty chemical companies outside Japan, and numerous Japanese banks and government departments have offices located in Houston. We have an ongoing commitment to the promotion of Houston - Japan trade, not only through the efforts of the Greater Houston Partnership, but also through the Japan American Society in Houston and the Japan Business Association. We also have a sister city relationship with Chiba, Japan.

Despite these major trading connections and close community ties, as well as the City's extensive efforts over a period of nearly three decades to obtain the Japan air service we need, we have no nonstop or direct air service to Japan. This major void in our international air transportation network has a significant adverse impact on our ability to compete in the ever-growing Asian marketplace. It is unacceptable that the U.S.'s fourth largest city should be deprived of the critical air transportation links that are the lifeblood of our economic health and well-being.

Why the absence of this greatly needed service? The principal reason is, of course, the outdated and highly restrictive air services agreement that exists between the U.S. and Japan, an agreement which precludes the kind of service between Houston and Japan that we seek. This antiquated agreement between two of the world's largest trading partners has no place in the global network of the 1990s, where international air access and transportation links can spell the difference between economic success and failure.

We in Houston understand that, given the restrictive nature of the U.S. - Japan agreement and the desire on the part of the Japanese Government to allow only limited access to the valuable Japanese markets, our own negotiators face inordinate obstacles in opening up access to Japan. We recognize that in the face of such obstacles there are limits to what our negotiators can achieve.

In that regard, and notwithstanding the limited nature of the new rights agreed to, we are extremely pleased to hear that progress has recently been made on further expanding access to Japan for cargo services. We hope that the U.S. will continue to press ahead with further liberalization of the Japan agreement, and in particular will insist that a major expansion of U.S. - Japan passenger rights be among the U.S.'s highest priorities in the international aviation arena.

However, as with the U.K. agreement, there are aspects of the U.S. Government approach to expanding Japan access that we find troubling, and which we believe sometimes work against the interests of U.S. citizens, namely the emphasis that all too often is given to serving the needs of U.S. carriers at the expense of the U.S. community as a whole. Just as with the Heathrow situation, there are incumbent U.S. carriers in the Japan market and U.S. cities that already enjoy extensive air service between our two countries. And then there are the "have-nots", including Houston, the fourth largest city in the United States. The list of have-nots is large, and the U.S. - Japan traffic rights that the incumbents enjoy are a highly valuable and precious commodity.

Despite the long list of carriers and communities waiting in line for their first nonstop or direct Japan service, the U.S. Government's emphasis in discussions with Japan appears constantly to be placed on obtaining additional rights for incumbent carriers, while the have-nots remain exactly where they have been for years -- namely without any such service. This makes absolutely no sense, and fails to serve the public interest as a whole, which extends well beyond the needs and desires of incumbent carriers. Accordingly we believe that it should be a fundamental tenet of U.S. international aviation policy that priority be given not only to obtaining additional traffic rights for U.S. carriers, but to distributing those rights fairly among U.S. citizens throughout the United States.

Obviously new traffic rights given to U.S. carriers also benefit U.S. consumers. However, when the emphasis is placed on obtaining even more access for incumbent carriers, the U.S. consumer does not always benefit. Take, for example, the enormous emphasis placed by our Government on obtaining fifth freedom rights beyond Japan for U.S. carriers. Such rights clearly are important and valuable for the U.S. carriers that already enjoy third and fourth freedom traffic rights between the U.S. and Japan. And certainly where the U.S. has already obtained and paid for fifth freedom rights, we should vigorously contest any efforts by Japan to take away those rights.

But unless it can be shown that particular fifth freedom rights are vital to the interests of the U.S. traveling public, and are more important than third and fourth freedom rights, there is simply no justification for allowing fifth freedom rights to dominate U.S. aviation policy towards Japan. The first priority for the U.S. <u>must</u> first be to obtain third and fourth freedom access for the U.S. carriers and communities that are currently totally excluded from such access. Nothing less can fairly serve the interests of the U.S. consumer and the U.S. public interest as a whole. We in the City of Houston strongly urge you to insist that our Government make this its first consideration and goal insofar as aviation relations with Japan are concerned.

Thank you for your attention to our concerns.

REPORT ON ACTIONS TAKEN TO ELIMINATE DISCRIMINATION AND UNFAIR COMPETITIVE PRACTICES IN INTERNATIONAL AIR TRANSPORTATION

(FY 1995)

EXECUTIVE SUMMARY

During Fiscal Year (FY) 1995, the Department of Transportation, through its Office of the Secretary, dealt with several complaints of discriminatory and unfair competitive practices filed by U.S. air carriers. While none of the proceedings were terminated during FY 1995, the Department continued intergovernmental efforts toward their resolution. These complaints were filed under the International Air Transportation Fair Competitive Practices Act of 1974 (IATFCPA), which was recodified in July 1994 under title 49, U.S.C.

Two new complaints were filed during FY 1995. They involved Fine Airlines' services to Ecuador and Peru. The complaint against Ecuador remained pending at the end of FY 1995 as intergovernmental contacts regarding the complaint continued. The Peru complaint was filed three days before the end of FY 1995 and was, therefore, under review at the end of FY 1995.

Eight additional complaints, filed before fiscal year 1995, also remained pending at the end of FY 1995. Those complaints involved services to Brazil (three complaints), the Caribbean, Italy, Japan (two complaints), and Germany. The Department approved the three Brazil complaints, the Caribbean complaint, and the two Japan complaints filed before FY 1995. As to all of these, the issue of sanctions remained pending at the end of FY 1995. The Department also approved in part and denied in part the complaint against Italy filed before FY 1995. American Airlines petitioned for reconsideration of the Department's partial denial, and the matter remained pending at the end of FY 1995. Intergovernmental contacts regarding the complaint against Germany continued during the course of FY 1995, and the complaint remained pending at the end of FY 1995.

The complaints and the disposition of each are described below. This annual report on unfair practices is required by §41310(e)(2) of title 49, U.S.C., formerly §2 (b) of the IATFCPA.

Cases Pending And Their Status At The End Of FY 1995

The Flying Tiger Line Inc., vs. the Government of Brazil and Varig, S.A.
Docket 41653

Description of Complaint: On August 17, 1983, The Flying Tiger Line Inc. (Flying Tiger), filed a complaint against the Government of Brazil and Varig, S.A. Flying Tiger alleged that certain Brazilian laws and regulations worked to favor the movement on Brazilian carriers of airfreight between the United States and Brazil in violation of the civil aviation agreement between the two countries.

Action Requested: Flying Tiger requested that, until such time as Brazil removes the preferences and currency restrictions, Brazil's scheduled flag carrier, Viacao Aerea Rio-Grandense (Varig), should be prohibited from offering any main-deck cargo capacity other than that offered on freighter aircraft operated pursuant to the capacity limits placed upon such aircraft by the aviation agreement.

Disposition: By Order 84-1-83, the Department approved Flying Tiger's complaint but deferred on the issue of sanctions because of negotiations that were scheduled. The issues raised in the complaint were the subject of numerous formal and informal intergovernmental consultations. These negotiations concluded in 1989 with the signing of a new air transport agreement. This agreement removed the cargo preferences and instituted an acceptable regime for the conversion and remittance of currency. The withdrawal of the complaint, however, was not immediately forthcoming due, in part, to actual implementation of the new policies and, in part, to Federal Express Corporation's acquisition of Flying Tiger around this same time. The matter remained pending at the end of FY 1995.

Pan American World Airways, Inc., vs. the Government of Brazil and Varig, S.A.
Docket 46439, and **Pan American World Airways, Inc., vs. Transbrasil S.A. Linhas Aereas** Docket 46522

Description of Complaints: On August 8, 1989, Pan American World Airways, Inc. (Pan American), filed a complaint against the Government of Brazil and its flag carrier, Empresa de Viacao Aerea Rio-Grandense, S.A. (Varig) (Docket 46439). In addition, on October 2, 1989, Pan American filed a complaint against Transbrasil S.A. Linhas Aereas (Transbrasil) (Docket 46522). In the complaints, Pan American alleged that Brazil had refused to permit it to remit to the United States in U.S. currency the local revenues in excess of local expenses accruing to the carrier for its services in the U.S.-Brazil market, and had restricted the carrier's right to use its converted revenues to pay its expenses in Brazil, in violation of the aviation agreement between the two countries.

Action Requested: Pan American requested that the Department impose appropriate sanctions to ensure that the Government of Brazil fulfills its obligations under the aviation agreement.

Disposition: By Order 89-11-7, the Department approved the complaints but deferred on the issue of sanctions because of ongoing intergovernmental efforts to resolve the issues raised. The matter remained pending at the end of FY 1995.

Florida West Airlines, Inc., vs. Caribbean Air Cargo Company, Ltd., and BWIA International Docket 46829

Description of Complaint: On March 6, 1990, Florida West Airlines, Inc. (Florida West), filed a complaint against Caribbean Air Cargo Company, Ltd. (Caricargo), and BWIA International (BWIA). Florida West alleged that the Government of Barbados violated the U.S.-Barbados Air Transport Agreement by failing to grant Florida West operating authority to perform scheduled cargo service between the United States and points in Barbados.

Action Requested: Florida West requested that the Department: (1) require Caricargo and BWIA to file their U.S.-Barbados schedules in advance under Part 213 of Title 14 of the Department's regulations; (2) formally consult with the Government of Barbados to demand that it fulfill its commitment under the aviation agreement; and (3) institute, if necessary, proceedings to cancel Caricargo's foreign air carrier permit and exemption authority to operate in the United States.

Disposition: By Order 90-4-18, the Department approved Florida West's complaint and required BWIA to file its schedules for U.S.-Barbados service. The order also required Caricargo to notify the Department before it operated any non-scheduled service. The issue of Florida West's licensing authority was the subject of numerous informal intergovernmental consultations. The matter remained pending at the end of FY 1995.

<u>American vs. Italy, the Directorate General of Civil Aviation of the Ministry of Transport, Societa Esercizi Aeroportuali, and Alitalia Linee Aeree Italiane S.p.A.</u>, Docket 47956

Description of Complaint: On January 21, 1992, American filed an IATFCPA complaint against the Government of the Republic of Italy, the Directorate General of Civil Aviation of the Ministry of Transport, Societa Esercizi Aeroportuali (SEA), and Alitalia Linee Aeree Italiane S.p.A. (Alitalia). American cited the fact that, at Milan's Malpensa Airport, the Government of Italy and SEA prohibited American from: (1) using its own CRS (SABRE) at check-in facilities; and (2) self-handling. American stated that these restrictions denied it a fair and equal opportunity to compete in the U.S.-Italy market.

Action Requested: American proposed that appropriate sanctions be taken against the U.S. operations of Alitalia unless the Government of Italy and SEA immediately grant American the right to use its SABRE CRS and to self-handle at Malpensa. American specifically recommended suspension of future Alitalia tariff filings, or temporary operating restrictions on Alitalia's U.S. operations or in the alternative, prohibition of Alitalia's self-handling in the United States and requirement that Alitalia deal with an appointed agent.

Status: The Department extended the period for taking action on this complaint several times while informal discussions between representatives of the United States and Italy were conducted regarding this complaint and other matters. Various meetings were held between the parties in June and July 1992, during which they agreed to conduct a test of American's SABRE system in early September 1992. That test was successfully conducted on September 9, 1992, and SEA and Alitalia accepted in principle that American's system was compatible with the existing infrastructure at Malpensa and could be used at check-in positions. Additional meetings were held between the parties on October 14, 1992, at Milan. By Order 92-10-33, the Department approved, in part, American's complaint, finding that the Government of Italy, SEA, *et al.*, by restricting American's use of its SABRE computer reservation system at Milan's Malpensa Airport, denied American's right to a fair and equal opportunity to compete in the U.S.-Italy market; but deferred action on the issue of appropriate sanctions based on continuing progress of the SABRE implementation. The Department denied American's complaint with respect to self-handling on the basis that both American and Alitalia were precluded from self-handling, and, thus, no discrimination existed warranting sanctions against Alitalia. On November 9, 1992, American petitioned for reconsideration of the Department's denial of the self-handling aspect of its complaint. The petition remained pending at the end of FY 1995.

<u>**United vs. The Government of Japan**</u>, Docket 48457.

Description of Complaint: On November 5, 1992, United filed an IATFCPA complaint against the Government of Japan. United cites the fact that Japan's denial of United's twice weekly New York-Tokyo-Sydney schedules violates an agreement between the countries under which Japan agreed to accept such filings and allow the schedules to take effect on the date proposed.

Action Requested: United proposes that the Department should require Japanese carriers to file all schedules to and from the United States and to specify on each segment of those flights the percentage of passengers on board originating or terminating their journey in a third country so that the Department can determine appropriate countermeasures.

Status: By Order 92-12-40, the Department extended through February 3, 1993, the period for taking action on the complaint of United, based on upcoming negotiations scheduled with respect to this matter. A number of informal discussions with the Government of Japan were held and negotiations were conducted the week of January 11, 1993. No progress toward resolution of the complaint was achieved at the negotiations and no further talks were scheduled. By Order 93-2-9, the Department approved the complaint of United, finding that Japan's actions with respect to the Tokyo-Sydney portion of United's New York-Tokyo-Sydney services violated the provisions of the U.S.-Japan aviation agreement by denying United access to a beyond-Japan market it is entitled to serve under the Agreement. The order also requested comments from interested parties on appropriate sanctions against Japan Air Lines Company, Ltd., in response to our findings on United's complaint. A number of responses were received. On October 11, 1994, United filed a motion to withdraw its complaint, stating that it was no longer pursuing operations beyond Japan to Australia. The motion remained pending at the end of FY 1995.

<u>**Federal Express Corporation vs. the Government of Japan,**</u> Docket 49094

Description of Complaint: On August 20, 1993, Federal Express Corporation (Federal Express), filed a complaint against the Government of Japan, citing that, contrary to the U.S.-Japan bilateral aviation agreement, Japan has refused to approve its summer schedules providing for Fifth Freedom operations on one weekly flight beyond Japan to Cebu, Philippines.

Action Requested: Federal Express proposes that the Department issue an order requiring that one or both Japanese carriers (Japan Air Lines Company (JAL) and/or Nippon Cargo Airlines (NCA)), suspend one all-cargo flight per week between Japan and the United States during the period that Federal Express is prevented from operating its service between Japan and Cebu.

Status: By Order 93-10-36, the Department approved Federal Express' complaint against the Government of Japan finding that the actions of the Japanese Government to prevent unrestricted implementation of Federal Express' Japan-Cebu schedules, have, over the objection of the U.S. Government, denied Federal Express rights to which it is entitled under the agreement. We deferred on the issue of sanctions, however, stating that the issue of U.S. carrier Fifth Freedom services has been the subject of numerous informal and formal consultations with the Japanese. The matter remained pending at the end of FY 1995.

Delta Air Lines, Inc., vs. the Government of Germany and Flughafen Frankfurt Main AG, Docket OST-95-683 (formerly Docket 49338)

Description of Complaint: On December 29, 1993, Delta Air Lines, Inc. (Delta), filed a complaint against the Government of Germany and the Frankfurt Airport, Flughafen Frankfurt Main AG (FAG), alleging that Germany, through FAG, had denied Delta the right to perform its own ground handling at Frankfurt in violation of the U.S.-Germany agreement, including understandings memorialized in the September 1993 MOC.

Action Requested: Delta proposed that the Department not grant any new code-share authority to Lufthansa under the September 1993 MOC until the U.S. Government receives written assurances from Germany that Delta will be permitted to exercise its self-handling rights and that FAG will not impose excessive user fees on Delta's Frankfurt flights.

Status: In September 1993 and March 1994, the United States and Germany reached understandings which addressed, inter alia, ground handling issues and pointed toward resolution of Delta's complaint. Those understandings formed the basis for a May 24, 1994, Transitional Arrangement for Air Transport Services between the U.S. and Germany. During this period, the Department extended the deadline for action on Delta's complaint for the full 180 days provided for under the IATFCPA statute to provide for implementation of a resolution to Delta's complaint (Orders 94-2-42, 94-3-46, 94-4-36, and 94-5-37). Delta subsequently advised that commercial implementation of the provisions of the agreement between Delta and the Frankfurt Airport had not yet been completed. By Order 94-6-42, the Department granted Delta's motion to waive, through July 27, 1994, its rights to a final decision on its complaint (absent the waiver, the 180-day statutory deadline for action on the complaint was June 27). And, by Orders 94-7-38, 94-9-37, 94-11-15, 95-2-45, 95-5-31, and 95-9-28 we granted Delta's motions to defer a final decision on its complaint to provide for an additional opportunity to resolve the issues raised in its complaint. The matter remained pending at the end of FY 1995.

Fine Airlines, Inc., vs. Aeroservicios Ecuatorianos, C.A. and the Government of Ecuador Docket OST-95-300 (formerly Docket 50002)

Description of Complaint: On January 5, 1995, Fine Airlines, Inc. (Fine), filed a complaint against the Government of Ecuador and Aeroservicios Ecuatorianos, C.A. (AECA), alleging that Ecuador had refused to grant Fine U.S.-Ecuador charter authority, in violation of the U.S.-Ecuador aviation agreement.

Action Requested: Fine requested that the Department take appropriate sanctions against AECA, a carrier of Ecuador. Fine proposed that the Department immediately suspend all U.S. operating authority held by AECA or, alternatively, require that AECA apply in advance for, and obtain prior Department approval of, all nonscheduled or charter flights to or from the United States.

Status: By Order 95-1-29, we invited interested parties to file answers to the complaint. A number of responses were received. By Orders 95-3-20, 95-4-12, 95-5-9, and 95-6-9, we extended the date for taking action on the complaint while intergovernmental and carrier efforts continued to resolve the complaint. On July 7, 1995, Fine requested a further extension of the action deadline, stating that while it had now been awarded a form of operating authority by Ecuador, matters related to this authority remained to be resolved. By Orders 95-7-5, 95-8-13, and 95-9-9, the Department granted Fine's motions to defer action on the complaint while efforts continued to resolve the issues raised. The matter remained pending at the end of FY 1995.

Fine Airlines, Inc., vs. the Government of the Republic of Peru
Docket OST-95-691

Description of Complaint: On September 27, 1995, Fine Airlines filed a complaint against the Government of the Republic of Peru, alleging that Peru had summarily banned Fine from conducting air transportation to, from, or over the territory of Peru based on a report that Fine had operated flights transporting arms to Ecuador at a time when Ecuador and Peru were engaged in hostilities. Fine stated that it had been conducting flights in the market pursuant to wet lease agreements, and that Peru took its action without any consultation with the United States and without any notice, hearing, or explanation offered to Fine.

Action Requested: Fine requested that the Department take appropriate sanctions against Peruvian carriers. Fine proposed that the Department immediately deny all pending applications by Peruvian carriers for additional economic authority, and immediately rescind any existing authority held by any Peruvian carrier to conduct any extrabilateral services.

Status: The complaint was under review at the end of FY 1995.

U.S. Department of Transportation

News:

Office of the Assistant Secretary for Public Affairs
Washington, D.C. 20590

FOR IMMEDIATE RELEASE

Contact: Bill Schulz
Tel.: (202) 366-4570

STATEMENT ON U.S.-JAPAN AVIATION DISCUSSIONS

Wednesday, May 1, 1996

United States and Japanese aviation officials met informally April 29-30 for talks on outstanding issues related to passenger services.

Considering heavy tourist travel during the summer season, the two sides agreed that the following services would be permitted to operate:

- United Airlines' Osaka-Seoul services for the summer, 1996 season.
- United's increase of capacity on its Los Angeles-Tokyo service for five weeks commencing May 2.
- Japan Airlines' Tokyo-Kona, Hawaii service for the summer, 1996 season.
- Japan Airlines' Sendai-Honolulu service for up to seven weekly frequencies for five weeks commencing May 2.

The two sides also agreed to meet again in Tokyo June 3-4 to discuss other passenger issues currently outstanding, including the Japanese requests for consultations on passenger services.

Secretary of Transportation Federico Peña said, "I am pleased that our staffs were able to make some progress with the Japanese negotiators during informal discussions over the last two days in clearing up some of our current disputes over air routes. While there remains work to be done on resolving current disputes before we can consider moving toward more comprehensive discussions on our significant aviation disagreements, we are hopeful that we can continue to move in a positive direction with Japan."

####

An electronic version of this document can be obtained via the World Wide Web at:
http://www.dot.gov/affairs/index.htm

Bimonthly Summary of International Aviation Negotiations
November and December, 1996

FRANCE: During negotiations in Paris, on December 16-17, 1996, we told the French that our objective continued to be to negotiate a "transition" agreement leading to a full "open-skies" regime. The French seek a formal relationship that would provide for growth, but would fall short of "open skies." They are preparing a proposal which they promised to send to us soon. We made it clear that we were not prepared to entertain a proposal that was limited to only the 1997 summer season, a position that the French accepted while noting their interest in an eight-year agreement. We made it clear that we could not agree to specific dates for a next round until after we reviewed their promised proposal. The immediate French objective is to achieve an agreement that allows U.S. carrier growth in return for limited 3rd/4th Freedom transatlantic code-share authority for the Air France-Delta and Air France-Continental alliances, including service to Atlanta--a new point for Air France.

PORTUGAL: On December 9, 1996, informal discussions with Portuguese aviation officials were held in Lisbon. Portugal is considering the United States proposal for an open-skies agreement, but, given the weakness of TAP Air Portugal, will not be ready to enter open-skies discussions for the next few months.

UNITED KINGDOM: On December 4-6, 1996, in London, U.S. and U.K. delegations held the first round of negotiations on replacing the Bermuda 2 Air Services Agreement with an open-skies accord since talks stalled last summer. Progress at this latest round of talks was minimal. No resolution was reached on such key questions as regulation of pricing, establishing a dispute resolution, access to Fly America traffic for British carriers and European cargo fifth freedom rights for U.S. airlines. Some progress was made on CRS and groundhandling issues. Another round of negotiations has been agreed to for February 4 in Washington, D.C.

ISBN 0-16-054141-7
90000
9 780160 541414